HEDDA GABLER
AND
THREE OTHER PLAYS

THE PLAYS OF HENRIK IBSEN
(1828-1906)

WITH THEIR DATES OF COMPOSITION

Cataline (1849)
The Warrior's Barrow
    (1849–50)
Norma (1851)
St. John's Eve (1852)
Lady Inger of Oestraat (1854)
The Feast at Solhaug (1855)
Olaf Liljekrans (1856)
The Vikings at Helgeland (1857)
Love's Comedy (1862)
The Pretenders (1863)
Brand (1865)
Peer Gynt (1867)
The League of Youth (1868–69)

Emperor and Galilean
    (1864–73)
The Pillars of Society
    (1875–77)
A Doll's House (1879)
Ghosts (1881)
An Enemy of the People (1882)
The Wild Duck (1884)
Rosmersholm (1886)
The Lady from the Sea (1888)
Hedda Gabler (1890)
The Master Builder (1892)
Little Eyolf (1894)
John Gabriel Borkman (1896)
When We Dead Awaken (1899)

HENRIK IBSEN, the most influential dramatist since Shakespeare, was born at Skien, Norway, in 1828. After years of failure and poverty, he emigrated at the age of thirty-six to Italy, and there wrote *Brand,* which brought him immediate fame. He remained in self-imposed exile for twenty-seven years, living in Rome, Dresden, and Munich. In 1891 he returned to Norway, and spent the last fifteen years of his life in Christiania (now Oslo). He died there in 1906 at the age of seventy-eight. Ibsen wrote twenty-six plays, sixteen of which are still performed in England and America.

MICHAEL MEYER, the translator, was born in London in 1921. After studying at Oxford he was for three years lecturer in English Literature at Upsala University in Sweden and now lives partly in Stockholm and partly in London. Author of one novel, two plays, and one television play, he is best known as a translator from the Scandinavian languages and has established a unique reputation for himself in this field in England.

The Pillars of Society
The Wild Duck
Hedda Gabler
Little Eyolf

BY

HENRIK IBSEN

NEWLY TRANSLATED FROM
THE NORWEGIAN BY
MICHAEL MEYER

Anchor Books
Doubleday & Company, Inc.
Garden City, New York

Library of Congress Catalog Card Number 61–13811

ACKNOWLEDGMENTS

Permission to quote from Ibsen's letters has been kindly granted by Gyldendal Norsk Forlag of Oslo, Norway.

Permission to use material by George Bernard Shaw has been granted by the Public Trustees, London, England, and The Society of Authors, London, England.

CONTENTS

FOREWORD

By the time he was forty-five, Ibsen had raised poetic drama to something near perfection in *Brand* and *Peer Gynt,* and had done the same for historical drama in *Emperor and Galilean.* He then abandoned both poetry and history, and spent the rest of his life experimenting with the form that has come to be most commonly associated with his name, the tightly plotted drama of social realism. The four plays translated in this volume show him at various stages of the experiment. *The Pillars of Society* (1875–77) was his first real essay in this field, and in a sense the whole of modern prose drama may be said to stem from it. Then having perfected this type of play in *A Doll's House* and *Ghosts,* or at any rate done it better than anyone has managed to since, he moved restlessly on into new territory. *The Wild Duck* (1884) marks a return to symbolism; but instead of being scattered with symbols like *Brand* and *Peer Gynt, The Wild Duck* is an experiment in the use of symbol as a cornerstone; the play is dependent on and held together by a single and precise symbol, the crippled bird which holds the characters captive and from which they cannot escape any more than it can escape from the loft in which they have imprisoned it. *Hedda Gabler* (1890), a return to the simpler and more straightforward method of *A Doll's House,* is at the same time an unconscious and revealing exercise in self-analysis. The last of the four plays included here, *Little Eyolf* (1894), is one of Ibsen's least-known plays and is, to my mind, the greatest he wrote, at any rate in prose. After a dynamic first act all external action virtually ceases, and the characters spend the rest of the play stripping each other of their protective spiritual padding until at the end they are left humbled and bare like criminals shaved for execution.

One still occasionally hears the parrot-cry about Ibsen being a polemical writer whose subjects, women's rights and the like, were ephemeral and whose plays have therefore lost their urgency. This view is partly a hangover from the time when Ibsen was best known as the author of *A Doll's House, Ghosts* and *An Enemy of the People;* it is also largely the fault of Bernard Shaw, who tried in *The Quintessence of Ibsenism* to prove that Ibsen was really a sociologist like himself. (The book originated from a series of lectures given to the Fabian Society as part of a course entitled Socialism in Contemporary Literature). Ibsen was a sociologist only in a very limited sense. He never, for example, concerned himself with bettering the lot of the working classes, and there is only one attempt at a sympathetic portrayal of a working man in all his plays (Aune in *The Pillars of Society*). In a letter to Georg Brandes, he expressed his lack of interest in "special revolutions, revolutions in externals, in the political sphere," asserting that "what is really wanted is a revolution in the spirit of man." His letters contain only a passing reference to Garibaldi's march on Rome, although he was in Rome when it took place and witnessed it, and he sided with British Imperialism in the Boer War. Ibsen's theme was timeless, and was the same as that of Sophocles, Shakespeare, Racine and every other major dramatist who has ever lived: the behaviour of passionate men and women ravaged by love, hatred, sexual desire and guilt as they approach the moment when they are finally forced to settle accounts with themselves and their Maker. As Bernard Shaw once observed: "There is not one of Ibsen's characters who is not, in the old phrase, the temple of the Holy Ghost, and who does not move you, at moments, by the sense of that mystery."

M. M.

The Pillars of Society

INTRODUCTION

Ibsen completed THE PILLARS OF SOCIETY a few months after his forty-ninth birthday; he wrote it in Munich between 1875 and 1877. Enormously successful and influential at the time of its appearance, and indeed for the next quarter of a century, it has rarely been performed during the past fifty years, having rather glibly been relegated to the category of polemical dramas that have lost their topicality, and is usually thought of nowadays as an apprentice work of documentary rather than practical interest. In fact, however, the whole question of which plays of Ibsen are still theatrically valid is in serious need of reappraisal. Recent productions in London of *Brand* and *Little Eyolf*, which had both long been dismissed as unactable, have shown them to be full of theatrical life, and the same is probably true of THE PILLARS OF SOCIETY. It is tightly plotted and beautifully characterised; and at this distance of time we can see that its true subject is not women's rights or the evil practices of nineteenth-century shipowners, but human emotions and relationships. The ending has been condemned as facilely happy, but the same accusation was, until recently, made against *Little Eyolf* and *The Lady from the Sea*, and has been proved false if the plays are capably handled. The chief obstacles to a professional production are the size of the cast and a tendency to verbosity on the part of Bernick and, more particularly, Dr. Roerlund, the schoolmaster. Trim him down, and THE PILLARS OF SOCIETY stands as an absorbing example of Ibsen in his less familiar mood of humane comedy—the mood which pervades *Love's Comedy*, *The League of Youth*, and much of *Peer Gynt* and *The Wild Duck*, and of which isolated characters in his more sombre plays, such as George Tesman in *Hedda Gabler*, Ballested in *The Lady from the Sea* and Vilhelm Foldal in *John Gabriel Borkman*, are belated manifestations.

THE PILLARS OF SOCIETY is often referred to as the first of Ibsen's social prose dramas. That honour in fact belongs to *The League of Youth*, a vigorous and delightful comedy completed eight years earlier which hardly deserves the oblivion which has enveloped it. To *The League of Youth*, too, belongs the credit of being Ibsen's first attempt to write dialogue that was genuinely modern and colloquial. His earlier prose plays, such as *St. John's Eve*, *Lady Inger of Oestraat*, *The Vikings at Helgeland* and *The Pretenders*, had been written in a formalised style. But *The League of Youth*, often assumed by those who have not read it to be an earnest political tract, is a loosely constructed and light-hearted frolic almost in the manner of Restoration comedy,* which happens to have a pushing young politician as its chief character—"Peer Gynt as a politician," someone has described it. THE PILLARS OF SOCIETY is in a much truer sense the forerunner of the eleven great plays that followed it. Apart from the tightness of its construction, it contains, as *The League of Youth* does not, the elements we commonly associate with an Ibsen play—a marriage founded on a lie, passionate women stunted and inhibited by the conventions of their time, and an arrogant man of high intellectual and practical gifts who destroys, or nearly destroys, the happiness of those nearest to him. It also, unlike his earlier plays, exhibits what Henry James admiringly described as "the operation of talent without glamour . . . the ugly interior on which his curtain inexorably rises and which, to be honest, I like for the queer associations it has taught us to respect: the hideous carpet and wallpaper (one may answer for them), the conspicuous stove, the lonely central table, the 'lamps with green shades' as in the sumptuous first act of *The Wild Duck*, the pervasive air of small interests and standards, the sign of

---

* It was influenced by the eighteenth-century Danish dramatist, Ludvig Holberg, one of the few authors Ibsen really admired.

limited local life." Above all, THE PILLARS OF SOCIETY has, despite its overtones of comedy, that peculiarly Ibsenish quality of austerity; what Henry James, on another occasion, described as "the hard compulsion of his strangely inscrutable art."

It is indicative of the technical problems posed by this new form of tightly plotted social realism that THE PILLARS OF SOCIETY took Ibsen longer to write than any of his other plays except the triple-length *Emperor and Galilean.* No less than five separate drafts of the first act have survived, and over a period of nearly eight years his letters are scattered with excuses for its lack of progress. He began to brood on it as early as December 1869, just after finishing *The League of Youth.* On the fourteenth of that month he wrote to his publisher, Frederik Hegel: "I am planning a new and serious contemporary drama in three acts, and expect to start work on it in the immediate future." The following month (January 25, 1870) he informed Hegel that he hoped to have it ready by the following October, but on April 11 he wrote: "My new play has not yet got beyond the draft, and since I have to get my travel notes into order it looks like being delayed for some time." These travel notes referred to the visit he had made to Egypt in November 1869 to attend, as official Norwegian representative, the opening of the Suez Canal.

October 1870 arrived, and so far from having the play ready he could only tell Hegel that it "has sufficiently developed in my mind for me to hope that any day now I may be able to start writing it." Two sets of notes have survived from this year which contain the first germs of the play. By now he had found a more impressive excuse than the Suez Canal; the Franco-Prussian War, which had started in July of that year. In such an atmosphere (he was living in Germany) how could he concentrate on writing a social drama set in a small Norwegian seaport? He returned instead to the broader historical canvas of *Emperor and Galilean,* on which he had been working intermittently since 1864.

It was in fact another five years before he began the actual writing of THE PILLARS OF SOCIETY. Apart from completing

Emperor and Galilean, he prepared for publication a selection of his poems covering the past twenty years; it was his deliberate farewell to poetry, the form which had been his earliest love. He explained this decision in a letter written to Edmund Gosse on January 15, 1874, shortly after the publication of *Emperor and Galilean,* and although his remarks were made with specific reference to that play, they apply even more strongly to the works which followed. I quote the passage in Gosse's own translation:

"The illusion I wanted to produce is that of reality. I wished to produce the impression on the reader that what he was reading was something that had really happened. If I had employed verse, I should have counteracted my own intention and prevented the accomplishment of the task I had set myself. The many ordinary and insignificant characters whom I have introduced into the play would have become indistinct, and indistinguishable from one another, if I had allowed all of them to speak in one and the same rhythmical measure. We are no longer living in the age of Shakespeare. Among sculptors, there is already talk of painting statues in the natural colours. Much can be said both for and against this. I have no desire to see the Venus de Milo painted, but I would rather see the head of a negro executed in black than in white marble.

"Speaking generally, the style must conform to the degree of ideality which pervades the representation. My new drama [i.e., *Emperor and Galilean*] is no tragedy in the ancient acceptation; what I desired to depict were human beings, and therefore I would not let them talk in 'the language of the gods.'"

In the summer of 1874 Ibsen returned to Norway for the first time since he had left it ten years earlier. There the strife between the conservatives and the liberals had reached its height and, as a result of *The League of Youth,* which was an attack on the hollowness of radical politicians, Ibsen found the conservatives hailing him as their champion. He had, however, no intention of attaching himself to any political party, and when he read in the right-wing newspaper *Morgen-bladet* an editorial demand that a candidate for a professorship at the university should be rejected on the grounds that he was a free-thinker, Ibsen seized the opportunity to advertise his independence. He withdrew his subscription to *Morgen-bladet* and changed to the left-wing newspaper *Dagbladet*. The uneasiness of the conservatives on hearing this—Ibsen was famous enough by now for the students to arrange a torch-light procession in his honour before he left—would have been considerably increased if they had known what he was pre-paring for them.

After two and a half months in Norway, he returned briefly to Dresden and then, the following spring (1875), he moved to Munich, a city which he found much more to his liking and where he was to spend most of the next sixteen years. At last, in the autumn of that year, nearly six years after he had first begun to brood on it, he settled down to the actual writ-ing of THE PILLARS OF SOCIETY. At first things went well. On October 23 he wrote to Hegel: "My new play is progressing swiftly; in a few days I shall have completed the first act, which I always find the most difficult part. The title will be: THE PILLARS OF SOCIETY, a Play in Five [*sic*] Acts. In a way it can be regarded as a counterblast to *The League of Youth*, and will touch on several of the more important questions of our time." On November 25 he writes: "Act 1 of my new play is finished and *fair-copied;* I am now working on Act 2." By December 10 he is "working at it daily and am now doubly anxious to get the manuscript to you as quickly as possible." On January 26, 1876, he expects to "have it ready by May."

But now things began to go less smoothly. After February 26, when he writes to the director of the Bergen Theatre that it "will probably be printed during the summer," there is no further mention of the play in his letters until September 15, when he explains rather lengthily to Hegel that he has been so distracted by productions or plans for productions of his earlier plays—*The Pretenders* in Meiningen, Schwerin, and Berlin, *The Vikings at Helgeland* in Munich, Leipzig, Vienna, and Dresden—that he has been "compelled to postpone completion of my new play; but on my return to Munich at the beginning of next month, I intend to get it polished off." But progress continued to be slow. 1877 arrived, and on February 9 he could only tell Hegel, who must by now have been growing a little impatient: "I shall have my new play ready in the summer, and will send you the manuscript as soon as possible." However, on April 20 he wrote that it "is now moving rapidly towards its conclusion," and at last, on June 24, 1877, he was able to report: "Today I take advantage of a free moment to tell you that on the 15th inst. I completed my new play and am now going ahead with the fair-copying." He posted the fair copy to Hegel in five instalments between July 29 and August 20, 1877.

THE PILLARS OF SOCIETY was published by Hegel's firm, Gyldendals of Copenhagen, on October 11, 1877, and achieved immediate and widespread success. Throughout Scandinavia, the liberals and radicals hailed it with as much delight as that with which the conservatives had greeted *The League of Youth*. The first edition of 6000 copies sold out in seven weeks, and a further 4000 had to be printed. It was first performed on November 18, 1877, in Copenhagen, where it was received with great enthusiasm, and it was equally acclaimed in Christiania,* Stockholm and Helsinki. It also gave Ibsen his first real break-through in Germany. In the absence of any copyright protection, three separate German translations were published early in 1878 (one of them by a man described by Ibsen as "a frightful literary bandit"), and in February of that year it was produced at five different theatres in Berlin within a fortnight. Twenty-seven German and Austrian theatres staged it within the year. In England, William Archer, then aged twenty-two, made a "hurried translation" entitled, rather uninspiringly, *The Supports of Society;* an analysis by him of the play, with extracts from his translation, was published in the *Mirror of Literature* on March 2, 1878. Since "no publisher

---

* In Swedish at the Moellergaten Theatre. Ibsen refused to allow the Christiania Theatre to stage it because "the new director is a quite useless man," and the play was not performed in Norwegian in the capital until the following spring.

would look at" this version, he made another more careful one, under the new title of *Quicksands,* and this was performed for a single matinée at the Gaiety Theatre, London, on December 15, 1880—a noteworthy occasion, for it was the first recorded performance of any Ibsen play in England. THE PILLARS OF SOCIETY was not staged in America, at any rate in English—though it had been acted there in German—until March 13, 1891, when it was produced at the Lyceum Theatre, New York. In 1892 it was performed in Australia and South Africa, in 1893 in Rome; and in 1896 Lugné-Poë staged it at his Théâtre de l'Oeuvre in Paris. By the end of the century, according to Archer, it had been performed no less than 1200 times in Germany and Austria, a remarkable record for those days.

THE PILLARS OF SOCIETY dealt with two problems of extreme topicality for the 1870s, and it is a measure of the play's emotional and dramatic content that it has retained its validity despite the fact that both issues have long since been settled. One was the question of women's rights; the other, that of "floating coffins," i.e., unseaworthy ships which were deliberately sacrificed with their crews so that their owners could claim insurance. Controversy over the former problem reached its height in Norway during the seventies. The Norwegian novelist Camilla Collett had fired a warning shot as long ago as 1853, with her novel *The Judge's Daughters.* In 1869 John Stuart Mill had published *The Subjection of Women,* which Ibsen's friend Georg Brandes translated into Danish the same year. Matilda Schjoett's *Conversation of a Group of Ladies about the Subjection of Women* (published anonymously in 1871) and Camilla Collett's *Last Papers* (1872) set the issue squarely before the Norwegian public; in 1874 a Women's Reading Society was founded in Christiania, and in 1876 Asta Hanseen, a great champion of the cause, began a series of lectures on women's rights, but was so furiously assailed that in 1880 she emigrated to America. She was the original of Lona Hessel (Ibsen at first gave her the surname of Hassel, but changed it, presumably so as to avoid too direct an identification with Hanseen). Camilla Collett exerted a direct influence on Ibsen, for he had seen a good deal of her in Dresden in 1871, and again in Munich in the spring of 1877 when he was writing the play, and when they had many arguments about marriage and other female problems. Another influence was Ibsen's wife, Susannah; the subject of women's rights was one about which she had long felt strongly. Ibsen had already touched tentatively on this problem in *The League of Youth*, and he was to deal with it more minutely in his next play, *A Doll's House*. His original intention in THE PILLARS OF SO- CIETY was to be even more outspoken than he finally was, for in one of the preliminary drafts Dina announces her decision to go off with her lover without marrying him; but he evidently doubted whether the theatres would stage a play which suggested anything quite so daring, and legalised their relationship.

The problem of the "floating coffins" was first forced upon Ibsen's attention by an English Member of Parliament. In 1868 Samuel Plimsoll had sought in the House of Commons to have the State interfere against the cold-blooded and unscrupulous sacrifice of human life by sending men to sea in rotten ships. In 1873 he succeeded in getting a law passed to enforce seaworthiness; but this proved too slack. On July 22, 1875, he created a tremendous commotion in Parliament by a boldly outspoken attack on the people responsible for such a policy; he called the owners of such ships murderers and the politicians who supported them scoundrels, and so roused the conscience of the nation that a temporary bill went through in a few days, and its principles were made permanent by the Merchant Shipping Act of the following year. Plimsoll's protest echoed throughout the world, and in a seafaring country such as Norway it rang especially loudly. A particularly scandalous case had occurred in Christiania during Ibsen's visit there in 1874. On September 2 of that year, at the annual general meeting of the shipping insurance company Norske Veritas, questions were asked about a ship which, after having been declared seaworthy, sprang a leak while at sea and was shown to be completely rotten. At the annual general meeting a year later two similar cases were mentioned, and a storm of indignation was aroused. The matter was reported in detail in the newspapers, and Ibsen can hardly have failed to read about it.

THE PILLARS OF SOCIETY is full of memories of Grimstad, the little port where Ibsen had spent his years as a chemist's apprentice (just as *The League of Youth* is full of memories of his birthplace, Skien). The *Palm Tree* was the name of a Grimstad ship. Touring theatrical companies played in the hall of a sailmaker named Moeller; an actress belonging to one of them had returned there after being involved in a scandal, and had tried to keep herself by taking in washing and sewing like Dina Dorf's mother, but had been shooed out of town by the local gossips. Foreign ships came in for repairs, and foreign visitors turned the place upside down, like the crew of the *Indian Girl*. In the autumn of 1849, six months before Ibsen left for Christiania, the Socialist Marcus Thrane had arrived in Grimstad and founded a Workers' Association, like the one Aune belonged to. And the Bernicks had their origin in a family named Smith Petersen. Morten Smith Petersen, the original of Karsten Bernick, returned to Grimstad from abroad in the 1840s, and ran his aged mother's business for a while, but finally had to close it down. He then started his own shipyard and an insurance company, and eventually founded the Norske Veritas company which earned the notoriety referred to above. He had died in 1872, but his sister Margrete Petersen survived. She was an elementary school teacher, and the original of Martha Bernick.

The rich quantity of notes and draft material which has been preserved enables us to plot the development of THE PILLARS OF SOCIETY in some detail. Ibsen's first notes, made in 1870, begin: "The main theme must be how women sit modestly in the background while the men busily pursue their petty aims with an assurance which at once infuriates and impresses." The main characters are to be an "old white-haired lady" with two sons, one a shipowner, the other a ship's officer who has been abroad for ten years on foreign service. The shipowner's wife, "a feted beauty before she married, is full of poetry but is bitter and unsatisfied; she makes demands of life which are,

or seem, excessive." In other words, Mrs. Bernick, as originally
conceived, is the forerunner of the great line of Ibsen heroines
—Nora Hellmer, Mrs. Alving, Rebecca West, Ellida Wangel,
Hedda Gabler, Rita Allmers, the Rentheim twins in *John
Gabriel Borkman*, and Maja and Irene in *When We Dead
Awaken*. Martha, too, appears in these early notes, jotted down
five years before the play was written: "her sister, still unsure
of herself; has grown up quietly admiring the man who is absent and far away." But although several of the characters of
THE PILLARS OF SOCIETY as we know it are here, the plot as first
conceived bears little relation to that of the final version; the
naval officer falls in love with the sister (i.e., Martha), but she
is already in love with a student, and the officer's mother per-
suades him to give up the girl and go away. "The greatest
victory," she tells him, "is to conquer oneself"—a kind of echo
of Brand's "The victory of victories is to lose everything." There
is also reference to "the foster-daughter of 16, sustained by
daydreams and expectations" (i.e., Dina). The play at this
stage was to be "a comedy," presumably of the same genre
as *The League of Youth*.

In his next notes, made five years later, we find much more
of the play as we know it. A scenic synopsis includes the schoolmaster reading to the assembled wives, the husbands discussing the railway, the foster-daughter (here called Valborg)
impatient and longing to get away (to her mother, who is still
alive), and Lona's arrival with the steamer; Act 1 ends with
her "appearing in the doorway to the garden as the curtain
falls." In Act 2 "the returned wanderers [i.e., Lona and the
Captain] start turning things upside down in the town. Rumours about the Captain's great wealth and the earlier scandal
concerning Valborg's mother. The schoolmaster begins to think
of getting engaged to Valborg. Conflict begins between the
factory-owner and the Captain." Act 3: "News about irregu-
larities in the repairs to the ship. The engagement is announced
and celebrated. The Captain decides to leave the country.
Fresh information from the yards. The factory-owner hesitates;
for the moment, nothing must be said." Act 4: "Secret understanding between the Captain and Valborg. The railway proj-

ect secured. Great ovations. Olaf runs away with the Captain and Valborg. Exciting final catastrophe."

The list of characters has by now grown considerably. Apart from Bennick [*sic*], his wife, his blind mother and his sister Margrete (Martha), Miss "Hassel," the schoolmaster "Roerstad," Valborg (who suddenly becomes Dina), and Captain John Tennyson (later Rawlinson), we also have Madame Dorf, young Mrs. Bernick's father, Mads Toennesen (a "ship-owner and master builder nicknamed 'The Badger'"), his other son Emil (altered to Hilmar), and Evensen, "a supply teacher." As synopsis follows synopsis, the list of characters changes; Aune, Sandstad, and "Knap" appear, Bennick becomes Bernick, and the whole of the older generation is removed— Bernick's mother, Madame Dorf, Evensen the supply teacher and, eventually, Mads Toennesen, though he was to reappear three plays later as Morten Kiil in *An Enemy of the People.*

The drafts which follow comprise four versions of Act 1 or part of it, a draft of the whole play, and Ibsen's final fair copy in the version familiar to us. The first draft of Act 1 is different from the final version in numerous respects, and makes interesting reading. Among other things it contains a rare example of Ibsen trying to write English. The clerk Knap announces (in Norwegian) that since "the Captain fell overboard in the North Sea and the mate has delirium tremens," the *Indian Girl* has arrived under the command of "a sailor who was on board as a passenger . . . John Rawlinson, Esqr., New Orleans." Captain Rawlinson then appears and the following spirited exchange takes place in English:

BERNICK. Good morning, master Rawlinson! This way, if you please, sir! I am master Bernick!

CAPTAIN RAWLINSON *waves his handkerchief and cries.* Very well, Karsten; but first three hurrah for the old graevling!*

The draft makes very spirited reading, and it is only when we compare it with the final version that we realize how much

* The Norwegian word for badger.

Ibsen gained in the rewriting. Bernick has much superfluous talk trimmed down, Lona is given a far more effective entrance, Aune (the only sympathetic portrait of a working-class man Ibsen ever attempted) is introduced quickly instead of having to wait until Act 2, a good deal of argument as to the pros and cons of the railway is cut, and we are told far more about the characters' past, notably Lona's quarrel with Bernick and the returned brother's supposed intrigue with Madame Dorf. Hilmar (who with his hypochondria and fanciful speech surely anticipates Hjalmar Ekdal in *The Wild Duck*) and Lona are much more sharply characterised; and the "floating coffin" issue, absent from the first draft, is introduced. The subsequent drafts show Ibsen groping painfully towards his final conception, and together they chart his progress from the vigorous but rather artless method of *The League of Youth* towards the compactness and inevitability of *A Doll's House*.

THE PILLARS OF SOCIETY was not the first realistic prose play. Apart from *The League of Youth,* Bjoernson's two plays *A Bankrupt* and *The Editor,* both written in 1875, are explorations in this field. But these are not plays in the truest sense; they are melodramas which indict individual figures. THE PILLARS OF SOCIETY was the first play to combine the three elements of colloquial dialogue, objectivity, and tightness of plot which are the requirements and characteristics of modern prose drama. The effect of the play on the younger generation of its time has been recorded by Otto Brahm, one of the founders of the Freie Buhne in Berlin, a theatre comparable in influence to Antoine's Théâtre Libre and Stanislavsky's Moscow Art. In 1878, when Brahm was twenty-two, he saw THE PILLARS OF SOCIETY at a small theatre in Berlin. Many years later he recalled that this was "the first strong theatrical impression" that he received. "It was," he said, "my first intimation of a new world of creative art."

M. M.

CHARACTERS

KARSTEN BERNICK
BETTY, his wife
OLAF, their son, aged 13
MARTHA, Karsten's sister
JOHAN TOENNESEN, Betty's younger brother
LONA HESSEL, her elder half sister
HILMAR TOENNESEN, Betty's cousin
DR. ROERLUND, a schoolmaster
MR. RUMMEL, a wholesale dealer
MR. VIGELAND, a merchant
MR. SANDSTAD, a merchant
DINA DORF, a young girl living with the Bernicks
KRAP, chief clerk
AUNE, a shipyard foreman
MRS. RUMMEL
MRS. HOLT, the postmaster's wife
MRS. LYNGE, wife of the local Doctor
MISS RUMMEL
MISS HOLT

Townspeople and other residents, foreign seamen, steamship passengers, etc.

The action takes place in KARSTEN BERNICK's *house in a small Norwegian seaport.*

This translation was commissioned by Peter Bridge Productions, Ltd., for production in the West End of London during the 1961–62 season.

ACT ONE

A spacious garden room in KARSTEN BERNICK'S *house. Downstage left, a door leading to* BERNICK'S *room; upstage in the same wall is a similar door. In the centre of the opposite wall is a large entrance door. The rear wall is composed almost entirely of fine, clear glass, with an open door giving on to a broad verandah over which an awning is stretched. Steps lead down from the verandah into the garden, part of which can be seen, enclosed by a fence with a small gate. Beyond the fence is a street, the far side of which is lined with small wooden houses painted in bright colours. It is summer, and the sun is shining warmly. Now and then people wander along the street; they stop and speak to each other, buy things from a little corner shop, etc.*

In the garden room a group of ladies is seated round a table. At the head of it sits MRS. BERNICK; *on her left,* MRS. HOLT *and her daughter; beyond them,* MRS. RUMMEL *and* MISS RUMMEL. *On* MRS. BERNICK'S *right sit* MRS. LYNGE, MARTHA BERNICK *and* DINA DORF. *All the ladies are busy sewing. On the table lie large heaps of linen cut into shapes and half finished, and other articles of clothing. Further upstage, at a little table on which stand two potted plants and a glass of lemonade,* DR. ROERLUND, *the schoolmaster, sits reading aloud from a book with gilt edges, though only the odd word can be heard by the audience. Outside in the garden,* OLAF BERNICK *is running about, shooting at a target with a bow and arrow.*

After a few moments, AUNE, *a shipyard foreman, enters quietly through the door on the right. The reading is interrupted briefly;* MRS. BERNICK *nods to* AUNE *and points to the door on the left.* AUNE *walks quietly over and knocks softly on* BERNICK'S *door. Pause. He knocks again.* KRAP, *the chief clerk, comes out of the room with his hat in his hand and papers under his arm.*

KRAP. Oh, it's you, is it?

AUNE. Mr. Bernick sent for me.

KRAP. I know; but he can't see you himself. He's deputed me to tell you—

AUNE. You? I'd much rather speak to—

KRAP. He's deputed me to tell you this. You're to stop giving these talks to the men on Saturday evenings.

AUNE. Oh? I thought my free time was my own—

KRAP. You don't get free time in order for you to stop the men working. Last Saturday you told them their interests were threatened by the new machines, and by these new methods we've introduced down at the yard. Why d'you do it?

AUNE. For the good of the community.

KRAP. That's odd. Mr. Bernick says this kind of thing will disintegrate the community.

AUNE. I don't mean by community what Mr. Bernick does, Mr. Krap. As chairman of the Workers' Association I—

KRAP. You're Mr. Bernick's foreman. And the only community to which you owe allegiance is the Bernick Shipbuilding Company. That's where we all get our living. Well, now you know what Mr. Bernick had to say to you.

AUNE. Mr. Bernick wouldn't have said it like that, Mr. Krap. But I know whom I've to thank for this. It's that damned American ship that's put in for repairs. Those people expect us to work like they do over there, and it isn't—

KRAP. Yes, well I haven't time to go into all that. Now you've heard Mr. Bernick's orders, so stop it. Run back to the yard, now; I'm sure they need you there. I'll be down myself shortly. Pardon me, ladies!

He bows and goes out through the garden and down the street. AUNE *exits quietly, right.* DR. ROERLUND, *who has continued his reading during the foregoing dialogue, which has been conducted in subdued voices, finishes his book and closes it with a snap.*

ROERLUND. And that, dear ladies, concludes our story.

MRS. RUMMEL. Oh, what an instructive book!

MRS. HOLT. And so moral!

MRS. BERNICK. Yes, a book like that certainly gives one food for thought.

ROERLUND. Indeed, yes. It provides a salutary contrast to the horrors that confront us daily in the newspapers and magazines. This rouged and gilded exterior which Society flaunts before our eyes—what does it really hide? Hollowness and corruption—if I may use such words. No solid moral foundation. These so-called great modern communities are nothing but whited sepulchres.

MRS. HOLT. How true!

MRS. RUMMEL. We only need look at the crew of that American ship that's in port.

ROERLUND. I would rather not sully your ears by speaking of such human refuse. But even in respectable circles, what do we see? Doubt and unrest fermenting on every side; spiritual dissension and universal uncertainty. Out there, family life is everywhere undermined. An impudent spirit of subversion challenges our most sacred principles.

DINA, *without looking up.* But hasn't there been great progress too?

ROERLUND. Progress? I don't understand—

MRS. HOLT, *amazed.* Dina, really!

MRS. RUMMEL, *simultaneously.* Dina, how can you?

ROERLUND. I hardly think it would be healthy if this progress you speak of were to gain favour in our community. No; we in this little town should thank God that we are as we are. The occasional tare is, alas, to be found among the wheat here as elsewhere; but we strive with all the might that God has given us to root it up. We must keep our community pure, ladies. We must hold these untried theories which an impatient age would force upon us at arm's length.

MRS. HOLT. Yes, there are many too many of them about.

MRS. RUMMEL. Yes, last year we were only saved from having that horrible railway forced upon us by the skin of our teeth.

MRS. BERNICK. Karsten put a stop to that.

ROERLUND. Providence, Mrs. Bernick, Providence. You may rest assured that in refusing to countenance the scheme your husband was but the instrument of a Higher Purpose.

MRS. BERNICK. But the way they attacked him in the newspapers! Oh, but dear Dr. Roerlund, we've completely forgotten to thank you. It really is more than kind of you to sacrifice so much of your time for us.

ROERLUND. Oh, nonsense. My school has its holidays.

MRS. BERNICK. Well, yes, but it's still a sacrifice, Dr. Roerlund.

ROERLUND, *moves his chair closer.* Pray do not speak of it, dear lady. Are you not all making sacrifices for a noble cause? And do you not make them gladly and willingly? These depraved sinners whose moral condition we are striving to ameliorate are as wounded soldiers upon a battlefield; and you, dear ladies, are the Sisters of Mercy, the ministering angels who pick lint for these fallen creatures, wind your bandages gently round their wounds, tend and heal them—

MRS. BERNICK. How wonderful to be able to view everything in such a charitable light.

ROERLUND. It is a gift one is born with; but much can be done to foster it. It is merely a question of having a serious vocation in life and viewing everything in the light of that vocation. What do you say, Miss Bernick? Do you not find that life has a more solid moral foundation since you decided to devote yourself to the noble task of educating the young?

MARTHA. I don't really know what to say. Sometimes as I sit there in the schoolroom I wish I were far away, on the wild sea.

ROERLUND. Temptation, my dear Miss Bernick! You must bar

the door against such unruly guests! The wild sea—well, of course you don't mean that literally; you are thinking of the turbulent ocean of modern society in which so many human souls founder. Do you really envy that life you hear murmuring, nay, thundering outside? Only look down into the street. People walk there in the sunshine sweating and wrestling with their petty problems. No, we are better off who sit coolly here behind our windows with our backs turned on the direction from which unrest and disturbance might come.

MARTHA. Yes, of course. I'm sure you're right—

ROERLUND. And in a house such as this—a good, clean home, where family life may be seen in its fairest form—where peace and harmony reign—

To MRS. BERNICK.

Are you listening for something, Mrs. Bernick?

MRS. BERNICK *has turned towards the door downstage left.* How loudly they're talking in there!

ROERLUND. Is something important being discussed?

MRS. BERNICK. I don't know. My husband seems to have someone with him.

HILMAR TOENNESEN, *with a cigar in his mouth, enters through the door on the right, but stops when he sees the ladies.*

HILMAR. Oh, I beg your pardon—

Turns to leave.

MRS. BERNICK. No, come in, Hilmar; you're not disturbing us. Did you want something?

HILMAR. No, I was just looking in. Good morning, ladies.

To MRS. BERNICK.

Well, what's going to be the outcome?

MRS. BERNICK. How do you mean?

HILMAR. Your husband's called a council of war.

MRS. BERNICK. Oh? But what on earth about?

HILMAR. Oh, it's some nonsense about that confounded railway again.

MRS. RUMMEL. How disgraceful!

MRS. BERNICK. Poor Karsten! As if he hadn't enough worries already!

ROERLUND. But how is this possible, Mr. Toennesen? Mr. Bernick made it perfectly clear last year that he wouldn't have anything to do with any railway.

HILMAR. Yes, that's what I thought. But I met Krap just now, and he tells me that the question's being reconsidered, and that Bernick's having a meeting with three of the other local plutocrats.

MRS. RUMMEL. Yes, I thought I heard my husband's voice.

HILMAR. Oh yes, Rummel's there all right; and Sandstad who owns that big store up the hill; and Michael Vigeland—you know, the one they call Holy Mick—

ROERLUND *coughs.*

Oh, sorry, Doctor.

MRS. BERNICK. Just when everything was so nice and peaceful here.

HILMAR. Well, personally I shouldn't be sorry if they started squabbling again. Give us a bit of fun—

ROERLUND. I think we can do without that kind of fun.

HILMAR. Depends on your temperament. Certain natures need to be harrowed by conflict occasionally. Provincial life doesn't provide many opportunities, worse luck; and not everybody has the guts to—

Glances at ROERLUND'S *book.*

Woman as the Servant of Society. What's this nonsense?

MRS. BERNICK. Good heavens, Hilmar, you mustn't say that! You can't have read it.

HILMAR. No, and I don't intend to.

MRS. BERNICK. You don't seem in a very good temper today.

HILMAR. I'm not.

MRS. BERNICK. Didn't you sleep well last night?

HILMAR. No, I slept rottenly. I took a walk yesterday evening —for my health, you know—and wandered into the club and read a book some chap had written about the North Pole. I find it very good for my nerves to read about man's struggle with the elements.

MRS. RUMMEL. It doesn't appear to have agreed with you, Mr. Toennesen.

HILMAR. No, it didn't really agree with me. I tossed and turned all night. Dreamed I was being chased by a horrible walrus.

OLAF, *who has come up on to the verandah.* Have you been chased by a walrus, Uncle?

HILMAR. I dreamed it, you young jackass. Are you still playing with that silly bow? Why don't you get yourself a proper rifle?

OLAF. Oh, I'd love one! But—

HILMAR. There's some sense in having a rifle. That slow pressure on the trigger, you know—good for the nerves.

OLAF. And I could shoot bears with it, Uncle! But Father won't let me.

MRS. BERNICK. You mustn't put such ideas into his head, Hilmar.

HILMAR. Hm! Fine lot his generation's going to be! All this talk about the importance of sport, and all they do is play silly games, when they ought to be toughening their characters by staring danger unflinchingly in the face. Don't stand there pointing that bow at me, you little fool, it might go off.

OLAF. But Uncle, there's no arrow in it.

HILMAR. You can never be sure. There might be. Point it somewhere else, I tell you. Why the devil don't you go over to America on one of your father's ships? You could hunt buffalos there. Or fight redskins.

MRS. BERNICK. Hilmar, really!

OLAF. Oh yes, Uncle, I'd love to! And I might meet Uncle Johan and Aunt Lona!

HILMAR. Hm—I shouldn't bother about that.

MRS. BERNICK. You can go back into the garden now, Olaf.

OLAF. Can I go out into the street too, Mother?

MRS. BERNICK. Yes, but not too far.

OLAF *runs out through the garden gate.*

ROERLUND. You ought not to stuff the child's head with such ideas, Mr. Toennesen.

HILMAR. Oh, no. Of course not. He's got to spend the rest of his life sitting safe at home, like all the others.

ROERLUND. Why don't you go to America yourself?

HILMAR. I? In my state of health? But of course no one in this town bothers about that. Besides, one has certain responsibilities towards the community one lives in. There's got to be someone here to keep the flag of ideals flying. Ugh, now he's started shouting again.

LADIES. Who? Shouting? Who is shouting?

HILMAR. I don't know. They're raising their voices in there, and it's very bad for my nerves.

MRS. RUMMEL. Ah, that's my husband, Mr. Toennesen. He's so used to addressing public meetings.

ROERLUND. The others aren't doing too badly either, by the sound of it.

HILMAR. But of course! The moment their pockets are threatened— Oh, everyone here's so petty and materialistic. Ugh!

MRS. BERNICK. Well anyway, that's better than the old days, when people thought of nothing but dissipation.

MRS. LYNGE. Were things really so dreadful here before?

MRS. RUMMEL. Indeed they were, Mrs. Lynge. You may think yourself fortunate that you didn't live here then.

MRS. HOLT. Yes, there have certainly been great changes. When I think of what things were like when I was a young girl—

MRS. RUMMEL. Oh, you only need to look back fifteen years. My word, the goings-on there used to be! Why, there was a dance club, *and* a musical society—

MARTHA. And a dramatic society. I remember that well.

MRS. RUMMEL. Yes, it was they who put on that play of yours, Mr. Toennesen.

HILMAR, *upstage.* Really? Oh, I don't—er—

ROERLUND. Mr. Toennesen wrote a play?

MRS. RUMMEL. Why, yes. Long before you came here, Dr. Roerlund. It only ran for one night.

MRS. LYNGE. Wasn't that the play you were telling me about in which you acted one of the young lovers, Mrs. Rummel?

MRS. RUMMEL, *shoots a glance at* ROERLUND. I? I really don't recall that, Mrs. Lynge. But I do remember all the dreadful parties that used to go on.

MRS. HOLT. Yes, I know houses where they used to hold big parties twice a week.

MRS. LYNGE. And I hear there was a company of strolling players that used to come here.

MRS. RUMMEL. Yes, they were the worst of all—

MRS. HOLT *coughs uneasily.*

Er—strolling players, did you say? No, I don't remember them.

MRS. LYNGE. But I hear they got up to all kinds of wicked pranks. Tell me, is there any truth in those stories?

MRS. RUMMEL. None whatever, Mrs. Lynge, I assure you.

MRS. HOLT. Dina, my love, pass me that piece of linen, will you?

MRS. BERNICK, *simultaneously.* Dina dear, run out and ask Katrine to bring us some coffee.

MARTHA. I'll come with you, Dina.

DINA *and* MARTHA *go out through the door upstage left.*

MRS. BERNICK. If you'll excuse me for a moment, ladies, I think we'll take coffee outside.

She goes out onto the verandah and lays a table. DR. ROER-LUND *stands in the doorway talking to her.* HILMAR TOEN-NESEN *sits down outside and smokes.*

MRS. RUMMEL, *quietly.* My goodness, Mrs. Lynge, how you frightened me!

MRS. LYNGE. I?

MRS. HOLT. Yes, but you started it really, Mrs. Rummel.

MRS. RUMMEL. I? How can you say such a thing, Mrs. Holt? I never let a single word pass my lips.

MRS. LYNGE. But what is all this?

MRS. RUMMEL. How could you bring up the subject of—! I mean, really! Didn't you see Dina was here?

MRS. LYNGE. Dina? But good heavens, is there anything the matter with—?

MRS. HOLT. And in this house? Don't you know it was Mrs. Bernick's brother who—?

MRS. LYNGE. What about him? I don't know anything—I'm a newcomer here—

MRS. RUMMEL. You mean you haven't heard about—? Hm.

To MISS RUMMEL.

Hilda dear, run down into the garden for a few minutes.

MRS. HOLT. You too, Netta. And be sure you're nice to poor dear Dina when she comes back.

MISS RUMMEL *and* MISS HOLT *go into the garden.*

MRS. LYNGE. Well? What was this about Mrs. Bernick's brother?

MRS. RUMMEL. Don't you know it was he who was involved in that dreadful scandal?

MRS. LYNGE. Mr. Toennesen was involved in a dreadful scandal?

MRS. RUMMEL. Oh good heavens no, Mr. Toennesen is her cousin, Mrs. Lynge. I'm talking about her brother—

MRS. HOLT. The Prodigal of the family—

MRS. RUMMEL. His name was Johan. He ran away to America.

MRS. HOLT. Had to, you understand.

MRS. LYNGE. And it was he who was involved in this dreadful scandal?

MRS. RUMMEL. Yes. It was a kind of a—what shall I call it?—a kind of a—with Dina's mother. Oh, I remember it as if it had happened yesterday. Johan Toennesen was working in old Mrs. Bernick's office. Karsten Bernick had just come back from Paris—he hadn't got engaged yet—

MRS. LYNGE. Yes, but the dreadful scandal?

MRS. RUMMEL. Well you see, that winter a theatrical troupe was here in town—

MRS. HOLT. And among them was an actor named Dorf, and his wife. All the young men were quite crazy about her.

MRS. RUMMEL. Yes, heaven knows what they could see in her. Well, Mr. Dorf came home later one night—

MRS. HOLT. Unexpectedly, you understand—

MRS. RUMMEL. And what should he find but—no, I really can't bring myself to speak of it.

MRS. HOLT. No, Mrs. Rummel, he didn't *find* anything. The door was locked. From the inside.

MRS. RUMMEL. Yes, well, that's what I'm saying—he found the door locked. And, would you believe it, he—the man who was inside—had to jump out of the window!

MRS. HOLT. Right out of one of the top windows!

MRS. LYNGE. And the man was Mrs. Bernick's brother?

MRS. RUMMEL. It was indeed.

MRS. LYNGE. And that was why he ran away to America?

MRS. HOLT. Yes. Well, of course he had to.

MRS. RUMMEL. And then afterwards they discovered something almost equally dreadful. Would you believe it, he'd stolen some of the firm's money!

MRS. HOLT. But we don't know that for sure, Mrs. Rummel. It may only have been gossip.

MRS. RUMMEL. Oh, but now really! Didn't the whole town know about it? Didn't old Mrs. Bernick practically go bankrupt because of it? My husband told me so himself. But heaven forbid that *I* should say anything!

MRS. HOLT. Well anyway, Mrs. Dorf didn't get the money, because she—

MRS. LYNGE. Yes, what happened between Dina's parents after
that?

MRS. RUMMEL. Well, Dorf went away and left his wife and
child. But Madam had the cheek to stay here a whole year
more. Of course, she didn't dare show her face at the theatre. She kept herself by taking in washing and sewing—

MRS. HOLT. And tried to start a dancing academy.

MRS. RUMMEL. Of course, nothing came of it. What parents
would entrust their children to the care of a person like
that? Besides, as things turned out she didn't last long. She
wasn't used to hard work, not that fine lady. She picked up
some chest trouble, and died.

MRS. LYNGE. Well, that was a dreadful scandal indeed.

MRS. RUMMEL. Yes, it's been a terrible cross for the Bernicks
to bear. It's been the one skeleton in their cupboard, as my
husband once phrased it. So don't ever mention the subject
in this house, Mrs. Lynge.

MRS. HOLT. Or the half sister, for heaven's sake!

MRS. LYNGE. Mrs. Bernick has a half sister too?

MRS. RUMMEL. Did have—fortunately. It's all over between
them now. Oh, she was a queer one all right. Would you
believe it, she cut her hair off, and when it rained she walked
round in gumboots just like a man!

MRS. HOLT. And when the half brother—the Prodigal—ran
away, and the whole town quite naturally raised a hue and
cry against him, do you know what she did? Went over and
joined him!

MRS. RUMMEL. Yes, but the scandal she created before she
went, Mrs. Holt!

MRS. HOLT. Hush, let's not talk of that.

MRS. LYNGE. My goodness, was she involved in a scandal too?

MRS. RUMMEL. Well, it was like this. Karsten Bernick had just
got engaged to Betty Toennesen; and he was going in to

announce the news to her aunt, with his newly betrothed on
his arm—

MRS. HOLT. The Toennesens had lost their parents, you see—

MRS. RUMMEL. —when Lona Hessel got up from the chair she
was sitting on and gave Karsten Bernick for all his fine airs
and breeding such a box on the ears she nearly split his
eardrums.

MRS. LYNGE. You don't mean it!

MRS. RUMMEL. As heaven is my witness.

MRS. HOLT. And packed her bags and went to America.

MRS. LYNGE. Then she must have had her eye on him too!

MRS. RUMMEL. Of course she had! She'd been flouncing round
here imagining that he'd marry her the moment he got back
from Paris.

MRS. HOLT. Yes, fancy her being able to believe that! A man
of the world like Karsten Bernick—so genteel and well-bred
—the perfect gentleman—every woman's dream—

MRS. RUMMEL. And so virtuous with it all, Mrs. Holt. So moral.

MRS. LYNGE. But what has this Miss Hessel been doing in
America?

MRS. RUMMEL. Ah. Over that hangs a veil which had best not
be lifted, as my husband once phrased it.

MRS. LYNGE. What do you mean?

MRS. RUMMEL. Well, the family's no longer in contact with
her, as you can imagine. But the whole town knows this
much, that she's sung for money over there in—hm—places
of entertainment—

MRS. HOLT. And given lectures in public—

MRS. RUMMEL. And brought out a wicked book.

MRS. LYNGE. My goodness!

MRS. RUMMEL. Yes, Lona Hessel is another skeleton in the
Bernick family cupboard. Well, now you know the whole
story, Mrs. Lynge. Of course I've only told you all this so
that you'll be on your guard.

MRS. LYNGE. My goodness yes, you can be sure I will. But
that poor Dina Dorf! I feel really sorry for her.

MRS. RUMMEL. Oh, it was a great stroke of luck as far as she
was concerned. Just imagine if she'd been left in the hands
of those parents of hers! We all lent her a helping hand, of
course, and did what we could to try to guide her along
the right paths. Then Miss Bernick arranged for her to come
and live here.

MRS. HOLT. But she's always been a difficult child. Well, what
can you expect, when you think of the example she's been
set? A girl like that isn't like one of us. We have to take
her as we find her, Mrs. Lynge.

MRS. RUMMEL. Hush, here she is.

Loudly.

Yes, dear Dina's a very clever girl. Oh hullo, Dina, are you
back? We're just finishing.

MRS. HOLT. Dina my sweet, how lovely your coffee smells.
There's nothing like a nice cup of morning coffee—

MRS. BERNICK, *outside on the verandah.* Everything is ready,
ladies.

MISS BERNICK *and* DINA *have meanwhile been helping the*
MAID *to bring in the coffee things. All the* LADIES *go out on
to the verandah and sit down. They talk to* DINA *with osten-
tatious amiability. After a few moments, she comes into the
room and looks for her sewing.*

MRS. BERNICK, *outside at the coffee table.* Dina, won't you
join us?

DINA. No, thank you. I don't want any.

She sits down to her sewing. MRS. BERNICK *and* DR. ROER-
LUND *exchange a few words; then he comes into the room.*

ROERLUND, *pretends to need something from the table: then
says softly.* Dina.

DINA. Yes.

ROERLUND. Why don't you want to sit outside with us?

DINA. When I came in with the coffee I could see from the

expression on that new lady's face that they'd been talking about me.

ROERLUND. But didn't you also notice how friendly she was to you on the verandah?

DINA. That's just what I can't bear.

ROERLUND. You have a stubborn nature, Dina.

DINA. Yes.

ROERLUND. Why?

DINA. That's the way I am.

ROERLUND. Couldn't you try to make yourself different?

DINA. No.

ROERLUND. Why not?

DINA, *looks at him*. I'm one of the depraved sinners.

ROERLUND. Dina!

DINA. Mother was a depraved sinner too.

ROERLUND. Who has told you about these things?

DINA. No one. They never tell me anything. Why don't they? They all treat me so gently, as though I might break into pieces if— Oh, how I hate all this kindness!

ROERLUND. Dina dear, I understand so well how confined you feel here, but—

DINA. Yes, if only I could go far away. I'm sure I could manage on my own if only I didn't live among people who were so—so—

ROERLUND. So what?

DINA. So virtuous and moral.

ROERLUND. Dina, you can't mean that.

DINA. Oh, you know what I mean. Every day Hilda and Netta are brought here so that I can model myself on them. I can never be as clever as them. I don't want to be. Oh, if only I were far away! Then I might be able to become someone.

ROERLUND. You are someone, Dina.

DINA. What's the use, here?

ROERLUND. Then you mean you're seriously thinking of going away?

DINA. I wouldn't stay a day longer, if you weren't here.

ROERLUND. Tell me, Dina. Why do you like being with me?

DINA. Because you teach me so much about what's beautiful.

ROERLUND. I teach you about what is beautiful?

DINA. Yes. Or rather—you don't teach me anything; but when I hear you talk, I understand what beauty is.

ROERLUND. What do you mean by beauty?

DINA. I've never thought.

ROERLUND. Well, think now. What do you mean by beauty?

DINA. Beauty—is something that is big—and far away.

ROERLUND. Hm. Dina my dear, I'm deeply concerned about you.

DINA. Is that all?

ROERLUND. You know how very dear you are to me.

DINA. If I were Hilda or Netta you wouldn't be afraid to let people see it.

ROERLUND. Oh, Dina, you don't understand all the little things a man has to— When a man is chosen to be a moral pillar for the society he lives in—well, he can't be sufficiently careful. If only I could be sure that people would not misinterpret my motives— Well, it can't be helped. You must and shall be rescued. Dina, is it a bargain that when I come—when circumstances permit me to come to you and say: "Here is my hand"—you will take it and be my wife? Will you promise me that, Dina?

DINA. Yes.

ROERLUND. Thank you—thank you! Because I, too—oh, Dina, you are so very dear to me. Hush, someone's coming. Dina—please—for my sake—go outside and join the others.

She goes out and joins the LADIES. *As she does so* MR. RUMMEL, MR. SANDSTAD *and* MR. VIGELAND *enter from the room downstage left, followed by* MR. BERNICK, *with a sheaf of papers in his hand.*

BERNICK. Right, then, we're agreed.

VIGELAND. Yes, yes. May God's blessing rest upon our plans!

RUMMEL. Never you fear, Bernick. A Norseman's word is his bond. You know that.

BERNICK. There's to be no going back, now. No one's to drop out, whatever opposition we may encounter.

RUMMEL. We stand or fall together, Bernick.

HILMAR, *who has come to the door of the verandah.* Fall? What's going to fall? Railway shares?

BERNICK. On the contrary. The railway is to go ahead.

RUMMEL. Full steam, Mr. Toennesen.

HILMAR, *comes closer.* Really?

ROERLUND. What?

MRS. BERNICK, *at the verandah door.* But Karsten dear, surely you—?

BERNICK. Betty dear, how can these things possibly interest you?

To the THREE GENTLEMEN.

Well, we must get out a prospectus as quickly as possible. Our names will head the list, of course. The positions we occupy in the community render it our duty to support this cause to the fullest limit of our generosity.

SANDSTAD. Of course, of course.

RUMMEL. We'll see it through, Bernick. You have our word.

BERNICK. Oh yes, I'm not worried about the outcome. But we must use our authority and influence; once we can show that every section of the community is actively participating, the municipality will feel compelled to subscribe its shares.

MRS. BERNICK. Karsten, you must come outside and tell us all about it.

BERNICK. My dear Betty, this is not a matter for women to concern themselves with.

HILMAR. You seriously mean you're letting this railway project go through after all?

BERNICK. Yes, of course.

ROERLUND. But Mr. Bernick, last year you—

BERNICK. Last year the situation was different. The plan then was for a line to run along the coast—

VIGELAND. Which would have been utterly superfluous, Dr. Roerlund. After all, we have ships—

SANDSTAD. And it'd have been prohibitively expensive—

RUMMEL. Yes, and would have damaged important interests in our town.

BERNICK. The main point is that the project as then conceived would not have benefited the community as a whole. That is why I opposed it; and as a result, they have decided to run the line inland.

HILMAR. Yes, but then it won't touch any of the towns round here.

BERNICK. It will touch our town, my dear Hilmar. We have arranged for a branch line to be built.

HILMAR. Oh? That's a new idea, isn't it?

RUMMEL. Yes—magnificent idea, isn't it? What?

ROERLUND. Hm.

VIGELAND. There's no denying that Providence might almost have designed that little valley especially so as to accommodate a branch line.

ROERLUND. Do you really think so, Mr. Vigeland?

BERNICK. Yes, I must confess that I, too, feel it was the hand of Providence that sent me up country on business last spring and directed my footsteps into this valley, which I had never seen before. Suddenly it struck me like an inspiration that through this valley we could lay a branch line to our little town. I arranged for an engineer to survey the land and I have here his provisional calculations and estimates. Nothing now stands in our way.

MRS. BERNICK, *still in the doorway, with the other* LADIES. But Karsten dear, why have you kept all this hidden from us?

BERNICK. My dear Betty, you wouldn't have been able to understand what it was all about. In any case, I haven't mentioned it to anyone until today. But now the decisive moment has arrived. Now we can work openly and with all our strength. Yes, I shall force this project through, even if it means staking everything I possess.

RUMMEL. Us too, Bernick. You can rely on us.

ROERLUND. You really expect so much from this project then, gentlemen?

BERNICK. Of course we do! Think what a stimulus it will give to our whole community! Think of the great tracts of forest it will render accessible! Think of the mines it will enable us to work! Think of the river, with its waterfalls one above the other, and the factories we could build to utilise their power! A whole wealth of new industries will spring into being!

ROERLUND. But are you not afraid of the possible consequences of more frequent contact with the depraved world outside?

BERNICK. No need to fear that, my dear Doctor. Nowadays our industrious little community rests, thank God, on a sound moral foundation. We have all, if I may say so, helped to cleanse it; and we shall continue to keep it clean, each in his own way. You, Dr. Roerlund, will maintain your splendid work at the school and in the home. We, the practical men of affairs, will strengthen the community by spreading prosperity over as broad a circle as possible. And our womenfolk —yes, ladies, come closer, you may listen to what I have to say—our womenfolk, I say, our wives and daughters—continue, ladies I beseech you, to labour untiringly in the cause of charity, and to be a help and a shield to your dear ones, as my beloved Betty and Martha are to me and to Olaf—

Looks round.

Yes, where is Olaf today?

MRS. BERNICK. Oh, now the holidays have begun it's hopeless to try to keep him indoors.

BERNICK. I suppose that means he's down on the water front

again. He'll have an accident before he's finished, you mark my word.

HILMAR. Oh, rubbish. A little skirmish with the elements—

MRS. RUMMEL. Oh, I think it's so wonderful the love you show your family, Mr. Bernick.

BERNICK. Well, the family is the basis on which society rests. A good home, loyal and truthworthy friends, a small close-knit circle with no intrusive elements to cast their shadow—

KRAP *enters right with letters and newspapers.*

KRAP. The foreign mail, Mr. Bernick. And a telegram from New York.

BERNICK *takes it.* Ah, this'll be from the owners of the *Indian Girl.*

RUMMEL. Has the post come? Then I must ask you to excuse me—

VIGELAND. Me too.

SANDSTAD. Good-bye, Mr. Bernick.

BERNICK. Good-bye, gentlemen, good-bye. And don't forget, we meet at five o'clock this afternoon.

THE THREE GENTLEMEN. Yes, yes. Of course.

They go out right.

BERNICK *reads the telegram.* Oh no, really, this is typically American! How absolutely disgraceful!

MRS. BERNICK. Oh, Karsten, what is it?

BERNICK. Look at this, Mr. Krap. Here, read it.

KRAP *reads.* "Execute minimum repairs. Despatch *Indian Girl* as soon as seaworthy. Safe season. At worst, cargo will keep her afloat." Well, bless my soul!

BERNICK. "Cargo will keep her afloat"! Those fellows know perfectly well that if anything goes wrong that cargo'll send the ship to the bottom like a stone.

ROERLUND. Well, that only goes to show what the moral climate is like in these so-called great communities.

BERNICK. You're right. They don't even respect human life, as long as they make their profit.

To KRAP.

Can we make the *Indian Girl* seaworthy in four or five days?

KRAP. Yes, if Mr. Vigeland lets us stop work on the *Palm Tree*.

BERNICK. Hm. He won't do that. Well, look through the mail. By the way, did you see Olaf down on the jetty?

KRAP. No, sir.

He goes into the room downstage left.

BERNICK *reads the telegram again.* Eighteen human lives at stake! And those gentlemen don't turn a hair.

HILMAR. Well, it's a sailor's job to brave the elements. It must be exhilarating to have nothing but a thin plank between yourself and eternity. Good for the nerves—

BERNICK. I'd like to meet the shipowner in this town who could reconcile his conscience to giving an order like this. There isn't a man in this community, not one—

Sees OLAF.

Ah, here he is. Thank goodness for that.

OLAF, *with a fishing line in his hand, has run up the street and in through the garden gate.*

OLAF, *still in the garden.* Uncle Hilmar, I've been down looking at the steamer!

BERNICK. Have you been on that jetty again?

OLAF. No, I only went out in a boat. Just fancy, Uncle Hilmar, a whole circus has come ashore, with horses and animals! And there were lots of tourists too!

MRS. RUMMEL. I say, are we going to see a circus?

ROERLUND. We? I hardly think so.

MRS. RUMMEL. No, no—of course, I didn't mean *us*—I only—

DINA. I should like to see a circus.

OLAF. Yes, so would I!

HILMAR. You little fool, what's worth seeing there? Dressage, and all that nonsense. Now to see a Gaucho galloping across the pampas on his snorting mustang—that'd be different! Oh dear, these provincial backwaters—

OLAF *tugs* MARTHA's *sleeve.* Look, Aunt Martha, look! There they are!

MRS. HOLT. Oh, my goodness.

MRS. LYNGE. Dear me, what horrible people.

A crowd of TOURISTS *and* TOWNSPEOPLE *appears in the street.*

MRS. RUMMEL. My word, they're proper vagabonds. Look at that woman in the grey dress, Mrs. Holt. She's carrying a knapsack on her back!

MRS. HOLT. Yes. Fancy, she's got it tied to her parasol! I expect she's the ringmaster's—er—wife.

MRS. RUMMEL. There's the ringmaster! The one with the beard. I say, he looks just like a pirate! Don't look at him, Hilda.

MRS. HOLT. Nor you, Netta.

OLAF. Mother, he's waving to us!

BERNICK. What!

MRS. BERNICK. Olaf, what on earth do you mean?

MRS. RUMMEL. My goodness, yes! The woman's waving too!

BERNICK. This really is intolerable.

MARTHA *gives an involuntary cry.* Oh!

MRS. BERNICK. What is it, Martha?

MARTHA. Oh, nothing. I thought for a moment it—

OLAF *cries excitedly.* Look, look! Here come the horses and animals! And there are the Americans, too! All the sailors from the *Indian Girl!*

Yankee Doodle is heard, accompanied by a clarinet and drum.

HILMAR *puts his hands over his ears.* Ugh, ugh, ugh!

ROERLUND. I think we should isolate ourselves for a while, ladies. This is not for us. Let us return to our work.

MRS. BERNICK. Ought we perhaps to draw the curtains?

ROERLUND. That is exactly what I had in mind.

The LADIES *take their places again at the table.* DR. ROER-

LUND *closes the verandah door and draws the curtains across it and the windows. The room is plunged into semi-darkness.*

OLAF, *peering out.* Mother, now the ringmaster's lady's washing her face at the pump.

MRS. BERNICK. What! In the middle of the market place?

HILMAR. Well, if I was crossing a desert and happened on a well, I don't suppose I'd bother to look round to see if— ugh, that dreadful clarinet!

ROERLUND. This is becoming a matter for the police.

BERNICK. Ah well, they're foreigners; one mustn't judge them too severely. These people are not born with the sense of decorum which makes us instinctively obey the laws of propriety. Let them go their way. What are they to us? This ribald behaviour, offensive to every standard of decency, has fortunately no place in our community. What the—!

The STRANGE LADY *strides in through the door, right.*

THE LADIES, *in terrified whispers.* The circus woman! The ringmaster's—er—!

MRS. BERNICK. Good heavens! What is the meaning of this?

MARTHA *jumps to her feet.* Oh!

THE LADY. Morning, Betty dear. Morning, Martha. Morning, brother-in-law.

MRS. BERNICK, *with a scream.* Lona!

BERNICK *takes a step backwards.* Good God!

MRS. HOLT. Oh, dear heaven!

MRS. RUMMEL. It can't be possible!

HILMAR. Well! Ugh!

MRS. BERNICK. Lona! Is it really you!

MISS HESSEL. Really me? Sure it's me. Come on, kiss me and prove it!

HILMAR. Ugh! Ugh!

MRS. BERNICK. You mean you've come here to—?

BERNICK. To perform?

MISS HESSEL. Perform? What do you mean, perform?

BERNICK. In the—er—circus.

MISS HESSEL *roars with laughter*. Karsten, have you gone nuts? You think I've joined the circus? No—I've learned a few tricks, and acted the clown in more ways than one—

MRS. RUMMEL *coughs*.

—but I haven't started jumping through hoops yet.

BERNICK. Then you're not—!

MRS. BERNICK. Thank heaven for that!

MISS HESSEL. No, we came respectably, with the other tourists. Steerage—but we're used to that.

MRS. BERNICK. Did you say *we?*

BERNICK *takes a step towards her*. Who do you mean by *we?*

MISS HESSEL. Me and the kid, of course.

THE LADIES *shriek*. Kid?

HILMAR. What!

ROERLUND. Well, really!

MRS. BERNICK. But Lona, what do you mean?

MISS HESSEL. Whom do you think I mean? John, of course; he's the only kid I have, to my knowledge. Johan, you used to call him.

MRS. BERNICK. Johan!

MRS. RUMMEL, *sotto voce to* MRS. LYNGE. The Prodigal!

BERNICK, *unwillingly*. Is Johan with you?

MISS HESSEL. Yes, of course. Never go anywhere without him. Say, you *are* all looking down in the mouth. Why are you sitting in the dark? What's that white stuff you're all sewing? Is someone dead?

ROERLUND. Madam, you find yourself at a meeting of the Society for the Redemption of Fallen Women.

MISS HESSEL *lowers her voice*. What! You mean all these respectable-looking ladies are—?

MRS. RUMMEL. Now, really!

MISS HESSEL. Oh, I get it, I get it. Well, if it isn't Mrs. Rummel! And Mrs. Holt! Say, we three haven't grown any shorter in the tooth since we last met! Now, listen, all of you. Let the Fallen Women wait for twenty-four hours; they won't fall any further. This is an occasion for celebration!

ROERLUND. A homecoming is not always an occasion for celebration.

MISS HESSEL. Is that so? How do you interpret your Bible, Reverend—

ROERLUND. I am not a Reverend.

MISS HESSEL. Never mind, you'll become one. Say, this charity stuff stinks awful. Just like a shroud. Of course, I'm used to the prairies. Air's fresher there.

BERNICK *mops his brow.* Yes, it is rather close in here.

MISS HESSEL. Take it easy, Karsten; you'll surface.

Pulls aside the curtains.

Let's have some daylight in here for when the kid comes. Wait till you see him! He's scrubbed himself as clean as a—

HILMAR. Ugh!

MISS HESSEL *opens the door and windows.* That's to say, he *will* have, once he gets a chance up at the hotel. On that ship he got as filthy as a pig.

HILMAR. Ugh! Ugh!

MISS HESSEL. Ugh? Well, bless me if it isn't—!

Points at HILMAR *and asks the others.*

Does he still sit around here saying 'Ugh!'?

HILMAR. I *don't* sit around. I only stay here because my health doesn't permit me to work.

ROERLUND *coughs.* Ladies, I hardly think—

MISS HESSEL *catches sight of* OLAF. Is this yours, Betty? Give us your paw, kid. Are you afraid of your ugly old aunt?

ROERLUND *puts his book under his arm.* Ladies, I hardly think the atmosphere here is conducive to further work today. We meet again as usual tomorrow?

MISS HESSEL, *as the other* LADIES *rise to leave.* Sure, why not? You can count me in.

ROERLUND. You? Forgive my asking, Madam, but what can you possibly contribute to our Society?

MISS HESSEL. Fresh air—Reverend.

ACT TWO

The garden room in BERNICK'S *house.* MRS. BERNICK *is seated alone at the worktable with her sewing. After a few moments,* BERNICK *enters right with his hat on, carrying gloves and a stick.*

MRS. BERNICK. Home already, Karsten?

BERNICK. Yes. I have an appointment here.

MRS. BERNICK *sighs*. Oh, dear. Johan again, I suppose.

BERNICK. No, no, it's with one of the men.

Takes off his hat.

Where are all the ladies today?

MRS. BERNICK. Mrs. Rummel and Hilda hadn't time.

BERNICK. Oh? They sent their excuses?

MRS. BERNICK. Yes; they had so much to do at home.

BERNICK. But of course. And the others won't be coming either, I suppose?

MRS. BERNICK. No, they're busy too.

BERNICK. I could have told you that yesterday. Where's Olaf?

MRS. BERNICK. I sent him out for a walk with Dina.

BERNICK. Hm. Dina. Flighty young hussy. Striking up like that with Johan the very first day he arrived—

MRS. BERNICK. But Karsten dear, Dina knows nothing about—

BERNICK. Well, he ought to have had the tact not to pay her so much attention. I saw the look Vigeland gave them.

MRS. BERNICK *puts her sewing in her lap.* Karsten, why do you think they've come?

BERNICK. Well, I dare say that farm of his isn't doing too well —she said yesterday they'd had to travel steerage—

MRS. BERNICK. Yes, I'm afraid you must be right. But fancy *her* coming with him! After the dreadful way she insulted you!

BERNICK. Oh, that was a long time ago. Forget about it.

MRS. BERNICK. How can I forget about it? After all, he is my brother—but it's not so much him I'm thinking of as all the unpleasantness it's causing you. Oh, Karsten, I'm so dreadfully frightened—

BERNICK. Frightened? Of what?

MRS. BERNICK. Mightn't they arrest him for stealing that money from your mother?

BERNICK. Don't be so silly. No one can prove anything was taken.

MRS. BERNICK. Oh, but the whole town knows. And you've said yourself that—

BERNICK. I have said nothing. The town knows nothing. All they heard was just vague gossip.

MRS. BERNICK. You are so magnanimous, Karsten.

BERNICK. Try to forget these old memories, Betty. You don't know how it distresses me to be reminded about all this. *Walks up and down; then he throws down his stick.*

Why on earth must they come home just at this moment, when I don't want any trouble in the town, or in the press? It'll get into every local paper for miles around. Whether I welcome them or whether I turn my back on them, people will talk about it and read something into it. They'll dig the whole story up again, just the way you're doing. And in a community like ours—

Throws down his gloves on the table.

And I haven't a single person I can talk to or look to for support.

MRS. BERNICK. Have you no one, Karsten?

BERNICK. No, who could there be? Oh, why in God's name must they come *now?* They're sure to create a scandal of some kind or another. Especially she. It really is intolerable having people like that in one's own family.

MRS. BERNICK. Well, I can't help it if—

BERNICK. You can't help what? That they're your relations? No, you can't help that.

MRS. BERNICK. I didn't ask them to come.

BERNICK. Oh, here we go again. "I didn't ask them to come. I didn't write and beg them. I didn't drag them here by the hair." I know it all by heart!

MRS. BERNICK *begins to cry.* Oh, why must you be so unkind.

BERNICK. That's right. Start crying, and give the town something else to talk about. Stop this foolishness, Betty. Go and sit outside, someone might come. Do you want people to see you've been crying? A fine thing it'd be if people got to hear that— Hush, someone's coming.

There is a knock on the door.

Come in!

MRS. BERNICK *goes out on to the verandah with her sewing.* AUNE *enters, right.*

AUNE. Good morning, Mr. Bernick.

BERNICK. Good morning. Well, I suppose you can guess why I've sent for you?

AUNE. Mr. Krap said something yesterday about your not being satisfied with—

BERNICK. I'm dissatisfied with the way things are going down at the yard, Aune. You're not getting on with those repairs. The *Palm Tree* ought to have been under sail days ago. Mr. Vigeland comes here to complain every day. He's a difficult man to have as a partner.

AUNE. The *Palm Tree* can sail the day after tomorrow.

BERNICK. At last! But that American ship, the *Indian Girl*, has been lying here for five weeks—

AUNE. The American? I understood we were to put all our men on to your ship till she was ready.

BERNICK. I gave no such orders. My instructions were that you should go full steam ahead with the American too. You haven't.

AUNE. But her bottom's rotten, Mr. Bernick. The more we patch her the worse she gets.

BERNICK. That's not the real reason. Mr. Krap's told me the whole story. You don't understand how to use these new machines I've bought—or rather, you won't use them.

AUNE. Mr. Bernick, I'm nearly sixty and ever since I was a boy I've been accustomed to the old methods—

BERNICK. We can't use those nowadays. Look, Aune, you mustn't think I'm doing this for money. Luckily I don't need any more of that. I've got to think of the community of which I'm a member, and of the business of which I am the head. Progress has got to come from me or it won't come at all.

AUNE. I want progress too, Mr. Bernick.

BERNICK. Yes, for your own narrow circle, the working class. Oh, I know you agitators. You make speeches and get the people worked up, but the moment anyone takes any practical steps towards improving matters, as with these machines, you refuse to co-operate, and get frightened.

AUNE. I am frightened, Mr. Bernick. I'm frightened for all the mouths from which these machines will take the bread. You keep on saying we've got to think of the community, but I reckon the community owes us a duty too. What's the use of society employing knowledge and capital to introduce all these new inventions before it's educated a generation that knows how to use them?

BERNICK. You read and think too much, Aune. And what good do you get from it? It just makes you discontented with your position in society.

AUNE. It isn't that, Mr. Bernick. I can't bear to see one good man after another getting sacked and their families going hungry to make way for these machines.

BERNICK. When printing was invented, many scribes went hungry.

AUNE. Would you have welcomed it if you'd been a scribe?

BERNICK. I didn't send for you to argue with you. The *Indian Girl's* got to be ready to sail the day after tomorrow.

AUNE. But Mr. Bernick—

BERNICK. The day after tomorrow, do you hear? At the same time as our own ship; not an hour later. I've good reasons for wanting to get the job done quickly. Have you read the newspaper this morning? Then you know that the Americans have been causing trouble again. Those ruffians are turning the whole town upside down; not a night goes by without them starting a brawl in the streets or in a drinking house. To say nothing of other things I'd rather not mention.

AUNE. Yes, they seem a bad lot.

BERNICK. And who gets the blame for all this? I do! It all comes back on to my head. These newspaper fellows grumble and try to insinuate that we've put all our labour strength on to the *Palm Tree.* And I, who am supposed to influence my fellow citizens by setting them a good example, have all this dirt thrown at me. Well, I'm not standing for it. I'm not used to having my name dragged in the mud like this.

AUNE. Oh, you don't need to bother about that kind of thing, Mr. Bernick.

BERNICK. Just now I do. I need all the respect and good will I can muster from my fellow citizens. I've big plans afoot, as I dare say you've heard, and if malicious-minded people succeed in shaking the community's trust in me, it could cause me very great difficulties. So I want at all costs to avoid giving these damned scribblers any food for gossip, and that's why I say the job's got to be done by the day after tomorrow.

AUNE. Mr. Bernick, you might as well tell me it's got to be done by this afternoon.

BERNICK. You mean I'm demanding the impossible?

AUNE. With our present labour strength, yes.

BERNICK. Very well. Then I'll have to start looking elsewhere.

AUNE. You don't mean you're going to dismiss still more of the older men?

BERNICK. No, that's not what I was thinking.

AUNE. It'd create bad feeling in the town if you did that. And in the newspapers.

BERNICK. Probably it might, so I won't. But if the *Indian Girl* isn't ready to sail by the day after tomorrow, there'll be a notice of dismissal served on you.

AUNE. On me!

Laughs.

You're joking with me, sir.

BERNICK. I shouldn't take that for granted if I were you.

AUNE. Dismiss me? But my father and his father worked all their lives in this yard. And so have I.

BERNICK. Who's making me do this?

AUNE. You're asking the impossible, Mr. Bernick.

BERNICK. A good worker doesn't know the meaning of the word impossible. Yes or no? Give me a straight answer, or you'll get your notice now.

AUNE *takes a step towards him.* Mr. Bernick, have you ever seriously thought what it means to give an old worker the sack? You think he can look round for something else? Oh, yes; he can do that; but that isn't the whole story. You ought to be present some time in a workman's house on the evening when he comes home and throws down his bag of tools behind the door.

BERNICK. Do you think I'm finding it easy to do this? Haven't I always been a good master to you?

AUNE. So much the worse for me, sir. It means no one at home will put the blame on you. They won't say anything to my face—they wouldn't dare—but they'll shoot a glance at me when they think I'm not looking and say to themselves: "Oh well, he must have deserved it." Don't you see, sir, that's the one thing I can't bear! Poor as I am, I've always been used to being regarded as lord and master in my own house. My humble home is a little community just as yours is, Mr. Bernick, and I've been able to sustain it and keep it going because my wife has believed in me and my children have believed in me. And now it's all going to fall to the ground.

BERNICK. Well, if there's no other way, the lesser must make way for the greater. The individuals must be sacrificed for the common cause. That's the only answer I can give you; it's the way of the world. You're a stubborn man, Aune. You oppose me, not because you must but because you won't accept the fact that machines can work better than flesh and blood.

AUNE. And you're so dead set on this, Mr. Bernick, because you know that if you sack me at least you'll have shown the press you're anxious to do as they say you should.

BERNICK. Well, suppose I am? I've told you how much this means to me; either I have every newspaper in the district putting me in the pillory, or else I get them on my side just at the moment when I'm working to get a big project under way for the good of the community. Well then, how else can I act? My choice is either to keep your home going or to suppress the building of hundreds of new homes—hundreds of homes that will never be built, never have a fire in their hearth, unless I succeed in achieving what I'm now working for. Well, I leave the choice to you.

AUNE. I see. In that case I've no more to say.

BERNICK. Hm. My dear Aune, it really grieves me deeply that we have to part.

AUNE. We're not parting, Mr. Bernick.

BERNICK. What do you mean?

AUNE. Working men have a sense of honour too.

BERNICK. Of course they have. Then you think you can promise—?

AUNE. The *Indian Girl* will be ready to sail the day after tomorrow.

Touches his forehead and goes out right.

BERNICK. Well, I've made that obstinate old fool see sense. That's a good omen, anyway.

HILMAR TOENNESEN *enters through the garden gate, smoking a cigar.*

HILMAR, *on the verandah.* Morning, Betty. Morning, Bernick.

MRS. BERNICK. Good morning.

HILMAR. You've been crying. You know, then?

MRS. BERNICK. Know what?

HILMAR. That the scandal's started. Ugh!

BERNICK. What do you mean?

HILMAR *comes into the room.* Those two Americans are walking round the town in broad daylight with our little Dina Dorf.

MRS. BERNICK *follows him.* Hilmar, you're joking!

HILMAR. I'm afraid it's the truth. Lona was actually so tactless as to shout at me. Of course I pretended not to hear her.

BERNICK. And I suppose this hasn't exactly passed unnoticed.

HILMAR. You bet your life it hasn't. People stood still and stared at them. The news spread through the town like wildfire; like a prairie blaze. In every house people stood at their windows and waited for the procession to pass; they were packed behind their curtains like sardines—ugh! You must forgive me, Betty; I can't help saying "Ugh!", this makes me so nervous. If it goes on, I shall have to think about taking a holiday. Rather a long one.

MRS. BERNICK. But you ought to have spoken to him and made it clear that—

HILMAR. What, in public? No, I'm sorry. But fancy him daring to show his face in this town at all! Well, we'll see if the newspapers can't put a spoke in his wheel. I'm sorry, Betty, but—

BERNICK. The newspapers, did you say? Have you heard anything to suggest that they may take action?

HILMAR. Oh yes, there's no doubt about that. When I left you yesterday afternoon, I took a walk up to the club, for my health. It was quite evident from the silence that fell when I entered that they'd been talking about our American friends. Well, then that tactless editor fellow—you know, Hammer—came in and congratulated me out loud on my rich cousin's return home.

BERNICK. Rich—?

HILMAR. Yes, that's what he said. Of course I gave him a pretty piercing look and made it quite clear that I knew nothing about any riches as far as Johan Toennesen was concerned. "Oh really?" he said, "that's strange. People usually do all right in America provided they have some capital, and your cousin didn't go empty-handed, did he?"

BERNICK. Hm. Look, do me the goodness to—

MRS. BERNICK, *worried*. There you are, Karsten—

HILMAR. Yes, well anyway, he's given me a sleepless night. And he has the cheek to stroll round this town looking as innocent as an angel. Why didn't that illness he had knock him off? It's really monstrous how indestructible some people are.

MRS. BERNICK. Hilmar, what are you saying?

HILMAR. Oh, I'm not saying anything. But look at him; he's survived railway accidents and attacks by grizzlies and Blackfoot Indians without a scratch to show for it all. Didn't even get scalped. Ugh, here they are!

BERNICK *glances up the street*. Olaf's with them!

HILMAR. But of course. They want to remind everyone that they belong to the best family in town. Look at all those people coming out of the chemist's to stare at them and make remarks. My nerves won't stand this; how a man can be expected to keep the flag of ideals flying under circumstances like these I really don't know.

BERNICK. They're coming here. Now listen, Betty, it's my express wish that you treat them with every courtesy.

MRS. BERNICK. May I, Karsten?

BERNICK. Yes, yes; and you too, Hilmar. With luck they won't stay long, and while we're alone together I don't want there to be any insinuations. We must on no account embarrass them.

MRS. BERNICK. Oh, Karsten, how magnanimous you are!

BERNICK. Yes well, never mind that.

MRS. BERNICK. No, you must let me thank you; and forgive me for becoming so emotional just now. Oh, you were quite justified in—

BERNICK. Never mind, I say, never *mind*.

HILMAR. Ugh!

JOHAN TOENNESEN *and* DINA *enter through the garden, followed by* MISS HESSEL *and* OLAF.

MISS HESSEL. Morning, everyone.

JOHAN. We've been giving the old place the once-over, Karsten.

BERNICK. Yes, so I hear. Plenty of changes, eh?

MISS HESSEL. Everywhere there's evidence of Karsten Bernick's great and good works. We've been around the gardens you presented to the town—

BERNICK. Oh, you've been there?

MISS HESSEL. "The Gift of Karsten Bernick," it says over the entrance. Yes, you seem to be the kingpin here all right.

JOHAN. Fine ships you've got too. I ran into the captain of the *Palm Tree*—he's an old school friend of mine—

MISS HESSEL. And you've built a new school; and I hear we can thank you for the waterworks and the gas tank.

BERNICK. Well, one must do something for the community one lives in.

MISS HESSEL. The sentiment does you credit, brother-in-law.

It made me proud to see what a high opinion everyone has of you. I don't reckon myself vain, but I couldn't resist reminding one or two people we spoke to that Johan and I belong to the family.

HILMAR. Ugh!

MISS HESSEL. What's "Ugh!" about that?

HILMAR. All I said was "Hm!"

MISS HESSEL. Did you? Oh, that's all right. Well, you don't seem to have any visitors today.

MRS. BERNICK. No, we're alone.

MISS HESSEL. We met a couple of your Salvationists in the market place. They seemed to be in a great hurry. But, we haven't had a real chance to talk yet, have we? Yesterday you had those three Railway Kings and the Reverend—

HILMAR. Schoolmaster.

MISS HESSEL. Well, I call him Reverend. But tell me, what do you think of what I've been doing for the past fifteen years? Hasn't he grown into a fine boy? Who'd ever think he was the same as that young good-for-nothing who ran away from home?

HILMAR. Hm.

JOHAN. Oh Lona, stop boasting.

MISS HESSEL. O.K., so I'm proud of it! Hell, it's the only thing I've ever achieved in the world; but it makes me feel I've done something to justify my existence. Yes, Johan, when I think how you and I started out there, with just our four bare paws—

HILMAR. Hands—

MISS HESSEL. I said paws. They were black.

HILMAR. Ugh!

MISS HESSEL. Yes, and empty.

HILMAR. Empty? Well, I must say—

MISS HESSEL. What must you say?

BERNICK *coughs.*

HILMAR. I must say—ugh!

Goes out on to the verandah.

MISS HESSEL. What's the matter with him?

BERNICK. Oh, never mind him; he's been rather nervous these last few days. Er—wouldn't you like to have a look round the garden? You haven't seen it properly yet, and I happen to have an hour free just now.

MISS HESSEL. That's a fine idea. I'd love to.

MRS. BERNICK. There've been some big changes there too, as you'll see.

BERNICK, MRS. BERNICK *and* MISS HESSEL *descend into the garden. We see them occasionally during the following scene.*

OLAF, *in the doorway to the verandah.* Uncle Hilmar, do you know what Uncle Johan asked me? He asked if I'd like to go with him to America?

HILMAR. You, you jackass! Why, you spend your whole time clinging to your mother's petticoats.

OLAF. I don't want to do that any longer. You wait—once I'm big, I'll—

HILMAR. Oh, stuff; you've no stomach for danger.

They go together into the garden.

JOHAN, *to* DINA, *who has taken off her hat and is standing in the doorway on the right, shaking the dust from her dress.* I'm afraid that walk must have made you very hot.

DINA. No, I enjoyed it. I've never enjoyed a walk so much before.

JOHAN. You don't often go for walks in the morning, perhaps?

DINA. Oh, yes. But only with Olaf.

JOHAN. I see. Er—perhaps you'd rather go into the garden than stay inside here?

DINA. No, I'd rather stay here.

JOHAN. So would I. Good, that's agreed then, we'll take a walk like this every morning.

DINA. No, Mr. Toennesen. You mustn't.

JOHAN. Mustn't? But you promised—

DINA. Yes, but now I think about it— You ought not to be seen with me.

JOHAN. But why not?

DINA. Oh, you're a stranger here. You don't understand. I'm not—

JOHAN. Yes?

DINA. No, I'd rather not talk about it.

JOHAN. Come on. You can tell me.

DINA. Well, if you want to know—I'm not like other girls. There's something—well, something. So you mustn't.

JOHAN. Look, I don't understand this at all. You haven't done anything wrong, have you?

DINA. No—I haven't—but—no, I don't want to talk any more about it. You'll hear all about it from the others, I expect.

JOHAN. Hm.

DINA. But there was something else I wanted to ask you.

JOHAN. What?

DINA. Is it as easy as they say to become—someone—over there in America?

JOHAN. No, it isn't always easy. You often have to work your fingers to the bone at first, and live pretty rough.

DINA. I wouldn't mind that.

JOHAN. You?

DINA. I can work. I'm healthy and strong, and Aunt Martha's taught me a lot.

JOHAN. Well, for heaven's sake then, come back with us.

DINA. Oh, you're only joking. You said that to Olaf. But tell me one thing. Are people as—as moral over there as they are here?

JOHAN. Moral?

DINA. Yes. I mean—are they as good and virtuous as they are here?

JOHAN. Well, they haven't all got horns, the way people here seem to imagine. You needn't be afraid of that.

DINA. You don't understand. I want to go somewhere where people aren't good and virtuous.

JOHAN. Where they *aren't?* What do you want them to be, then?

DINA. I want them to be natural.

JOHAN. They're that all right.

DINA. Then I think it'd be good for me if I could go and live there.

JOHAN. I'm sure it would. You must come back with us.

DINA. No, I don't want to go with you. I must go alone. Oh, I'd manage. I'd make something of myself—

BERNICK, *below the verandah with the two* LADIES. No, no, stay here, Betty dear. I'll fetch it. You might easily catch cold.

He enters the room and starts looking for MRS. BERNICK'S *shawl.*

MRS. BERNICK, *in the garden.* You must come with us, Johan. We're going down to the grotto.

BERNICK. No, I'm sure Johan would rather stay here. Dina, take my wife's shawl down to her, will you, and go along with them? Johan'll stay here with me, Betty dear. I want to hear about what life is like on the other side.

MRS. BERNICK. All right, but come soon. You know where we'll be.

MRS. BERNICK, MISS HESSEL *and* DINA *go out left through the garden.*

BERNICK *watches them go for a moment, then walks across to the door upstage left and closes it. Then he goes over to* JOHAN, *clasps both his hands, shakes and presses them.* Johan! Now we're alone—thank you! Thank you!

JOHAN. Oh, nonsense.

BERNICK. My house and home, the happiness of my family, my position in the community—I owe it all to you.

JOHAN. Well, I'm glad to hear it, my dear Karsten. Some good came out of that silly business after all, then.

BERNICK *shakes his hands again.* Thank you, thank you! There isn't one man in ten thousand who'd have done as you did.

JOHAN. Forget it! We were both young and wild, weren't we? One of us had to take the rap.

BERNICK. But who deserved to, if not the guilty one?

JOHAN. Now wait a minute! On this occasion it was the innocent one who deserved the rap. I had no worries or responsibilities; and no parents. I was glad of a chance to get away from that drudgery at the office. You had your old mother still alive; besides, you'd just got secretly engaged to Betty, and she was deeply in love with you. What would have happened to her if she'd found out that you—?

BERNICK. I know, I know; all the same—

JOHAN. And wasn't it just for Betty's sake that you broke off that business with Mrs. Dorf? You'd only gone along that evening to put an end to it all—

BERNICK. Yes; why did that drunken ruffian have to come home just that evening? Yes, Johan, it was for Betty's sake; even so —that you could be so unselfish as to take the blame on yourself, and go away—

JOHAN. Forget it, my dear Karsten. After all, we agreed that this was the best solution; we had to get you out of it somehow, and you were my friend. Yes, how proud I was of that friendship! I was a poor country lad working in an office; you were rich and of good family, just back from Paris and London—and yet you chose me as your friend, though I was four years younger than you. Oh, I realise now it was because you were in love with Betty, but how proud I was! And who wouldn't have been? Who wouldn't gladly have sacrificed himself for you, especially when all it meant was giving the town something to gossip about for a month and having an excuse to get away from it all into the great wide world outside?

BERNICK. Hm. My dear Johan, to be frank I must tell you that the matter hasn't quite been forgotten yet.

JOHAN. Hasn't it? Well, what's that to me? Once I'm back on my ranch—

BERNICK. You're going back, then?

JOHAN. Of course.

BERNICK. But not too soon, I hope?

JOHAN. As soon as I can. I only came here to please Lona.

BERNICK. Oh? How do you mean?

JOHAN. Well, you see, Lona isn't young any longer, and these last few months she's been pining her heart out to get back here; but she wouldn't ever admit it.

Smiles.

She didn't dare leave an irresponsible young fellow like me on my own, when by the age of nineteen I'd already gone and—

BERNICK. Yes, well?

JOHAN. Karsten, I've got a confession to make to you which I'm a little ashamed about.

BERNICK. You didn't tell her?

JOHAN. Yes, I did. It was wrong of me, but I had to. You've no idea what Lona has been to me. I know you could never get along with her, but to me she's been like a mother. Those first years over there, when we were so poor—you've no idea how she worked! And when I had that long illness and couldn't earn anything, she went off and sang in cafés—I tried to stop her but I couldn't—and gave lectures which people laughed at, and wrote a book which she's since laughed over herself—yes, and cried over—all just to keep me alive. I couldn't sit there last winter and watch her pining her heart out after the way she'd slaved and toiled for me. Karsten, I couldn't. So I said to her: "Go, Lona. You needn't worry about me. I'm not as irresponsible as you think." And then—well, I told her.

BERNICK. And how did she take it?

JOHAN. Well, she quite rightly decided that since I'd proved myself innocent, there was no reason why I shouldn't come back with her. But you don't need to worry. Lona won't talk, and I can keep my mouth shut. Like I did before.

BERNICK. Oh, yes, yes. I trust you.

JOHAN. Here's my hand on it. Well now, we'll say no more about that business; luckily it's the only crazy thing either of us has ever done. I intend to enjoy the few days I'm going to be here. You can't imagine what a lovely walk we had this morning. Who'd ever have imagined that that little girl who used to run around here and act cherubs at the theatre would ever—by the way, Karsten, what happened to her parents—afterwards?

BERNICK. My dear chap, I don't know any more than what I wrote to you just after you sailed. You got my two letters all right?

JOHAN. Yes, yes, I have both of them. That drunken scoundrel left her, then?

BERNICK. Yes, and got himself killed in a brawl.

JOHAN. She died not long afterwards, didn't she? But you did all you could for her, I presume? Secretly, I mean?

BERNICK. She was proud. She revealed nothing, and refused to accept a penny.

JOHAN. You did the right thing in bringing Dina to live with you.

BERNICK. Of course, of course. Actually, it was Martha who arranged that.

JOHAN. Was it Martha? Yes, by the way, where is Martha today?

BERNICK. Where is she? Oh, when she isn't at the school she's busy with her invalids.

JOHAN. So it was Martha who took care of her?

BERNICK. Yes, Martha's always had rather a weakness for looking after children. That was why she took this job at the council school. Damn stupid idea.

JOHAN. Yes, she looked pretty worn out yesterday. I'm afraid you're right, she isn't really strong enough for that kind of work.

BERNICK. Oh, she's strong enough for it. But it's so unpleasant for me. It makes it look as though I wasn't prepared to maintain my own sister.

JOHAN. Maintain her? I thought she had money of her own—

BERNICK. Not a penny. You remember what a difficult situation Mother was in when you left? Well, she managed to keep going for a while, with my help, but I wasn't really happy with that as a long-term policy. I thought I'd go in with her, but even that wasn't enough. In the end, I had to take over the whole business, and when we finally drew up the accounts there was scarcely anything left of Mother's share. Soon afterwards she died and of course Martha was left practically penniless.

JOHAN. Poor Martha!

BERNICK. Poor? What do you mean? You don't imagine I let her want for anything? Oh no, I think I may say I'm a good brother to her. She lives with us, naturally, and eats at our table; her teacher's salary is sufficient for her clothing needs, and—well she's a single woman, what more does she want?

JOHAN. Hm; we don't reason like that in America.

BERNICK. No, I dare say not, in an unstable society like theirs. But here in our little community, which immorality hasn't yet, thank God, begun to corrupt, the women are content to occupy a modest and unassuming position. Anyway, it's Martha's own fault; she could have been provided for long ago if she'd been so minded.

JOHAN. Could have married, you mean?

BERNICK. Yes, and very advantageously. She's had several good offers; strangely enough, considering she's a woman with no money and no longer young, and really rather ordinary.

JOHAN. Ordinary?

BERNICK. Oh, don't think I hold it against her. Indeed, I

wouldn't have it otherwise. You know how it is, in a big house like ours it's always useful to have a—well—placid-natured person around whom one can ask to do anything.

JOHAN. Yes, but what about her?

BERNICK. What do you mean, what about her? Oh, I see. Well, she's got plenty to interest herself; she's got me and Betty and Olaf and—me. It isn't good for people to be always thinking of themselves first, least of all women. After all, each of us has a community of one kind or another to work for, be it great or small. I do so, anyway.

Indicates KRAP, *as the latter enters right.*

Here's an example for you. This business I have to deal with now, do you suppose it's to do with my own company? Not a bit of it.

Quickly, to KRAP.

Well?

KRAP *shows him a sheaf of papers and whispers.* All the documents for the transaction are in order.

BERNICK. Good! Splendid! Well, brother-in-law, I'm afraid you'll have to excuse me for a while.

Lowers his voice as he presses his hand.

Thank you, Johan, thank you! You may rest assured that anything I can ever do for you—well, you understand.

To KRAP.

Come with me.

They go into BERNICK's *office.*

JOHAN *looks after him for a moment.* Hm.

He turns to go down into the garden. As he does so, MARTHA *enters right with a small basket on her arm.*

JOHAN. Why, Martha!

MARTHA. Oh—Johan—is it you?

JOHAN. You've been out early too.

MARTHA. Yes. Wait here a minute, I'm sure the others will be along soon.

Turns to go out, left.

JOHAN. Look, Martha, are you always in such a hurry?

MARTHA. Am I—

JOHAN. Yesterday you seemed to be avoiding me—I didn't manage to get a word with you—and today—

MARTHA. Yes, but—

JOHAN. We always used to be inseparable. Ever since we were children.

MARTHA. Oh, Johan. That's many, many years ago.

JOHAN. For heaven's sake! It's only fifteen years. You think I've changed?

MARTHA. You? Oh yes—you have too—although—

JOHAN. What do you mean?

MARTHA. Oh, nothing.

JOHAN. You don't sound very glad to see me again.

MARTHA. I've waited so long, Johan. Too long.

JOHAN. Waited? For me to come back?

MARTHA. Yes.

JOHAN. Why did you think I'd want to come back?

MARTHA. To repair the wrong you did.

JOHAN. I?

MARTHA. Have you forgotten that a woman died in destitution and disgrace because of you? Have you forgotten that because of you the best years of a young child's life were embittered?

JOHAN. You don't mean that you—? Martha, did your brother never—?

MARTHA. Do what?

JOHAN. Did he never—I mean—did he never say anything in mitigation of what I did?

MARTHA. Oh, Johan, you know how strict Karsten's principles are.

JOHAN. Hm. Yes, yes, I know how strict my old friend Karsten's principles are. But this is—! Oh, well. I spoke to him just now. I think he's changed somewhat.

MARTHA. How can you say that? Karsten has always been a fine man.

JOHAN. Yes, I didn't mean it like that; but never mind. Hm. Well, now I understand how you've been thinking about me. You've been awaiting the return of the Prodigal.

MARTHA. Listen, Johan. I'll tell you how I've been thinking about you.

Points down into the garden.

You see that girl playing down there on the grass with Olaf? That is Dina. You remember that strange letter you wrote to me when you ran away? You wrote that I must believe in you. I have believed in you, Johan. Those wicked things people talked about afterwards—you did them in a fit of madness, you didn't know what you were doing—

JOHAN. What do you mean?

MARTHA. Oh, you know what I mean; don't let's talk about it any more. Anyway, you had to go away and—start a new life. Listen, Johan. You remember how we two used to play games together when we were children? Well, I have acted as your proxy. The duties that you forgot to fulfil here, or couldn't fulfil, I have fulfilled for you. I tell you this so that you shan't have that to reproach yourself with too. I have been a mother to that wronged child; I've brought her up, as well as I could—

JOHAN. And wasted your whole life for her sake.

MARTHA. It hasn't been wasted. But you took so long in coming, Johan.

JOHAN. Martha—if only I could tell you the— Well, anyway let me thank you for being such a loyal friend to me.

MARTHA *smiles sadly*. Hm. Well, now we've had our talk, Johan. Hush, someone's coming. Good-bye; I can't wait now.

She goes out through the door upstage left. MISS HESSEL *enters from the garden, followed by* MRS. BERNICK.

MRS. BERNICK, *still in the garden*. For heaven's sake, Lona, what are you thinking of?

MISS HESSEL. Let me go, I tell you! I must speak with him.

MRS. BERNICK. But it'd create the most dreadful scandal. Oh, Johan, are you still here?

MISS HESSEL. Get along now, son. Don't stand hanging around indoors; go down into the garden and talk to Dina.

JOHAN. Yes, I was just thinking of doing that.

MRS. BERNICK. But—

MISS HESSEL. Johan, have you bothered to take a close look at Dina?

JOHAN. Why, yes, I think so.

MISS HESSEL. So you damn well should. Now there *is* something for you.

MRS. BERNICK. But, Lona—!

JOHAN. Something for me?

MISS HESSEL. Yes, well, something to look at anyway. O.K, then, get going!

JOHAN. Yes, yes, I'm going. I'm going!

He goes down into the garden.

MRS. BERNICK. Lona, I'm speechless. Surely you can't be serious about this?

MISS HESSEL. Of course I'm serious! She's a healthy, honest girl, and in her right mind, isn't she? She'd make just the wife for Johan. That's the kind of girl he needs over there, not an old half sister.

MRS. BERNICK. Dina! Dina Dorf! But Lona, think—

MISS HESSEL. All I'm thinking about is the boy's happiness. He needs me to give him a push, he's a bit timid where these things are concerned; never really had an eye for girls.

MRS. BERNICK. What, Johan? I should have thought we had sufficient evidence to the contrary—unfortunately—

MISS HESSEL. Oh, to hell with that, that's ancient history! Where's Karsten? I want to talk to him.

MRS. BERNICK. Lona, you mustn't do this, I tell you.

MISS HESSEL. I'm going to do it. If the boy likes her, and she likes him, let them have one another. Karsten's a clever guy, he'll manage to find a way—

MRS. BERNICK. Do you really imagine that these American improprieties will be permitted here?

MISS HESSEL. Betty, don't talk nonsense.

MRS. BERNICK. And that a man with such strict moral principles as Karsten—

MISS HESSEL. Oh, nonsense, they're not that strict.

MRS. BERNICK. How dare you!

MISS HESSEL. All I'm saying is that Karsten isn't any more moral than most other men.

MRS. BERNICK. You still hate him, don't you? But what do you want here, if you can't forget—? I don't understand how you dare to look him in the face after the disgraceful way you behaved towards him.

MISS HESSEL. Yes, Betty, I did overstep the mark a bit that time.

MRS. BERNICK. And he's forgiven you so generously, though he never did you any wrong. It wasn't his fault that you set your cap at him. But ever since that moment you've hated me too.

Bursts into tears.

You've always begrudged me my happiness. And now you come here to shame me, by showing the town what kind of a family I've made Karsten marry into! I'm the person everyone will blame, and that's what you want. Oh, it's hateful of you!

She goes out weeping through the door upstage left.

MISS HESSEL *watches her go.* Poor Betty!

BERNICK *enters from his office.*

BERNICK, *still in the doorway.* Yes, yes, Krap. Good. Excellent. Send four hundred crowns to provide food for the poor. *Turns.*

Lona!

Comes closer.

Are you alone? Isn't Betty with you?

MISS HESSEL. No. Shall I go and fetch her?

BERNICK. No, no, it doesn't matter. Oh, Lona, you can't imagine
how I've been longing for a chance to talk frankly with you.
To ask your forgiveness.

MISS HESSEL. Look, Karsten, don't let's get sentimental. It
doesn't suit us.

BERNICK. You must listen to me, Lona. I know appearances
seem to be against me now that you know about Dina's
mother. But I swear to you it was only a temporary infatuation. I did love you once, honestly and truly.

MISS HESSEL. Why do you think I've come back?

BERNICK. Whatever you have in mind, I beseech you not to do
anything before you have given me the chance to vindicate
myself. I can, Lona; at any rate I can explain to you why
I acted as I did.

MISS HESSEL. Now you're afraid. You once loved me, you say.
Yes, you told me so often enough in your letters—and perhaps it was true in a way, as long as you were living out
there in a world which was big and free and gave you the
courage to think bigly and freely yourself. You probably
thought I had a bit more character and will and independence than most of the others here. Besides, it was a secret
between the two of us; no one could make funny remarks
about your vulgar taste.

BERNICK. Lona, how can you think that—?

MISS HESSEL. But when you came back here and heard how
people were laughing at me, and making fun of what they
called my peculiarities—

BERNICK. Well, you were rather headstrong in those days.

MISS HESSEL. Only because I wanted to shock the prudes this
town was full of—the ones in trousers as well as the ones in
petticoats. Well, then you met that charming young actress—

BERNICK. It was a momentary infatuation, nothing more. I swear to you that not a tenth part of all the rumours and slander that went round about me was true.

MISS HESSEL. Possibly. But then Betty came home, pretty and rich, and everyone's darling; and the news got around that she was to inherit all her aunt's money and I was to get nothing—

BERNICK. Yes, that was the crux of it, Lona. I shan't beat about the bush. I didn't love Betty; I didn't break with you because my affections had changed. It was only for the money. I needed it; I *had* to make sure I got it.

MISS HESSEL. And you can tell me that to my face!

BERNICK. Yes, I do. Please listen to me, Lona—

MISS HESSEL. But you wrote to me that you'd fallen passionately in love with Betty, asked me to be magnanimous, begged me for Betty's sake to say nothing about the fact that there had been anything between us—

BERNICK. I had to, I tell you.

MISS HESSEL. Then, by God, I don't regret what I did.

BERNICK. Let me explain to you calmly and objectively how things stood. My mother, you recall, was head of the family business; but she had no business sense whatever. I was urgently summoned home from Paris; things had become critical; I had to get the firm back on its feet again. What did I find? I found a business tottering on the verge of bankruptcy. We had to keep it absolutely secret, of course, but this ancient and respected house which had flourished for three generations was facing ruin. I was her son, her only son—I had to look round for some means of saving it.

MISS HESSEL. So you saved the House of Bernick at the expense of a woman.

BERNICK. You know quite well that Betty loved me.

MISS HESSEL. What about me?

BERNICK. Believe me, Lona, you would never have been happy with me.

MISS HESSEL. Was it out of consideration for my happiness that you jilted me?

BERNICK. You think I acted from selfish motives? If it had only been my interests that had been at stake, I would gladly and fearlessly have started again from nothing. But you don't understand how a man of business identifies himself with the business he inherits and with the vast responsibilities it brings with it. Do you realise that the happiness or misery of hundreds, even thousands, of people depends on him? Has it ever occurred to you that the whole of our community, which both you and I call our home, would have been shattered if the House of Bernick had failed?

MISS HESSEL. Is it also for the sake of the community that for the past fifteen years your life has been based upon a lie?

BERNICK. A lie?

MISS HESSEL. How much does Betty know about the circumstances that lay behind her marriage with you?

BERNICK. Do you really believe I'd hurt her by revealing such things? What dividends would that pay?

MISS HESSEL. What dividends, did you say? Ah, well, you're a businessman—I suppose you know best about dividends. Now listen to me, Karsten. I'm going to talk calmly and objectively to you. Tell me; are you really happy?

BERNICK. In my family life, you mean?

MISS HESSEL. Of course.

BERNICK. Yes, Lona, I am. The sacrifice you made for me wasn't in vain. I think I can say I've grown happier year by year. Betty's so good and acquiescent. During the years we've lived together she has learned to mould her character to mine—

MISS HESSEL. Hm.

BERNICK. She used to have a lot of over-romantic ideas about love; she couldn't accept that as the years pass it must shrink into the calm candle flame of friendship.

MISS HESSEL. But she accepts that now?

BERNICK. Completely. As you can imagine, her daily association with me hasn't been without a maturing influence on her. People have to learn to reduce their demands on each other if they are to fulfil their functions in the community in which it has pleased God to place them. Betty has gradually learned to realise this, with the result that our house is now an example to our fellow citizens.

MISS HESSEL. But these fellow citizens know nothing about this lie?

BERNICK. Lie?

MISS HESSEL. Yes, the lie on which your life has been resting for the past fifteen years.

BERNICK. You call that a—?

MISS HESSEL. I call it a lie. A triple lie. You lied to me, you lied to Betty and you lied to Johan.

BERNICK. Betty has never asked to be told the truth.

MISS HESSEL. Because she doesn't know.

BERNICK. And you won't ask it. For her sake you won't.

MISS HESSEL. Oh, no. I can put up with ridicule; I've a broad back.

BERNICK. Johan won't, either. He's told me so.

MISS HESSEL. But what about you, Karsten? Isn't there something in you that cries out to be freed from this lie?

BERNICK. Do you expect me voluntarily to sacrifice the happiness of my family and my position in society?

MISS HESSEL. What right have you to that position?

BERNICK. Every day for the past fifteen years I have purchased a grain of that right—by my conduct, and my work, and my achievements.

MISS HESSEL. Yes, you've achieved plenty all right—for yourself and for others. You're the richest and most powerful man in town; no one dares oppose you, because you're supposed to be a man without fault or dishonour; your home is regarded as a pattern for other homes; your career as an example for other men to follow. But all this honour, and you too, rest on a quicksand. A moment may come, a word

may be spoken, and you and all your honour will sink to
the bottom if you don't save yourself in time.

BERNICK. Why have you come, Lona?

MISS HESSEL. I want to help you to get firm ground under your
feet, Karsten.

BERNICK. Revenge! You want revenge? Yes, that's it, of course.
But you won't succeed! There's only one person who knows
the truth, and he'll hold his tongue.

MISS HESSEL. Johan?

BERNICK. Yes, Johan. If anyone else accuses me, I shall deny
everything. If anyone tries to destroy me, I shall fight for
my life! You'll never succeed, I tell you! The only person
who could destroy me is silent. And he's going away.

RUMMEL *and* VIGELAND *enter right.*

RUMMEL. Good morning, good morning, my dear Bernick. You
must come along with us to the Chamber of Commerce;
you know, to discuss the railway.

BERNICK. I can't. Not just now.

VIGELAND. But Mr. Bernick, you must—

RUMMEL. You must, Bernick. There are people working against
us. That damned newspaper editor, Hammer, and the others
who wanted the coast line, are saying there are private
interests behind this new proposal.

BERNICK. Well, tell them—

VIGELAND. It won't help what *we* tell them, Mr. Bernick.

RUMMEL. No, no, you must come yourself. No one will dare
to suspect you of anything like that.

MISS HESSEL. Why, the very idea!

BERNICK. I can't, I tell you. I'm not well. That is—well, anyway,
wait a minute and give me time to collect myself.

ROERLUND *enters right.*

ROERLUND. Excuse me, Mr. Bernick. I've just seen something
that has deeply disturbed me.

BERNICK. Yes, yes, what is it?

ROERLUND. I must ask you a question. Is it with your consent that the young girl who has found asylum beneath your roof is walking the public streets in the company of a person who—

MISS HESSEL. What person, Reverend?

ROERLUND. Of the person from whom, of all people, she should be kept at the greatest possible distance.

MISS HESSEL *laughs loudly.*

ROERLUND. Is it with your consent, Mr. Bernick?

BERNICK *looks for his hat and gloves.* I know nothing about it. Excuse me, I'm in a hurry—I have to attend a meeting of the Chamber of Commerce.

HILMAR *enters from the garden and goes over to the door upstage left.* Betty, Betty!

MRS. BERNICK, *in the doorway.* What is it?

HILMAR. You really must go down into the garden and put a stop to the way a certain person is flirting with Dina Dorf. It made me quite nervous to listen to them.

MISS HESSEL. Oh? What did this person say?

HILMAR. Only that he wants her to go with him to America! Ugh!

ROERLUND. Can this be possible!

MRS. BERNICK. What are you saying!

MISS HESSEL. But it'd be a wonderful thing!

BERNICK. Impossible. You must have misheard.

HILMAR. Ask him yourself, then. Here come the happy pair. Keep me out of it, though.

BERNICK, *to* RUMMEL *and* VIGELAND. Go ahead, I'll join you in a moment.

RUMMEL *and* VIGELAND *go out right.* JOHAN *and* DINA *enter from the garden.*

JOHAN. Lona, Lona, she's coming with us!

MRS. BERNICK. Johan, you must be mad!

ROERLUND. I refuse to believe my ears! This is the most disgraceful scandal! By what arts of seduction have you—?

JOHAN. Now, take it easy—!

ROERLUND. Answer me, Dina. Do you seriously intend to do this? Have you made this decision freely and voluntarily?

DINA. I must get away from here.

ROERLUND. But with him! With him!

DINA. Name me any other man here who would have the courage to take me away with him.

ROERLUND. Right, then you'll have to be told who he is.

JOHAN. Be quiet!

BERNICK. Don't say another word!

ROERLUND. If I remained silent I should be betraying the community whose morals and manners I have been chosen to protect; and I should be failing my duty towards this young girl in whose upbringing I have had no small share and who is to me—

JOHAN. Be careful what you say!

ROERLUND. She shall know the truth! Dina, it was this man who was responsible for your mother's misery and shame.

BERNICK. Dr. Roerlund!

DINA. He!

To JOHAN.

Is this true?

JOHAN. Karsten, you answer her.

BERNICK. Silence, all of you! The subject is closed.

DINA. It is true, then.

ROERLUND. Of course it is true. And that's not all. This person in whom you have placed your trust did not leave home empty-handed. Old Mrs. Bernick's money— Her son can testify.

MISS HESSEL. Liar!

BERNICK. Ah!

MRS. BERNICK. Oh my God, oh my God!

JOHAN *raises his arm.* You dare to—

MISS HESSEL. Don't hit him, Johan.

ROERLUND. Yes, go on, hit me! The truth shall out—and it is the truth—Mr. Bernick has said so himself, and the whole town knows it. Well, Dina, now you know the kind of man he is.

Short silence.

JOHAN, *quietly, grips* BERNICK's *arm.* Karsten, Karsten, what have you done?

MRS. BERNICK, *in tears, softly.* Oh, Karsten, that I should have involved you in such a scandal!

SANDSTAD *hurries in right and shouts, with his hand still on the door handle.* Mr. Bernick, you must come at once! The railway is hanging by a thread!

BERNICK, *abstractedly.* What? What must I do?

MISS HESSEL, *earnestly, meaningly.* You must do your duty to the community, brother-in-law.

SANDSTAD. Yes, hurry! We need all your moral authority behind us.

JOHAN, *close to* BERNICK. Bernick, you and I will talk about this tomorrow.

He goes out through the garden. BERNICK *helplessly and blindly walks out right with* SANDSTAD.

ACT THREE

The same. BERNICK *enters angrily through the door upstage left with a cane in his hand, leaving the door ajar behind him.*

BERNICK. There, now! He's been asking for that. I fancy he won't forget that hiding in a hurry.

Speaks to someone through the open door.

What? Oh, Betty, you mother the boy too much. You make excuses for him and take his side whatever he does. Irresponsible little brat! Not irresponsible? What would you call it, then? Sneaking out of the house at night, stealing one of the fishermen's boats, stays away half the day and frightens the life out of me! As if I hadn't enough on my mind already! And then the young puppy has the nerve to threaten me that he'll run away! Well, just let him try! You? No, I'm sure you don't; you don't care what happens to him. I really believe if he went and killed himself, you'd— Oh, don't you? Possibly, but when I die I shall leave something behind me that I want carried on; I don't fancy the idea of being left childless. Don't argue, Betty, I've given my orders; he's not to leave the house.

Listens.

Be quiet now, I don't want anyone to notice anything.

KRAP *enters right.*

KRAP. Can you spare me a moment, Mr. Bernick?

BERNICK *throws down the cane.* Yes, yes, by all means. Have you come from the yard?

KRAP. Yes, I've just left there. Hm.

BERNICK. Well? Everything's going ahead all right with the *Palm Tree*, isn't it?

KRAP. Oh, the *Palm Tree* will be able to sail tomorrow, but—

BERNICK. Is it the *Indian Girl*? Don't tell me that stubborn old fool—

KRAP. The *Indian Girl* will be able to sail tomorrow too—but she won't get very far.

BERNICK. What do you mean?

KRAP. Excuse me, Mr. Bernick, but that door's open and I think there's someone in there.

BERNICK *closes the door.* Well, what have you got to tell me that mustn't be overheard?

KRAP. It's this. Your foreman seems determined to send the *Indian Girl* to the bottom with all hands.

BERNICK. Aune? Good God, what on earth makes you think that?

KRAP. Can't think of any other explanation, Mr. Bernick.

BERNICK. Well, tell me. But be brief.

KRAP. Yes, Mr. Bernick. Well, you know how slowly the work's been going since we got those new machines and took on those new untrained workmen.

BERNICK. Yes, yes.

KRAP. But when I went down there this morning I noticed they'd made the most extraordinary progress on the American ship. That big patch on her hull—you know, where she's gone rotten—

BERNICK. Yes, yes, what about it?

KRAP. Completely repaired! Apparently. They've sheathed it; looks as good as new. Aune himself had been working on her all night with a lantern.

BERNICK. Well?

KRAP. I thought about it. Didn't like it. The men were having lunch, so I went and took a good look at her, outside and in. No one saw me. I had difficulty in getting down into the hold because they've reloaded the cargo, but I saw enough to confirm my suspicions. There's something funny going on, Mr. Bernick.

BERNICK. You must be mistaken, Mr. Krap. I can't believe Aune would do a thing like that.

KRAP. I don't like saying it, but it's the truth. Something funny going on, I said to myself. He hadn't put in any new timbers, as far as I could see; just plugged and caulked her, and covered it up with plates and tarpaulins and so on. Real shoddy workmanship! The *Indian Girl* will never reach New York. She'll go to the bottom like a cracked kettle.

BERNICK. This is dreadful! But what motive do you suppose he can have?

KRAP. Probably wants to bring the machines into discredit. Revenge; wants to force you to take the old workmen back.

BERNICK. And for that he's willing to sacrifice all those human lives.

KRAP. He said the other day: "There aren't any human beings in the *Indian Girl*. Only beasts."

BERNICK. Possibly; but what about all the capital investment that will be lost? Hasn't he thought of that?

KRAP. Aune doesn't hold with capital investment, Mr. Bernick.

BERNICK. True enough. He's a troublemaker, a demagogue. All the same—to be so devoid of conscience! Look here, Krap, we must check on this. Not a word about it to anyone. It'll be bad for the yard if this leaks out.

KRAP. Of course, but—

BERNICK. You must try to get down there again during the dinner break. I must have the truth about this.

KRAP. I'll get it for you, Mr. Bernick. But may I ask—what will you do if—?

BERNICK. Report the matter, of course. We can't let ourselves be accessories to a criminal action. I can't afford to have that on my conscience. Besides, it will make a good impression on both the press and the community if they see that I am putting personal considerations aside so that justice may take its course.

KRAP. Very true, Mr. Bernick.

BERNICK. But first we must have the truth. Meanwhile, not a word to anyone.

KRAP. You can trust me, Mr. Bernick. I'll get the truth for you. *He goes out through the garden and down the street.*

BERNICK, *to himself.* Terrible! But—no, it's impossible! It couldn't happen.

He turns to enter his office. HILMAR TOENNESEN *enters right.*

HILMAR. Morning, Bernick. Well, congratulations on your triumph at the Chamber of Commerce yesterday.

BERNICK. Oh, thank you.

HILMAR. Brilliant victory, they tell me. Public-spirited visionary routs chauvinistic self-interest. Like a colonial power disciplining the savages. Remarkable achievement after that unpleasant little scene you'd—

BERNICK. Yes, yes, never mind that.

HILMAR. I gather the final *coup de grâce* hasn't been delivered yet, though.

BERNICK. You mean the railway?

HILMAR. Yes. You know what our beloved editor Mr. Hammer is cooking up, I presume?

BERNICK, *tensely.* No. What?

HILMAR. He's cottoned on to that rumour that's floating around. Says he's going to make it front-page news.

BERNICK. What rumour?

HILMAR. Why all that buying up of property along the route of the branch line.

BERNICK. What? Is there a rumour to that effect?

HILMAR. Yes, it's all over town. I heard about it at the club.

It seems one of our lawyers has been secretly buying up all
the forests and mines and waterfalls on behalf of an anony-
mous client.

BERNICK. Do they say who this client is?

HILMAR. The members thought he must be acting for a syndicate in some other town that had heard about your plans
and thought they'd get in quickly before property values
began to soar. Disgusting, isn't it, what? Ugh!

BERNICK. Disgusting?

HILMAR. Yes, strangers trespassing on our property like that.
And fancy one of our own lawyers lending himself to such
a scheme! Now it'll be these damned outsiders who'll reap
all the profit.

BERNICK. But it's only an unconfirmed rumour.

HILMAR. Yes, but everyone believes it, and tomorrow or the
day after Hammer will publish it as a fact. Everyone at the
club's feeling very bitter about it already. I heard several
people say that if the rumour's confirmed they'll withdraw
their support.

BERNICK. But that's impossible!

HILMAR. Oh? Why do you suppose those hucksters were so
keen to go in with you? Do you think they hadn't already
started licking their lips at the—

BERNICK. Impossible, I tell you! We have *some* public spirit in
this little community—

HILMAR. Here? Look, you're an optimist and you judge other
people by yourself. But I know our town pretty well, and
I tell you there isn't one person here—apart from ourselves,
of course—not one, I tell you, who attempts to keep the flag
of ideals flying.

Upstage.

Ugh, here they are!

BERNICK. Who?

HILMAR. The two Americans.

Looks out, right.

Who's that with them? Oh dear, isn't that the captain of the *Indian Girl?* Ugh!

BERNICK. What on earth can they want with him?

HILMAR. Birds of a feather, I suppose. He's probably been a pirate, or a slave trader; and heaven knows what they haven't got up to in the past fifteen years.

BERNICK. No, you've no right to think of them like that.

HILMAR. You *are* an optimist. Well, if they're descending on us again, I'll be off.

He goes towards the door, left. MISS HESSEL *enters right.*

MISS HESSEL. Hullo, Hilmar. Am I chasing you away?

HILMAR. Not at all. I just happen to be in a hurry. I've something I have to say to Betty.

Enters the room upstage left.

BERNICK, *after a short silence.* Well, Lona?

MISS HESSEL. Well?

BERNICK. How do you feel about me today?

MISS HESSEL. The same as yesterday. One lie more or less—

BERNICK. I must make you understand. Where is Johan?

MISS HESSEL. He's coming. He had something he wanted to ask someone.

BERNICK. After what you heard yesterday, surely you must understand that everything I have built up here will be destroyed if the truth gets out.

MISS HESSEL. I understand that.

BERNICK. I need hardly tell you that I was not guilty of this theft which was rumoured to have been committed.

MISS HESSEL. Oh, naturally. But who was the thief, then?

BERNICK. There was no thief. No money was stolen. Not a penny was missing.

MISS HESSEL. What?

BERNICK. I repeat; not a penny.

MISS HESSEL. Then how did that monstrous rumour get round that Johan—?

BERNICK. Lona, I can talk to you as I wouldn't to anyone else. I shan't hide anything from you. I was partly responsible for spreading that rumour.

MISS HESSEL. You? You could do a thing like that to him, when to save your skin he'd—?

BERNICK. You mustn't judge me without remembering how things stood at the time. I explained it to you yesterday. I came home and found my mother involved in a whole string of stupid enterprises. One misfortune followed after another; every disaster that could happen to us happened; our house stood on the verge of ruin. I felt desperate and reckless. Oh, Lona, I think it was mainly in the hope of trying to forget it all that I got myself involved in that—business which ended in Johan going away.

MISS HESSEL. Hm.

BERNICK. You can imagine how all sorts of rumours spread about after you and he had left. It wasn't the first thing of that kind he'd done, they said; Dorf had been well paid to go away and keep his mouth shut; others said she'd been given the money. Just then it was beginning to get whispered that our house was having difficulty in fulfilling its obligations. What more natural than that the scandalmongers should put two and two together? When she stayed on here in obvious poverty, people said he'd taken the money with him to America; the gossip increased, and the sum multiplied like a snowball.

MISS HESSEL. And you, Karsten—?

BERNICK. I seized on this rumour as a drowning man clutches at a raft.

MISS HESSEL. You encouraged it?

BERNICK. I didn't contradict it. Our creditors were beginning to get restive; I had to find some way of calming them; it was essential that no one should doubt our solidarity. We'd had a temporary setback; they mustn't foreclose on us; we only needed a little time, and everyone would get their money.

MISS HESSEL. And everyone got their money?

BERNICK. Yes, Lona. This rumour saved our house, and made me the man I am now.

MISS HESSEL. In other words, a lie made you the man you are now.

BERNICK. Who suffered by it—then? Johan had sworn he'd never come back.

MISS HESSEL. You ask who suffered by it. Look at yourself, Karsten, and tell me honestly; don't you think you've suffered?

BERNICK. Look at any man you choose to name; you'll find every one of them has at least one skeleton hidden in his cupboard.

MISS HESSEL. And you call yourselves pillars of society?

BERNICK. Society has none better.

MISS HESSEL. If that's what your society is like, what does it matter whether it survives or is destroyed? What do people here set store by? Lies and pretences—that's all. You, the chief citizen of the town, sit here in honour and happiness, power and glory, simply because you once branded an innocent man as a criminal.

BERNICK. Do you think I don't know how deeply I wronged him? And do you think I'm not ready to right that wrong?

MISS HESSEL. How? By talking?

BERNICK. I can't do that, Lona.

MISS HESSEL. How else can such a wrong be righted?

BERNICK. I am rich, Lona. Johan can ask anything he wants—

MISS HESSEL. Yes, offer him money, and see what he replies.

BERNICK. Do you know what he intends to do?

MISS HESSEL. No. Since yesterday he's said nothing. It's as though all this has suddenly made him into a man.

BERNICK. I must talk to him.

MISS HESSEL. Here he is.

JOHAN *enters right*.

BERNICK *goes towards him.* Johan—!

JOHAN *waves him aside.* First you listen to me. Yesterday morning I gave you my word to keep my mouth shut.

BERNICK. You did.

JOHAN. I didn't know then that—

BERNICK. Johan, just let me briefly explain the circumstances—

JOHAN. There's no need; I know all about the circumstances. The firm was in difficulties; I'd left the country; you had a name and a reputation at stake. Oh, I don't blame you so much for that; we were young and reckless in those days. But now the truth will have to be revealed. I need it.

BERNICK. I can't reveal the truth just now. I need all the moral credit I can muster.

JOHAN. I don't mind about the lies you've been spreading about me. It's this business with Dina's mother. You've got to admit it was you. Dina's going to become my wife, and I want to live with her here, and build a new life with her here, in this town.

MISS HESSEL. You want to do that?

BERNICK. With Dina? As your wife? Here?

JOHAN. Yes, here. I want to stay here to silence all these liars and scandalmongers. But she won't marry me unless you clear my name.

BERNICK. Don't you realise that if I admit to the one I'm automatically confessing to the other? You think I only need to show the firm's books to prove nothing was stolen? But I can't do that—our books weren't kept very carefully in those days. And even if I could, what good would it do? I'd stand revealed as a man who'd saved his skin by telling a lie, and had allowed this lie with all its consequences to be believed for fifteen years without raising a finger to contradict it. You don't know this community as well as you used to, or you'd realise that to do this would ruin me completely.

JOHAN. All I can say is that I intend to make Mrs. Dorf's daughter my wife and live with her here in this town.

BERNICK *wipes the sweat from his forehead.* Listen, Johan—and you too, Lona. I'm in a very particular position just now. If you do this to me you'll destroy me, and not only me but a future of great prosperity and happiness for the community which nurtured you.

JOHAN. And if I don't I shall destroy my own chances of happiness for ever.

MISS HESSEL. Go on, Karsten.

BERNICK. Now listen. It's to do with this question of the railway, and that isn't such a simple matter as you may think. I suppose you've heard there was talk last year about building a coast line? A good many influential voices were raised in support of it, both here and elsewhere in the neighbourhood, especially in the press; but I managed to stop it, because it would have damaged our steamship trade along the coast.

MISS HESSEL. Have you an interest in this steamship trade?

BERNICK. Yes. But no one dared to suspect me of acting from that motive. My name and my reputation forbade that. In any case, I could have carried the loss; but the town couldn't have. So they decided to run the line inland. Once this had been decided I took steps secretly to assure myself that it would be practicable for a branch line to be extended here.

MISS HESSEL. Why secretly, Karsten?

BERNICK. Have you heard about the big purchases that have been made of forests and mines and waterfalls—?

MISS HESSEL. Yes, by a syndicate from one of the other towns.

BERNICK. Under present conditions these properties are virtually worthless to their various owners, so they went comparatively cheaply. If one had waited till the project of the branch line had been made public, the prices of these properties would have rocketed exorbitantly.

MISS HESSEL. Yes, well; what of it?

BERNICK. Now we come to something that could bear two different interpretations—something that a member of our community could only admit to if his name and reputation were such as to set him above suspicion.

MISS HESSEL. Yes?

BERNICK. It was I who bought all those properties.

MISS HESSEL. You?

JOHAN. On your own?

BERNICK. On my own. If the branch line gets built, I am a millionaire. If it doesn't get built, I am ruined.

MISS HESSEL. That was a big risk, Karsten.

BERNICK. I have risked all the money I possess.

MISS HESSEL. I'm not thinking of your money. When it gets known that—

BERNICK. Yes, that's the point. With the reputation I have now I can accept the responsibility for this act, carry it through to its conclusion and say to my fellow citizens: "Look! I have taken this risk for the sake of the community."

MISS HESSEL. Of the community?

BERNICK. Yes. And no one will question my motive.

MISS HESSEL. But there are others here who've acted more openly than you, and with no ulterior motive.

BERNICK. Who?

MISS HESSEL. Rummel, Sandstad and Vigeland, of course.

BERNICK. In order to win their support I was compelled to take them into my confidence.

MISS HESSEL. Oh?

BERNICK. They demanded a fifth of the profit, to be shared amongst them.

MISS HESSEL. Oh, these pillars of society!

BERNICK. Doesn't society itself force us to use these backstairs methods? What would have happened if I hadn't acted secretly? Everyone would have charged in, they'd have divided and dispersed the properties and bungled and wrecked the whole enterprise. There isn't one man in this town apart from me who understands how to organise a project of this magnitude. Up here, it's only the families who have migrated from the cities who have any talent for big business. That's why my conscience tells me I have acted correctly in this matter. Only in my hands can these properties be of any permanent value to the thousands of people whom I intend that they shall benefit.

MISS HESSEL. I think you're right there, Karsten.

JOHAN. But I don't know these thousands of people, and my life and my happiness are at stake.

BERNICK. The prosperity of your birthplace is also at stake. If anything comes to light which casts a shadow on my early career, all my enemies will unite to destroy me. A youthful indiscretion won't be forgiven in this community. People will examine my whole life under a microscope, dig up a hundred trivial incidents and reinterpret them in the light of this revelation. They will destroy me with their rumours and innuendoes. I shall have to withdraw from the railway project; and if I do that, it will fail, and I shall be ruined and ostracized.

MISS HESSEL. Johan, after what you've just heard you must go away and keep your mouth shut.

BERNICK. Yes, yes, Johan, you must!

JOHAN. All right. I'll go. And I'll keep my mouth shut. But I shall come back, and when I do I shall speak.

BERNICK. Stay over there, Johan. Keep quiet about this, and I'll gladly give you a share of—

JOHAN. Keep your money. Give me back my name and my honour.

BERNICK. And sacrifice my own?

JOHAN. You and your community must work that out between you. I want to marry Dina; I must and shall marry her. So I'm leaving tomorrow. In the *Indian Girl*—

BERNICK. The *Indian Girl?*

JOHAN. Yes. The captain's promised to take me with him. I'm going back to America, to sell my ranch and put my affairs in order. In two months, I shall be here again.

BERNICK. And then you'll talk?

JOHAN. Then the guilty will have to pay for his crime.

BERNICK. Are you forgetting that I shall also have to pay for a crime of which I am not guilty?

JOHAN. Who was it who profited by the false rumour of fifteen years ago?

BERNICK. You're making me desperate. If you speak, I shall deny everything. I shall say there's a conspiracy against me; a plot for revenge. I shall say you have come here to blackmail me.

MISS HESSEL. Karsten!

BERNICK. I'm desperate, I tell you; and I'm fighting for my life. I shall deny everything, everything!

JOHAN. I have your two letters. I found them in my trunk with my other papers. I read them again this morning. They're plain enough.

BERNICK. And you intend to publish them?

JOHAN. If you force me to.

BERNICK. And in two months you say you will be back?

JOHAN. I hope so. The winds are favourable. In three weeks I shall be in New York—if the *Indian Girl* doesn't sink—

BERNICK *starts*. Sink? Why should the *Indian Girl* sink?

JOHAN. No, why should she?

BERNICK, *scarcely audibly*. Sink?

JOHAN. Well, Bernick, now you know how things are. You'd better start thinking. Good-bye. You can give my love to Betty, though she's hardly received me in a very sisterly manner. But I want to see Martha. She must tell Dina—she must promise me—

He goes out through the door upstage left.

BERNICK, *to himself*. The *Indian Girl*?

Quickly.

Lona, you must stop him!

MISS HESSEL. You can see for yourself, Karsten. I haven't any power over him any longer.

She follows JOHAN *into the room left.*

BERNICK *ponders uneasily.* Sink?

AUNE *enters right.*

AUNE. Excuse me, Mr. Bernick. Can you spare me a moment?

BERNICK *turns angrily.* What do you want?

AUNE. I'd like permission to ask you a question.

BERNICK. All right, but be quick. What is it?

AUNE. I wanted to ask if you're still resolved to dismiss me if the *Indian Girl* doesn't sail tomorrow?

BERNICK. Why ask me that? She'll be ready now, won't she?

AUNE. She'll be ready. But if she wasn't, it'd mean my dismissal?

BERNICK. Why are you asking me these foolish questions?

AUNE. I'd like to know, Mr. Bernick. Answer me; would it mean my dismissal?

BERNICK. Do I usually stand by my word?

AUNE. Then tomorrow I'd lose my position in my home, and among the people I belong to. I'd lose my influence among the workmen; lose my chance to do anything for the poor and humble of this community.

BERNICK. Aune, we've discussed all that.

AUNE. Right, then the *Indian Girl* can sail.

Short silence.

BERNICK. Look, I can't have eyes everywhere; I can't be personally responsible for everything. You give me your promise, don't you, that the repairs have been executed satisfactorily?

AUNE. You didn't give me much time, Mr. Bernick.

BERNICK. But the work has been done properly?

AUNE. The weather's good, and it's midsummer.

Another silence.

BERNICK. Have you anything else to say to me?

AUNE. I don't know of anything else, Mr. Bernick.

BERNICK. Then—the *Indian Girl* will sail—

AUNE. Tomorrow?

BERNICK. Yes.

AUNE. Very good.

Touches his forehead and goes. BERNICK *stands for a moment, torn by doubt; then he strides quickly over to the door as though to call* AUNE *back, but stops uneasily with his hand on the door handle. As he does so, the door is opened from the outside and* KRAP *enters.*

KRAP, *quietly.* Oh, so he's been here. Has he confessed?

BERNICK. Hm—did you discover anything?

KRAP. What's the need? Couldn't you see from his eyes that he had a guilty conscience?

BERNICK. Oh, nonsense, one can't *see* things like that. I asked you if you discovered anything?

KRAP. Couldn't get to her. Too late; they'd already started hauling her out of the dock. But the very fact that they were in such a hurry proves—

BERNICK. It proves nothing. They've completed the inspection, then?

KRAP. Of course, but—

BERNICK. There, you see! And they've found nothing to complain of.

KRAP. Mr. Bernick, you know what these inspections are, especially in a yard with a reputation like ours.

BERNICK. Nevertheless, it means that no blame can be attached to us.

KRAP. But, Mr. Bernick, surely you could see from the way Aune—

BERNICK. Aune has convinced me that there is nothing to fear.

KRAP. And I tell you I'm morally convinced that—

BERNICK. Look here, Krap, what the devil are you getting at? I know you've a grudge against this man, but if you want to pick a quarrel with him you'll have to find other grounds than this. You know how vitally important it is for me—for the company—that the *Indian Girl* sails tomorrow.

KRAP. All right. Let her sail. But how far she'll go—hm!

VIGELAND *enters right.*

VIGELAND. Good morning, Mr. Bernick, good morning! Can you spare me a moment?

BERNICK. Yes, of course, Mr. Vigeland.

VIGELAND. I just wanted to ask if you agree that the *Palm Tree* shall sail tomorrow.

BERNICK. Why, yes. It's all settled.

VIGELAND. Only that the captain came just now to tell me there's a gale warning.

KRAP. The barometer's fallen heavily since this morning.

BERNICK. Oh? Do they expect a storm?

VIGELAND. Well, a stiff breeze. But no headwind; on the contrary—

BERNICK. Hm. Well, what do you say?

VIGELAND. I say, as I said to the captain: "The *Palm Tree* rests in the hand of Providence." Besides, she's only got the North Sea to cross on her first leg; and freight charges are pretty high in England just now, so—

BERNICK. Yes, it'd certainly be expensive to delay her.

VIGELAND. She's solidly built; and anyway, she's fully insured. She's a good risk; not like that *Indian Girl*—

BERNICK. What do you mean?

VIGELAND. She's sailing tomorrow, too.

BERNICK. Yes, we've worked overtime on her; besides—

VIGELAND. Well, if that old coffin can sail—especially with the crew she's got—it'd be a poor thing if we were afraid to—

BERNICK. Quite, quite. You have the ship's papers with you?

VIGELAND. Yes, here.

BERNICK. Good. Mr. Krap, will you see to them?

KRAP. This way, Mr. Vigeland. We'll soon get this settled.

VIGELAND. Thank you. And the outcome, Mr. Bernick, we leave in the hands of the Almighty.

He goes with KRAP *into the room downstage left.* ROERLUND *enters through the garden.*

ROERLUND. Why, fancy seeing you here at this time of day, Mr. Bernick.

BERNICK, *abstractedly.* Mm?

ROERLUND. I really came to speak to your wife. I thought she might need a few words of consolation.

BERNICK. I'm sure she does. But I'd like to have a word with you too.

ROERLUND. With pleasure, Mr. Bernick. Is something the matter. You look quite pale and upset.

BERNICK. Oh? Do I? Well, what can you expect with everything piling up on me the way it has these last few days? I've got my own business to look after without this railway. Listen, Dr. Roerlund: tell me something. Let me ask you a question.

ROERLUND. By all means, Mr. Bernick.

BERNICK. It's just a thought that occurred to me. When a man stands on the threshold of a great and ambitious enterprise which has as its object the creation of prosperity for thousands of people—suppose this enterprise should claim one, just one victim—?

ROERLUND. How do you mean?

BERNICK. Well, say a man is thinking of building a great factory. He knows for certain, because all his experience has taught him, that sooner or later in this factory human life will be lost.

ROERLUND. Yes, I fear that is only too likely.

BERNICK. Or a man is planning to start a mine. He employs men with children, and young men with all their lives before them. It's certain, is it not, that some of these men will lose their lives in his service?

ROERLUND. Alas, yes.

BERNICK. Well. A man in such a position knows before he starts that the project he is launching will at some stage of its development cost human life. But this project is for the general good. For every life it takes it will, equally beyond doubt, provide the means of happiness for many hundreds of people.

ROERLUND. Ah, you're thinking of the railway—all that dangerous quarrying and dynamiting and so on—

BERNICK. Yes, yes, exactly. I'm thinking of the railway. And the railway will mean mines and factories— Remembering all this, do you still feel—?

ROERLUND. My dear Mr. Bernick, your conscience is too tender. I believe that as long as one entrusts one's work to the hands of Providence—

BERNICK. Yes; yes, of course; Providence—

ROERLUND. One is absolved from guilt. Build your railway, and have no fear.

BERNICK. Yes, but now I want to give you a particular example. Suppose a mountainside has to be blasted at a dangerous spot; and if this isn't done, the railway cannot be completed. I know, and the engineer knows, that it will cost the life of the man who lights the fuse; but it must be lit, and it is the engineer's duty to send a man to do it.

ROERLUND. Hm—

BERNICK. I know what you're going to say. The engineer ought to take the match and go himself to light the fuse. But such things aren't done. He must sacrifice one of his men.

ROERLUND. No engineer in this country would do it.

BERNICK. No engineer in a big country would think twice about doing it.

ROERLUND. Yes, I can quite believe that. In those depraved and unscrupulous societies—

BERNICK. Oh, there's some merit in those societies—

ROERLUND. How can you say that? Why, you yourself—

BERNICK. In big countries men at least have elbowroom to plan ambitiously for the general good. They have courage to make sacrifices for the sake of a cause; but here one's hands are tied by all kinds of petty scruples and considerations.

ROERLUND. Is a human life a petty consideration?

BERNICK. When it's weighed against the general good, yes.

ROERLUND. But the examples you suggest are quite unrealistic, Mr. Bernick. I really can't make you out today. These great communities you speak of—what is a human life worth there? They think of human life simply as capital. Our ethical standpoint is completely different. Look at our great shipyards! Name one shipowner in this town who would think of sacrificing a human life for mercenary motives! And then think of those scoundrels in your great communities who, to increase their profits, send out one unseaworthy ship after another—

BERNICK. I'm not talking about unseaworthy ships!

ROERLUND. But I am talking about them, Mr. Bernick.

BERNICK. Why bring that up? That's got nothing to do with it. Oh, this wretched narrowness and timidity! If a general in this country sent his men into battle and saw them shot down, he'd have sleepless nights. It isn't so in big countries. You should hear that fellow in there talking about—

ROERLUND. What fellow? The American?

BERNICK. Yes. You should hear him describe how people in America—

ROERLUND. Is he in there? Why didn't you tell me? I'll soon see to him—

BERNICK. Oh, it's no use. You won't get anywhere with him.

ROERLUND. We'll see about that. Ah, here he is.

JOHAN TOENNESEN *enters from the room on the left.*

JOHAN *talks back through the open door.* All right, Dina, as you wish. But I'm not giving you up. I'm coming back, and when I do everything's going to be all right.

ROERLUND. May I ask what you mean by those words? What exactly do you want?

JOHAN. That young girl, before whom you slandered me yesterday, is going to be my wife.

ROERLUND. *Your—?* Do you really imagine that—?

JOHAN. I want her as my wife.

ROERLUND. Very well. I suppose you'll have to be told.

Goes across to the door, which is still ajar.

Mrs. Bernick, will you please come and witness this? You too, Miss Martha. And let Dina come too.

Sees MISS HESSEL.

Oh. Are you here?

MISS HESSEL, *in the doorway.* Can I come too?

ROERLUND. By all means. The more the better.

BERNICK. What are you going to do?

MISS HESSEL, MRS. BERNICK, MARTHA, DINA *and* HILMAR *enter from the room.*

MRS. BERNICK. Oh, Dr. Roerlund, I tried to stop him, but—

ROERLUND. I shall stop him, Mrs. Bernick. Dina, you are a rash and thoughtless girl. But I do not reproach you. For too long you have lacked the moral support which you so grievously need. I reproach myself for not having provided you with that support earlier.

DINA. You mustn't tell them now!

MRS. BERNICK. What is all this?

ROERLUND. I must tell them now, Dina, although your conduct yesterday and today has made it ten times more difficult for me. But you must be saved, and all other considerations must yield to that. You remember the promise I made you, and the answer you promised to give me when I should decide that the time had come. Now I dare delay no longer; therefore—

To JOHAN.

This young girl after whom you lust is betrothed to me.

MRS. BERNICK. What!

BERNICK. Dina!

JOHAN. She? To you?

MARTHA. No, Dina, no!

MISS HESSEL. It's a lie!

JOHAN. Dina. Is that man speaking the truth?

DINA, *after a brief pause*. Yes.

ROERLUND. Let us pray that by this the arts of the seducer will
be rendered powerless. This decision, which I have resolved
to take in order to secure Dina's happiness, may be revealed
to the rest of our community; I raise no objection. I sin-
cerely trust it will not be misinterpreted. Meanwhile, Mrs.
Bernick, I think it would be wisest to remove her to her
room and to try to restore her calm and equilibrium.

MRS. BERNICK. Yes, come with me. Oh, Dina, what a lucky
girl you are!

She leads DINA *out, left.* DR. ROERLUND *goes with them.*

MARTHA. Good-bye, Johan.

She goes.

HILMAR, *in the verandah doorway.* Hm. Well, really! I must
say—!

MISS HESSEL, *who has watched* DINA *go out; to* JOHAN. Don't
lose heart, son. I'll stay here to keep an eye on the Reverend.

She goes out right.

BERNICK. Well, Johan, this means you won't be sailing in the
Indian Girl.

JOHAN. It means I shall.

BERNICK. But you won't be coming back?

JOHAN. I'll come back.

BERNICK. After this? But what can you want here now?

JOHAN. To take my revenge on you all. To break as many of
you as I can.

He goes out right. VIGELAND *and* KRAP *enter from* BERNICK's
office.

VIGELAND. Well, all the papers are in order now, Mr. Bernick.

BERNICK. Good, good.

KRAP *whispers.* You still want the *Indian Girl* to sail tomorrow, then?

BERNICK. Yes.

He goes into his office. VIGELAND *and* KRAP *go out right.* HILMAR *is about to follow them when* OLAF *pokes his head cautiously out of the doorway to the room left.*

OLAF. Uncle! Uncle Hilmar!

HILMAR. Ugh, is it you? Why aren't you upstairs? You're under house arrest.

OLAF *takes a step towards him.* Ssh! Uncle Hilmar, have you heard the news?

HILMAR. Yes, I hear you've had a hiding today.

OLAF *scowls towards his father's office.* He won't hit me again. But have you heard that Uncle Johan's sailing to America tomorrow?

HILMAR. What's that to do with you? Now you run upstairs again.

OLAF. I'll fight those redskins yet.

HILMAR. Oh, stuff! A little coward like you?

OLAF. Just you wait till tomorrow. You'll see.

HILMAR. Jackass!

He goes out through the garden. OLAF *runs back into the room and shuts the door as he sees* KRAP *enter right.*

KRAP *goes over to* BERNICK's *door and half opens it.* Excuse me disturbing you again, Mr. Bernick, but there's a dreadful storm blowing up.

Waits for a moment; there is no reply.

Is the *Indian Girl* to sail?

Short pause.

BERNICK, *from his room.* The *Indian Girl* will sail.

KRAP *closes the door and goes out right.*

ACT FOUR

*The same. The worktable has been moved out. It is a stormy
afternoon, already twilight; during the scene it grows gradually darker. A* FOOTMAN *lights the chandelier. Two* MAIDS
*bring in pots of flowers, lamps and candles, and place them
on the tables and in brackets on the walls.* RUMMEL, *in tails,
with gloves and a white cravat, is standing in the room giving orders.*

RUMMEL, *to the* FOOTMAN. Only every second candle, Jacob.
We mustn't look too festive; it's meant to be a surprise. Oh,
and all these flowers—? Ah, well, let them stay. People will
think they're always here—

BERNICK *enters from his office.*

BERNICK, *in the doorway.* What's the meaning of all this?

RUMMEL. Oh dear, you weren't meant to see.

To the SERVANTS.

All right, you can go now.

The FOOTMAN *and* MAIDS *go out through the door upstage
left.*

BERNICK *comes closer.* Rummel, what on earth does all this
mean?

RUMMEL. It means that your proudest moment has come. The
whole town is marching here in procession this evening to
pay homage to its foremost citizen.

BERNICK. What!

RUMMEL. With banners and a brass band. We were going to

have torches, but the weather was so doubtful we didn't
dare risk it. Still, there's to be an illumination. That'll look
well in the newspapers.

BERNICK. Look, Rummel, I'd rather we didn't have this.

RUMMEL. Well, it's too late now. They'll be here in half an
hour.

BERNICK. But why didn't you tell me about it before?

RUMMEL. I was afraid you might object to the idea. I had
a word with your wife, and she gave me permission to make
a few arrangements. She's looking after the refreshments
herself.

BERNICK listens. What's that? Are they coming already? I
think I hear singing.

RUMMEL, at the verandah door. Singing? Oh, that's only the
Americans. The Indian Girl is being hauled out to the buoy.

BERNICK. Is she hauling out? Yes. No, I can't this evening,
Rummel. I'm not feeling well.

RUMMEL. Yes, you look off colour. But you must pull yourself together. Damn it, man, you must! I and Sandstad and
Vigeland attach the utmost importance to this ceremony.
Such a spectacular display of public feeling will completely
crush our opponents. Rumours are spreading in the town;
the news of the property deals is bound to come out soon.
You must let them know this evening, against a background
of songs and speeches, and the merry clink of glasses—in
short, in an atmosphere of holiday and carnival—how much
you have staked for the welfare of the community. In such
an atmosphere of holiday and carnival, as I have just
phrased it, we can get the hell of a lot done. But we've
got to have that atmosphere, or it'll be no good.

BERNICK. Yes, yes, yes—

RUMMEL. Especially when the issue is such a delicate and
ticklish one. Thank heaven you've the name and reputation
to carry it off. But listen, now. I must tell you about the
arrangements. Hilmar Toennesen has written a song in your
honour. It's very beautiful; it begins: "Wave high the ban-

ner of ideals!" And Dr. Roerlund is to make the speech.
You'll have to reply, of course.

BERNICK. I can't do that this evening, Rummel. Couldn't
you—?

RUMMEL. Impossible! Much as I'd like to. The speech will
naturally be addressed mainly to you. Possibly just a word
or two about us, too. I've been discussing it with Vigeland
and Sandstad. We thought you might reply with a toast to
the prosperity of the community. Sandstad will say something about the harmony that exists between the various
strata of our society; Vigeland will want to stress how important it is that this new enterprise should not disturb the
moral foundations on which our life is so firmly based; and
I'm thinking of paying a brief tribute to the ladies, whose
contribution to the welfare of our community, while humble and unassuming, must not be overlooked. But you're
not listening.

BERNICK. Yes, yes, I am. But tell me—is the sea very rough
this evening?

RUMMEL. Are you worrying about the *Palm Tree?* She's well
insured.

BERNICK. Insured, yes. But—

RUMMEL. And in good trim. That's the main thing.

BERNICK. Hm. If anything should happen to a ship, it doesn't
necessarily follow that human lives will be lost. The ship
and her cargo, perhaps—chests and papers—

RUMMEL. Damn it man, chests and papers aren't that important.

BERNICK. Of course not. No, no—I only meant— Quiet! They're
singing again.

RUMMEL. That'll be the crew of the *Palm Tree.*

VIGELAND *enters right.*

VIGELAND. Well, the *Palm Tree's* hauling out now. Good evening, Mr. Bernick.

BERNICK. You're a seaman. Do you still feel confident that—?

VIGELAND. Providence will decide, Mr. Bernick; of that I am confident. Besides, I've been on board myself and distributed a few little tracts which I hope will ensure God's blessing on her.

SANDSTAD *and* KRAP *enter right.*

SANDSTAD, *still in the doorway.* Well, if that ship survives, I'll believe in miracles. Oh—good evening, good evening!

BERNICK. Anything wrong, Mr. Krap?

KRAP. I said nothing, Mr. Bernick.

SANDSTAD. The whole crew of the *Indian Girl* is drunk. If those brutes get that ship safely across the Atlantic, I'm a Dutchman.

MISS HESSEL *enters right.*

MISS HESSEL, *to* BERNICK. He asked me to say good-bye to you.

BERNICK. Is he aboard already?

MISS HESSEL. He will be any moment. I left him outside the hotel.

BERNICK. And he's still determined—?

MISS HESSEL. Absolutely determined.

RUMMEL, *over by the windows.* Confound these new-fangled contraptions. I can't get these curtains down.

MISS HESSEL. You want them down? I thought they were to stay up.

RUMMEL. Down to begin with, madam. I suppose you know what's going to happen?

MISS HESSEL. Yes, I know. Let me help you.
Takes the cords.
Yes, I'll lower the curtain on my brother-in-law; though I'd sooner lift it.

RUMMEL. You can do that later. When the garden is filled with the surging throng, the curtains will be raised to reveal an amazed and happy family circle. A citizen's home should be as a house of glass, open to the gaze of all.

BERNICK *seems about to speak, but turns quickly and goes into his room.*

RUMMEL. Well, let's just run through the arrangements. Come along, Mr. Krap. We need your help on a few details.

All the GENTLEMEN *go into* BERNICK'S *room.* MISS HESSEL *has drawn the curtains over the windows and is just about to do the same across the open glass door when* OLAF *jumps down on to the verandah from above. He has a plaid over his shoulder and a bundle in his hand.*

MISS HESSEL. Oh, my goodness, Olaf, how you frightened me!

OLAF, *hiding his bundle.* Ssh!

MISS HESSEL. Did you jump out of that window? Where are you going?

OLAF. Ssh! Don't tell anyone! I'm going to Uncle Johan. Only down to the jetty, of course—just to say good-bye to him. Good night, Aunt Lona!

He runs out through the garden.

MISS HESSEL. No, wait! Olaf, Olaf!

JOHAN TOENNESEN, *in travelling clothes, with a bag over his shoulder, enters cautiously right.*

JOHAN. Lona!

MISS HESSEL *turns.* What! Are you here again?

JOHAN. I've still got a few minutes. I must see her just once more. We can't part like this.

MARTHA *and* DINA, *both wearing overcoats, and the latter with a small travelling bag in her hand, enter through the door upstage left.*

DINA. I must see him, I must see him!

MARTHA. Yes, Dina. You'll see him.

DINA. There he is!

JOHAN. Dina!

DINA. Take me with you.

JOHAN. What?

MISS HESSEL. You want to go with him?

DINA. Yes! Take me with you! That man says he's going to make a public announcement this evening in front of the whole town about—

JOHAN. Dina! You don't love him?

DINA. I have never loved him. I'd die rather than be engaged to him. Oh, how he humiliated me yesterday with his fine phrases! He made me feel he was raising something contemptible up to his own level. I'm not going to be humiliated like that any more. I'm going away. Can I come with you?

JOHAN. Yes! Yes!

DINA. I shan't trouble you for long. Just help me to get over there; help me to find my feet—

JOHAN. Yippee! Don't you worry about that, Dina!

MISS HESSEL *points towards* BERNICK's *door*. Ssh! Quiet, quiet!

JOHAN. I'll take care of you, Dina!

DINA. No. I won't let you do that. I'm going to look after myself. I'll manage to do that over there. If only I can get away from here. Oh, these women—you've no idea! They've written to me today begging me to realise how lucky I am, and reminding me how noble and magnanimous he's been. Tomorrow and the next day and every day they'll be squinting at me to see whether I'm proving myself worthy of him. Oh, all this respectability frightens me so much!

JOHAN. Tell me, Dina. Is that the only reason you're leaving? Am I nothing to you?

DINA. Oh, no, Johan. You mean more to me than anyone else in the world.

JOHAN. Oh, Dina!

DINA. Everyone here tells me I ought to hate you and detest you. They say it's my duty. But I don't understand all this about duty. I never shall.

MISS HESSEL. That's right, child! Don't you!

MARTHA. Yes, Dina. Go with him. As his wife.

JOHAN. Yes! Yes!

MISS HESSEL. What? I'll have to kiss you for that, Martha. I hadn't expected that from you.

MARTHA. No, I suppose not. I hadn't expected it myself. But I've got to speak out some time. Oh, how we suffer here under this tyranny of duty and convention! Rebel against it, Dina! Marry him. Do something to defy all their stupid ideals!

JOHAN. What do you say, Dina?

DINA. Yes. I will be your wife.

JOHAN. Dina!

DINA. But first I want to work and become someone. The way you have. I don't just want to be something someone takes.

MISS HESSEL. Sensible girl! That's the way!

JOHAN. Right! I'll wait, and hope—

MISS HESSEL. You'll win her, son. But now it's time for you both to go aboard.

JOHAN. Yes—aboard! Oh, Lona, my dear sister! Here, I want a word with you—

He leads her upstage and whispers quickly to her.

MARTHA. Dina, my dear, let me look at you. Let me kiss you once again. For the last time.

DINA. Not for the last time. No, dear, dear Aunt Martha! We'll meet again!

MARTHA. No; we never shall. Promise me, Dina—don't ever come back.

Clasps both DINA's *hands and looks at her.*

Go, my dear child—go to your happiness across the sea. Oh, down in that schoolroom I've so often longed to be over there! It must be beautiful there. The sky is larger and the clouds fly higher than they do here. The air that blows on the faces of the people is freer—

DINA. Oh, Aunt Martha, you must come and join us. Someday.

MARTHA. I? Never; never. My little task lies here. Now I think I can resign myself to being what I must be.

DINA. I can't imagine being without you.

MARTHA. Oh, one can learn to manage without almost anything, Dina.

Kisses her.

But you'll never have to test the truth of that, my dear. Promise me you'll make him happy.

DINA. I won't promise anything. I hate promises. What will be will be.

MARTHA. Yes, yes, my dear. Always be as you are now. Be true to yourself. And believe in yourself.

DINA. I will, Aunt Martha.

MISS HESSEL *puts some papers, which* JOHAN *has given her into her pocket.* Good boy, Johan! All right, I'll do that. But now be off with you!

JOHAN. Yes, we've no time to waste. Good-bye, Lona—thanks for everything you've done for me. Good-bye, Martha. Thank you too. You've been a wonderful friend.

MARTHA. Good-bye, Johan! Good-bye, Dina! God bless you and make you happy—always!

MARTHA *and* MISS HESSEL *hurry them to the verandah door.* JOHAN *and* DINA *run out through the garden.* MISS HESSEL *closes the door and draws the curtain over it.*

MISS HESSEL. Now we're alone, Martha. You've lost her, and I've lost him.

MARTHA. *You've* lost him?

MISS HESSEL. Oh, I'd half lost him already over there. The boy wanted to stand on his own feet, so I pretended I was pining to come back here.

MARTHA. Was that why? Now I see why you came. But he wants you to go back and join them.

MISS HESSEL. An old half sister? What good can she be to him now? Men destroy a lot of things to find happiness.

MARTHA. It happens sometimes.

MISS HESSEL. But we'll stick together, Martha.

MARTHA. Can I be of any use to you?

MISS HESSEL. Who better? We two foster mothers—haven't we both lost our children? Now we're alone.

MARTHA. Yes; alone. You might as well know now. I loved him more than anything else in the world.

MISS HESSEL. Martha!

Grips her arm.

Is this true?

MARTHA. That's been my life. I loved him, and waited for him. Every summer I waited for him to come through that door. At last he came; but he didn't see me.

MISS HESSEL. You loved him! But it was you yourself who put happiness into his hands.

MARTHA. What else should I have done, if I loved him? Yes, I loved him. I've only lived for him, ever since he went away. What ground did I have for hope, you're wondering? Oh, I thought I had a little. But then, when he came back, it was just as though everything had been wiped clean from his memory. He didn't see me.

MISS HESSEL. Because of Dina, Martha. You stood in her shadow.

MARTHA. I'm glad. When he left, we were the same age; but when I saw him again—oh, that dreadful moment!—I suddenly realised that now I was ten years older than him. He'd been walking over there in the bright, quivering sunlight, drawing in youth and strength with every breath, while I'd been sitting in here, spinning and spinning—

MISS HESSEL. The thread of his happiness, Martha.

MARTHA. Yes, it was gold I was spinning. I mustn't be bitter. It's true, isn't it, Lona—we two have been good sisters to him?

MISS HESSEL *throws her arms round her.* Martha!

BERNICK *enters from his room.*

BERNICK, *to the* GENTLEMEN *inside his room.* Yes, yes, yes, make what arrangements you please. I'll manage when the time comes—

Closes the door.

Oh, are you here? Look, Martha, you'd better go and dress up a bit. And tell Betty to do the same. Nothing grand, of course. Just something neat and simple. You must be quick, though.

MISS HESSEL. And you must look happy and excited, Martha. This is a joyful occasion for us all.

BERNICK. Olaf must come down too. I want to have him by my side.

MISS HESSEL. Hm. Olaf—

MARTHA. I'll go and tell Betty.

She goes out through the door upstage left.

MISS HESSEL. Well. Now the great moment's arrived.

BERNICK *paces uneasily up and down.* Yes, so it has.

MISS HESSEL. I imagine a man must feel very proud and happy at such a moment.

BERNICK *looks at her.* Hm.

MISS HESSEL. The whole town's to be illuminated, I hear.

BERNICK. Yes, they've planned something of the kind.

MISS HESSEL. All the guilds are to march here with their banners. Your name is to shine in letters of fire. Tonight the news will be telegraphed to every corner of the land: "Surrounded by his happy family, Karsten Bernick was acclaimed by his fellow citizens as a pillar of society."

BERNICK. Yes, that's right. And they're going to give three cheers for me outside there, and the crowd will demand that I show myself in the doorway here, and I shall be forced to bow and make a speech of thanks.

MISS HESSEL. Forced?

BERNICK. Do you think I feel happy at this moment?

MISS HESSEL. No, I don't imagine you can feel all that happy.

BERNICK. You despise me, don't you, Lona?

MISS HESSEL. Not yet.

BERNICK. You've no right to do that. To despise me. Oh, Lona, you can't imagine how dreadfully alone I am in this narrow, stunted society—how, year by year, I've had to renounce my hopes of really fulfilling myself and becoming what I might and could have become. What have I accomplished? It seems a lot, but really it's nothing—a patchwork of trivialities. But they wouldn't tolerate anything else here, or any-

thing bigger. If I tried to move a step outside their conception of right and wrong, my power would vanish. Do you
know what we are, we whom they call the pillars of society?
We are the instruments of society. Nothing more.

MISS HESSEL. Why have you only begun to realise this now?

BERNICK. Because I've been thinking a great deal lately—since
you came back. Especially this evening. Oh, Lona, why
didn't I appreciate you then for what you were?

MISS HESSEL. And if you had?

BERNICK. I'd never have let you go. And if I'd had you beside
me, I wouldn't stand where I do today.

MISS HESSEL. What about Betty? Haven't you ever thought
what she might have been to you?

BERNICK. I only know she hasn't been the wife I needed.

MISS HESSEL. Because you've never let her share your work
with you, or tried to establish a free and truthful relationship with her. Because you've allowed her to spend her life
reproaching herself for the disgrace to her family for which
you yourself are responsible.

BERNICK. Yes, yes, yes. Lying and cheating—that's the cause
of it all.

MISS HESSEL. Then why don't you start telling the truth?

BERNICK. Now? It's too late now, Lona.

MISS HESSEL. Tell me, Karsten. What satisfaction does all this
lying and cheating bring you?

BERNICK. None. I shall be destroyed, like the whole of this
rotten society. But a generation will grow up after us. It's my
son I'm working for; it's for him that I'm doing all this. A
time will come when society will be founded on honesty
and truth, and then he will be able to live a happier life
than his father has.

MISS HESSEL. With a lie as the cornerstone of his existence?
Think what an inheritance you're leaving your son.

BERNICK, *in subdued despair*. I am leaving him an inheritance

a thousand times worse than you know. But some time the curse must end. And yet—in spite of everything—
Violently.

How could you do all this to me? Well, now it's happened. Now I must go on. I won't let you destroy me!

HILMAR TOENNESEN, *an open letter in his hand, hastens in right, confused.*

HILMAR. But this is utterly—! Betty, Betty!

BERNICK. What is it now? Have they come already?

HILMAR. No, no. I must speak to someone—
He goes out through the door upstage left.

MISS HESSEL. Karsten, you say we came here to destroy you. Then let me tell you the metal he's made of, this prodigal whom your virtuous community treated like a leper. He can manage without you now. He's gone.

BERNICK. But he's coming back.

MISS HESSEL. Johan will never come back. He's gone for ever, and Dina has gone with him.

BERNICK. Never come back? And Dina—gone with him?

MISS HESSEL. Yes, to become his wife. There's a slap in the face for your virtuous community! Reminds me of the day I gave you—ah well!

BERNICK. Gone? She too? In the *Indian Girl?*

MISS HESSEL. No. He didn't dare to risk so precious a cargo with that gang of ruffians. Johan and Dina have sailed in the *Palm Tree.*

BERNICK. Ah! Then it was all for nothing—!
Goes quickly to the door of his room, flings it open and shouts.

Krap, stop the *Indian Girl!* She mustn't sail tonight!

KRAP, *from the other room.* The *Indian Girl* is already standing out to sea, Mr. Bernick.

BERNICK *closes the door and says dully.* Too late! And for nothing—!

MISS HESSEL. What do you mean?

BERNICK. Nothing, nothing. Get away from me—!

MISS HESSEL. Hm. Look here, Karsten. Johan told me to tell you that he's entrusted to me the keeping of his good name, which he once entrusted to you and which you robbed him of while he was away. Johan will keep his mouth shut. And I can do as I choose. Look. I have your two letters here in my hand.

BERNICK. You have them! And now—now you're going to—to-night—when the procession arrives—?

MISS HESSEL. I didn't come here to unmask you. I came to shake you from your sleep, so that you'd stand up and tell the truth. I have failed. Very well, then. Go on living your lie. Look. I'm tearing your two letters up. Take the pieces. Now you have them. There's no evidence against you now, Karsten. You've nothing left to fear. Be happy— if you can.

BERNICK, *a shiver runs through his whole body*. Lona, why didn't you do this before. Now it's too late. Now my whole life is ruined. After today, I can't go on living.

MISS HESSEL. What has happened?

BERNICK. Don't ask me. And yet—I must live! I shall live! For Olaf's sake! He'll make everything right—he'll atone for everything—!

MISS HESSEL. Karsten!

HILMAR TOENNESEN *hurries back*.

HILMAR. I can't find him. He's gone. Betty, too.

BERNICK. What's the matter with you?

HILMAR. I daren't tell you.

BERNICK. What is it? You must tell me!

HILMAR. Very well. Olaf has run away. He's gone—in the *Indian Girl*.

BERNICK *recoils*. Olaf! In the *Indian Girl*! No! No!

MISS HESSEL. Yes, it's true. Now I understand. I saw him jump out of the window.

BERNICK, *in the doorway to his room, cries desperately.* Krap, stop the *Indian Girl!* Stop her at all costs!

KRAP *comes out.* Impossible, Mr. Bernick. How can we?

BERNICK. We must stop her. Olaf is on board.

KRAP. What!

RUMMEL *enters from* BERNICK's *room.* Olaf run away? Impossible!

SANDSTAD *enters.* They'll send him back with the pilot, Mr. Bernick.

HILMAR. No, no. He's left me a letter.

Shows it.

He says he'll hide among the cargo until they've reached the open sea.

BERNICK. I shall never see him again.

RUMMEL. Oh, rubbish. She's a good, strong ship, newly repaired—

VIGELAND, *who has also come out.* In your own yard, Mr. Bernick.

BERNICK. I shall never see him again, I tell you. I've lost him, Lona. No—I realise it now. He never belonged to me.

Listens.

What's that?

RUMMEL. Music. The procession's arriving.

BERNICK. I can't receive anyone. I won't!

RUMMEL. What on earth do you mean? You must!

SANDSTAD. You must, Mr. Bernick. Remember what you have at stake.

BERNICK. What does that matter now? Whom have I to work for now?

RUMMEL. What a question to ask! You have us. And the community.

VIGELAND. Of course!

SANDSTAD. And you surely haven't forgotten that we too—

MARTHA *enters through the door upstage left. The music can be faintly heard from far down the street.*

MARTHA. The procession's arriving. I can't find Betty anywhere. I can't think where she—

BERNICK. Can't find her! You see, Lona! In sorrow as in joy, I stand alone.

RUMMEL. Up with those curtains! Come and help me, Mr. Krap. You too, Mr. Sandstad. Most regrettable that the whole family isn't here. That's not at all according to programme.

The curtains are raised from the windows and the door. The whole street is illuminated. On the house opposite is a big transparency, bearing the inscription: "Long live Karsten Bernick, The Pillar of our Society!"

BERNICK *recoils.* Take that away! I don't want to see it! Put it out, put it out!

RUMMEL. My dear fellow, have you taken leave of your senses?

MARTHA. What's the matter with him, Lona?

MISS HESSEL. Ssh!

Whispers to her.

BERNICK. Take away this nonsense, I tell you! Can't you see that all these lights are a mockery!

RUMMEL. Well, really!

BERNICK. Oh, how could you understand? But I—I—! These are torches to light the dead to their graves!

KRAP. Hm!

RUMMEL. Now look! You're making too much of this.

SANDSTAD. The boy'll just take a trip across the Atlantic, and then you'll have him back home again.

VIGELAND. Put your trust in the hand of the Almighty, Mr. Bernick.

RUMMEL. That ship's not ready to sink yet.

KRAP. Hm.

RUMMEL. It's not as though she was one of these floating coffins they send out in foreign countries—

MRS. BERNICK, *a big shawl over her head, enters from the verandah.*

MRS. BERNICK. Karsten, Karsten, have you heard?

BERNICK. Yes, I've heard. But you—you see nothing! You're his mother, why didn't you look after him?

MRS. BERNICK. Karsten, listen—

BERNICK. Why didn't you keep a watch on him? I've lost him! Give him back to me, if you can.

MRS. BERNICK. Yes, I can. I have him safe.

BERNICK. You have him?

THE OTHERS. Ah!

HILMAR. Yes, I thought as much.

MARTHA. You've got him back, Karsten!

MISS HESSEL. Yes. Now you must win him too.

BERNICK. You have him safe! Do you really mean it? Where is he?

MRS. BERNICK. I shan't tell you until you've forgiven him.

BERNICK. Forgiven—! But how did you find out—?

MRS. BERNICK. Do you think a mother hasn't eyes? I was terrified you might find out. Those few words he let fall yesterday—then I found his room was empty and his clothes and rucksack missing—

BERNICK. Yes, yes.

MRS. BERNICK. So I ran down and got hold of Aune. We went out in his boat. The American ship was just getting ready to sail. Thank heaven, we got there in time—went aboard—had the ship searched—found him. Oh, Karsten, you mustn't punish him!

BERNICK. Betty!

MRS. BERNICK. Or Aune, either!

BERNICK. Aune? What do you know about him? Is the *Indian Girl* under sail again?

MRS. BERNICK. No, that's just it—

BERNICK. Speak, speak!

MRS. BERNICK. Aune was as frightened as I was. It took a long time to search the ship—darkness was falling, the pilot began to complain—so Aune took his courage in his hands and told them in your name—

BERNICK. Yes?

MRS. BERNICK. To hold the ship until morning.

KRAP. Hm.

BERNICK. Oh, what luck! What incredible luck!

MRS. BERNICK. You aren't angry?

BERNICK. Oh, Betty, thank God, thank God!

RUMMEL. Come, man, you're being oversensitive.

HILMAR. Yes, as soon as anyone's bold enough to risk a little skirmish with the elements—ugh!

KRAP, *by the windows.* The procession's just coming through the garden gate!

BERNICK. Let them come.

RUMMEL. The whole garden's filling with people.

SANDSTAD. The street's crammed too.

RUMMEL. The entire town's here, Bernick. This is really an inspiring moment.

VIGELAND. Let us accept it in a humble spirit, Mr. Bernick.

RUMMEL. All the flags are out. What a procession! There's the festival committee, with Dr. Roerlund at its head.

BERNICK. Let them come, I say!

RUMMEL. Look, you're in a rather disturbed state of mind just now—

BERNICK. So?

RUMMEL. Well, if you don't feel up to it, I wouldn't mind saying a few words on your behalf.

BERNICK. No, thank you. This evening I shall speak myself.

RUMMEL. But do you know what you have to say?

BERNICK. Yes, Rummel. Don't worry. I know what I have to say.

The music has ceased. The verandah door is thrown open.

DR. ROERLUND *enters at the head of the festival committee,
accompanied by two* FOOTMEN *carrying a covered basket.
After them come* CITIZENS *of all classes, as many as the
room will hold. A huge crowd, with banners and flags, can
be glimpsed outside in the garden and the street.*

ROERLUND. Most honoured sir! I see by the amazement on
your face that our intrusion into this happy family circle,
where you sit gathered at your peaceful fireside surrounded
by active and honourable friends and fellow citizens, takes
you completely by surprise. But our hearts commanded that
we should come and pay you homage. It is not the first time
we have done this, but it is the first time we have done so
on such a comprehensive scale. We have often expressed
to you our thanks for the solid moral foundation on which
you have, as one might say, grounded our community. But
tonight we hail you as the far-sighted, indefatigable and
selfless—nay self-sacrificing—fellow citizen who has seized
the initiative in launching an enterprise which, so expert
opinion assures us, will give a powerful impetus to the temporal welfare and prosperity of our community.

VOICES FROM THE CROWD. Bravo, bravo!

ROERLUND. Mr. Bernick, you have for many years been a shining example to our town. I am speaking now not of your
model family life, nor of your untarnished moral record.
These are matters for private admiration rather than public
acclaim. I speak rather of your work as a citizen, which is
apparent for all to see. Stately ships sail forth from your
shipyards and show our country's flag upon the furthest
corners of the globe. A numerous and contented family of
workers reveres you as a father. By calling into existence
new branches of industry you have given prosperity to hundreds of homes. You are, in a word, the cornerstone of our
community.

VOICES. Hear, hear! Bravo!

ROERLUND. But what we especially bless in you is the shining
altruism which irradiates your every action—a rare quality
indeed in this modern age. You are now in the process of

procuring for the community a—I do not flinch from the plain, prosaic word—a railway.

MANY VOICES. Bravo, bravo!

ROERLUND. But this enterprise is threatened by obstacles deliberately placed in its path by narrow and selfish interests.

VOICES. Hear, hear!

ROERLUND. It is not unknown that certain individuals who do not belong to our community have stolen a march on our own industrious citizens, and have secured certain advantages which rightly belonged to this town.

VOICES. Yes, yes. Hear, hear!

ROERLUND. This regrettable information has, sir, doubtless come to your knowledge. None the less you are pursuing your project inflexibly, knowing that a true patriot's vision cannot be confined by the needs of his own parish.

VARIOUS VOICES. Hm. No, no! Yes, yes!

ROERLUND. It is therefore to the patriot and, in the largest sense, the model citizen, that we are gathered here tonight to pay homage. May God grant that your enterprise may result in true and lasting prosperity for this community! The railway is a road which may expose us to corrupting influences from without, but it will also be a road by which we shall swiftly be able to rid ourselves of them. We can, alas, no longer hope to isolate ourselves completely from the evil of the outside world. But the fact that on this evening of rejoicing we have, it is rumoured, been rid with unexpected speed of one such influence—

VOICES. Ssh! Ssh!

ROERLUND. —I take as a happy omen for this enterprise. I only mention this as evidence that we stand here in a house in which ethical considerations carry greater weight than the ties of blood.

VOICES. Hear, hear! Bravo!

BERNICK, *simultaneously*. Allow me to—

ROERLUND. One word more, sir. What you have done for this parish you have, of course, done with no ulterior motive or thought of material advantage. But we trust you will not refuse to accept a small token of appreciation from your fellow citizens, least of all at this significant moment when, so men of practical experience assure us, we stand on the threshold of a new era.

MANY VOICES. Bravo! Hear, hear!

He nods to the FOOTMEN, *who bring the basket closer. During the following, members of the* COMMITTEE *take out and present the objects described.*

ROERLUND. We therefore have the honour, Mr. Bernick, to present you with this silver coffee service. May it adorn your table when, in the days to come, as so often in days gone by, we shall enjoy the pleasure of gathering in your hospitable house. And you too, gentlemen, who have so steadfastly supported our foremost citizen, we beg to accept these small tokens of our affection. To you, Mr. Rummel, this silver cup. You have often, in well-winged words, amid the clinking of cups, championed the civic interests of this community. May you often find worthy opportunities for raising and emptying this cup. To you, Mr. Sandstad, I present this album containing photographs of your fellow citizens. Your famed and acknowledged generosity places you in the agreeable position of numbering friends in every stratum of the community, regardless of political differences. And to you, Mr. Vigeland, to adorn your bedside, I offer this book of sermons, printed on vellum, and luxuriously bound. Under the ripening influence of the years you have arrived at a mature wisdom; your interest in temporal matters has been purified and sublimated by reflection upon loftier and less worldly things.

Turns to the CROWD.

And now, my friends, three cheers for Mr. Bernick and his fellows in the fight! Three cheers for the pillars of our society!

WHOLE CROWD. Long live Mr. Bernick! Long live the pillars of our society! Hurrah! Hurrah! Hurrah!

MISS HESSEL. Good luck, brother-in-law.

An expectant silence.

BERNICK *begins slowly and earnestly.* Fellow citizens! Your Chairman has said that we stand this evening on the threshold of a new era; and I hope this will prove to be the case. But for this to happen, we must face the truth, which until this evening has been an outcast from this community.

General amazement.

I must therefore begin by rejecting the words of praise with which you, Dr. Roerlund, as is the custom on such occasions, addressed me. I am unworthy of them, for until today I have not acted selflessly. If I have not always acted from pecuniary motives, I none the less now realise that a desire for power, for influence and for reputation, has been the driving force behind most of my actions.

RUMMEL, *aside.* What's this?

BERNICK. However, I do not therefore reproach myself before my fellow citizens. For I still believe that I can be reckoned among the most useful of us who stand here tonight.

MANY VOICES. Hear, hear! Yes, yes!

BERNICK. I condemn myself most for having so often been weak enough to use backstairs methods, because I knew and feared our community's fondness for scenting impure motives behind everything a man does here. And that brings me to a case in point.

RUMMEL, *uneasily.* Hm-hm!

BERNICK. Rumours have been spreading about the big purchases of land that have been made in the neighbourhood. All these purchases have been made by me, and by me alone.

VOICES *whisper.* What did he say? Him? Mr. Bernick?

BERNICK. All that land belongs, at this moment, to me. I have of course confided this information to my partners in this enterprise, Messrs. Rummel, Vigeland, and Sandstad, and we have agreed that—

RUMMEL. It isn't true! Where's the proof? Show us the proof?

VIGELAND. We agreed nothing!

SANDSTAD. Well, I must say!

BERNICK. That is quite correct; we have not yet agreed on what I was about to propose. But I am confident that these three gentlemen will agree with me now when I say that I have this evening convinced myself that these properties should be turned into a public company, so that any citizen who wishes may buy a share in them.

MANY VOICES. Hurrah! Long live Mr. Bernick!

RUMMEL, *quietly to* BERNICK. You damned traitor!

SANDSTAD, *also quietly*. You've cheated us!

VIGELAND. May the Devil— Oh good heavens, what am I saying?

CROWD, *outside*. Hurrah, hurrah, hurrah!

BERNICK. Quiet, gentlemen! I am unworthy of this applause, for the decision I have now reached is not what I originally intended. I intended to keep all the land for myself, and I still believe that these properties can be best exploited if they come under the control of a single hand. But that is for you to decide. If it is the general wish, I am willing to administer them to the best of my ability.

VOICES. Yes! Yes! Yes!

BERNICK. But first my fellow citizens must know me as I really am. Let each man look into his own heart, and let us resolve that from tonight we shall in fact enter upon a new era. Let the old life, with its painted façade, its hypocrisy and its hollowness, its sham propriety and its miserable prejudices, survive only as a museum. And to this museum we shall give—shall we not, gentlemen?—our coffee service, our silver cup, our photograph album and our book of sermons printed on vellum and luxuriously bound.

RUMMEL. Yes, of course.

VIGELAND *mutters*. You've taken all the rest from us, so why not this?

SANDSTAD. Yes, yes.

BERNICK. And now to the chief issue that remains between me and my community. You have heard it asserted that evil influences have left us this evening. To that piece of news I can add another. The man in question did not leave alone. A girl went with him, to become his wife—

MISS HESSEL, *loudly*. Dina Dorf!

ROERLUND. What?

MRS. BERNICK. Lona!

Great excitement.

ROERLUND. Fled? Run away—with him? Impossible!

BERNICK. To become his wife, Dr. Roerlund. And I will tell you something else.

Quietly.

Prepare yourself, Betty, for what I am about to say.

Loudly.

I say: "Hats off to that man, for he had the courage to shoulder the blame for another man's crime." Oh, fellow citizens, I am weary of lies. They have poisoned every fibre of my being. You shall know everything. It was I who was guilty fifteen years ago.

MRS. BERNICK, *quietly, emotionally*. Karsten!

MARTHA, *similarly*. Oh—Johan—!

MISS HESSEL. At last!

Dumb astonishment among the onlookers.

BERNICK. Yes, fellow citizens! I was the guilty one, and he was the one who fled. The false and evil rumours which were afterwards spread about him it is now too late to refute. But who am I to complain of this? Fifteen years ago I raised myself on these rumours. Whether they are now to bring me down is a question that each one of you must argue with his own conscience.

ROERLUND. What a thunderbolt! The town's foremost citizen!

Softly, to MRS. BERNICK.

Oh, Mrs. Bernick, I feel most deeply sorry for you.

HILMAR. What an admission! Well, I must say—!

BERNICK. But you must not decide tonight. I beg each of you

to return home to collect your thoughts and to look into your hearts. When you are calm again you will decide whether by speaking thus openly I have lost or won. Goodbye. I still have much to atone for; but that is between myself and my own conscience. Good night. Take away these trappings. This is not the time nor the place for them.

ROERLUND. I should think not indeed!

Softly, to MRS. BERNICK.

Run away! She was quite unworthy of me after all.

Half aloud to the COMMITTEE.

Well, gentlemen, after this I think we had better depart as quietly as we can.

HILMAR. How anyone is to wave the banner of ideals high after this I really—ugh!

The news meanwhile has been whispered from mouth to mouth. The CROWD *drifts away.* RUMMEL, SANDSTAD *and* VIGELAND, *also go, arguing in subdued but vehement tones.* HILMAR *wanders out right. Silence.* BERNICK, MRS. BERNICK, MARTHA, MISS HESSEL *and* KRAP *are left in the room.*

BERNICK. Betty, can you forgive me?

MRS. BERNICK *smiles*. Do you know, Karsten, this has been the happiest moment I have had for years?

BERNICK. What do you mean?

MRS. BERNICK. For years now I have believed that you were once mine, but I had lost you. Now I know you were never mine; but I shall win you.

BERNICK *throws his arms round her*. Oh, Betty, you have won me! Lona has taught me to understand for the first time what kind of woman you really are. But Olaf—Olaf!

MRS. BERNICK. Yes, now you can see him. Mr. Krap—

She talks quietly to KRAP *upstage. He goes out through the verandah door. During the following, all the transparencies, and the lights in the houses outside, are gradually extinguished.*

BERNICK, *quietly.* Thank you, Lona. You have saved what was best in me—and for me.

MISS HESSEL. What else do you think I wanted?

BERNICK. Yes—was it this you came back for—or was it something else? I don't understand you, Lona.

MISS HESSEL. Hm—

BERNICK. It wasn't hatred, then? And it wasn't revenge? Then why did you come back here?

MISS HESSEL. Old friendship doesn't rust, Karsten.

BERNICK. Lona!

MISS HESSEL. When Johan told me about that lie, I vowed to myself: "The hero of my youth shall stand free and true."

BERNICK. Lona, Lona! How little I have deserved this from you!

MISS HESSEL. Ah, Karsten! If we women demanded our deserts—!

AUNE *enters from the garden with* OLAF.

BERNICK *runs towards him.* Olaf!

OLAF. Father, I promise you I won't ever again—

BERNICK. Run away?

OLAF. Yes, yes, I promise, Father.

BERNICK. And I promise you, you shall never have cause to. From now on you shall be allowed to grow up, not as the heir to my life's work, but as one who has his own life's work awaiting him.

OLAF. And may I become anything I like?

BERNICK. Yes, you may.

OLAF. Thank you. Then I don't want to become a pillar of society.

BERNICK. Oh? Why not?

OLAF. I think it must be so dull.

BERNICK. You shall be yourself, Olaf. That is all that matters. As for you, Aune—

AUNE. I know, Mr. Bernick. I'm dismissed.

BERNICK. We'll stay together, Aune. And please forgive me.

AUNE. What! But the ship didn't sail this evening—

BERNICK. She shall not sail tomorrow, either. I gave you too little time. The work must be attended to more thoroughly.

AUNE. It will, Mr. Bernick. And with the new machines!

BERNICK. Good. But it must be done thoroughly and honestly. There is much in us which needs to be repaired thoroughly and honestly. Well, good night, Aune.

AUNE. Good night, Mr. Bernick—and thank you. Thank you! *He goes out right.*

MRS. BERNICK. They have all gone now.

BERNICK. And we are alone. My name does not shine in letters of fire any longer. All the lights in the windows are out.

MISS HESSEL. Would you like them lit again?

BERNICK. Not for all the money in the world. Where have I been? You will be appalled when you know. I feel as though I had just returned to health and sanity after being poisoned. But I feel it—I *can* become young and strong again. Oh, come closer, come closer around me! Come, Betty! Come, Olaf, my son! And you, Martha. Oh, Martha! It's as though I had never seen you all these years.

MISS HESSEL. I can well believe that. Your society is a society of bachelors. You don't notice the women.

BERNICK. True, true. And because of that—now I don't want any arguing, Lona—you must not leave Betty and me.

MRS. BERNICK. No, Lona, you mustn't!

MISS HESSEL. How could I run away and abandon all you youngsters just when you're beginning to start a new life? Being a foster mother is my job, isn't it? You and I, Martha —we two old maids— What are you looking at?

MARTHA. How light the sky has grown! It's bright and calm over the sea. The *Palm Tree* has good luck in her sails.

MISS HESSEL. And good luck on board.

BERNICK. And we—we have a long, hard day ahead of us. I most of all. But let it come. Oh, gather close around me, you loyal and true women. That is something else I've learned in these past few days. It is you women who are the pillars of society.

MISS HESSEL. Then it's a poor wisdom you've learned, brother-in-law.

Puts her hand firmly on his shoulder.

No, Karsten. The spirit of truth and the spirit of freedom—they are the pillars of society.

The Wild Duck

INTRODUCTION

On January 11, 1883, Ibsen wrote from Rome to his publisher, Frederik Hegel: "I am already at work again planning a new play about contemporary life. It will be in 4 acts, and I hope to be able to get down to the actual writing within a couple of months at most. The Italian air, and the pleasant way of life down here, greatly increase my eagerness to create. I find it much easier to work here than in Germany."

Ibsen was now fifty-four, and the reception of *Ghosts* in Scandinavia a year earlier might well have deterred a less resilient spirit than his from setting pen to paper for some while. It had been reviled, not merely by the conservative press, which he had expected, but also by the radical press; even such an old admirer as Henrik Jaeger had lectured against it, and Hegel had been forced to take back large quantities of the book from booksellers who refused to stock it; indeed, it was thirteen years before the first printing of 10,000 copies was sold out. The theatres of Christiania, Copenhagen and Stockholm had been unanimous in declaring it unfit for public presentation.

So far from being silenced by this reception, however, Ibsen had reacted swiftly with the most buoyant play he had written since *Peer Gynt. An Enemy of the People* was immediately accepted by the Christiania Theatre, the management of which seems not to have appreciated, or to have been insensitive to, the fact that its theme was the unworthiness of "those who do not dare" and its conclusion: "The strongest man is he who stands alone." The play was in its last days of rehearsal when Ibsen wrote to Hegel with plans for its successor.

In the event, it was to be another fifteen months before he began the actual writing of THE WILD DUCK, and a further eleven weeks of intensive revision before he completed it. The slowness and difficulty with which it took shape contrasts markedly with the swiftness and ease with which he had written *An Enemy of the People*. THE WILD DUCK represented yet another departure into new country. Just as he had abandoned poetic drama as soon as he had mastered it in *Peer Gynt*, so now he threw aside almost contemptuously the new anti-poetic, anti-symbolic form which he had perfected in *A Doll's House*, *Ghosts* and *An Enemy of the People*. He explained his restlessness and passion for experiment in a letter to Georg Brandes that summer (June 12, 1883):

"An intellectual pioneer," he wrote, "can never gather a majority about him. In ten years the majority may have reached that standpoint which Dr. Stockmann had reached when the people held their meeting. But during those ten years the Doctor has not remained stationary; he still stands at least ten years ahead of the others. The majority, the masses, the mob, will never catch him up; he can never rally them behind him. I myself feel a similarly unrelenting compulsion to keep pressing forward. A crowd now stands where I stood when I wrote my earlier books. But I myself am there no longer. I am somewhere else—far ahead of them—or so I hope. At present I am struggling with the draft of a new play in four acts. As time passes, various odd ideas settle in one's head, and one must find some outlet for them. Though since it won't deal with the High Court, or the absolute veto, or even the 'pure' flag,* it is hardly likely to arouse any interest in Norway. However, I hope it may obtain a hearing in other quarters."

Ibsen does not seem to have made any progress with THE WILD DUCK during the remainder of 1883, apart from a few pages of rough notes and a provisional list of characters. On January 22, 1884, he wrote to Laura Grundtvig: "I have been having one of those periods when I can only with the greatest

---

* I.e., without the mark of union with Sweden.

reluctance sit down to my desk." On April 21, however, he was able to send better tidings to his publisher. "The political complications in Norway," he wrote to Hegel, "have prevented me all this winter from working seriously, and with undivided attention, on my new play. But now at last I have managed to free my mind from this chaos, and am writing at full stretch. The first act will be finished this week, and I reckon that by the middle of June I should be able to let you know that the play is ready."

He completed Act 1 according to schedule; his manuscript draft of this act is dated April 20–28, 1884. On May 2 he began Act 2; but when he was halfway through it, he stopped, and started to rewrite the play from the beginning. By May 24 he had completed Acts 1 and 2 in their new form. Act 3 occupied him from May 25–30; Act 4 from June 2–8; and Act 5 from June 9–13. The following day, June 14, 1884, he wrote to Hegel:

"I am glad to be able to tell you that yesterday I completed the draft of my new play. It comprises five acts and will, as far as I can calculate, occupy some 200 printed pages, possibly a little more. It still remains for me to make the fair copy and I shall start on that tomorrow. As usual, however, this will involve not just copying the draft but a comprehensive rewriting of the dialogue. So it will take time. Still, unless some unforeseen obstacle presents itself I reckon that the whole manuscript should be in your hands by mid-September. The play doesn't touch on political or social problems, or indeed any matters of public import. It takes place entirely within the confines of family life. I dare say it will arouse some discussion; but it can't offend anyone."

On June 30, he left Rome for the little mountain resort of Gossensass in the Tyrol—that village that was later to prove so fateful to him. There he settled down in his usual strictly methodical manner to revise the play.

"My routine," he wrote to his wife on July 4, 1884, "has so far been as follows. Rise at 6.30; breakfast brought up half an hour later; then I go out while they do the room; then write from 9 to 1. Then lunch, with a ravenous appetite. In the afternoons, too, I have managed to write a little, or at any rate do groundwork. The second act will be ready in 5–6 days. I am not drinking any beer; which suits me well. But I am drinking milk, and a little—not much—white wine, with water. A light evening meal at 7.30. Up to now I have been in bed each evening by 10, and have been sleeping well."

Ibsen's wife and son were holidaying in Norway, and his fairly frequent letters to them enable us to date the progress of his revision. He finished Act 2 in its final form on July 12. Act 3 took him from July 14 until either July 29 or 30; Act 4 was ready by August 17. On August 27 he wrote to his son Sigurd: "My play is now fast nearing its conclusion. In 3–4 days it will be ready; then I shall read it through carefully and send it off. I take great joy in working on this play; it grows all the time in little details, and I shall miss it when I have to part from it; though, at the same time, I shall be glad . . . The German sculptor Professor Kopf, from Rome, has with him a 13-year-old daughter who is the most perfect model for my Hedvig that could be imagined; she is pretty, has a serious face and manner, and is a little *gefräsig*." Three days later, on August 30, he wrote to his wife: "Although I don't know when or where my letters reach you, while you continue to move from town to town, I must nevertheless send you the good news that I have just finished my manuscript. The play will be very rich in content, and bigger than any other of my recent works. I have said everything I wanted to say; and I don't think it could easily have been said better. Now to the business of reading it through, which will take 2–3 days; then off it goes to Hegel."

On September 2 he wrote to Hegel (still from Gossensass): "I enclose the manuscript of my new play, THE WILD DUCK, which has occupied me daily for the past 4 months, and from which I cannot now part without a certain feeling of loss. The characters in it have, despite their many failings, grown dear to me as a result of this long daily association. But I cherish the hope that they will also find good friends and well-wishers among the great reading public and, not least, among theatre folk; for they all, without exception, offer rewarding opportunities. But the study and representation of them will not be found easy. . . . This new play occupies, in some ways, a unique position among my dramatic works. Its method differs in certain respects from that which I have previously employed. However, I don't wish to enlarge on that subject here. The critics will, I trust, see this for themselves; at any rate, they will find something to argue about, something to construe. I believe, too, that The Wild Duck may possibly tempt some of our younger dramatists to explore new territories, and this I regard as a desirable thing."

Hegel's firm, Gyldendals of Copenhagen, published The Wild Duck on November 11, 1884, in a printing of 8000 copies. This sold so quickly that a new edition appeared on December 1. The play received its première on January 9, 1885, at Bergen; before the month was out it had also been staged in Christiania, Helsinki and Stockholm, and the following month it was presented in Copenhagen. Germany, surprisingly, had to wait three years to see the play; its German première was on March 4, 1888, at the Residenztheater, Berlin. Berne, Wiesbaden and Dresden saw it in 1889, and Paris in 1891, when Antoine staged it at the Théâtre Libre (the only Ibsen play, apart from *Ghosts,* which he presented there). William Archer had not yet begun his association with Janet Achurch and J. T. Grein, and it was not performed in London until 1894.

The Wild Duck greatly perplexed Norwegian readers when it first appeared. "The public does not know what to make of it," commented the *Christiania Intelligentssedler.* "One paper says one thing and the other just the opposite." *Aftenposten* complained: "One may study and study to find what Ibsen wants to say, and not find it." *Morgenbladet* found the plot "as queer as it is thin . . . The total impression can hardly be other than a strong sense of emptiness and unpleasantness." *Bergens Tidende* thought the play proved Ibsen's inferiority to Bjoernson. "He does not speak from the depths of his heart as does Bjoernson. He does not make demands of the individual with the same strength, he has no faith in his own ability to ennoble humanity by means of his writings. He states the

problems excellently as he sees them, but makes no attempt
to show the way beyond them; he chastises as one who has
authority, but makes no demand for improvement." The only
newspaper critic in Norway who seemed to appreciate the
point of the play was Irgens Hansen in *Dagbladet;* he recognised that Ibsen "here stands on humanity's ground and speaks
humanity's cause, even though it be the cause of a very shabby
humanity."

Across the North Sea, Ibsen's admirers were equally baffled.
His earliest English champion, Edmund Gosse, condemned it
in the *Fortnightly Review* as "a strange, melancholy and pes-
simistic drama, almost without a ray of light from beginning
to end . . . There is really not a character in the book that
inspires confidence or liking . . . There can be no doubt that
it is by far the most difficult of Ibsen's dramas for a reader to
comprehend." Gosse himself does not seem to have compre-
hended it very well, for he concluded that "the ideal spirit
of goodness is the untamed bird in its close and miserable
garret, captive to circumstances and with no hope of escape."
William Archer also failed to understand it at first, though he
later came to admire it greatly, and named it "Ibsen's greatest
play." Arthur Symons thought it "a play of inferior quality,"
and Havelock Ellis dismissed it as "the least remarkable of
Ibsen's plays." Almost the only critic to see the point of the
play during the next ten years was Bernard Shaw, who de-
voted to it one of his most penetrating passages in *The Quintessence of Ibsenism:*

"After *An Enemy of the People,* Ibsen . . . left the vulgar
ideals for dead and set about the exposure of those of the
choicer spirits, beginning with the incorrigible idealists who
had idealized his very self, and were becoming known as Ib-
senites. His first move in this direction was such a tragi-comic
slaughtering of sham Ibsenism that his astonished victims
plaintively declared that THE WILD DUCK, as the new play
was called, was a satire on his former works; while the pious,
whom he had disappointed so severely by his interpretation of
Brand . . . began to hope that he was coming back repentant
to the fold."

Shaw concluded: "The busybody [i.e., Gregers] finds that people cannot be freed from their failings from without. They must free themselves."

THE WILD DUCK at first received a mixed reception on the stage. It was admired in Christiania, thanks largely to Arnoldus Reimers's rendering of Hjalmar; but it was hissed in Helsinki. In Stockholm, at that time the most theatrically enlightened of the Scandinavian capitals, it aroused deep interest, not least because the production was so daringly realistic as to include real doors with actual handles and even, which caused a great buzz, a commode in Hjalmar's studio. When it was staged in Rome in January 1892, the audience became so irritated by Gregers's behaviour that they harassed the unfortunate actor who played him with shouts of "Basta!" and "Imbecile!", while at the Paris première at the Théâtre Libre some of the spectators showed their displeasure by quacking like ducks. As an illustration of how little people understood the play, Francisque Sarcey, the famous critic of *Le Temps*, thought that Hedvig had shot herself out of grief because the wild duck was dead. The first London performance, in 1894, was only moderately good, but in 1897 there was a much better one, directed by Charles Charrington with Laurence Irving (Sir Henry's younger son) as Hjalmar. Bernard Shaw paid the play a memorable tribute in the *Saturday Review*:

"Where shall I find an epithet magnificent enough for THE WILD DUCK? To sit there getting deeper and deeper into that Ekdal home, and getting deeper and deeper into your own life all the time, until you forget that you are in a theatre; to look on with horror and pity at a profound tragedy, shaking with laughter all the time at an irresistible comedy; to go out, not from a diversion, but from an experience deeper than real life ever brings to most men, or often brings to any man; that is what THE WILD DUCK was like last Monday at the Globe."

Subsequent generations proved similarly receptive, and THE WILD DUCK now shares with *A Doll's House, Ghosts, Hedda Gabler* and *The Master Builder* the honour of being the most frequently staged of Ibsen's plays.

A rich quantity of Ibsen's draft material for the play has survived: nine sets of notes, the unfinished first draft (comprising one and a half acts) and the full second draft, which differs considerably from the final version. The first set of notes, undated but probably written in late 1882 or early 1883, contains a quantity of aphorisms, often rather vapid, but is chiefly of interest in that it shows Ibsen making his first sketches for the characters of Hjalmar and Gregers. Hjalmar seems to have been originally based on a photographer named Edvard Larsen with whom Ibsen had lodged in earlier days, and who had taken the oldest known photograph of him (in 1861–62).

"E.L. . . . is a naïve and pretentious pessimist, devoid of energy, an idle dreamer. . . . [His] marriage with a simple wife has, in one way, been a 'true' marriage, in that it has caused him to shrink, or at any rate stopped him developing. Now he can't manage without her; or she without him . . . He has to spend the evening with people of quality. It bores and irritates him. He longs to get back to his own narrow, homely surroundings . . . Like A. the printer [Aslaksen of *The League of Youth* and *An Enemy of the People*] he has been afforded a glimpse into a higher world; that is his tragedy. . . . 'The sixth sense.' Magnetic [i.e., hypnotic] influence is E.L.'s favourite subject. . . . Photographer, failed poet, dreams of a socialist revolution, the revolution of the future, of science. Poison in the breakfast . . . Is a socialist at heart but dares not admit it; he has a family, and so is not free."

Gregers was at first based on the Norwegian novelist and playwright, Alexander Kielland (1849–1906), whose radicalism Ibsen appears to have regarded as bogus:

"A.K., the sybarite, enjoys an aesthetic indignation at poverty and misery. Enjoys his visits to his old schoolfriend who has come down in the world, without realizing why he enjoys them. . . . A.K-d.: to lie tucked up in a soft bed with a well-filled belly and hear the rain pouring down and think of difficult journeys in the wet and cold, is a great pleasure."

As Ibsen's plans developed, however, Hjalmar and Gregers became more and more different from the E.L. and A.K-d. of these first notes. The Gregers we know has little in common with the character of A.K-d. as sketched here. It is the contrast between the two characters rather than the characters themselves that has survived into the play. The rich man's son visiting his old schoolfellow who has come down in the world seems to have been the idea which first ignited Ibsen's imagination. Gregers gradually developed into a kind of *reductio ad absurdum* of Dr. Stockmann, the hero of Ibsen's previous play—a living illustration of the danger of a single-minded pursuit of truth if not tempered by common sense and an understanding of human limitations. Similarly, Ibsen soon found Edvard Larsen inadequate as a model for Hjalmar, and borrowed characteristics from two other Norwegians of his acquaintance, a poet named Kristofer Janson and, especially, a failed artist, Magnus Bagge, from whom Ibsen had taken drawing lessons around 1860. Halvdan Koht has said of Bagge that he had "a constant longing to lift himself above everyday prose"; it was typical of him that when he went to live in Germany he called himself von Bagge. Hjalmar's mode of speech was fairly ordinary at first; it is only in the final (third) draft that it acquires its peculiarly florid quality and its excess of adjectives. He is perhaps the most difficult of all Ibsen's characters to translate, at any rate in the prose dramas.

Hedvig, in Ibsen's early notes, is described as being "drawn to the sea." There is a reference to "the first time she saw a big expanse of water looking down from a height," and a note that "Human beings are sea-creatures—like the wild duck—not land creatures. Gregers was made for the sea. In time, all people will live on it, when the land becomes swallowed up. Then family life will cease." Ibsen discarded these ideas from THE WILD DUCK, but returned to them two plays later in *The Lady from the Sea*. Hedvig's impending blindness was an afterthought. There is no reference to it until the final draft; indeed, until that draft she is rather a commonplace child. Hjalmar's "invention," too, which figures so largely in the play as we know it, is barely touched on in the preliminary drafts. Ibsen, in a letter to Georg Brandes (June 25, 1884) described his revisionary work as "polishing the language and

giving a sharper individuality to the characters and dialogue"
and, as William Archer remarked: "Everywhere, on a close
comparison of the texts, we see an intensive imagination lighting up, as it were, what was at first somewhat cold and colour-
less. In this case, as in many others, the draft suggests a transparency before the electricity has been switched on."

THE WILD DUCK is full of echoes from Ibsen's own childhood. The family home at Venstoep had contained a library
of old books left, like the ones in the Ekdals' loft, by a previous
owner of the house known as "The Flying Dutchman," a Norwegian who had been a prison convict in England and a slave
in the Barbary States, and had died the year Ibsen was born.
These books had included *Harrison's* (or, as Ibsen originally
wrote it, *Harryson's*) *History of London* (1775), which so
delighted Hedvig. Hedvig herself seems to have got her name,
and probably some of her character, from Ibsen's sister Hedvig; and Old Ekdal contains many traits of the playwright's
father, Knud Ibsen, who had been a lieutenant in the militia
and a great huntsman before he went bankrupt and brought
the family name into disgrace. Ibsen also borrowed certain
details from a trial which had caused a sensation during his
student days in Christiania, when an army officer accused of
embezzlement tried unsuccessfully to shoot himself. (He was
to return to this source for much of his material for *John
Gabriel Borkman*.) And, perhaps the most significant echo
from Ibsen's past, at the age of sixteen he had, like Haakon
Werle, given a servant girl an illegitimate child.

Wherein does the "method" of THE WILD DUCK differ, as
Ibsen told Hegel, from that which he had previously employed? At first sight there is no immediately obvious difference; it seems, like *A Doll's House, Ghosts* and *An Enemy of
the People*, to be a realistic play about realistic people, and
the method seems to be his old method of raking over apparently dead ashes and exposing the live embers beneath. The
symbolism? But Ibsen had used symbolism at least as freely
in *Brand*.

Nevertheless, I think there is little doubt that it was the

symbolism in THE WILD DUCK to which Ibsen was referring when he wrote of a new method. In *Brand* the symbols are incidental to the play, or at any rate are not fully integrated into it. The Ice Church and the hawk are left deliberately imprecise; there is room for intelligent argument about their meaning; perhaps, indeed, they are intended to mean different things to different people. In THE WILD DUCK, however, there is a single and precise symbol, that of the bird itself; and, so far from being incidental to the play, it is the hub and heart of it. *Brand* is a play into which symbols have worked their way; THE WILD DUCK is a play dependent on, and held together by, a symbol, as though the wild duck were a magnet and the characters in the play so many iron filings held together by this centripetal force. This was not a method that Ibsen was to use invariably in his subsequent plays; *Rosmersholm*, for example, and *Hedda Gabler* seem to me to have more in common with *Ghosts* than with THE WILD DUCK. But we find him returning to it in the later plays; the towers and spires in *The Master Builder* and the crutch in *Little Eyolf* serve a structural purpose similar to the wild duck. They are images from which the characters cannot escape, any more than the iron filings can escape the magnet.

Ibsen probably borrowed the image of the wild duck from a poem called "The Sea Bird" by Johan Sebastian Welhaven which describes how a wild duck is wounded and dives down to die on the sea-bed; and Professor Francis Bull suggests that he may also have been influenced by Darwin's account in *The Origin of Species* of how wild ducks degenerate in captivity. Some astonishing theories have been advanced as to what the bird is intended to stand for. Surely Ibsen makes it abundantly clear that he intended it as a double symbol with two precise and obvious references. Firstly, it is, like Hedvig, a by-product of Haakon Werle's fondness for sport which has been rejected by him and is now cared for by the Ekdal family. Secondly, with a more general application, it represents the refusal of most people, once they have been wounded, to go on living and face reality. Both Hjalmar and his father have sought to hide themselves in the deep blue sea of illusion, and Gregers,

like the "damned clever dog" trained by his father, hauls them
back to the surface. The cynics (Relling and Haakon Werle)
watch this operation; so do the two sensible, earthbound
women, Gina and Mrs. Soerby. These women, Ibsen seems
to imply, offer the only real refuge: love. Mrs. Soerby can
save Haakon Werle, despite Gregers's cynicism, just as she
could have saved Relling, who had also once loved her; Relling knows this, and it is hinted that the loss of her is partly
responsible for his having turned into a drunkard. And Gina,
if Gregers had not intervened, could have saved Hjalmar. Yet
Ibsen leaves a question mark here; is love simply another illusion, like the Ekdals' loft? And if so, then is not the illusion of
the loft justified, just as much as the illusion of love?

At the same time, while the wild duck has these two specific significances within the play, it is possible that, consciously or unconsciously, it also reflects Ibsen's impression of
himself when he wrote it; one who has forgotten what it means
to live wild, and has grown plump and tame and content with
his basket; as unlike the author of *Brand* as the duck is unlike
the hawk of the earlier play, of which, too, the climax had
been a shot fired at (or supposedly at) a bird by a girl of
fourteen. How far, Ibsen must have asked himself—and he
was to ask the question again, through Allmers in *Little Eyolf*
and Rubek in *When We Dead Awaken*—does the artist, like the
Ekdals, shut himself off from life? Is his world so very different
from their loft with its imitations of reality? Which is the more
cowardly refuge, the Ekdals' loft or Brand's Ice Church?

Hjalmar and Gregers both represent different aspects of Ibsen; on the one hand the evader of reality, on the other the
impractical idealist who pesters mankind with his "claims of
the ideal" because he has a sick conscience and despises himself. How far, one wonders, did Ibsen identify himself with
Gregers in that curious episode when the latter, finding that
the stove smokes, throws water on it to put out the fire and only
makes the stink worse? He had already portrayed these two
conflicting aspects of himself in *Brand* and *Peer Gynt,* and the
conflict between Gregers and Hjalmar is as though Brand and
Peer Gynt had been brought face to face.

Two main dangers confront anyone who produces THE WILD DUCK: the temptation to play Hjalmar as ridiculous and farcical, and the temptation to play Gregers as spiteful. A perusal of the notices of London productions of the play during the past seventy years reveals how often actors and producers have fallen into these traps. Ibsen foresaw the danger of Hjalmar being made a figure of fun, and warned against it in a letter which he wrote to H. Schroeder, the manager of the Christiania Theatre, on November 14, 1884. Hjalmar, he wrote, "must not be played with any trace of parody. The actor must never for a moment show that he is conscious that there is anything funny in what he says. His voice has, as Relling observes, something endearing about it, and this quality must be clearly brought out. His sentimentality is honest, his melancholy, in its way, attractive; no hint of affectation. Between ourselves, I would suggest you cast your mind towards Kristofer Janson, who still contrives to give an effect of beauty whatever drivel he may be uttering. There is a pointer for whoever plays the part. . . . Where can one find a Hedvig? I don't know. And Mrs. Soerby? She must be beautiful and witty, *not* vulgar. . . . Gregers is the most difficult part in the play, from the acting point of view. Sometimes I think Hammer would be best, sometimes Bjoern B. . . . I hope you will spare me Isachsen, as he always carries on like some strange actor instead of like an ordinary human being. However, I suppose he might possibly make something out of Molvik's few lines. The two servants must not be cast too casually; Pettersen might possibly be played by Bucher, and Jensen by Abelsted, if the latter is not required for one of the dinner guests. Yes, those guests! What about them? You can't just use ordinary extras; they'd ruin the whole act. . . . This play demands absolute naturalness and truthfulness both in the ensemble work and in the staging. The lighting, too, is important; it is different for each act, and is calculated to establish the particular atmosphere of that act. I just wanted to pass on these random reflections. As regards everything else, please do as you think best."

Further evidence of Ibsen's anxiety that his actors should

not overstep the boundary dividing comedy from farce is given
in an account by P. A. Rosenberg of a conversation he and
some acquaintances had with Ibsen in Copenhagen fourteen
years later (April 3, 1898). "Ibsen spoke also of the Royal
Theatre's presentation of THE WILD DUCK, of which strangely
enough he did not approve. The rest of us were unanimous
in praising Bloch's masterly *mise-èn-scene*, Mrs. Henning's en-
chanting Hedvig, Olaf Poulsen's Old Ekdal and Miss Anthon-
sen's incomparable Gina. But Ibsen declared it had been
played too much for farce. "It must be played as tragi-
comedy," he said; "otherwise Hedvig's death makes no sense."

As a postscript, one may remark how in THE WILD DUCK,
as in almost every play he wrote, Ibsen anticipated one of the
main discoveries of modern psychology. "Liberation," he had
noted in his preliminary jottings, "consists in securing for individuals the right to free themselves, each according to his
particular need." To free *themselves;* how many of Ibsen's contemporaries who regarded themselves as revolutionaries realised that? Ibsen understood that the demand must come from
within, and that truth, if it comes from without, is often regarded as an attack on the defensive system which the "life-
lie" represents.

M. M.

CHARACTERS

HAAKON WERLE, a wholesale merchant
GREGERS WERLE, his son
OLD EKDAL
HJALMAR EKDAL, his son, a photographer
GINA EKDAL, HJALMAR's wife
HEDVIG, their daughter, aged 14
MRS. SOERBY, housekeeper to HAAKON WERLE
RELLING, a doctor
MOLVIK, sometime student of theology
GRAABERG, a clerk
PETTERSEN, servant to HAAKON WERLE
JENSEN, a hired waiter
A PALE, FLABBY GENTLEMAN
A BALDING GENTLEMAN
A SHORT-SIGHTED GENTLEMAN
SIX OTHER GENTLEMEN, dinner guests of HAAKON WERLE
SEVERAL HIRED WAITERS

The first act takes place in HAAKON WERLE's *house, the remaining acts in* HJALMAR EKDAL's *studio.*

ACT ONE

The home of HAAKON WERLE, *a wholesale merchant. A study, expensively and comfortably furnished; bookcases, upholstered furniture. A desk, with papers and ledgers on it, stands in the middle of the room. Lighted lamps with green shades throw a soft light. In the rear wall folding doors stand open; the curtains across the entrance are drawn aside, and within can be seen a large and elegant room, brilliantly lit by lamps and candelabra. Downstage right in the study a small concealed door leads to the offices. Downstage left, a fireplace with coals glowing in it. Upstage of this a double door leads to the dining room.*

WERLE'S *servant,* PETTERSEN, *in livery, and a hired waiter,* JENSEN, *in black, are arranging the study. In the larger room two or three other hired waiters are moving around putting things in order and lighting more lamps. From the dining room can be heard the buzz of conversation and laughter. Someone taps a knife against a glass; silence; a toast is proposed; cries of "Bravo!"; then the buzz of conversation begins again.*

PETTERSEN *lights a lamp on the mantelpiece above the fireplace, and puts a shade over it.* You hear that, Jensen? Now the old man's at it, proposing a toast to Mrs. Soerby.

JENSEN *moves a chair forward.* Is it true what they say, that there's something between them?

PETTERSEN. I wouldn't know.

JENSEN. They say he's been a regular old billy goat in his time.

PETTERSEN. Could be.

JENSEN. Did you say he's giving this party for his son?

PETTERSEN. Yes. He came home yesterday.

JENSEN. I never knew old Werle had a son.

PETTERSEN. Oh yes, he's got a son. The boy spends all his time up at the sawmill, though, out at Hoydal. He's never set foot in town all the years I've worked in this house.

A HIRED WAITER, *in the doorway to the large room.* Pettersen, there's an old fellow here who wants to—

PETTERSEN, *beneath his breath.* What the devil—oh, not now!

OLD EKDAL *enters from the large room, right. He is wearing a threadbare coat with a high collar, and woollen gloves, and carries a stick and a fur hat in his hand and a brown paper parcel under his arm. He has a dirty, reddish-brown wig and small grey moustaches.*

Goes towards him.

Oh, Jesus! What do *you* want here?

EKDAL, *in the doorway.* Got to get into the office, Pettersen. It's very important.

PETTERSEN. The office has been shut for an hour—

EKDAL. They told me that downstairs, my boy. But Graaberg's still in there. Be a good lad, Pettersen, and let me nip in this way.

Points at the concealed door.

I've been this way before.

PETTERSEN. Oh, all right.

Opens the door.

But make sure you leave by the proper way. We've got company.

EKDAL. Yes, I know that—hm! Thanks, Pettersen, my boy. You're a good pal.

Mutters quietly.

Damn fool!

Goes into the office. PETTERSEN *shuts the door after him.*

JENSEN. Does he work in the office, too?

PETTERSEN. No, he just takes stuff home to copy, when they've more than they can manage. Mind you, he's been quite a gentleman in his time, has old Ekdal.

JENSEN. Yes, he looked as if he might have been around a bit.

PETTERSEN. Oh, yes. He was a lieutenant.

JENSEN. What—him a lieutenant?

PETTERSEN. That's right. But then he went into timber or something of that sort. They say he did the dirty on old Werle once. The two of them used to work together at Hoydal. Oh, I know old Ekdal well. We often have a nip and a bottle of beer together down at Madame Eriksen's.

JENSEN. But he can't have much to spend, surely?

PETTERSEN. I'm the one who does the spending. The way I look at it, it's only right to lend a helping hand to gentry who've come down in the world.

JENSEN. What, did he go bankrupt?

PETTERSEN. Worse. He went to prison.

JENSEN. Went to prison!

PETTERSEN. Ssh, they're getting up now.

The doors to the dining room are thrown open from inside by waiters. MRS. SOERBY *comes out, engaged in conversation by two gentlemen. A few moments later, the rest of the company follow,* HAAKON WERLE *among them. Last come* HJALMAR EKDAL *and* GREGERS WERLE.

MRS. SOERBY, *as she goes through.* Pettersen, have the coffee served in the music room.

PETTERSEN. Very good, Mrs. Soerby.

She and the two gentlemen go into the large room and out towards the right. PETTERSEN *and* JENSEN *follow them.*

A PALE, FLABBY GENTLEMAN, *to one with little hair.* Whew—that dinner! Pretty exhausting work, eh?

BALDING GENTLEMAN. Ah, it's remarkable what one can get through in three hours, when one puts one's mind to it.

FLABBY GENTLEMAN. Yes, but afterwards, my dear sir! Afterwards!

A THIRD GENTLEMAN. I hear the—er—mocha and maraschino are to be served in the music room.

FLABBY GENTLEMAN. Capital! Then perhaps Mrs. Soerby will play something for us.

BALDING GENTLEMAN, *sotto voce.* Let's hope it isn't a marching song!

FLABBY GENTLEMAN. No fear of that. Berta won't give her old friends the shoulder.

They laugh and pass into the large room.

WERLE, *quietly, unhappily.* I don't think anyone noticed, Gregers.

GREGERS *looks at him.* What?

WERLE. Didn't you notice, either?

GREGERS. Notice what?

WERLE. We were thirteen at table.

GREGERS. Thirteen? Oh, really?

WERLE *glances at* HJALMAR EKDAL. We're usually twelve.

To the others.

Gentlemen—please!

He and the rest, except for HJALMAR *and* GREGERS, *go out upstage right.*

HJALMAR, *who has overheard their conversation.* You shouldn't have invited me, Gregers.

GREGERS. What! But this dinner is said to be in my honour. So why shouldn't I invite my one and only friend?

HJALMAR. I don't think your father approves. I mean, I never get invited to this house.

GREGERS. No, so I've heard. But I had to see you and speak with you; I'm not staying very long, you know. Yes, we've lost touch with each other since we were at school, Hjalmar.

We haven't seen each other for—why, it must be sixteen or seventeen years.

HJALMAR. Is it as long as that?

GREGERS. I'm afraid so. Well, how is everything with you? You look well. You've filled out a bit; you're quite stout now.

HJALMAR. Oh—I wouldn't say stout. I dare say I'm a bit broader across the shoulders than I used to be. After all, I'm a man now.

GREGERS. Oh, yes. You're as handsome as ever.

HJALMAR, *sadly*. But within, Gregers! There has been a change there. You must know how disastrously my world has crashed about me—and my family—since we last met.

GREGERS, *more quietly*. How is your father now?

HJALMAR. My dear friend, let us not talk about it. My poor unfortunate father lives with me, of course. He has no one else in the world to lean on. But all this is so distressing for me to talk about. Tell me now, how have things been for you up at the sawmill?

GREGERS. Oh, I've been wonderfully lonely. I've had plenty of time to brood over things. Come, let's make ourselves comfortable.

He sits in an armchair by the fire and motions HJALMAR *into another beside him.*

HJALMAR, *softly*. Thank you all the same, Gregers. I'm grateful to you for inviting me to your father's house. I know now that you no longer have anything against me.

GREGERS, *amazed*. What makes you think I have anything against you?

HJALMAR. You did at first.

GREGERS. At first?

HJALMAR. After the great disaster. Oh, it was only natural that you should. It was only by a hairsbreadth that your father himself escaped being dragged into all this—this dreadful business.

GREGERS. And I should hold that against you? Who gave you this idea?

HJALMAR. I know—I know you did, Gregers. Your father himself told me so.

GREGERS. Father! I see. Hm. Was that why you never wrote me a line?

HJALMAR. Yes.

GREGERS. Not even when you went and became a photographer?

HJALMAR. Your father said there would be no purpose in my writing to you about anything whatever.

GREGERS, *thoughtfully*. No, no; perhaps he was right. But, tell me, Hjalmar—are you quite satisfied the way things are now?

HJALMAR, *with a little sigh*. Oh yes, indeed I am. I can't complain. At first, you know, I found it a little strange. It was such a different way of life from what I'd been used to. But everything had changed. The great disaster that ruined my father—the disgrace and the shame, Gregers—

GREGERS, *upset*. Yes, yes, of course, yes.

HJALMAR. Naturally, I had to give up any idea of continuing with my studies. We hadn't a shilling to spare—quite the reverse in fact. Debts. Mostly to your father, I believe—

GREGERS. Hm—

HJALMAR. Well, so I thought it'd be best, you see, to make a clean break. Cut myself off from everything that had to do with my old way of life. In fact, it was your father who advised me to do it—and as he was being so very helpful to me—

GREGERS. Father?

HJALMAR. Yes, surely you must know? How else could I have found the money to learn photography and equip a studio and set myself up? That costs a lot of money, you know.

GREGERS. And Father paid for all this?

HJALMAR. Yes, my dear fellow, didn't you know? I understood him to say he'd written to you.

GREGERS. He never said he was behind it. He must have forgotten. We never write to each other except on business. So it was Father—

HJALMAR. Why, yes. He's never wanted people to know about it; but it was he. And of course it was he who made it possible for me to get married. But—perhaps you don't know that either?

GREGERS. I had no idea.

Shakes him by the arm.

But, my dear Hjalmar, I can't tell you how happy I feel—and guilty. Perhaps I've been unjust to Father after all—in some respects. This proves that he has a heart, you see. A kind of conscience—

HJALMAR. Conscience?

GREGERS. Yes, or whatever you like to call it. No, I can't tell you how happy I am to hear this about Father. Well, and you're married, Hjalmar! That's more than I shall ever dare to do. Well, I trust you've found happiness in marriage.

HJALMAR. Oh, indeed I have. She's as capable and good a wife as any man could wish for. And she's not by any means uncultured.

GREGERS, *a little surprised.* I'm sure she isn't.

HJALMAR. Yes. Life is a great teacher. Being with me every day—and we have a couple of very gifted friends who visit us daily. I can assure you, you wouldn't recognise Gina.

GREGERS. Gina?

HJALMAR. Yes, my dear fellow, don't you remember? Her name's Gina.

GREGERS. Whose name is Gina? I have no idea what you're—

HJALMAR. But don't you remember? She used to work here once.

GREGERS *looks at him.* You mean Gina Hansen?

HJALMAR. Of course I mean Gina Hansen.

GREGERS. Who kept house for us when my mother was ill? The year before she died?

HJALMAR. Yes, that's right. But, my dear fellow, I'm absolutely certain your father wrote and told you I'd got married.

GREGERS *has got up.* Yes, he told me that. But what he didn't tell me was that—

Begins to pace up and down.

Ah, but wait a minute. Perhaps he did after all, now I think about it. But Father always writes such brief letters.

Half sits on the arm of his chair.

Look, tell me now, Hjalmar—this is very funny—how did you come to meet Gina—I mean, your wife?

HJALMAR. Oh, it was quite straightforward. As you know, Gina didn't stay long with your father—everything was so upside down at that time—your mother's illness—it was all too much for Gina, so she gave notice and left. It was the year before your mother died. Or was it the same year?

GREGERS. The same year. And I was up at the sawmill. But then what happened?

HJALMAR. Yes, well, then Gina went home to live with her mother, a Mrs. Hansen, a very excellent hard-working woman who ran a little café. Well, she had a room to let; a very nice, comfortable room.

GREGERS. And you were lucky enough to find out about it?

HJALMAR. Yes—in fact, it was your father who suggested it. And it was there, you see, that I really got to know Gina.

GREGERS. And the engagement followed?

HJALMAR. Yes. Well, you know how quickly young people become fond of each other—hm—

GREGERS *gets up and walks up and down for a little.* Tell me —when you were engaged—was that when Father got you to—I mean, was that when you began to take up photography?

HJALMAR. Yes, that's right. I was very keen to get married as soon as possible. And your father and I both came to the conclusion that photography would be the most convenient profession for me to take up. And Gina thought so too. Oh, and there was another thing. By a lucky chance, Gina had learned how to retouch photographs.

GREGERS. What a fortunate coincidence.

HJALMAR, *pleased, gets up.* Yes, wasn't it? Amazingly lucky, don't you think?

GREGERS. I certainly do. Father seems almost to have been a kind of fairy godfather to you.

HJALMAR, *emotionally.* He did not forget his old friend's son in his time of need. He's got a heart, you see, Gregers.

MRS. SOERBY *enters with* HAAKON WERLE *on her arm.* Not another word, now, Mr. Werle. You mustn't walk around any longer in there with all those bright lights. It's not good for you.

WERLE *lets go of her arm and passes his hand over his eyes.* Yes, I think you may be right.

PETTERSEN *and* JENSEN *enter with trays.*

MRS. SOERBY, *to the guests in the other room.* Gentlemen, please! If anyone wants a glass of punch, he must come in here.

FLABBY GENTLEMAN *comes over to* MRS. SOERBY. Dammit, madame, is it true that you have deprived us of our sacred privilege, the cigar?

MRS. SOERBY. Yes. This is Mr. Werle's sanctum, sir, and here there is no smoking.

BALDING GENTLEMAN. When did you introduce this austere edict, Mrs. Soerby?

MRS. SOERBY. After our last dinner, sir; when certain persons permitted themselves to overstep the mark.

BALDING GENTLEMAN. And it is not permitted to overstep the mark a little, Madame Berta? Not even an inch or two?

MRS. SOERBY. No. Not in any direction, my dear Chamberlain. *Most of the guests have come into the study. The* SERVANTS *hand round glasses of punch.*

HAAKON WERLE, *to* HJALMAR, *who is standing apart, by a table.* What's that you're looking at, Ekdal?

HJALMAR. It's only an album, sir.

BALDING GENTLEMAN, *who is wandering around.* Ah, photographs! Yes, that's rather down your street, isn't it?

FLABBY GENTLEMAN, *in an armchair.* Haven't you brought any
of your own with you?

HJALMAR. No, I haven't.

FLABBY GENTLEMAN. You should have. It's so good for the
digestion to sit and look at pictures.

BALDING GENTLEMAN. Adds to the fun. We've each got to contribute our mite, haven't we?

A SHORT-SIGHTED GENTLEMAN. All contributions will be grate-
fully received.

MRS. SOERBY. I think the gentlemen mean that if one is invited
out one should work for one's dinner, Mr. Ekdal.

FLABBY GENTLEMAN. Where the table is so exquisite, that duty
becomes a pleasure.

BALDING GENTLEMAN. Yes, by God! Particularly when it's a
question of fighting for survival—

MRS. SOERBY. *Touché!*

They continue amid joking and laughter.

GREGERS, *quietly.* You must join in, Hjalmar.

HJALMAR *twists uncomfortably.* What should I talk about?

FLABBY GENTLEMAN. Wouldn't you agree, Mr. Werle, that
Tokay may be regarded as a comparatively safe drink for
the stomach?

WERLE, *by the fireplace.* I'd guarantee the Tokay you drank
tonight, anyway. It's an exceptional year, quite exceptional.
But of course you would have noticed that.

FLABBY GENTLEMAN. Yes, it had a remarkably *soigné* bouquet.

HJALMAR, *uncertainly.* Is there some difference between the
various years?

FLABBY GENTLEMAN *laughs.* I say, that's good!

WERLE *smiles.* It's a waste to offer you good wine.

BALDING GENTLEMAN. Tokay's like photography, Mr. Ekdal. It needs sunshine. Isn't that right?

HJALMAR. Oh yes, light is important, of course.

MRS. SOERBY. But that's like you, gentlemen. You're drawn towards the sun, too.

BALDING GENTLEMAN. For shame! That's not worthy of you.

SHORT-SIGHTED GENTLEMAN. Mrs. Soerby is displaying her wit.

FLABBY GENTLEMAN. At our expense.

Threateningly.

Oh, madame, madame!

MRS. SOERBY. But it's perfectly true. Vintages do differ greatly. The oldest are the best.

SHORT-SIGHTED GENTLEMAN. Do you count me among the old ones?

MRS. SOERBY. By no means.

BALDING GENTLEMAN. Indeed? And what about me, dear Mrs. Soerby?

FLABBY GENTLEMAN. Yes, and me. What vintage are we?

MRS. SOERBY. A sweet vintage, gentlemen!

She sips a glass of punch. The GENTLEMEN *laugh and flirt with her.*

WERLE. Mrs. Soerby always finds a way out—when she wants to. Fill your glasses, gentlemen! Pettersen, look after them. Gregers, let us take a glass together.

GREGERS *does not move.*

Won't you join us, Ekdal? I didn't get a chance to drink with you at dinner.

GRAABERG, *the bookkeeper, looks in through the concealed door.*

GRAABERG *to* HAAKON WERLE. Excuse me, sir, but I can't get out.

WERLE. What, have you got locked in again?

GRAABERG. Yes. Flakstad's gone off with the keys.

WERLE. Well, you'd better come through here, then.

GRAABERG. But there's someone else—

WERLE. Well, let him come, too. Don't be frightened.

GRAABERG and OLD EKDAL come out of the office.

Involuntarily.

Oh, God!

The laughter and chatter of the GUESTS dies away. HJALMAR shrinks at the sight of his father, puts down his glass and turns away towards the fireplace.

EKDAL *does not look up, but makes little bows to either side as he walks, mumbling.* Beg pardon. Come the wrong way. Door locked. Beg pardon.

He and GRAABERG go out upstage right.

WERLE, *between his teeth.* Damn that Graaberg!

GREGERS *stares open-mouthed at* HJALMAR. Surely that wasn't—?

FLABBY GENTLEMAN. What's all this? Who was that?

GREGERS. Oh, no one. Just the bookkeeper and someone else.

SHORT-SIGHTED GENTLEMAN, *to* HJALMAR. Did you know that man?

HJALMAR. I don't know—I didn't notice—

FLABBY GENTLEMAN *gets up.* What the devil's going on?

He goes over to some of the others, who are talking quietly amongst themselves.

MRS. SOERBY *whispers to* PETTERSEN. Take something out to him. Something really nice.

PETTERSEN *nods.* Very good, ma'am.

Goes out.

GREGERS, *quietly, emotionally, to* HJALMAR. Then it *was* he!

HJALMAR. Yes.

GREGERS. And you stood here and denied him!

HJALMAR *whispers violently.* What could I do?

GREGERS. You denied your own father?

HJALMAR, *in pain.* Oh—if you were in my place, you'd—

The talk among the GUESTS, *which has been carried on in a low tone, now switches over to a forced loudness.*

BALDING GENTLEMAN *goes amiably over to* HJALMAR *and* GREGERS. Hullo, reviving old college memories, what? Don't you smoke, Mr. Ekdal? Want a light? Oh, I'd forgotten—we mustn't—

HJALMAR. Thank you, I won't.

FLABBY GENTLEMAN. Haven't you some nice little poem you could recite to us, Mr. Ekdal? You used to recite so beautifully.

HJALMAR. I'm afraid I can't remember one.

FLABBY GENTLEMAN. Pity. What else can we find to amuse ourselves with, Balle?

The TWO GENTLEMEN *walk into the next room.*

HJALMAR, *unhappily.* Gregers, I want to go. You know, when a man has been as buffeted and tossed by the winds of Fate as I have— Say good-bye to your father for me.

GREGERS. I will. Are you going straight home?

HJALMAR. Yes?

GREGERS. In that case I may drop in on you later.

HJALMAR. No, don't do that. You mustn't come to my home. It's a miserable place, Gregers; especially after a brilliant gathering like this. We can always meet somewhere in town.

MRS. SOERBY *has come over to them, and says quietly.* Are you leaving, Ekdal?

HJALMAR. Yes.

MRS. SOERBY. Give my regards to Gina.

HJALMAR. Thank you.

MRS. SOERBY. Tell her I'm coming out to see her one of these days.

HJALMAR. I will. Thank you.

To GREGERS.

Stay here. I don't want anyone to see me go.

Saunters into the other room and out to the right.

MRS. SOERBY, *to* PETTERSEN, *who has returned.* Well, did you give the old man something?

PETTERSEN. Yes, I put a bottle of brandy into his pocket.

MRS. SOERBY. Oh, you might have found him something nicer than that.

PETTERSEN. Why no, Mrs. Soerby. Brandy's what he likes best.

FLABBY GENTLEMAN, *in the doorway, with a sheet of music in his hand.* Shall we play a duet together, Mrs. Soerby?

MRS. SOERBY. Yes, with pleasure.

GUESTS. Bravo, bravo!

She and all the GUESTS *go out to the right.* GREGERS *remains standing by the fireplace.* HAAKON WERLE *starts looking for something on his desk, and seems to wish that* GREGERS *would go. Seeing that* GREGERS *does not move, he goes towards the door.*

GREGERS. Father, would you mind waiting a moment?

WERLE *stops.* What is it?

GREGERS. I've got to speak with you.

WERLE. Can't it wait till we're alone together?

GREGERS. No, it can't. We may never be alone together.

WERLE *comes closer.* What does that mean?

During the following scene, piano music can be heard distantly from the music room.

GREGERS. How has that family been allowed to sink into this pitiable condition?

WERLE. You mean the Ekdals, I presume?

GREGERS. Yes, I mean the Ekdals. Lieutenant Ekdal and you used to be such close friends.

WERLE. Unfortunately, yes. Too close. All these years I've had to pay for it. It's him I have to thank for the stain I have suffered on my name and reputation.

GREGERS, *quietly.* Was he really the only one who was guilty?

WERLE. Who else?

GREGERS. You and he bought those forests together.

WERLE. But it was Ekdal who drew up that misleading map. It was he who had all that timber felled illegally on government property. He was in charge of everything up there. I was absolutely in the dark as to what Lieutenant Ekdal was doing.

GREGERS. Lieutenant Ekdal seems to have been pretty much in the dark himself.

WERLE. Quite possibly. But the fact remains that he was found guilty and I was acquitted.

GREGERS. Oh yes, I know nothing was proved against you.

WERLE. An acquittal means not guilty. Why do you rake up these old troubles, which turned me grey before my time? Is that what you've been brooding about all these years up there? I can assure you, Gregers, in this town the whole business has been forgotten long ago, as far as my reputation is concerned.

GREGERS. But what about those wretched Ekdals?

WERLE. What would you have had me do for them? When Ekdal was released he was a broken man, past help. There are some people in this world who sink to the bottom the moment they get a couple of pellets in their body, and never rise to the surface again. Upon my honour, Gregers, I did everything I could short of exposing myself to gossip and suspicion—

GREGERS. Suspicion? Oh, I see.

WERLE. I've arranged for Ekdal to do copying for the office, and I pay him a great deal more than the work's worth—

GREGERS, *without looking at him.* I don't doubt it.

WERLE. You laugh? You don't think it's true? Oh, you won't find anything about it in the books. I don't keep account of that kind of payment.

GREGERS *smiles coldly.* No, there are certain payments of which it's best to keep no account.

WERLE. What do you mean by that?

GREGERS, *screwing up his courage.* Have you any account of what it cost you to have Hjalmar Ekdal taught photography?

WERLE. Why should I have any account of that?

GREGERS. I know now that it was you who paid for it. And I also know that it was you who so generously enabled him to set himself up.

WERLE. And still you say I've done nothing for the Ekdals? I can assure you, that family's cost me a pretty penny.

GREGERS. Have you accounted any of those pennies in your books?

WERLE. Why do you ask that?

GREGERS. Oh, I have my reasons. Tell me—when you began to take such a warm interest in your old friend's son—wasn't that just about the time he was about to get married?

WERLE. Yes, how the devil—how do you expect me to remember after all these years—?

GREGERS. You wrote me a letter at the time—a business letter, of course—and in a postscript you said—quite briefly—that Hjalmar Ekdal had married a Miss Hansen.

WERLE. Yes, so he did. That was her name.

GREGERS. But what you didn't say was that this Miss Hansen was Gina Hansen—our former maid.

WERLE *laughs scornfully, but with an effort.* No. It didn't occur to me that you were particularly interested in our former maid.

GREGERS. I wasn't. But—

Lowers his voice.

—there was someone else in this house who was interested in her.

WERLE. What do you mean?

Angrily.

You're not referring to me?

GREGERS, *quietly but firmly.* Yes, I am referring to you.

WERLE. You dare to—you have the impertinence—! That ungrateful—that photographer—how dare he make such insinuations!

GREGERS. Hjalmar has never said a word about this. I don't think he suspects anything.

WERLE. Where do you get it from, then? Who has said such a thing to you?

GREGERS. My unhappy mother told me. The last time I saw her.

WERLE. Your mother! I might have known it. She and you always clung together. She turned you against me from the first.

GREGERS. No. It was all the suffering and humiliation she had to endure before she finally succumbed and came to such a pitiful end.

WERLE. Oh, she didn't have to suffer. Not more than most people, anyway. But one can't do anything with people who are oversensitive and romantic. I've learned that much. And you nurse these suspicions and go around rooting up all kinds of old rumours and slanders about your own father! At your age, Gregers, it's time you found something more useful to do.

GREGERS. Yes, it's about time.

WERLE. It might enable you to be a little more at peace with yourself than you seem to be now. What good can it do for you to stay up at the sawmill, year after year, drudging away like a common clerk and refusing to accept a penny more than the standard wage? It's absolutely idiotic.

GREGERS. I wish I was sure of that.

WERLE. I understand how you feel. You want to be independent, you don't want to be in my debt. But now there is an opportunity for you to become independent, and be your own master in everything.

GREGERS. Oh? How?

WERLE. When I wrote and told you it was necessary for you to travel here at once—hm—

GREGERS. Yes, what do you want me for? I've been waiting all day to find out.

WERLE. I want to suggest that you become a partner in the firm.

GREGERS. I? Your partner?

WERLE. Yes. It wouldn't mean we'd have to be together all the time. You could take over the business here, and I'd move up to the mill.

GREGERS. You?

WERLE. Yes. You see, I'm not able to work as hard as I used to. I've got to take care of my eyes, Gregers. They've begun to grow a little weak.

GREGERS. They always were.

WERLE. Not like now. Besides—circumstances might make it desirable for me to live up there. For a while, anyway.

GREGERS. I hadn't imagined anything like this.

WERLE. Listen, Gregers. I know there are so many things that stand between us. But we're father and son. It seems to me we must be able to come to an understanding.

GREGERS. You mean, we must appear to come to an understanding?

WERLE. Well, that is something. Think it over, Gregers. Don't you think it might be possible? Well?

GREGERS *looks at him coldly*. What's behind all this?

WERLE. How do you mean?

GREGERS. You want to use me, don't you?

WERLE. In a relationship as close as ours, one can always be useful to the other.

GREGERS. That's what they say.

WERLE. I should like to have you living at home with me for a while. I'm a lonely man, Gregers. I've always felt lonely, all my life, but especially now that I'm growing old. I need to have someone near me—

GREGERS. You've got Mrs. Soerby.

WERLE. Yes, I have her. And she's become—well, almost indispensable to me. She's witty and good-humoured; she brightens the house for me. I need that—badly.

GREGERS. Well, then you have things the way you want them.

WERLE. Yes, but I'm afraid it can't continue like this. A woman in her situation may easily find herself compromised in the eyes of the world. Yes; and I dare say it's not very good for a man's reputation, either.

GREGERS. Oh, when a man gives dinners like this, he needn't worry about what people think.

WERLE. Yes, but what about her, Gregers? I'm afraid she won't want to put up with this for much longer. And even if she did—even if, for my sake, she were to set herself above the gossip and the slander— Don't you think then, Gregers—you with your stern sense of right and wrong—that—?

GREGERS *interrupts.* Answer me one thing. Are you thinking of marrying her?

WERLE. Suppose I were? Would you be so insuperably opposed to that?

GREGERS. Not in the least.

WERLE. I didn't know if perhaps—out of respect to your late mother's memory—

GREGERS. I'm not a romantic.

WERLE. Well, whatever you are, you've taken a great weight from my mind. I'm delighted that I may count on your agreement to the action I propose to take.

GREGERS *looks at him.* Now I see what you want to use me for.

WERLE. Use you? What kind of talk is that?

GREGERS. Oh, let's not be squeamish. Not when we're alone together.

Gives a short laugh.

I see. So that's why, at all costs, I had to come along and show myself here. So as to have a nice family reunion in Mrs. Soerby's honour. Father and son—*tableau!* That's something new, isn't it?

WERLE. How dare you take that tone?

GREGERS. When has there been any family life here? Not for as long as I can remember. But now of course there's got to be a little. It'll look splendid if people can say that the son of the family has flown home on the wings of filial piety to attend his ageing father's wedding feast. What'll become then of all those dreadful rumours about the wrongs his poor dead mother had to put up with? They will vanish. Her son will dissipate them into thin air.

WERLE. Gregers—I believe there's no one in the world you hate as much as you do me.

GREGERS, *quietly.* I've seen you at close quarters.

WERLE. You have seen me with your mother's eyes.

Lowers his voice a little.

But you should remember that her vision was sometimes a little—blurred.

GREGERS, *trembling.* I know what you're trying to say. But who was to blame for that? You were! You and all those—! And the last of them you palmed off on to Hjalmar Ekdal, when you no longer—oh!

WERLE *shrugs his shoulders.* Word for word as though I were listening to your mother.

GREGERS, *not heeding him.* And there he sits, childlike and trusting, caught in this web of deceit—sharing his roof with a woman like that, never suspecting that what he calls his home is built upon a lie!

Comes a step closer.

When I look back on your career, I see a battlefield strewn with shattered lives.

WERLE. It seems the gulf between us is too wide.

GREGERS *bows coldly.* I agree. Therefore I take my hat and go.

WERLE. Go? Leave the house?

GREGERS. Yes. Because now at last I see my vocation.

WERLE. And what is that vocation?

GREGERS. You'd only laugh if I told you.

WERLE. A lonely man does not laugh easily, Gregers.

GREGERS *points upstage.* Look, Father. The gentlemen are

playing blind man's buff with Mrs. Soerby. Good night, and
good-bye.

He goes out upstage right. Sounds of laughter and merri-
ment are heard from the GUESTS, *as they come into sight in*
the other room.

WERLE *mutters scornfully after* GREGERS. Hm! Poor wretch!
And he says he's not a romantic!

ACT TWO

HJALMAR EKDAL'S *studio. It is quite a large room, and is evidently an attic. To the right is a sloping ceiling containing large panes of glass, which are half covered by a blue curtain. In the corner upstage right is the front door. Downstage of this is a door to the living room. In the left-hand wall are two more doors, with an iron stove between them. In the rear wall are broad double sliding doors. The studio is humbly but comfortably furnished. Between the doors on the right, a little away from the wall, stands a sofa, with a table and some chairs. On the table is a lighted lamp, with a shade. In the corner by the stove is an old armchair. Here and there, various pieces of photographic apparatus are set up. Against the rear wall, to the left of the sliding doors, is a bookcase, containing some books, boxes, bottles containing chemicals, various tools, instruments and other objects. Photographs and small articles such as brushes, sheets of paper and so forth, lie on the table.*

GINA EKDAL *is seated on a chair at the table, sewing.* HEDVIG *is seated on the sofa with her hands shading her eyes and her thumbs in her ears, reading a book.*

GINA *glances at her a couple of times, as though with secret anxiety.* Hedvig!

HEDVIG *does not hear.* GINA *repeats more loudly.*

Hedvig!

HEDVIG *drops her hands and looks up.* Yes, Mother?

GINA. Hedvig darling, don't read any more.

HEDVIG. Oh, but Mother, can't I go on a little longer? Just a little?

GINA. No, no; put the book away. Your father doesn't like it. He never reads in the evenings.

HEDVIG *closes the book.* No, Father doesn't bother much about reading, does he?

GINA *puts down her sewing and picks up a pencil and a small notebook from the table.* Can you remember how much we paid for that butter?

HEDVIG. One crown sixty-five öre.

GINA. That's right.

Makes a note of it.

It's shocking how much butter gets eaten in this house. Then there was the sausages, and the cheese—let me see—

Writes.

And the ham—hm—

Adds it up.

Mm, that makes nearly—

HEDVIG. Don't forget the beer.

GINA. Oh yes, of course.

Writes.

It mounts up. But we've got to have it.

HEDVIG. But you and I didn't have to have a proper meal this evening, as Father was out.

GINA. Yes; that helped. Oh, and I got eight and a half crowns for those photographs.

HEDVIG. I say! As much as that?

GINA. Exactly eight and a half crowns.

Silence. GINA *takes up her sewing again.* HEDVIG *picks up a pencil and paper and starts to draw, her left hand shading her eyes.*

HEDVIG. Isn't it lovely to think of Father being invited by Mr. Werle to that big dinner?

GINA. He wasn't invited by Mr. Werle. It was his son who sent the invitation.

Short pause.

You know we've nothing to do with Mr. Werle.

HEDVIG. I'm so looking forward to Father coming home. He promised he'd ask Mrs. Soerby for something nice to bring me.

GINA. Yes, there's never any shortage of nice things in that house.

HEDVIG, *still drawing.* I think I'm beginning to get a bit hungry.

OLD EKDAL, *his package of papers under his arm and another parcel in his coat pocket, comes in through the front door.*

GINA. Hullo, Grandfather, you're very late tonight.

EKDAL. They'd shut the office. Graaberg kept me waiting. I had to go through the—hm.

HEDVIG. Did they give you anything new to copy, Grandfather?

EKDAL. All this. Look!

GINA. Well, that's good.

HEDVIG. And you've another parcel in your pocket.

EKDAL. Have I? Oh, nonsense—that's nothing.

Puts down his stick in a corner.

This'll keep me busy for a long time, this will, Gina.

Slides one of the doors in the rear wall a little to one side. Ssh!

Looks inside for a moment, then closes the door again carefully.

He, he! They're all asleep. And she's lied down in her basket. He, he!

HEDVIG. Are you sure she won't be cold in that basket, Grandfather?

EKDAL. What an idea! Cold? With all that straw?

Goes towards the door upstage left.

Are there any matches?

GINA. They're on the chest-of-drawers.

EKDAL *goes into his room.*

HEDVIG. Isn't it splendid Grandfather getting all that stuff to copy again, after so long?

GINA. Yes, poor old Father. It'll mean a bit of pocket money for him.

HEDVIG. And he won't be able to spend all morning down at that horrid Mrs. Eriksen's restaurant, will he?

GINA. Yes, there's that too.

Short silence.

HEDVIG. Do you think they're still sitting at table?

GINA. God knows. It wouldn't surprise me.

HEDVIG. Think of all that lovely food Father's getting to eat! I'm sure he'll be in a good humour when he comes back. Don't you think, Mother?

GINA. Oh, yes. But if only we were able to tell him we'd managed to let that room.

HEDVIG. But we don't have to worry about *that* tonight.

GINA. It wouldn't do any harm. It's no use to us standing empty.

HEDVIG. No, I mean we don't have to worry about it because Father'll be jolly anyway. It'll be better if we can save the news about the room for another time.

GINA *glances across at her.* Does it make you happy to have good news to tell Father when he comes home in the evening?

HEDVIG. Yes, it makes things more cheerful here.

GINA. Yes, there's something in that.

OLD EKDAL *comes in again and goes towards the door downstage left.*

Half turns in her chair.

Do you want something out of the kitchen, Grandfather?

EKDAL. Er—yes, yes. Don't get up.

Goes out.

GINA. He's not messing about with the fire, is he?

Waits a moment.

Hedvig, go and see what he's up to.

EKDAL *returns with a little jug of steaming water.*

HEDVIG. Are you getting some hot water, Grandfather?

EKDAL. Yes, I am. Need it for something. Got some writing to do; and the ink's like porridge—hm!

GINA. But, Grandfather, you should eat your supper first. I've put it in there for you.

EKDAL. Can't be bothered with supper, Gina. I'm busy, I tell you. I don't want anyone to disturb me. Not anyone—hm!

He goes into his room. GINA *and* HEDVIG *look at each other.*

GINA, *quietly.* Where do you think he's got the money from?

HEDVIG. From Graaberg, I suppose.

GINA. No, he can't have. Graaberg always sends the money to me.

HEDVIG. He must have got a bottle on tick somewhere, then.

GINA. Poor Grandfather! No one'll give him anything on credit.

HJALMAR EKDAL, *wearing an overcoat and a grey felt hat, enters right.*

GINA *drops her sewing and gets up.*

Why, Hjalmar, are you here already?

HEDVIG, *simultaneously, jumping to her feet.* Oh Father, fancy your coming back so soon!

HJALMAR *takes off his hat.* Yes, well, most of them had begun to leave.

HEDVIG. As early as this?

HJALMAR. Yes. It was a dinner party, you know.

Begins to take off his overcoat.

GINA. Let me help you.

HEDVIG. Me too.

They take off his coat. GINA *hangs it up on the rear wall.* Were there many people there, Father?

HJALMAR. Oh no, not many. We were, oh, twelve or fourteen at table.

GINA. And you talked to them all?

HJALMAR. Oh yes, a little. But Gregers monopolised me most of the time.

GINA. Is he still as ugly as ever?

HJALMAR. Well, he's not very much to look at. Hasn't the old man come home?

HEDVIG. Yes, Grandfather's in his room, writing.

HJALMAR. Did he say anything?

GINA. No, what should he say?

HJALMAR. Didn't he mention anything about—? I thought I heard someone say he'd been up to see Graaberg. I'll go in and have a word with him.

GINA. No, no—don't.

HJALMAR. Why not? Did he say he didn't want to see me?

GINA. I don't think he wants to see anyone this evening.

HEDVIG *makes signs to* HJALMAR. GINA *does not notice.*

He's been out and fetched some hot water.

HJALMAR. Oh. He's—?

GINA. Yes.

HJALMAR. Dear God! Poor old Father! Bless his white hairs! Let him have his little pleasure.

OLD EKDAL, *wearing a dressing gown and smoking a pipe, enters from his room.*

EKDAL. So you're home? I thought I heard your voice.

HJALMAR. Yes, I've just got back.

EKDAL. You didn't see me, did you?

HJALMAR. No. But they said you'd been through, and so I thought I'd follow you.

EKDAL. Hm. Decent of you, Hjalmar. Who were all those people?

HJALMAR. Oh, all sorts. There was Mr. Flor—the Chamberlain—and Mr. Balle—he's one, too—and so's Mr. Kaspersen—

and Mr.—what's his name, I don't remember what they were all called—

EKDAL *nods.* You hear that, Gina? People from the palace— and Hjalmar!

GINA. Yes, they're very grand up there nowadays.

HEDVIG. Did the Chamberlains sing, Father? Or recite anything?

HJALMAR. No, they just chattered. They tried to get me to recite something. But I said: "No."

EKDAL. You said "No," did you?

GINA. Oh, you might have obliged them.

HJALMAR. No. One can't go round pandering to everyone.

Begins to walk up and down the room.

I won't, anyway.

EKDAL. No, no. You won't get round Hjalmar as easily as that.

HJALMAR. I don't see why *I* should have to provide the entertainment on the few occasions when I go out to enjoy myself. Let the others do some work for a change. Those fellows go from one dinner table to the next stuffing themselves every night. Let them work for their food and drink.

GINA. You didn't say all this?

HJALMAR *hums to himself.* I gave them a piece of my mind.

EKDAL. You said this to their faces?

HJALMAR. Could be.

Nonchalantly.

Afterwards we had a little altercation about Tokay.

EKDAL. Tokay, did you say? That's a fine wine.

HJALMAR *stops walking.* It *can* be a fine wine. But, let me tell you, all vintages are not equally fine. It depends on how much sunshine the grapes have had.

GINA. Oh, Hjalmar! You know about everything!

EKDAL. And they tried to argue about that?

HJALMAR. They tried. But they soon learned that it's the same as with Chamberlains. All vintages are not equally fine.

GINA. The things you think of!

EKDAL *chuckles.* He, he! And they had to put that in their pipes and smoke it?

HJALMAR. Yes. It was said straight to their faces.

EKDAL. You hear that, Gina? He said it straight to the Chamberlains' faces.

GINA. Just fancy! Straight to their faces!

HJALMAR. Yes, but I don't want it talked about. One doesn't repeat such things. It was all very friendly, of course. They're decent, friendly people. Why should I hurt them?

EKDAL. But straight to their faces!

HEDVIG, *trying to please him.* What fun it is to see you in tails! You look splendid in tails, Father!

HJALMAR. Yes, I do, don't I? And it fits me perfectly; almost as though it had been made for me. Just a little tight under the arms, perhaps. Give me a hand, Hedvig.

Takes them off.

I think I'll put my jacket on. Where's my jacket, Gina?

GINA. Here it is.

Brings the jacket and helps him on with it.

HJALMAR. That's better! Don't forget to let Molvik have the tails back tomorrow morning.

GINA *puts them away.* I'll see he gets them.

HJALMAR *stretches.* Ah, now I feel more at home. Loose-fitting clothes suit my figure better. Don't you think, Hedvig?

HEDVIG. Yes, Father.

HJALMAR. When I loosen my tie so that the ends flow like this— Look! What do you think of that?

HEDVIG. Oh yes, that looks very good with your moustache and those big curls of yours.

HJALMAR. I wouldn't call them curls. Waves.

HEDVIG. Yes, they're such big curls.

HJALMAR. They are waves.

HEDVIG, *after a moment, tugs his jacket.* Father!

HJALMAR. Well, what is it?

HEDVIG. Oh, you know quite well what it is.

HJALMAR. No, I don't. Really.

HEDVIG *laughs and whimpers.* Oh yes, you do, Father. You mustn't tease me!

HJALMAR. But what *is* it?

HEDVIG. Oh, stop it! Give it to me, Father! You know! All those nice things you promised me!

HJALMAR. Oh, dear! Fancy my forgetting that!

HEDVIG. Oh, no, you're only teasing, Father! Oh, it's beastly of you! Where have you hidden it?

HJALMAR. No, honestly, I forgot. But wait a moment! I've something else for you, Hedvig.

Goes over to the tails and searches in the pockets.

HEDVIG *jumps and claps her hands.* Oh, Mother, Mother!

GINA. There, you see. Just be patient, and—

HJALMAR *holds out a card.* Look, here it is.

HEDVIG. That? That's only a piece of paper.

HJALMAR. It's the menu, Hedvig. The whole menu. Look here. It says *Déjeuner.* That means menu.

HEDVIG. Is that all?

HJALMAR. Well, I forgot the other things. But believe me, Hedvig, they're not much fun really, all those sickly sweet things. Sit over there at the table and read this menu, and then I'll describe to you how each dish tasted. Here you are, now, Hedvig.

HEDVIG *swallows her tears.* Thank you.

She sits down but does not read. GINA *makes a sign to her.* HJALMAR *notices.*

HJALMAR *starts walking up and down.* Really, it's incredible the things a breadwinner's expected to remember. If one forgets the slightest little thing, there are sour faces all round one. Well, one gets used to it.

Stops by the stove, where OLD EKDAL *is sitting.*

Have you looked in there this evening, Father?

EKDAL. Yes, of course I have. She's gone into the basket.

HJALMAR. Gone into the basket, has she? She's beginning to get used to it, then.

EKDAL. What did I tell you? Well, now, you see, there are one or two little—

HJALMAR. Little improvements, yes.

EKDAL. We've got to have them, Hjalmar.

HJALMAR. Yes. Let's have a word about those improvements, Father. Come along, let's sit on the sofa.

EKDAL. Yes, let's. Er—I think I'll fill my pipe first. Oh, I'd better clean it, too. Hm.

Goes into his room.

GINA *smiles at* HJALMAR. Clean his pipe!

HJALMAR. Oh, Gina, let him. Poor, shipwrecked old man! Yes, those improvements—I'd better get them done tomorrow.

GINA. But you won't have time tomorrow, Hjalmar.

HEDVIG *interrupts*. Oh, yes, he will, Mother!

GINA. Don't forget those prints have to be retouched. They've sent for them so many times.

HJALMAR. Oh, are you on about those prints again? They'll be ready. Have there been any new orders at all?

GINA. No, I'm afraid not. I've nothing tomorrow but those two portraits I told you about.

HJALMAR. Is that all? Well, if one doesn't put one's mind to it—

GINA. But what can I do? I advertise as much as I can—

HJALMAR. Advertise, advertise! You see what good that does. I don't suppose anyone's come to look at the room either?

GINA. No, not yet.

HJALMAR. I might have known it. If one doesn't bother to keep one's eyes and ears open— One must try to make an effort, Gina.

HEDVIG *goes towards him*. Can I bring your flute, Father?

HJALMAR. No. No flute. *I* don't need the pleasures of this world.

Starts walking again.

Yes, I'm going to work tomorrow. Don't you worry about that. I'll work as long as there's strength in these arms—

GINA. But my dear Hjalmar, I didn't mean it like that.

HEDVIG. Father, would you like a bottle of beer?

HJALMAR. Certainly not. I want nothing of anyone.

Stops.

Beer? Did you say beer?

HEDVIG, *alive.* Yes, Father. Lovely, cool beer.

HJALMAR. Well—if you want to, bring in a bottle.

GINA. Yes, do. That's a nice idea.

HEDVIG *runs towards the kitchen door.*

HJALMAR, *by the stove, stops her, looks at her, takes her head in his hands and presses her to him.* Hedvig! Hedvig!

HEDVIG, *happy, crying.* Oh, dear, kind, Father!

HJALMAR. No, don't call me that. I have been eating at the rich man's table. Gorging my belly at the groaning board. And yet I could—

GINA, *sitting at the table.* Oh, nonsense, nonsense, Hjalmar.

HJALMAR. It's true. But you mustn't judge me too harshly. You know I love you both. In spite of everything—

HEDVIG *throws her arms round him.* And we love you very, very much, Father.

HJALMAR. And if I should, once in a while, be unreasonable—dear God!—remember that I am a man besieged by a host of sorrows. Oh, well.

Dries her eyes.

This is not the moment for beer. Give me my flute.

HEDVIG *runs to the bookcase and fetches it.*

Thank you. Ah, this is better. With my flute in my hand, and you two by my side—ah!

HEDVIG *sits at the table by* GINA. HJALMAR *walks up and*

down, then begins to play a Bohemian folk dance, with spirit, in a slow and mournful tempo, and sensitively. Stops playing, stretches out his left hand to GINA *and says emotionally.*

Life may be poor and humble under our roof. But it is home. And I tell you, Gina—it is good to be here.

He begins to play again.

After a few moments, there is a knock on the front door.

GINA *gets up.* Hush, Hjalmar. I think there's someone at the door.

HJALMAR *puts the flute away in the bookcase.* Oh, here we go again.

GREGERS WERLE, *outside on the landing.* Excuse me, but—

GINA *starts back slightly.* Oh!

GREGERS. Doesn't Mr. Ekdal live here? The photographer.

GINA. Yes, he does.

HJALMAR *goes over to the door.* Gregers! Are you here? Well, you'd better come in.

GREGERS *enters.* But I told you I'd visit you.

HJALMAR. But—tonight? Have you left the party?

GREGERS. Yes. I have left the party. And my home, too. Good evening, Mrs. Ekdal. I don't suppose you recognise me?

GINA. Why, yes, Mr. Gregers. I recognise you.

GREGERS. Yes. I'm like my mother. And I've no doubt you remember her.

HJALMAR. Did you say you had left your father's house?

GREGERS. Yes. I've moved to a hotel.

HJALMAR. Oh, I see. Well, since you've come, take off your coat and sit down.

GREGERS. Thank you.

He takes off his coat. He has changed into a simple grey suit of a provincial cut.

HJALMAR. Here, on the sofa. Make yourself comfortable.

GREGERS *sits on the sofa,* HJALMAR *on a chair by the table.*

GREGERS *looks around.* So this is it, Hjalmar. This is where you live.

HJALMAR. This room is my studio, as you see.

GINA. We usually sit here, because there's more space.

HJALMAR. We had a nicer place before, but this apartment has one great advantage. The bedrooms—

GINA. And we've a spare room on the other side of the passage that we can let.

GREGERS *to* HJALMAR. Oh, I see. You take lodgers as well?

HJALMAR. No, not yet. It takes time, you know. One's got to keep one's eyes and ears open.

   To HEDVIG.

Let's have that beer now.

HEDVIG *nods and goes out into the kitchen.*

GREGERS. So that's your daughter?

HJALMAR. Yes, that is Hedvig.

GREGERS. Your only child?

HJALMAR. Yes, she is the only one. Our greatest joy.

   Drops his voice.

And also our greatest sorrow, Gregers.

GREGERS. What do you mean?

HJALMAR. There is a grave risk that she may lose her eyesight.

GREGERS. Go blind?

HJALMAR. Yes. As yet there are only the first symptoms, and she may be all right for some while. But the doctor has warned us. It will happen in the end.

GREGERS. What a terrible tragedy. What's the cause?

HJALMAR *sighs.* It's probably hereditary.

GREGERS *starts.* Hereditary?

GINA. Hjalmar's mother had weak eyes, too.

HJALMAR. So my father says. Of course, I can't remember.

GREGERS. Poor child. And how does she take it?

HJALMAR. Oh, you don't imagine we have the heart to tell

her? She suspects nothing. Carefree and gay, singing like a little bird, she will fly into the night.

Overcome.

Oh, it will be the death of me, Gregers.

HEDVIG *brings a tray with beer and glasses, and sets it on the table.* HJALMAR *strokes her head.*

Thank you, Hedvig.

She puts her arm round his neck and whispers in his ear.

No, no sandwiches now.

Glances at GREGERS.

Unless you'd like some, Gregers?

GREGERS. No, no, thank you.

HJALMAR, *still melancholy.* Well, you might bring a few in, anyway. A crust will be enough for me. Put plenty of butter on it, mind.

HEDVIG *nods happily and goes back into the kitchen.*

GREGERS *follows her with his eyes.* She looks quite strong and healthy, apart from that, I think.

GINA. Yes, there's nothing else the matter with her, thank God.

GREGERS. She's going to look very like you, Mrs. Ekdal. How old would she be now?

GINA. Almost exactly fourteen. It's her birthday the day after tomorrow.

GREGERS. Quite big for her age.

GINA. Yes, she's certainly shot up this last year.

GREGERS. Seeing these young people grow up makes one realise how old one's getting oneself. How long have you two been married now?

GINA. We've been married—er—yes, nearly fifteen years.

GREGERS. Good Lord, is it as long as that?

GINA, *suddenly alert; looks at him.* Yes, that's right.

HJALMAR. It certainly is. Fifteen years, all but a few months. *Changes his tone.*

They must have seemed long to you, those years up at the mill, Gregers.

GREGERS. They seemed long at the time. Looking back on them, I hardly know where they went.

OLD EKDAL *enters from his room, without his pipe but wearing his old army helmet. He walks a little unsteadily.*

EKDAL. Well, Hjalmar, now we can sit down and talk about that—er—. What was it we were going to talk about?

HJALMAR *goes over to him.* Father, we have a guest. Gregers Werle. I don't know if you remember him.

EKDAL *looks at* GREGERS, *who has got up.* Werle? The son? What does he want with me?

HJALMAR. Nothing. He's come to see me.

EKDAL. Oh. Nothing's wrong, then?

HJALMAR. No, of course not. Nothing at all.

EKDAL *waves an arm.* Mind you, I'm not afraid. It's just that—

GREGERS *goes over to him.* I only wanted to bring you a greeting from your old hunting grounds, Lieutenant Ekdal.

EKDAL. Hunting grounds?

GREGERS. Yes—up around Hoydal.

EKDAL. Oh, up there. Yes, I used to know that part well, in the old days.

GREGERS. You were a famous hunter then.

EKDAL. Oh, well. Maybe I was. I won't deny it. You're looking at my uniform. I don't ask anyone's permission to wear it in here. As long as I don't go out into the street in it—

HEDVIG *brings a plate of sandwiches and puts it on the table.*

HJALMAR. Sit down now, Father, and have a glass of beer. Gregers, please.

EKDAL *mumbles to himself and stumbles over to the sofa.* GREGERS *sits in the chair nearest to him,* HJALMAR *on the other side of* GREGERS. GINA *sits a little away from the table, sewing.* HEDVIG *stands beside her father.*

GREGERS. Do you remember, Lieutenant Ekdal, how Hjalmar

and I used to come up and visit you during the summer, and at Christmas?

EKDAL. Did you? No, no, no, I don't remember it. But though I say it myself, I was a first-rate shot. I've killed bears too, you know. Nine of them.

GREGERS *looks at him sympathetically.* And now your hunting days are over?

EKDAL. Oh, I wouldn't say that, my boy. Do a bit of hunting now and again. Not quite the way I used to. You see, the forest—the forest, you see, the forest—

Drinks.

How does the forest look up there now? Still good, eh?

GREGERS. Not as good as in your day. It's been thinned out a lot.

EKDAL. Thinned out? Chopped down?

More quietly, as though in fear.

That's dangerous. Bad things'll come of that. The forest'll have its revenge.

HJALMAR *fills his glass.* Have a little more, Father.

GREGERS. How can a man like you, a man who loves the open air as you do, bear to live in the middle of a stuffy town, boxed between four walls?

EKDAL *gives a short laugh and glances at* HJALMAR. Oh, it's not too bad here. Not bad at all.

GREGERS. But what about the cool, sweeping breezes, the free life in the forest, and up on the wide, open spaces among animals and birds? These things which had become part of you?

EKDAL *smiles.* Hjalmar, shall we show it to him?

HJALMAR, *quickly, a little embarrassed.* Oh, no, Father, no. Not tonight.

GREGERS. What does he want to show me?

HJALMAR. It's only something that—. You can see it another time.

GREGERS *continues speaking to* EKDAL. What I was going to

suggest, Lieutenant Ekdal, was that you should come with me back to the mill. I shall be returning there soon. I'm sure we could find you some copying to do up there, too. And there's nothing here to keep you cheerful and interested.

EKDAL *stares at him, amazed.* Nothing here—?

GREGERS. Of course you have Hjalmar; but then he has his own family. And a man like you, who has always been drawn to a life that is wild and free—

EKDAL *strikes the table.* Hjalmar, he *shall* see it!

HJALMAR. But, Father, what's the point of showing it to him now? It's dark.

EKDAL. Nonsense, there's the moonlight.

Gets up.

He shall see it, I tell you. Let me come through. Come and help me, Hjalmar.

HEDVIG. Oh, yes, do, Father!

HJALMAR *gets up.* Oh, very well.

GREGERS, *to* GINA. What are they talking about?

GINA. Oh, don't take any notice. It's nothing very much.

EKDAL *and* HJALMAR *go to the rear wall, and each of them pushes back one of the sliding doors.* HEDVIG *helps the old man.* GREGERS *remains standing by the sofa.* GINA *continues calmly with her sewing. Through the open doors can be seen a long and irregularly shaped loft, full of dark nooks and crannies, with a couple of brick chimney-pipes coming through the floor. Through small skylights bright moonlight shines on to various parts of the loft, while the rest lies in shadow.*

EKDAL, *to* GREGERS. You can come right in, if you like.

GREGERS *goes over to them.* What is it, exactly?

EKDAL. Have a look. Hm.

HJALMAR, *somewhat embarrassed.* This belongs to my father, you understand.

GREGERS, *in the doorway, peers into the loft.* Why, you keep chickens, Lieutenant Ekdal.

EKDAL. I should think we do keep chickens! They've gone to roost now. But you should just see them by daylight!

HEDVIG. And then there's the—!

EKDAL. Ssh! Don't say anything yet.

GREGERS. And you've pigeons, too, I see.

EKDAL. Why, yes! Of course we've pigeons. They've got their roosting-boxes up there under the roof. Pigeons like to nest high, you know.

HJALMAR. They're not all ordinary pigeons.

EKDAL. Ordinary! No, I should say not! We've tumblers. And a pair of pouters, too. But come over here! Do you see that hutch over there against the wall?

GREGERS. Yes. What do you use that for?

EKDAL. The rabbits go there at night.

GREGERS. Oh, you have rabbits, too?

EKDAL. You're damn right we've got rabbits. You hear that, Hjalmar? He asks if we've got rabbits! Hm! But now I'll show you! This is really something. Move over, Hedvig. Stand here. That's right. Now look down there. Can you see a basket with straw in it?

GREGERS. Yes. And there's a bird lying in the straw.

EKDAL. Hm! A bird!

GREGERS. Isn't it a duck?

EKDAL, *hurt*. Of course it's a duck.

HJALMAR. Ah, but what *kind* of a duck?

HEDVIG. It's not just an ordinary duck—

EKDAL. Ssh!

GREGERS. It's not one of those Muscovy ducks, is it?

EKDAL. No, Mr. Werle, it's not a Muscovy duck. It's a wild duck.

GREGERS. Oh, is it really? A wild duck?

EKDAL. Yes, that's what it is. That "bird," as you called it— that's a wild duck, that is. That's our wild duck, my boy.

HEDVIG. My wild duck. I own it.

GREGERS. But can it live up here in this loft? Is it happy here?

EKDAL. Well, naturally she has a trough of water to splash about in.

HJALMAR. Fresh water every other day.

GINA *turns towards* HJALMAR. Hjalmar dear, it's getting icy cold up here.

EKDAL. Mm. Well, let's shut up, then. It's best not to disturb them when they're sleeping, anyway. Give me a hand, Hedvig.

HJALMAR *and* HEDVIG *slide the doors together.*

Some other time you must have a proper look at her.

Sits in the armchair by the stove.

Ah, they're strange creatures, you know, these wild ducks.

GREGERS. But how did you manage to catch it, Lieutenant Ekdal?

EKDAL. I didn't catch it. There's a certain gentleman in this town whom we have to thank for that.

GREGERS *starts slightly.* You don't mean my father, surely?

EKDAL. Indeed I do. Your father. Hm.

HJALMAR. How odd that you should guess that, Gregers.

GREGERS. You told me earlier that you were indebted to my father for so many things, so I thought perhaps—

GINA. Oh, we didn't get it from Mr. Werle himself—

EKDAL. All the same, it's Haakon Werle we have to thank for her, Gina.

To GREGERS.

He was out in his boat, you see, and he shot her. But his eyesight isn't very good. Hm. So he only winged her.

GREGERS. Oh, I see. She got a couple of pellets in her.

HJALMAR. Yes, two or three.

HEDVIG. She got them under her wing, so that she couldn't fly.

GREGERS. Oh, and so she dived to the bottom, I suppose?

EKDAL, *sleepily, in a thick voice.* Of course. Wild ducks always do that. Dive down to the bottom, as deep as they can go, and hold on with their beaks to the seaweed or whatever they can find down there. And they never come up again.

GREGERS. But your wild duck did come up again, Lieutenant Ekdal.

EKDAL. He had such a damned clever dog, your father. And that dog—he dived down after the duck, and brought her to the surface.

GREGERS *turns to* HJALMAR. And then you took her in here?

HJALMAR. Not at once. To begin with, they took her home to your father's house. But she didn't seem to thrive there. So Pettersen was told to wring her neck.

EKDAL, *half asleep*. Hm. Yes. Pettersen. Damn fool—

HJALMAR *speaks more softly*. That was how we got her, you see. Father knows Pettersen, and when he heard all this about the wild duck he got him to give it to us.

GREGERS. And now she's thriving in your loft.

HJALMAR. Yes, she's doing extraordinarily well. She's got fat. Well, she's been in there so long now that she's forgotten what it's like to live the life she was born for; that's the whole trick.

GREGERS. Yes, you're right there, Hjalmar. Just make sure she never gets a glimpse of the sky or the sea. But I mustn't stay longer. I think your father's fallen asleep.

HJALMAR. Oh, never mind about that.

GREGERS. By the bye, you said you had a room to let.

HJALMAR. Yes, why? Do you know anyone who—?

GREGERS. Could I have it?

HJALMAR. You?

GINA. No, but Mr. Werle, it isn't—

GREGERS. Can I have that room? I'd like to move in right away. Tomorrow morning.

HJALMAR. Why, yes, with the greatest pleasure—

GINA. Oh no, Mr. Werle, it's not at all the kind of room for you.

HJALMAR. Why, Gina, how can you say that?

GINA. Well, it's dark and poky.

GREGERS. That won't bother me, Mrs. Ekdal.

HJALMAR. Personally I think it's quite a nice room. Not too badly furnished, either.

GINA. Don't forget those two who live down below.

GREGERS. Who are they?

GINA. Oh, one of them used to be a tutor—

HJALMAR. A Mr. Molvik.

GINA. And the other's a doctor called Relling.

GREGERS. Relling? I know him slightly. He had a practice up at Hoydal once.

GINA. They're a real couple of good-for-nothings. They often go out on the spree and come home very late at night, and aren't always—

GREGERS. One soon gets accustomed to that sort of thing. I hope I shall manage to acclimatise myself like the wild duck.

GINA. Well, I think you ought to sleep on it first, all the same.

GREGERS. You evidently don't want to have me living here, Mrs. Ekdal.

GINA. For heaven's sake! How can you think that?

HJALMAR. You're really behaving very strangely, Gina.

To GREGERS.

But tell me, are you thinking of staying in town for a while?

GREGERS *puts on his overcoat.* Yes, now I'm staying.

HJALMAR. But not at home with your father? What do you intend to do?

GREGERS. Ah, if only I knew that, Hjalmar, it wouldn't be so bad. But when one has the misfortune to be called Gregers— with Werle on top of it—Hjalmar, have you ever heard anything so awful?

HJALMAR. Oh, I don't think it's awful at all.

GREGERS. Oh, nonsense. Ugh! I'd want to spit on anyone who had a name like that.

HJALMAR *laughs.* If you weren't Gregers Werle, what would you like to be?

GREGERS. If I could choose, I think most of all I'd like to be a clever dog.

GINA. A dog?

HEDVIG, *involuntarily.* Oh, no!

GREGERS. Oh, yes. A tremendously clever dog. The sort that dives down after wild ducks when they have plunged to the bottom and gripped themselves fast in the seaweed and the mud.

HJALMAR. Honestly, Gregers, I don't understand a word of all this.

GREGERS. Oh, well, it doesn't mean much really. I'll move in tomorrow morning, then.

To GINA.

I shan't cause you any trouble. I do everything for myself.

To HJALMAR.

We'll talk about everything else tomorrow. Good night, Mrs. Ekdal.

Nods to HEDVIG.

Good night.

GINA. Good night, Mr. Werle.

HEDVIG. Good night.

HJALMAR, *who has lit a candle.* Wait a moment. I'll have to light you down. It's very dark on the stairs.

GREGERS *and* HJALMAR *go out through the front door.*

GINA, *thoughtfully, her sewing in her lap.* Wasn't that a funny thing, saying he'd like to be a dog?

HEDVIG. You know, Mother—I think when he said that he meant something else.

GINA. What could he mean?

HEDVIG. I don't know. But I felt as though he meant something different from what he was saying all the time.

GINA. You think so? Yes, it certainly was strange.

HJALMAR *comes back.* The light was still on.

Snuffs the candle and puts it down.

Ah, now I can get a little food inside me at last.

Begins eating the sandwiches.

Well, there you are, Gina. If one only keeps one's eyes and ears open—

GINA. How do you mean?

HJALMAR. Well, it's jolly lucky we've managed to let that room at last, isn't it? And, what's more, to a man like Gregers. A dear old friend.

GINA. Well, I don't know what to say about it.

HEDVIG. Oh, Mother! You'll see—it'll be such fun!

HJALMAR. You're very awkward. You were aching to let the room, and now we've done it you're not happy.

GINA. Oh, yes I am, Hjalmar. I only wish it had been to someone else. But what do you suppose the old man will say?

HJALMAR. Old Werle? It's none of his business.

GINA. Can't you see? They must have quarrelled again if his son's walked out of the house. You know how things are between those two.

HJALMAR. That may well be, but—

GINA. Now perhaps Mr. Werle'll think you're behind it all.

HJALMAR. All right, let him think so, if he wants to! Old Werle's done a great deal for me, I admit it. But that doesn't make me his vassal for life.

GINA. But, dear Hjalmar, he might take it out of Grandfather. Maybe now he'll lose the little bit of money he gets through Graaberg.

HJALMAR. Good riddance—I've half a mind to say. Don't you think it's a little humiliating for a man like me to see his grey old father treated like a leper? But I've a feeling the time is getting ripe.

Takes another sandwich.

As sure as I have a mission in life, it shall be fulfilled.

HEDVIG. Oh, Father, yes! It must, it must!

GINA. Ssh! For heaven's sake, don't wake him.

HJALMAR, *more quietly.* It shall be accomplished. The day will come, I tell you—and that's why it's good we've let that room—it makes me more independent.

Over by the armchair, emotionally.

My poor old father! Bless his white hairs! Put your trust in your son. He has broad shoulders—well, strong shoulders, anyway. One fine day you will wake up—

To GINA.

Don't you believe it?

GINA *gets up.* Of course I believe it. But let's get him to bed first.

HJALMAR. Yes, let's.

They take hold of the old man gently.

ACT THREE

HJALMAR EKDAL'S *studio. It is morning. The daylight is shining in through the large window in the sloping ceiling, from which the curtain is drawn back.*

HJALMAR *is seated at the table re-touching a photograph. Several others lie in front of him. After a few moments,* GINA *enters through the front door wearing a hat and coat. She has a lidded basket on her arm.*

HJALMAR. Back already, Gina?

GINA. Yes, I've no time to waste.

Puts the basket down on a chair and takes off her coat.

HJALMAR. Did you look in on Gregers?

GINA. I'll say I did. Lovely it looks. He's made it really nice and cosy for himself right from the start.

HJALMAR. Oh, how?

GINA. Manage for himself, he said he would. So he starts lighting the stove. Well, he shoved that damper in so far the whole room got full of smoke. Ugh! It stank like a—

HJALMAR. Oh dear, oh dear!

GINA. That's not all. Then he wants to put out the fire, so he throws all his washing water into the stove. That floor's swimming like a pigsty.

HJALMAR. Oh, I'm sorry about that.

GINA. I've got the caretaker's wife to clean up after him, the pig. But that room won't be fit to live in till this afternoon.

HJALMAR. What's he doing with himself meanwhile?

GINA. He said he'd go out for a bit.

HJALMAR. I went in there too for a moment. After you'd gone.

GINA. So I gathered. I hear you've invited him for lunch.

HJALMAR. Just a little snack, I thought. After all, it's his first day here—we can't very well not. You've got something, I suppose?

GINA. I'll have to find something, won't I?

HJALMAR. Don't skimp it too much. Relling and Molvik may be looking in, too, I think. I ran into Relling on the stairs just now, you see, so I couldn't very well—

GINA. Oh, we're having those two as well, are we?

HJALMAR. Good God, a couple more or less, what difference does that make?

OLD EKDAL *opens his door and looks out.* I say, Hjalmar—
Notices GINA.
Oh.

GINA. Do you want something, Grandfather?

OLD EKDAL. Oh, no. It doesn't matter. Hm!
Goes inside again.

GINA *picks up the basket.* Watch him. See he doesn't go out.

HJALMAR. All right, all right. I say, Gina, a little of that herring salad of yours mightn't be a bad idea. I think Relling and Molvik were out on the tiles again last night.

GINA. Well, as long as they don't come too soon—

HJALMAR. Of course, of course. You take your time.

GINA. Yes, well; and you can get a little work done in the meantime.

HJALMAR. I *am* working! I'm working as hard as I can!

GINA. I only meant, then you'll have it out of the way.

She goes out with her basket to the kitchen. HJALMAR *sits working at the photograph with a brush, slowly and listlessly.*

EKDAL *pokes his head in, looks around the room and says in a whisper.* Are you working?

HJALMAR. Yes, can't you see I'm struggling away at these pictures?

EKDAL. Oh. Well, never mind. If you're working so hard, I— Hm.

Goes out again. His door remains open.

HJALMAR *continues silently for a few moments, then puts down his brush and goes across to the door.* Are you working, Father?

EKDAL, *grumblingly, from the other room.* If you're working, I'm working, too. Hm!

HJALMAR. Yes, yes, of course.

Goes back to his work.

EKDAL, *after a moment, reappears in the doorway.* You know —I'm not working as hard as all that, Hjalmar.

HJALMAR. I thought you were writing.

EKDAL. Damn it, that Graaberg can wait a day or two. It's not a matter of life and death, is it?

HJALMAR. No. Anyway, you're not a slave, are you?

EKDAL. And then there's that thing in there—

HJALMAR. I was just thinking of that. Did you want to go in? Shall I open the door for you?

EKDAL. That's not a bad idea.

HJALMAR *gets up.* Then we'd have it out of the way.

EKDAL. That's what I was thinking. We've got to have it ready by tomorrow morning. It is tomorrow, isn't it? Eh?

HJALMAR. Yes, of course it's tomorrow.

HJALMAR *and* EKDAL *each slide back one of the doors. Within, the morning sun is shining in through the skylights. Some pigeons are flying back and forth, while others perch, cooing, on the rafters. Now and then the hens cackle further back in the loft.*

Well now. Get on with it, Father.

EKDAL *goes inside.* Aren't you going to help?

HJALMAR. You know, I think I—

Sees GINA *in the kitchen doorway.*

Me? No, I've no time. I've got to work. Oh—my contraption—

He pulls a cord. A curtain falls in the attic; the lower section of this consists of a strip of old sailcloth, the upper of a piece of fishing net, stretched taut. The floor of the attic is thus no longer visible.

Goes over to the table.

Good. Now perhaps I can be allowed to work in peace for a few minutes.

GINA. Is he messing around in there again?

HJALMAR. Would you rather he sneaked off down to Madame Eriksen's?

Sits.

Did you want something? You were saying—

GINA. I only wanted to ask whether you think it'd be all right if we eat in here.

HJALMAR. Yes, we haven't any early sittings today, have we?

GINA. Only those two young lovers who want to be taken together.

HJALMAR. Why the devil can't they be taken together some other day?

GINA. It's all right, dear. I've fixed for them to come after lunch, when you'll be having your nap.

HJALMAR. Oh, good. Very well, then, let's eat in here.

GINA. All right. But there's no hurry about laying the table just yet. You can go on using it for a bit longer.

HJALMAR. Surely you can see I'm working as hard as I can!

GINA. I only meant, then you'll be free later.

She goes back into the kitchen. Short pause.

EKDAL *peers through the net in the loft.* Hjalmar!

HJALMAR. What is it?

EKDAL. Afraid we'll have to move that water trough after all.

HJALMAR. That's what I've said all along.

EKDAL. Hm—hm—hm.

Goes away from the door again.

HJALMAR *works for a few moments, then glances towards the attic and half rises.* HEDVIG *comes in from the kitchen.*

HJALMAR *sits quickly down.* What do you want?

HEDVIG. I only wanted to be with you, Father.

HJALMAR, *after a moment.* What are you nosing around for? Have you been told to keep an eye on me?

HEDVIG. No, of course not.

HJALMAR. What's your mother up to now?

HEDVIG. Oh, she's in the middle of the herring salad.

Goes over to the table.

Isn't there some little thing I could help you with, Father?

HJALMAR. Oh, no. I'd better cope with it alone. While I still can. All will be well, Hedvig. As long as your father's strength holds out—

HEDVIG. Oh, no, Father, you mustn't say such dreadful things.

She wanders around for a little, then stops by the open doorway and looks into the loft.

HJALMAR. What's he up to, Hedvig?

HEDVIG. I think he's making a new path up to the water trough.

HJALMAR. He'll never manage that by himself! And I'm forced to sit here—

HEDVIG *comes over to him.* Let me take the brush, Father. I know how to do it.

HJALMAR. Oh, no, you'll only ruin your eyes.

HEDVIG. Nonsense. Come on, give me the brush.

HJALMAR *gets up.* Yes, well, it won't take more than a minute or two.

HEDVIG. Oh, what does it matter?

Takes the brush.

There, now.

Sits.

Here's one I can start on.

HJALMAR. But listen—if you ruin your eyes, I won't take the responsibility. On your own head be it. You hear?

HEDVIG, *busy on the photograph.* Yes, yes, I know.

HJALMAR. You're a clever girl, Hedvig. It'll only take a couple of minutes—

He squeezes into the loft past the edge of the curtain. HEDVIG *sits working.* HJALMAR *and* EKDAL *can be heard arguing in the loft.*

HJALMAR *comes back through the curtain.*

Hedvig, get me those pliers from that shelf. And the chisel.

Turns round towards the loft.

Now you'll see, Father. Just let me show you.

HEDVIG *gets the tools from the bookcase and hands them to him.*

HJALMAR. Ah, thanks. Good thing I came, Hedvig.

He goes away from the doorway. They can be heard working and chatting inside. HEDVIG *stands watching them. After a moment, there is a knock on the front door. She does not hear it.*

GREGERS *enters bareheaded and without an overcoat. He pauses in the doorway.* Hm—

HEDVIG *turns and goes towards him.* Good morning. Please come in.

GREGERS. Thank you.

Looks towards the attic.

Have you got workmen in the house?

HEDVIG. No, that's only Father and Grandfather. I'll tell them you're here.

GREGERS. No, no, don't do that. I'd rather wait.

Sits on the sofa.

HEDVIG. It's so untidy in here.

Begins to clear away the photographs.

GREGERS. Oh, never mind that. Are those photographs that have to be—er—finished off?

HEDVIG. Yes, just a few I'm helping Father with.

GREGERS. Please don't let me disturb you.

HEDVIG. All right.

Arranges the things again and sits down to work. GREGERS *watches her in silence.*

GREGERS. Did the wild duck sleep well last night?

HEDVIG. Yes, thank you, I think so.

GREGERS *turns towards the loft.* It looks quite different in there by daylight.

HEDVIG. Oh, yes. It varies a lot. In the morning it looks quite different from what it does in the afternoon. And when it's raining it looks different from when it's fine.

GREGERS. You've noticed that, have you?

HEDVIG. Yes, you can't help seeing it.

GREGERS. Do you like being in there with the wild duck, too?

HEDVIG. Yes, when I'm able to—

GREGERS. But you haven't so much spare time, I dare say. You go to school, of course?

HEDVIG. No, not any longer. Father's afraid I shall ruin my eyes.

GREGERS. Oh. So he reads with you himself?

HEDVIG. Father's promised to read with me, but he hasn't found time for it yet.

GREGERS. But isn't there someone else who could help you a little?

HEDVIG. Yes, there's Mr. Molvik—he's a student who lives downstairs—but he isn't always—er—altogether quite—

GREGERS. Does he drink?

HEDVIG. I think he does.

GREGERS. Oh. Then you've time for all sorts of things. In there, it's like a different world, I suppose?

HEDVIG. Quite, quite different. And there are so many strange things in there.

GREGERS. Oh?

HEDVIG. Yes. There are big cupboards with books in them. And a lot of the books have got pictures.

GREGERS. Ah.

HEDVIG. And there's an old bureau with drawers and bits that slide out, and a big clock with figures that are meant to pop out. But the clock doesn't work any more.

GREGERS. So time has stopped in there with the wild duck.

HEDVIG. Yes. And there are old paintboxes and things like that. And all the books.

GREGERS. And you read books, I suppose?

HEDVIG. Oh yes, when I can get the chance. But most of them are in English, and I can't understand that. But I look at the pictures. There's a great big book called *Harrison's History of London*—I should think it must be a hundred years old—and that's got heaps and heaps of pictures in it. On the front there's a picture of death with an hourglass, and a girl. That's horrid, I think. But then there are lots of other pictures of churches and castles and streets and great ships sailing on the sea.

GREGERS. But tell me, where have all these wonderful things come from?

HEDVIG. Oh, there was an old sea captain who used to live here once, and he brought them home. They called him The Flying Dutchman. It's funny, because he wasn't a Dutchman.

GREGERS. Wasn't he?

HEDVIG. No. But in the end he got lost at sea and left all these things behind.

GREGERS. Tell me—as you sit in there and look at the pictures, don't you feel you want to get out and see the world as it really is?

HEDVIG. Oh, no! I want to stay at home always, and help Father and Mother.

GREGERS. Help them retouch photographs?

HEDVIG. No, not only that. Most of all I'd like to learn to engrave pictures like the ones in the English books.

GREGERS. Hm. What does your father say to that?

HEDVIG. I don't think Father likes the idea. He's so strange about anything like that. Imagine, he talks about my learning how to plait straw and make baskets! I don't think there can be any future in that.

GREGERS. No, neither do I.

HEDVIG. But Father's right when he says that if I'd learned basket-making I could have made the new basket for the wild duck.

GREGERS. Yes, so you could. It was your job really, wasn't it?

HEDVIG. Yes, because it's my wild duck.

GREGERS. Of course it is.

HEDVIG. Oh, yes. I own it. But Father and Grandfather are allowed to borrow it whenever they want.

GREGERS. Oh, and what do they do with it?

HEDVIG. Oh, they look after it and build things for it, and that kind of thing.

GREGERS. I should think so. The wild duck's the most important thing in there, isn't it?

HEDVIG. Oh, yes. She's a real wild bird, you see. That's why I feel so sorry for her. She's got no one to care for, poor thing.

GREGERS. No family like the rabbits.

HEDVIG. No. The hens have got friends they used to be chicks with; but she's been separated from all her family. And there's so much that's strange about the wild duck. No one knows her. And no one knows where she came from.

GREGERS. And she's been down to the bottom of the deep blue sea.

HEDVIG *glances quickly at him and represses a smile.* Why do you say "the deep blue sea"?

GREGERS. What should I have said?

HEDVIG. You could have said the "sea bed," or just the "bottom of the sea."

GREGERS. Oh, why can't I say "the deep blue sea"?

HEDVIG. Yes, but it always sounds so odd to me when other people talk about "the deep blue sea."

GREGERS. Why? Tell me.

HEDVIG. No, I won't. It's silly.

GREGERS. Not at all. Tell me now, why did you smile?

HEDVIG. It's because if I suddenly—without thinking—remember what's in there, I always think of it all as being "the deep blue sea." But that's just silly.

GREGERS. No, you mustn't say that.

HEDVIG. Well, it's only a loft.

GREGERS *looks hard at her.* Are you so sure?

HEDVIG, *astonished.* That it's only a loft?

GREGERS. Yes. You are quite certain about that?

HEDVIG *stares silently at him, open-mouthed.* GINA *comes from the kitchen with cutlery and tablecloth.*

GREGERS *gets up.*

I'm afraid I've come too early.

GINA. Oh, you've got to sit somewhere. Anyway, I'll be ready in a minute. Clear the table, Hedvig.

HEDVIG *clears the table. She and* GINA *lay the cloth, etc., during the following scene.* GREGERS *sits in an armchair and turns the pages of an album.*

GREGERS. I hear you know how to retouch photographs, Mrs. Ekdal.

GINA *gives him a quick glance.* Why—yes, I know how.

GREGERS. That was a lucky chance, wasn't it?

GINA. Why lucky?

GREGERS. Since Hjalmar was to become a photographer, I mean.

HEDVIG. Mother can take photographs, too.

GINA. Oh, yes, I've had to teach myself that.

GREGERS. Then it's really you who run the business?

GINA. Yes, when Hjalmar hasn't time himself, I—

GREGERS. His old father takes up a lot of his time, I dare say.

GINA. Yes. And anyway it's no real job for a man like Hjalmar to have to take the portraits of just anyone.

GREGERS. I quite agree. But after all, he has chosen this profession—

GINA. Hjalmar isn't just an ordinary photographer, you know, Mr. Werle.

GREGERS. I'm sure he isn't. But—

A shot is fired inside the loft.

GREGERS *jumps up.*

What's that?

GINA. Ugh, they're shooting again.

GREGERS. Do they shoot too?

HEDVIG. They go hunting.

GREGERS. What!

By the door of the loft.

Are you hunting, Hjalmar?

HJALMAR, *from beyond the curtain.* Are you here? Oh, I didn't know. I was so busy with—

To HEDVIG.

Why didn't you tell us?

Comes into the studio.

GREGERS. Do you go shooting in the loft?

HJALMAR *shows him a double-barrelled pistol.* Oh, only with this.

GINA. You and Grandfather'll do yourselves an injury one of these fine days with that popgun.

HJALMAR, *irritated.* This is a pistol, as I think I've told you before.

GINA. I don't see that that improves matters.

GREGERS. So you've turned hunter, too, Hjalmar?

HJALMAR. Oh, I just go out after rabbits now and then. Mostly for the old man's sake, you know.

GINA. Men are funny creatures. Always got to have something to diverge themselves with.

HJALMAR, *bad-temperedly.* Quite so. As Gina says, we've always got to have something to divert ourselves with.

GINA. Isn't that what I said?

HJALMAR. Hm. Well—.

To GREGERS.

Yes, you see, as luck would have it the loft's placed in such a way that no one can hear us when we shoot.

Puts down the pistol on the top shelf of the bookcase.

Don't touch that pistol, Hedvig. One of the barrels is loaded. Now don't forget.

GREGERS *peers in through the net.* You've a shotgun too, I see.

HJALMAR. That's Father's old gun. It's no use any longer, something's gone wrong with the lock. But it's quite fun to have it around. We can take it to pieces now and then and clean it and grease it and put it together again. Of course it's mostly Father who fiddles around like that.

HEDVIG, *to* GREGERS. Now you can see the wild duck properly.

GREGERS. Yes, I was just looking at her. She droops a little on one wing, doesn't she?

HJALMAR. No wonder. That's where she was shot.

GREGERS. And she trails one foot a little. Am I right?

HJALMAR. Perhaps just a little.

HEDVIG. Yes, that's where the dog bit her.

HJALMAR. But otherwise there's nothing wrong with her. It's really marvellous when you think she's had a charge of shot in her and has been between the teeth of a dog—

GREGERS *glances at* HEDVIG. And has been on the bottom of the deep blue sea for so long.

HEDVIG *smiles.* Yes.

GINA, *laying the table.* Oh, that blessed wild duck. You make too much of a song and dance about her.

HJALMAR. Hm. Are you nearly ready with that?

GINA. Yes, I shan't be a minute. Hedvig, come and give me a hand.

GINA and HEDVIG *go out into the kitchen.*

HJALMAR, *in a low voice.* I think you'd better not stand there watching Father. He doesn't like it.

GREGERS *comes away from the loft door.*

HJALMAR. I'd better close up before the others arrive.

Claps his hands to frighten the birds.

Shoo, shoo! Get away with you!

Pulls up the curtain and closes the doors as he speaks.

I invented these gadgets myself. It's really rather fun to have something like this to fiddle with, and fix when it goes wrong. We've got to have it, because Gina doesn't like rabbits and hens in here.

GREGERS. No, no. It's your wife who runs the studio, I suppose?

HJALMAR. I generally leave the details of the business to her. Then I can lock myself away in the parlour and think about more important things.

GREGERS. What kind of things, Hjalmar?

HJALMAR. I wonder you haven't asked me that before. But perhaps you haven't heard about my invention?

GREGERS. Your invention? No.

HJALMAR. Really? Haven't you? Oh no, I suppose being cut off up there in those forests—

GREGERS. So you've invented something?

HJALMAR. It's not quite finished yet. But I'm working on it. As you can imagine, when I decided to give up my life to the service of photography it wasn't because I wanted to take portraits of the *bourgeoisie*.

GREGERS. No, that's what your wife said just now.

HJALMAR. I made a vow that if I was going to dedicate my powers to this craft, I would exalt it to the level of both an art and a science. And so I decided to make this astonishing invention.

GREGERS. But what *is* this invention? What's the idea behind it?

HJALMAR. Oh, my dear fellow, you mustn't ask me about details yet. It takes time, you know. And you mustn't think it's vanity that's inspiring me to do this. It isn't for myself that I'm doing it. Oh, no. I have a mission in life that I can never forget.

GREGERS. What kind of mission?

HJALMAR. Have you forgotten that old man with the silver hair?

GREGERS. Your poor father. Yes, but there isn't very much you can do for him, is there?

HJALMAR. I can rekindle his self-respect by restoring to the name of Ekdal the honour and dignity which it once had.

GREGERS. And that's your mission?

HJALMAR. I want to save that shipwrecked soul, yes. Right from the moment the storm broke over him, he was a wreck. And during those terrible investigations he was no longer himself. That pistol over there, Gregers—the one we use for shooting rabbits—has played its part in the tragedy of the House of Ekdal.

GREGERS. Really? That pistol?

HJALMAR. When sentence had been pronounced and he was about to be taken to prison—he had the pistol in his hand—

GREGERS. You mean—?

HJALMAR. Yes. But he didn't dare. He was a coward. His spirit had been broken. Can you understand it? He, a soldier, who had killed nine bears, and was descended from two lieutenant colonels—one after the other, of course— Can you understand it, Gregers?

GREGERS. Yes, I understand it very well.

HJALMAR. I can't. But that wasn't the last time that pistol
played a part in the history of our family. When he was in
his grey garb, under lock and key—oh, it was a terrible time
for me, believe me. I kept the blinds drawn over both my
windows. When I peeped out I saw that the sun still shone.
I couldn't understand it. I saw people in the street, laughing and chatting, about trivial things. I couldn't understand
it. I thought the whole world ought to stand still, as though
in eclipse.

GREGERS. That is how I felt when my mother died.

HJALMAR. At such a moment, Hjalmar Ekdal held the pistol
pointed at his own breast.

GREGERS. You mean you, too, thought of—?

HJALMAR. Yes.

GREGERS. But you didn't fire?

HJALMAR. No. At the critical moment, I triumphed over myself. I decided to remain alive. But I can tell you, Gregers,
it takes courage under such circumstances to choose life.

GREGERS. Yes, well—that depends on how one—

HJALMAR. Believe me, Gregers, I am right. Anyway, it was
better so. Now I shall make my invention; and then, Dr.
Relling agrees with me, Father may be allowed to wear
his uniform again. I shall demand it as my sole reward.

GREGERS. So it's the uniform he—?

HJALMAR. Yes, that's what he longs for most. You can't imagine how my heart bleeds for him. Every time we have
any little family celebration—for example, Gina's and my
wedding anniversary, or whatever it may be—the old man
appears as the lieutenant he used to be in happier days. But
if there's a knock on the door he scampers back to his room
as fast as his old legs will carry him, because he daren't
show himself to strangers. Oh, it's heart-rending for a son
to have to witness such things, Gregers.

GREGERS. How soon do you expect this invention to be ready?

HJALMAR. Good heavens, you can't expect me to work to a

schedule. An invention is something that even the inventor himself isn't completely master of. It depends largely on intuition—on inspiration—and it's almost impossible to predict when that's going to come.

GREGERS. But you're making progress?

HJALMAR. Of course I am. I think about it every day. It's always with me. Every afternoon, after I've eaten, I shut myself up in the parlour where I can meditate in peace. But I mustn't be rushed. That won't help at all. Relling says so too.

GREGERS. And you don't think that all that business in the loft distracts you too much, and dissipates your energies?

HJALMAR. No, no, no—quite the contrary. I can't spend all my time brooding over the same exhausting problem. I must have some distraction while I wait for the inspiration to come. Inspiration, you see, comes when it comes.

GREGERS. My dear Hjalmar, I really believe there is something of the wild duck in you.

HJALMAR. The wild duck? How do you mean?

GREGERS. You've plunged to the bottom and are holding on to the seaweed.

HJALMAR. Are you referring to that stroke of fate which crippled Father—and me as well?

GREGERS. Not that so much. I wouldn't say you've been crippled. You've wandered into a poisonous swamp, Hjalmar. You've got a creeping disease in your body, and you've sunk to the bottom to die in the dark.

HJALMAR. Me? Die in the dark? Now really, Gregers, you must stop that talk.

GREGERS. Don't worry. I shall get you up again. I've found a mission in life, too, you see. I found it yesterday.

HJALMAR. I dare say, but please leave me out of it. I can assure you that—apart from a certain melancholy, which is easily explained—I'm as contented with life as anyone could wish to be.

GREGERS. That's another effect of the poison.

HJALMAR. Oh, my dear Gregers, do stop talking about diseases and poisons. I'm not used to this kind of conversation. In my house we don't talk about disagreeable matters.

GREGERS. No, I can well believe that.

HJALMAR. Yes—it's not good for me, you see. And you won't find any poisonous fumes here, as you insinuate. In the poor photographer's home the roof is low, I know that well. And the circumstances are narrow. But I am an inventor, Gregers —the breadwinner for my family—and that lifts me above the poverty of my surroundings. Ah, lunch!

GINA *and* HEDVIG *bring in bottles of beer, a decanter of aquavit, glasses, etc. . . . At the same time* RELLING *and* MOLVIK *enter from the passage. Neither has a hat or overcoat.* MOLVIK *is dressed in black.*

GINA, *putting the things on the table.* Trust those two to come on time!

RELLING. Molvik thought he could smell herring salad, so there was no holding him. Good morning again, Ekdal.

HJALMAR. Gregers, may I present Mr. Molvik? Dr.—but of course you know Relling.

GREGERS. Yes, we have met.

RELLING. Oh, it's Mr. Werle Junior. Yes, we two have clashed before, up at Hoydal. You moved in here?

GREGERS. I moved in this morning.

RELLING. Molvik and I live underneath, so you haven't far to go for a doctor or a priest, if you should ever need either of them.

GREGERS. Thank you, I well may. Yesterday we were thirteen at table.

HJALMAR. Oh, don't start that awful business again.

RELLING. Take it easy, Ekdal. You were one of the twelve.

HJALMAR. I hope so, for my family's sake. But now let's sit down, and eat and drink and be merry.

GREGERS. Oughtn't we to wait for your father?

HJALMAR. No, he wants his taken in to him later. Come along now, everybody!

The men sit down at the table, and start eating and drinking. GINA *and* HEDVIG *come and go, waiting on them.*

RELLING. Molvik was as tight as a drum again last night, Mrs. Ekdal.

GINA. Oh? Last night again?

RELLING. Didn't you hear him when I brought him home?

GINA. No, I can't say I did.

RELLING. That's as well. Molvik was *awful* last night.

GINA. Is this true, Molvik?

MOLVIK. Let us draw a veil over the events of last night. It was not a manifestation of my better self.

RELLING, *to* GREGERS. It comes on him like an inspiration. And then I have to go out and paint the town with him. Molvik's daemonic, you see.

GREGERS. Daemonic?

RELLING. Yes, daemonic.

GREGERS. Hm.

RELLING. And people who are born daemonic can't keep a straight course through life. They have to go off the rails now and then. Well, so you're still sticking it out at that ugly black mill, are you?

GREGERS. I have stuck it out until now.

RELLING. And did you manage to enforce that claim you went round pestering everyone with?

GREGERS. Claim?

Understands him.

I see.

HJALMAR. Have you been acting as a debt collector, Gregers?

GREGERS. Oh, nonsense.

RELLING. Oh yes, he has. He went round all the workmen's cottages, shoving something in their faces which he called the "claim of the ideal."

GREGERS. I was young then.

RELLING. You're right there. You were very young. And as for that claim of the ideal—you never got anyone to honour it before I left.

GREGERS. Nor since, either.

RELLING. Then I hope you've grown wise enough to reduce your demands a little.

GREGERS. Not when I stand face to face with a man.

HJALMAR. Well, that sounds reasonable enough. A little butter, Gina.

RELLING. And a slice of pork for Molvik.

MOLVIK. Oh no, not pork!

There is a knock on the door of the loft.

HJALMAR. Open the door, Hedvig. Father wants to come out.

HEDVIG *goes across and opens the door a little.* OLD EKDAL *comes out with a fresh rabbit skin. She closes the door behind him.*

EKDAL. Morning, gentlemen. Good hunting today. I've shot a big one.

HJALMAR. Why did you have to skin it before I came?

EKDAL. Salted it, too. It's good, tender meat, rabbit meat. Sweet, too. Tastes like sugar. Enjoy your dinner, gentlemen!

Goes into his room.

MOLVIK *gets up.* Excuse me—I can't—I must—quickly—

RELLING. Drink some soda water, man!

MOLVIK *hurries out.* Ah—ah!

Goes out through the front door.

RELLING, *to* HJALMAR. Let's drink to the old huntsman.

HJALMAR *clinks glasses with him.* A great sportsman at the end of the road.

RELLING. His hair tempered with grey—

Drinks.

By the way, tell me, is his hair grey or white?

HJALMAR. Oh—somewhere between the two. Actually, he hasn't very many hairs left on his head.

RELLING. Well, one can get through the world with a wig, as one can with a mask. You're a lucky man, Ekdal. A beautiful mission to fight for—

HJALMAR. And I do fight for it, believe me.

RELLING. And a clever wife, jogging quietly in and out in her felt slippers, rocking her hips and making everything nice and comfortable for you.

HJALMAR. Yes, Gina.

Nods to her.

You are a good companion to have on life's journey.

GINA. Oh, get along with you!

RELLING. And then you have your little Hedvig.

HJALMAR, *moved.* My child, yes. Above all, my child. Hedvig, come to me.

Strokes her hair.

What day is it tomorrow, Hedvig?

HEDVIG *shakes him.* Oh no, Father, you mustn't tell them!

HJALMAR. It wounds me like a knife through the heart when I think how poor it must be. Just a little party in the attic—

HEDVIG. But Father, that's just what's so wonderful!

RELLING. And just you wait till your father's ready with his great invention, Hedvig.

HJALMAR. Yes, then you'll see! Hedvig, I have resolved to secure your future. You shall never want. I shall make it a condition that you get—er—something or other. That shall be the poor inventor's sole reward.

HEDVIG *whispers, her arm round his neck.* Oh, dear, kind Father!

RELLING, *to* GREGERS. Well, don't you find it pleasant for a change to sit down to a good meal surrounded by a happy family?

HJALMAR. Yes, I think I appreciate these hours at the table more than anything.

GREGERS. Personally I don't like poisonous fumes.

RELLING. Poisonous fumes!

HJALMAR. Oh, for heaven's sake, don't start that again.

GINA. By God, you'll find no fumes in here, Mr. Werle. I give the whole place a good airing every day.

GREGERS, *leaving the table.* You can't drive out the stench I mean by opening the windows.

HJALMAR. Stench!

GINA. How do you like that, Hjalmar!

RELLING. I beg your pardon—you couldn't possibly have brought the stench in yourself from those pits up there?

GREGERS. Yes, it's like you to call what I bring with me a stench.

RELLING *goes over to him.* Listen, Mr. Werle Junior. I've a strong suspicion you're still carrying that "claim of the ideal" unabridged in your back pocket.

GREGERS. I carry it in my heart.

RELLING. Well, wherever you have the bloody thing I'm damned if I'll let you blackmail anyone with it as long as I'm in this house.

GREGERS. And if I choose to ignore your warning?

RELLING. Then you'll go headfirst down those stairs. Now you know.

HJALMAR *gets up.* But—but, Relling—

GREGERS. All right, throw me out.

GINA *goes between them.* Relling, you can't do that. But I must say, Mr. Werle, after the mess you made with your stove you're in no position to come and complain to me about fumes.

There is a knock on the front door.

HEDVIG. Mother, someone's knocking.

HJALMAR. Oh, now that's going to start.

GINA. Let me take care of it.

Goes over, opens the door and steps back in surprise.

Oh! Oh, no!

HAAKON WERLE, *in a fur-lined coat with a fur collar, takes a step into the room.*

WERLE. I beg your pardon, but I believe my son is living in this house.

GINA *swallows.* Yes.

HJALMAR *goes towards him.* Wouldn't you do us the honour, sir, to—?

WERLE. Thank you, I only want to speak to my son.

GREGERS. Well? I'm here. What is it?

WERLE. I want to speak to you in your room.

GREGERS. Oh? In my room?

Moves towards the door.

GINA. No, for heaven's sake, that's in no state—

WERLE. Out in the passage, then. I want to speak with you alone.

HJALMAR. You can do that here, sir. Relling, come into the parlour.

HJALMAR *and* RELLING *go out to the right.* GINA *takes* HEDVIG *into the kitchen.*

GREGERS, *after a short pause.* Well. Now we're alone.

WERLE. You let drop a few remarks last night about— And since you've now come to lodge with the Ekdals I can only assume that you intend some action directed against me.

GREGERS. I intend to open the eyes of Hjalmar Ekdal. He must see his situation as it really is. That is all.

WERLE. And that is the mission in life you spoke of yesterday?

GREGERS. Yes. It's the only one you have left me.

WERLE. So it's I who have soured your mind, Gregers?

GREGERS. You have soured my whole life. Oh, I'm not just thinking of what happened to my mother. But it's you I have to thank for the fact that I'm continually haunted by a guilty conscience.

WERLE. Oh, so it's your conscience that's queasy, is it?

GREGERS. I ought to have stood up to you when those traps were laid for Lieutenant Ekdal. I ought to have warned him. I knew in my mind what was going on.

WERLE. Then you ought to have spoken out.

GREGERS. I was frightened. I was a coward. I was so miserably afraid of you then. And long afterwards.

WERLE. You seem to have got over that very well now.

GREGERS. Yes, thank God, I have. The crimes that have been committed against old Ekdal, by me and by—others—can never be undone. But at least I can free Hjalmar from the conspiracy of silence and deceit which is killing him here.

WERLE. And you think that'd be doing him a service?

GREGERS. I have no doubt of it.

WERLE. You think this photographer is the kind of man who would thank you for such a proof of friendship?

GREGERS. Yes. He is that kind of man.

WERLE. Well. We shall see.

GREGERS. And besides—if I am to go on living, I must try to find some cure for my sick conscience.

WERLE. Your conscience has been sickly ever since you were a child. There's no cure for it. That's an heirloom from your mother, Gregers. The only thing she left you.

GREGERS, *with a scornful smile.* Haven't you got over your disappointment yet? You miscalculated badly, didn't you, when you thought you'd get rich through her.

WERLE. Don't try to distract me with irrelevancies. Are you still resolved to carry out your intention of guiding Ekdal on to what you suppose to be the right path?

GREGERS. Yes. I am resolved.

WERLE. In that case I might have saved myself the trouble of climbing the stairs. I don't suppose it's any use now asking if you'll come back home?

GREGERS. No.

WERLE. And you won't enter the firm either, I suppose?

GREGERS. No.

WERLE. Very good. But since I am intending to enter into a new marriage, I will arrange for the estate to be divided between us.

GREGERS, *quickly*. No, I don't want that.

WERLE. You don't want it?

GREGERS. No. My conscience won't allow me.

WERLE, *after a moment*. Are you going back to the mill?

GREGERS. No. I have left your service.

WERLE. But what will you do?

GREGERS. I shall simply fulfil my mission. That is all.

WERLE. But afterwards? How will you live?

GREGERS. I have saved a little out of my salary.

WERLE. Yes, but how long will that last?

GREGERS. I think it will see me through.

WERLE. What does that mean?

GREGERS. I think you've asked me enough questions.

WERLE. Good-bye, then, Gregers.

GREGERS. Good-bye.

HAAKON WERLE *goes out*.

HJALMAR *looks in*. Has he gone?

GREGERS. Yes.

HJALMAR *and* RELLING *come in*. GINA *and* HEDVIG *enter from the kitchen*.

RELLING. Well, that's the end of our lunch.

GREGERS. Get your coat, Hjalmar. You and I must take a long walk together.

HJALMAR. Yes, let's. What did your father want? Was it anything to do with me?

GREGERS. Come along. We must have a little talk. I'll go and fetch my coat.

Goes out through the front door.

GINA. I don't like you going out with him, Hjalmar.

RELLING. She's right. Stay here with us.

HJALMAR *takes his hat and overcoat*. What! When an old schoolfellow feels the need to pour out his heart to me—?

RELLING. But, for Christ's sake—don't you see the fellow's mad, twisted, out of his mind?

GINA. There you are! Well, what do you expect? His mother had weird fits like that too, sometimes.

HJALMAR. All the more need for someone to keep a friendly eye on him, then.

To GINA.

Make sure dinner's ready in good time. Good-bye for now.

Goes out through the front door.

RELLING. What a pity that fellow didn't fall into one of his own mines and drop right down to Hell!

GINA. Mercy on us! Why do you say that?

RELLING *mutters*. Oh, I have my reasons.

GINA. Do you think young Mr. Werle's really mad?

RELLING. No, worse luck. He's no madder than most people. He's sick all right, though.

GINA. What do you think's wrong with him?

RELLING. I'll tell you, Mrs. Ekdal. He's suffering from a surfeit of self-righteousness.

GINA. Surfeit of self-righteousness?

HEDVIG. Is that a disease?

RELLING. Yes. It's a national disease. But it only very seldom becomes acute.

Nods to GINA.

Thanks for the lunch.

Goes out through the front door.

GINA *walks round uneasily*. Ugh! That Gregers Werle. He always was a queer fish.

HEDVIG *stands by the table and looks searchingly at her*. I think this is all very strange.

ACT FOUR

HJALMAR EKDAL's *studio. A photograph has just been taken; a camera with a cloth over it, a stand, two or three chairs, a folding table, etc., stand round the room. Afternoon light; the sun is just going down; a little later it begins to grow dark.* GINA *is standing in the open doorway with a small box and a wet glass plate in her hand, talking to someone outside.*

GINA. Yes, definitely. When I make a promise I always keep it. I'll have the first dozen ready by Monday. Good-bye, good-bye.

The other person goes downstairs. GINA *closes the door, puts the glass plate in the box and places the latter in the covered camera.*

HEDVIG *comes in from the kitchen.* Have they gone?

GINA, *tidying up.* Yes, thank God, I got rid of them at last.

HEDVIG. Why do you suppose Father hasn't come home yet?

GINA. Are you sure he's not down with Relling?

HEDVIG. No, he's not there. I've just run down the back stairs to ask.

GINA. And his dinner's getting cold too, I suppose?

HEDVIG. It's funny—Father's always on time for dinner.

GINA. Oh, he'll be here soon. You'll see.

HEDVIG. I wish he'd come. Everything seems so strange suddenly.

GINA *cries out.* Here he is!

HJALMAR EKDAL *comes in through the front door.*

HEDVIG *runs towards him.* Oh, Father! Oh, we've waited and
waited for you!

GINA *gives him a glance.* You've been a long time, Hjalmar.

HJALMAR, *without looking at her.* Yes, I have rather, haven't I?
He takes off his overcoat. GINA *and* HEDVIG *try to help him,
but he gestures them away.*

GINA. Have you eaten with Werle?

HJALMAR *hangs up his coat.* No.

GINA *goes towards the kitchen door.* I'll bring in your food,
then.

HJALMAR. No, never mind the food. I don't want any.

HEDVIG *goes closer.* Aren't you well, Father?

HJALMAR. Well? Oh yes, tolerably. We had rather a tiring
walk, Gregers and I.

GINA. You shouldn't do that, Hjalmar. You're not used to it.

HJALMAR. But there are a lot of things in life a man's got to
get used to.
Wanders round a little.
Anyone been here while I was out?

GINA. Only those two sweethearts.

HJALMAR. No new orders?

GINA. No, not today.

HEDVIG. There'll be some tomorrow, Father. You'll see.

HJALMAR. Let's hope so. Because tomorrow I intend to start
working in real earnest.

HEDVIG. Tomorrow? But don't you remember what day it is
tomorrow?

HJALMAR. Ah, that's true. Well, the day after tomorrow, then.
From now on I'm going to do everything myself. I'm going
to manage the whole business on my own.

GINA. But why should you do that, Hjalmar? It'll only make

you miserable. No, I'll take care of the photography, and you can go on puzzling with your invention.

HEDVIG. And think of the wild duck, Father. And all the hens and rabbits, and—

HJALMAR. Don't talk to me about all that nonsense. From now on I shall never set foot in that loft again.

HEDVIG. But Father, you promised tomorrow we'd have a party—

HJALMAR. Hm, that's true. Well, from the day after tomorrow, then. I'd like to wring the neck of that damned wild duck.

HEDVIG *screams*. The wild duck!

GINA. I never heard such nonsense!

HEDVIG, *shaking him*. But Father! It's my wild duck!

HJALMAR. That's why I won't do it. I haven't the heart to—I haven't the heart—because of you, Hedvig. But I know in my heart that I ought to do it. I ought not to allow any creature to live under my roof which has been in *his* hands.

GINA. For heaven's sake! Just because Grandfather got it from that wretched Pettersen—

HJALMAR, *wandering around*. There are certain demands—demands a man makes of himself—how shall I put it?—a striving for perfection—one might say the demands of an ideal—which a man may not ignore without danger to his soul.

HEDVIG *goes after him*. But Father, the wild duck! The poor wild duck!

HJALMAR *stops*. I've told you I shall spare it. For your sake. I shall not touch a hair of its—well, as I told you, I shall spare it. I have more important tasks than that to get down to. But you'd better go and take your walk now, Hedvig. It's getting dark—the light won't hurt your eyes now.

HEDVIG. No, I won't bother to go out today.

HJALMAR. Yes, you must. You screw up your eyes so; all these fumes in here are bad for you. The air under this roof is unclean.

HEDVIG. All right, all right. I'll run down the back stairs and go

for a little walk. My coat and hat? Oh, they're in my room.
Father, you won't hurt the wild duck while I'm out?

HJALMAR. Not a feather of its head shall be touched.

Presses her to him.

You and I, Hedvig—we two—! Well, run along.

HEDVIG *nods to her parents and goes out through the
kitchen.*

HJALMAR *walks around without looking up.* Gina.

GINA. Yes?

HJALMAR. From tomorrow—or let's say the day after tomorrow—I'd like to keep the household accounts myself.

GINA. You want to look after the household accounts too now?

HJALMAR. Yes. I want to find out where the money comes
from.

GINA. Well, heaven knows that won't take you long.

HJALMAR. One would imagine it would. You seem to make it
go a remarkably long way.

Stops and looks at her.

How do you do it?

GINA. It's because Hedvig and I need so little.

HJALMAR. Is it true that Father gets paid very generously for
the copying he does for Mr. Werle?

GINA. I don't know if it's so very generous. But then I don't
know what that kind of work is worth.

HJALMAR. Well, roughly how much does he get? Come on,
tell me!

GINA. It varies. On an average about what it costs us to keep
him, and a bit of pocket money over.

HJALMAR. What it costs us to keep him! And you never told
me!

GINA. How could I? You were so happy because you thought
he got everything from you.

HJALMAR. And all the time he gets it from Mr. Werle!

GINA. Oh, there's more where that comes from.

HJALMAR. I suppose we'd better light that lamp.

GINA *lights it.* Of course, we don't know if it's the old man himself. It might easily be Graaberg—

HJALMAR. Why drag in Graaberg?

GINA. No, I don't know. I just thought—

HJALMAR. Hm!

GINA. I didn't get this work for Grandfather. It was Berta— when she came to live there.

HJALMAR. Your voice has gone funny.

GINA *puts the shade on the lamp.* My voice?

HJALMAR. And your hands are trembling. Do you deny it?

GINA, *firmly.* Don't beat about the bush, Hjalmar. What's he been telling you about me?

HJALMAR. Is it true—can it be true—that there was a kind of relationship between you and Mr. Werle when you were in his service?

GINA. No, it's not true. Not at that time. Oh, he was after me, all right. And Mrs. Werle thought there was something doing; she created a great hullaballoo, and pulled my hair, she did, so I gave my notice and went.

HJALMAR. But it happened afterwards!

GINA. Yes, well I went home. And Mother—she wasn't such a simple soul as you thought, Hjalmar. She kept talking to me about one thing and another. Well, the old man was a widower by then, you see—

HJALMAR. Go on!

GINA. Well, I suppose you'd better know. He wouldn't give in till he'd had his way.

HJALMAR. And this is the mother of my child! How could you keep such a thing from me?

GINA. Yes, it was very wrong. I ought to have told you about it long ago.

HJALMAR. You ought to have told me at once. Then I'd have known what kind of woman you were.

GINA. If I had, would you have married me?

HJALMAR. What do you think?

GINA. Yes, well, that's why I didn't dare to say anything to you at the time. You know how fond I'd grown of you. How could I throw away my whole life?

HJALMAR, *walking about.* And this is the mother of my Hedvig! And to know that everything I see around me—

Kicks a chair.

—my entire home—I owe to a predecessor in your favours! Oh, that seductive old Werle!

GINA. Do you regret the fifteen years we have lived together?

HJALMAR *stops in front of her.* Have you not every day, every moment, regretted the web of concealment and deceit that you've spun around me like a spider? Answer me that! Do you mean to tell me that all this time you haven't been living in anguish and remorse?

GINA. Oh, my dear Hjalmar, I've had enough to think about trying to run the house without—

HJALMAR. Then you never probe your past with a questioning eye?

GINA. You know, I'd almost forgotten the whole dirty business.

HJALMAR. Oh, this soulless, unfeeling complacency! It always fills me with moral indignation. And what is more, you don't even regret it!

GINA. Yes, but tell me, Hjalmar. What would have become of you if you hadn't had a wife like me?

HJALMAR. Like you?

GINA. Yes; I've always been a little more down-to-earth and practical than you. Well, it's natural, I suppose, I'm just that much older.

HJALMAR. What would have become of me!

GINA. Yes. You'd gone a bit off the rails when you met me. You surely won't deny that.

HJALMAR. You call that going off the rails? Oh, you don't understand what it's like when a man is full of sorrow and despair. Particularly a man of my fiery temperament.

GINA. No, no. Perhaps I don't. Anyway, I'm not complaining; you became such a good man once you'd got a house and home of your own. And now it was getting to be so homely and nice here; and Hedvig and I were just thinking we might be able to spend a little on food and clothes.

HJALMAR. Yes, in this swamp of deceit.

GINA. Oh, why did that repulsive little man have to come to our house?

HJALMAR. I too used to think this was a good home. It was a delusion. Where shall I now find the strength I need to transfer my invention into terms of reality? Perhaps it will die with me. And it will be your past, Gina, which will have killed it.

GINA, *on the verge of tears.* No, you mustn't say things like that, Hjalmar. All our married life I've never thought of anyone but you.

HJALMAR. I ask you—what will become of the breadwinner's dream now? As I lay in there on the sofa brooding over the invention I had a feeling that it would devour my energies to the last drop. I sensed that the day on which I held the patent in my hands—that day would spell my release. And it was my dream that you should live on as the late inventor's prosperous widow.

GINA, *drying her tears.* Now you mustn't talk like that, Hjalmar. May the good Lord never let me live to see myself a widow.

HJALMAR. Oh, what does it matter? It's all finished now. Everything!

GREGERS WERLE *cautiously opens the front door and looks in.*

GREGERS. May one come in?

HJALMAR. Yes, come in.

GREGERS *comes forward with a radiant, gratified expression and holds out his hands to them.* Well, my dear friends! *Looks from one to the other and whispers to* HJALMAR.

Hasn't it happened yet?

HJALMAR. Oh, it has happened.

GREGERS. It has!

HJALMAR. I have just lived through the bitterest moment of my life.

GREGERS. But also, surely, the most sublime.

HJALMAR. Well, we've put that behind us. For the time being, anyway.

GINA. May God forgive you, Mr. Werle.

GREGERS, *greatly amazed.* But what I don't see is—

HJALMAR. What don't you see?

GREGERS. From such a crisis there must spring a mutual understanding on which a whole new life can be founded—a partnership built on truth, without concealment.

HJALMAR. Yes, I know, Gregers. I know.

GREGERS. I felt so sure, that when I walked through that door you would be standing there transfigured, and that my eyes would be dazzled by the light. And instead I see nothing but this dull heaviness and misery—

GINA. Oh, I see.

Takes the shade off the lamp.

GREGERS. You don't want to understand me, Mrs. Ekdal. Ah, well. I suppose you need a bit more time. But you, Hjalmar, you? Surely you must have gained a higher understanding now that the crisis is over?

HJALMAR. Yes, of course I have. That is—in a kind of way.

GREGERS. For there is nothing in the world that can compare with the joy of forgiving someone who has sinned, and raising her to one's heart in love.

HJALMAR. Do you think that a man can so easily digest the bitter draught that I have just drained?

GREGERS. Not an ordinary man, perhaps. But a man like you—

HJALMAR. Oh yes, I know, I know. But you mustn't rush me, Gregers. It takes time, you see.

GREGERS. There's a lot of the wild duck in you, Hjalmar.

RELLING *has entered through the front door.*

RELLING. So the wild duck's in the air again?

HJALMAR. Yes. Mr. Werle's winged victim.

RELLING. Mr. Werle? Are you talking about him?

HJALMAR. About him and—the rest of us.

RELLING, *aside, to* GREGERS. You bloody fool, why don't you go to Hell?

HJALMAR. What did you say?

RELLING. I was expressing my heartfelt desire to see this quack doctor back where he belongs. If he stays here he's quite capable of messing up both your lives.

GREGERS. You needn't fear for these two, Dr. Relling. I shan't speak about Hjalmar. We both know him. But in her too, deep in her heart, there is something of honesty and truthfulness.

GINA, *near to tears.* Then you ought to have let me stay as I was.

RELLING. Would it be impertinent to ask exactly what it is you're trying to do in this house?

GREGERS. I want to lay the foundations of a true marriage.

RELLING. Then you don't think their marriage is good enough as it stands?

GREGERS. It's probably as good a marriage as most others, I'm afraid. But it is not yet a true marriage.

HJALMAR. You've never had much faith in ideals, Dr. Relling.

RELLING. Rubbish, my boy! May I ask, Mr. Werle—how many true marriages have you seen in your life? Just roughly.

GREGERS. I hardly think I've seen a single one.

RELLING. Neither have I.

GREGERS. But I've seen so many, many marriages of the opposite kind. And I've had the opportunity to study one at sufficiently close quarters to realise how it can demoralise two human beings.

HJALMAR. The whole moral foundation of a man's life can crumble under his feet. That's the terrible thing.

RELLING. Yes, well, I've never been what you'd call married, so

I wouldn't presume to judge. But I do know this, that children are as much a part of any marriage as their parents. So you leave that child alone.

HJALMAR. Ah! Hedvig! My poor Hedvig!

RELLING. Yes, I'll thank you to keep Hedvig out of this. You two are adults; muck about with your own lives if you enjoy it. But I'm warning you, be gentle with Hedvig, or you may do her irreparable harm.

HJALMAR. Harm?

RELLING. Yes, or she may come to do herself harm—and perhaps others too.

GINA. What would you know about that, Relling?

HJALMAR. There isn't any immediate danger to her eyes, is there?

RELLING. This has nothing to do with her eyes. Hedvig's at a difficult age just now. She's capable of getting up to anything.

GINA. Yes, that's true—I've noticed it already. She's started fooling around with the kitchen stove. She calls it playing with fire. I'm often afraid she'll burn down the house.

RELLING. There you are. You see. I thought as much.

GREGERS, *to* RELLING. But how would you explain that kind of behaviour?

RELLING, *quietly*. My boy. Her voice is breaking.

HJALMAR. As long as the child has me— As long as my head is above the ground—

There is a knock on the door.

GINA. Quiet, Hjalmar. There's someone on the landing.

Calls.

Come in.

MRS. SOERBY *enters, in an overcoat.*

MRS. SOERBY. Good evening.

GINA *goes to greet her.* Berta, is it you?

MRS. SOERBY. Yes, it's me. But perhaps I've come at an inconvenient moment?

HJALMAR. Of course not. Any messenger from that house is always—

MRS. SOERBY, *to* GINA. To be honest, I hoped I might find you alone at this hour of the evening, so I looked in to have a chat and to say good-bye.

GINA. Oh? Are you going away?

MRS. SOERBY. Yes. Tomorrow morning. Up to Hoydal. Mr. Werle left this afternoon.

Casually, to GREGERS.

He asked to be remembered to you.

GINA. Well, fancy that!

HJALMAR. So Mr. Werle has gone away. And you're going after him?

MRS. SOERBY. Yes. What have you got to say about that, Ekdal?

HJALMAR. I say: take care!

GREGERS. I'd better explain. My father is marrying Mrs. Soerby.

HJALMAR. Going to *marry* her?

GINA. Berta! So it's happened at last!

RELLING, *with a slight tremor in his voice.* This isn't true, surely?

MRS. SOERBY. Yes, dear Relling, it's perfectly true.

RELLING. You want to get married again?

MRS. SOERBY. Yes, I've decided I do. Mr. Werle has obtained a special licence, and we're going to get married quite quietly up at Hoydal.

GREGERS. Well, in that case nothing remains but to wish you happiness, as a dutiful stepson.

MRS. SOERBY. Thank you; if you really mean it. I certainly hope it will bring happiness to Mr. Werle and to me.

RELLING. Oh, I'm sure it will. Mr. Werle never gets drunk—as far as I know—and I don't think he's in the habit of beating up his wives, as the late lamented horse-doctor used to.

MRS. SOERBY. Oh, let Soerby rest in peace. He had his good points.

RELLING. But Mr. Werle, we gather, has better ones.

MRS. SOERBY. At least he hasn't wasted all that was best in him. Men who do that must accept the consequences.

RELLING. I'm going out with Molvik tonight.

MRS. SOERBY. Don't do that, Relling. Please, for my sake.

RELLING. What else do you suggest?

To HJALMAR.

Care to join us?

GINA. No, thank you. Hjalmar doesn't go on that kind of spree.

HJALMAR, *aside, irritated.* Oh, be quiet.

RELLING. Good-bye, Mrs.—Werle.

Goes out through front door.

GREGERS, *to* MRS. SOERBY. It seems that you and Dr. Relling know each other pretty well.

MRS. SOERBY. Yes, we've known each other for many years. At one time it even seemed as though our friendship might lead to something more permanent.

GREGERS. Lucky for you it didn't.

MRS. SOERBY. I know. But I've always been wary of acting on impulse. A woman can't just throw herself away, can she?

GREGERS. Aren't you afraid I might tell my father about this old friendship?

MRS. SOERBY. You don't imagine I haven't told him myself?

GREGERS. Oh?

MRS. SOERBY. Anything anyone could truthfully say about me I have already told him. It was the first thing I did when I gathered his intentions.

GREGERS. In that case you've been uncommonly frank.

MRS. SOERBY. I've always been frank. It's by far the best policy for a woman.

HJALMAR. What do you say to that, Gina?

GINA. Oh, we women are so different. We can't all be like Berta.

MRS. SOERBY. Well, Gina, I really believe I did the only sensible thing. Mr. Werle hasn't hidden anything from me, either. And perhaps that's what binds us so closely. Now he can talk to me as freely as a child. He's never been able to do that with anyone before. Fancy a strong and vigorous man like him having to spend all his youth and the best years of his life listening to sermons—very often occasioned by quite imaginary offences, from what I've heard.

GINA. Yes, that's true enough.

GREGERS. If you ladies are going to discuss that subject, I had better go.

MRS. SOERBY. Don't bother. I've had my say. I haven't lied to him or kept anything from him. I dare say you think I've done very well for myself. Well, perhaps I have. But I don't think I'm taking more than I shall be able to give him. I shall never fail him. I shall serve him and look after him better than anyone, now that he's growing helpless.

HJALMAR. He? Growing helpless?

GREGERS, *to* MRS. SOERBY. Look, I'd rather we didn't discuss that.

MRS. SOERBY. It's no use trying to hide it any longer, though I know he wants to. He's going blind.

HJALMAR *starts*. Going blind? That's strange. Is he going blind, too?

GINA. It happens to lots of people.

MRS. SOERBY. It's not hard to imagine what that must mean to a man like him. Well, I shall try to make my eyes serve for the two of us as best I can. But I mustn't stay any longer, I've so much to do just now. Oh, what I wanted to tell you, Ekdal, was that if there's anything Mr. Werle can ever do for you, just go and speak to Graaberg.

GREGERS. I hardly think Hjalmar Ekdal will want to accept that offer.

MRS. SOERBY. Oh? I haven't noticed in the past that he—

GINA. Yes, Berta. Hjalmar doesn't need to take anything from Mr. Werle any longer.

HJALMAR, *slowly and emphatically*. Will you present my compliments to your future husband and tell him that I intend at the earliest opportunity to visit Mr. Graaberg—

GREGERS. Hjalmar!

HJALMAR. I repeat, to visit Mr. Graaberg and demand from him an account of the sum I owe his employer. I shall repay this debt of honour—
Laughs.

—debt of honour! But enough of that. I shall repay it to the last penny, with five per cent interest.

GINA. But my dear Hjalmar, we haven't the money to do that.

HJALMAR. Will you please tell your fiancé that I am working indefatigably at my invention. Will you tell him that my spirit is sustained throughout this exhausting struggle by the desire to be rid of the embarrassing burden of this debt. That is why I have become an inventor. The entire profits shall be used to free me from the money of which your prospective husband has seen fit to disgorge himself.

MRS. SOERBY. What's been going on in this house?

HJALMAR. Never mind.

MRS. SOERBY. Well, good-bye. There was something else I wanted to talk to you about, Gina; but it'll have to wait till another time. Good-bye.

HJALMAR *and* GREGERS *bow silently*. GINA *accompanies* MRS. SOERBY *to the door.*

HJALMAR. Not beyond the threshold, Gina.

MRS. SOERBY *goes*. GINA *closes the door behind her.*

There, Gregers. Thank God I've managed to get that debt off my conscience.

GREGERS. Well, you will soon, anyway.

HJALMAR. I think I can claim I behaved correctly.

GREGERS. You behaved exactly as I always knew you would.

HJALMAR. A time comes when a man can no longer ignore the command of his ideals. As the family breadwinner I am continually tormented by this command. I tell you,

Gregers, it isn't easy for a man of small means to repay an old debt on which, as one might say, there has settled the dust of oblivion. But there's no other way. I must do what is right.

GREGERS *puts his hand on* HJALMAR's *shoulders.* My dear Hjalmar. Aren't you glad I came?

HJALMAR. Yes.

GREGERS. Aren't you glad to see yourself as you really are?

HJALMAR, *a little impatiently.* Of course I'm glad. But there's one thing which troubles my sense of justice. Well, but I don't know whether I should speak so bluntly about your father.

GREGERS. Say what you like. I don't mind.

HJALMAR. Well, then—it offends me to think that it is he, and not I, who is going to make a true marriage.

GREGERS. What are you saying!

HJALMAR. But it's true. Your father and Mrs. Soerby are entering upon a marriage founded on absolute trust, with complete frankness on both sides. They are keeping nothing from each other. They have confessed their sins, if I may so put it, and have forgiven each other.

GREGERS. Well, what of it?

HJALMAR. But that's the whole point. You just said yourself that it's only by overcoming all that that you can found a true marriage.

GREGERS. But that's quite different, Hjalmar. You surely don't compare yourself or her with these two—? Well, you know what I mean.

HJALMAR. I can't get away from the fact that there's something here which wounds and offends my sense of justice. Well, it looks as though there's no just power ruling this world.

GINA. Oh, Hjalmar, really! You mustn't speak like that!

GREGERS. Hm—let's not get on to that subject!

HJALMAR. But on the other hand I seem to see the finger of fate at work restoring the balance. He is going blind.

GINA. Oh, we don't know for sure about that.

HJALMAR. Can we doubt it? At least, we ought not to; for there lie justice and retribution. He has blinded a loyal and trusting friend—

GREGERS. I'm afraid he has blinded many.

HJALMAR. And now comes the inexorable, the unfathomable, and demands his own eyes.

GINA. Oh, how can you say such a horrible thing? You make me feel quite frightened.

HJALMAR. It is useful to face up to the darker aspects of existence now and then.

HEDVIG, *in her hat and coat, enters happy and breathless through the front door.*

GINA. Are you back already?

HEDVIG. Yes, I didn't want to walk any more. And a good thing too, for I met someone coming out of the front door.

HJALMAR. That Mrs. Soerby, I suppose.

HEDVIG. Yes.

HJALMAR, *walking up and down.* I hope you have seen her for the last time.

Silence. HEDVIG *looks timidly from one to the other as though to find out what is the matter.*

HEDVIG *goes nearer him; wooingly.* Father.

HJALMAR. Well, what is it, Hedvig?

HEDVIG. Mrs. Soerby brought something for me.

HJALMAR *stops.* For you?

HEDVIG. Yes. Something for tomorrow.

GINA. Berta always brings something for your birthday.

HJALMAR. What is it?

HEDVIG. No, you mustn't know yet. Mother's going to bring it to me in bed tomorrow morning.

HJALMAR. Oh, this conspiracy to keep me out of everything!

HEDVIG, *quickly.* No, of course you can see it. It's a big letter. *Takes the letter from her coat pocket.*

HJALMAR. A letter too?

HEDVIG. Only a letter. The present'll come later, I suppose. But fancy—a letter! I've never had a letter before. And there's "Miss" written on the outside!

Reads.

"Miss Hedvig Ekdal." That's me!

HJALMAR. Let me see that letter.

HEDVIG *holds it out to him.* Here—look!

HJALMAR. This is Mr. Werle's writing.

GINA. Are you sure, Hjalmar?

HJALMAR. Look for yourself.

GINA. How should I know?

HJALMAR. Hedvig, may I open this letter and read it?

HEDVIG. Yes, certainly, if you want to.

GINA. No, Hjalmar, not tonight. It's for tomorrow.

HEDVIG, *quietly.* Oh, do let him read it, please! It's sure to be something nice, and then Father'll be happy, and it'll be nice here again.

HJALMAR. I may open it, then?

HEDVIG. Yes, do, Father. It'll be fun to know what's in it.

HJALMAR. Right.

Opens the letter, takes out a sheet of paper, reads it and looks bewildered.

What on earth—?

GINA. What does it say?

HEDVIG. Oh yes, Father! Do tell us!

HJALMAR. Be quiet!

Reads it through again. Then, pale but controlled, he says.

It's a deed of gift, Hedvig.

HEDVIG. I say! What do I get?

HJALMAR. See for yourself.

HEDVIG *goes over to the lamp and reads the letter under it.*

HJALMAR *softly, clenching his fists.*

The eyes! The eyes! And this letter!

HEDVIG *looks up from her reading.* But I think Grandfather ought to have it.

HJALMAR *takes the letter from her.* Gina, can you make any sense of this?

GINA. You know I don't understand anything. Tell me what it's about.

HJALMAR. Mr. Werle writes to Hedvig that her old grandfather need no longer trouble to copy letters but that he can henceforth draw from the office the sum of one hundred crowns per month—

GINA. Really?

HEDVIG. A hundred crowns, Mother! That's what it says!

GINA. Well, that'll be nice for Grandfather.

HJALMAR. One hundred crowns, for as long as he needs it. That means, of course, for as long as he lives.

GINA. Well, at least he's provided for then, poor old man.

HJALMAR. But there's something else. You didn't read this part, Hedvig. Afterwards, this money is to be paid to you.

HEDVIG. To me? All of it?

HJALMAR. "You are assured of this sum for the rest of your life," he writes. Did you hear that, Gina?

GINA. Yes, I heard.

HEDVIG. Imagine all the money I'm going to have!

Shakes him.

Oh, Father, Father, aren't you happy—?

HJALMAR *avoids her.* Happy!

Walks about.

Oh, what vistas, what perspectives begin to unroll before my eyes! It's Hedvig! She's the one he remembers so generously!

GINA. Yes—well, it's Hedvig's birthday.

HEDVIG. But you shall have it all, Father! I want to give all the money to you and Mother!

HJALMAR. Yes, to Mother! There we have it!

GREGERS. Hjalmar, this is a trap which has been laid for you.

HJALMAR. You think this is another trap?

GREGERS. When he was here this morning, he said to me: "Hjalmar Ekdal is not the man you think he is."

HJALMAR. Not the man—!

GREGERS. "You'll see," he said.

HJALMAR. Meaning that I would let myself be fobbed off with money!

HEDVIG. Mother, what are they talking about?

GINA. Go in there and take your coat off.

HEDVIG *goes out through the kitchen door, almost in tears.*

GREGERS. Well, Hjalmar, now we shall see which of us is right. He or I.

HJALMAR *slowly tears the letter in two and puts the pieces on the table.* There is my reply.

GREGERS. I knew it would be.

HJALMAR *goes over to* GINA *who is standing by the stove and says in a low voice.* And now let's have the truth. If it was all over between you and him when you—began to grow fond of me, as you put it—why did he make it possible for us to get married?

GINA. I suppose he thought he could have a key.

HJALMAR. Was that all? Wasn't he afraid of a certain possibility?

GINA. I don't know what you mean.

HJALMAR. I want to know if—your child has the right to live beneath my roof.

GINA *draws herself up; her eyes flash.* You ask me that?

HJALMAR. Answer me! Is Hedvig mine or—? Well?

GINA *looks at him in cold defiance.* I don't know.

HJALMAR *trembles slightly.* You don't know!

GINA. How could I? You know yourself what I'm like.

HJALMAR, *quietly, turning away from her.* Then I have no further business in this house.

GREGERS. Consider, Hjalmar!

HJALMAR *puts on his overcoat.* There's nothing for a man like me to consider.

GREGERS. You're wrong. There's a great deal to consider. You three must stay together if you are to win the forgiveness that comes with self-sacrifice.

HJALMAR. I don't want to win it! Never, never! My hat!

Takes his hat.

My home has crashed in ruins about me!

Bursts into tears.

Gregers, I have no child!

HEDVIG, *who has opened the kitchen door.* What are you saying!

Runs over to him.

Daddy, daddy!

GINA. There, you see!

HJALMAR. Don't come near me, Hedvig! Go—go far away! I can't bear to look at you! Ah—those eyes! Good-bye!

Goes towards the door.

HEDVIG *clings tightly to him and screams.* No! No! Don't leave me!

GINA *cries.* Look at the child, Hjalmar! Look at the child!

HJALMAR. I won't! I can't! I must get away! Away from all this!

Tears himself free from HEDVIG *and goes out through the front door.*

HEDVIG, *with despair in her eyes.* He's leaving us, Mother! He's leaving us! He'll never come back again!

GINA. Don't cry, Hedvig. Daddy will come back.

HEDVIG *throws herself sobbing on the sofa.* No, no. He'll never come back to us again.

GREGERS. Will you believe that I meant it all for your good, Mrs. Ekdal?

GINA. Yes, I believe it. But God forgive you.

HEDVIG, *lying on the sofa.* Oh, I shall die, I shall die! What have I done to him? Mother, you must make him come back home!

GINA. Yes, yes, yes, all right. Calm yourself, and I'll go out and and look for him.

Puts on her overcoat.

Perhaps he's just gone down to Relling. But you mustn't lie there and cry. Promise me?

HEDVIG, *sobbing convulsively.* Yes, I'll stop. When Father comes back.

GREGERS, *to* GINA, *as she is about to go.* Wouldn't it be better to let him fight his bitter battle to the end?

GINA. Oh, that'll have to wait. Now we must think of the child.

Goes out through the front door.

HEDVIG *sits up and dries her tears.* I want to know what all this means. Why won't Father look at me any more?

GREGERS. You mustn't ask that till you're grown up.

HEDVIG *catches her breath.* But I can't go on being unhappy like this all the time till I'm grown up. I know what it is. I'm not really Daddy's child.

GREGERS, *uneasily.* How on earth could that be?

HEDVIG. Mummy might have found me. And perhaps Father's got to know about it. I've read of things like that.

GREGERS. Well, but even if it were true—

HEDVIG. Yes, I think he should love me just the same. Or even more. After all, we got the wild duck sent to us as a present, but I love it very much.

GREGERS, *changing the conversation.* Yes, that's true. Let's talk for a moment about the wild duck, Hedvig.

HEDVIG. The poor wild duck. He can't bear to look at her any longer, either. Do you know, he wants to wring her neck!

GREGERS. Oh, I'm sure he won't do that.

HEDVIG. No, but he said it. And I think it was such a horrid thing for Father to say. I say a prayer for the wild duck every evening. I pray that she may be delivered from death and from all evil.

GREGERS *looks at her.* Do you always say your prayers at night?

HEDVIG. Oh, yes.

GREGERS. Who taught you to do that?

HEDVIG. I taught myself. Once when Father was very ill, and had leeches on his neck. He said death was staring him in the face.

GREGERS. Yes?

HEDVIG. So I said a prayer for him after I'd gone to bed. And since then I've kept it up.

GREGERS. And now you pray for the wild duck, too?

HEDVIG. I thought I'd better include her, because she was so ill when she first came to us.

GREGERS. Do you say your prayers in the morning, too?

HEDVIG. Oh, no. Of course not.

GREGERS. Well, why not in the morning?

HEDVIG. In the morning it's light, and then there's nothing to be afraid of any more.

GREGERS. And your father wanted to wring the neck of the wild duck, which you love so much?

HEDVIG. No, he said he ought to, but he'd spare her for my sake. That was kind of him, wasn't it?

GREGERS, *a little closer.* Yes, but what if you now gave up the wild duck for his sake?

HEDVIG *rises.* The wild duck?

GREGERS. Yes. Suppose you sacrificed for him the most precious of your possessions—the thing you love most dearly?

HEDVIG. Do you think that would help?

GREGERS. Try it, Hedvig.

HEDVIG, *quietly, her eyes aglow.* Yes, I will try it.

GREGERS. Do you think you have the strength to do it?

HEDVIG. I'll ask Grandfather to shoot the wild duck for me.

GREGERS. Yes, do that. But not a word to your mother about this!

HEDVIG. Why not?

GREGERS. She doesn't understand us.

HEDVIG. The wild duck! I'll do it tomorrow morning.

GINA *comes in through the front door.*

HEDVIG *goes to meet her.*

Did you find him, Mother?

GINA. No. But I heard he'd called in to see Relling and they'd gone off together.

GREGERS. Are you sure?

GINA. Yes, the caretaker told me. Molvik went with them too, she said.

GREGERS. Now, when he needs to wrestle with his soul alone!

GINA *takes off her coat.* Well, men are difficult creatures. God knows where Relling's dragged him off to. I ran over to Mrs. Eriksen's, but they weren't there.

HEDVIG, *trying not to cry.* Oh, suppose he never comes back!

GREGERS. He'll come back. I shall tell him the news tomorrow, and then you'll see how quickly he will come. Don't worry, Hedvig. You can sleep in peace. Good night.

Goes out through the front door.

HEDVIG *throws her arms, sobbing, round* GINA's *neck.* Mummy, mummy!

GINA *pats her on the back and sighs.* Oh, yes, Relling was right. This is what happens when people go round preaching about the commands of the ideal.

ACT FIVE

HJALMAR EKDAL's *studio. A cold, grey morning light. Wet snow lies on the large panes of glass in the roof.* GINA, *wearing an apron, enters from the kitchen with a brush and duster and goes towards the parlour door. At the same moment,* HEDVIG *runs in from the passage.*

GINA *stops.* Well?

HEDVIG. Yes, Mother, I think he's down with Relling—

GINA. There you are!

HEDVIG. The caretaker said Relling had two people with him when he came back last night.

GINA. I thought as much.

HEDVIG. But that's no good, if he won't come up and see us.

GINA. You leave it to me. I'll go down and have a word with him.

OLD EKDAL, *in a dressing gown and slippers and with a lighted pipe, appears in the doorway of his room.*

EKDAL. Hjalmar, I! Isn't Hjalmar at home?

GINA. No, he seems to have gone out.

EKDAL. What, already? And in this blizzard? Oh, well. Let him. I can go for a walk by myself.

He pushes aside the door of the loft. HEDVIG *helps him. He goes in, and she closes the door behind him.*

HEDVIG, *softly.* Poor Grandfather! What will he say when he hears Father's leaving us?

GINA. Don't be silly, Grandfather mustn't be told about that. Thank God he wasn't here yesterday when all the hullaballoo was going on.

HEDVIG. Yes, but—

GREGERS *enters through the front door.*

GREGERS. Well? Have you found where he is?

GINA. They say he's downstairs with Relling.

GREGERS. With Relling! Has he really been out with those people?

GINA. So it seems.

GREGERS. But he needed so much to be alone, and to collect his thoughts—

GINA. Yes, you may well say that.

RELLING *enters from the passage.*

HEDVIG *goes towards him.* Is Father with you?

GINA, *simultaneously.* Is he there?

RELLING. He certainly is.

HEDVIG. And you didn't tell us!

RELLING. Yes, I'm a beast. But I had to put the other beast to bed first—I refer of course to our daemonic friend—and then I fell asleep—

GINA. What has Hjalmar got to say today?

RELLING. Nothing.

HEDVIG. Doesn't he say anything?

RELLING. Not a damn thing.

GREGERS. No, no. I can understand that so well.

GINA. But what's he doing, then?

RELLING. He's on the sofa, snoring.

GINA. Is he? Yes, Hjalmar's a terrible snorer.

HEDVIG. You mean he's asleep?

RELLING. It certainly sounds like it.

GREGERS. It's quite understandable. After the spiritual conflict that's been rending him—

GINA. And he's not used to wandering around outside at night.

HEDVIG. Perhaps it's a good thing he's getting some sleep, Mother.

GINA. Yes, I was just thinking that. We'd better not wake him up too soon. Thanks, Relling. I must just clean the place up a bit, and then I'll— Come and give me a hand, Hedvig.

GINA *and* HEDVIG *go into the parlour.*

GREGERS *turns to* RELLING. Can you explain this spiritual turmoil in Hjalmar Ekdal?

RELLING. Can't say I've ever noticed any spiritual turmoil in him.

GREGERS. What! At such a crisis, when his whole life has been given a new moral foundation—! How do you suppose a man of Hjalmar's personality—?

RELLING. Personality—*him?* If he ever had any tendency to the kind of abnormalities you call personality, they were nipped out of him, root and branch, before his voice broke. You take my word for it.

GREGERS. That's surprising, considering the love and care with which he was brought up.

RELLING. By those two twisted, hysterical maiden aunts, you mean?

GREGERS. At least they were idealists—but I suppose you'll laugh at me again for saying that.

RELLING. No, I'm not in the mood for that. I know all about it. I've had to endure vomits of rhetoric about his "two spiritual mothers." But I don't think he's got much to be grateful to them for. Hjalmar's tragedy is that all his life he's been regarded by everyone around him as a genius—

GREGERS. Well, isn't he? Deep down inside?

RELLING. I've never noticed any evidence of it. Oh, his father thought so, but—well, *he's* been a bloody fool all his life.

GREGERS. No, he has kept the innocence of a child all his life. That's something you can't understand.

RELLING. All right, have it your way. But when dear little

Hjalmar somehow got to university, he was at once hailed as the great white hope there too. Well, he was handsome of course—that helps—you know, peaches and cream, the shopgirl's dream—and with his romantic temperament and throbbing voice and talent for declaiming other people's poetry and ideas—

GREGERS, *indignantly.* Are you talking about Hjalmar Ekdal?

RELLING. Yes. With your permission, that's what this idol you grovel to really looks like when you take him apart.

GREGERS. Well, I don't think I'm completely blind.

RELLING. You're not far off. You're a sick man too, you know.

GREGERS. Yes, you're right there.

RELLING. Oh, yes. Yours is a complicated case. To begin with, you've this tiresome rash of righteousness; and what's worse, you live in a perpetual delirium of hero-worship. You've always got to have something outside yourself that you can idolise.

GREGERS. That's true. I have to seek it outside myself.

RELLING. It's pathetic the way you make a fool of yourself over these supermen you imagine you see all around you. This is just another of those workmen's cottages where you started hawking your ideals. We're all insolvent here.

GREGERS. If that's your opinion of Hjalmar Ekdal, how can you spend so much time with him?

RELLING. I'm meant to be a doctor of sorts, God forgive me. I've got to do something for these wretched cripples I share a roof with.

GREGERS. I see. So Hjalmar Ekdal is sick too?

RELLING. Well, who isn't?

GREGERS. And what medicine are you giving him?

RELLING. My usual one. I feed the life-lie in him.

GREGERS. Life-*lie*, did you say?

RELLING. Yes, that's right. The universal stimulant.

GREGERS. And what is the life-lie with which Hjalmar Ekdal is infected, if I may ask?

RELLING. You may not. I don't betray professional secrets to quacks. I wouldn't put it past you to make an even worse mess of him. But my remedy's infallible. I've used it on Molvik for years. I've made him daemonic. That's the serum I've injected into his skull.

GREGERS. Isn't he daemonic, then?

RELLING. What the hell does it mean, daemonic? It's just a bit of claptrap I thought up to keep him alive. If I hadn't done it the poor swine would have succumbed to self-contempt and despair years ago. And what about the old lieutenant? Well, he found the cure himself.

GREGERS. Lieutenant Ekdal? How do you mean?

RELLING. What about that? The great bear hunter going into that musty old loft to chase rabbits? There isn't a happier sportsman in the world than that old man when they let him potter around in there among all that junk. Those four or five withered Christmas trees smell the same to him as the great forests of Hoydal; the chickens are the wild game in the pine tops; and the rabbits that flop across the floor are bears to challenge the strength and skill of the mighty hunter.

GREGERS. Poor Lieutenant Ekdal! Yes, he's had to abandon his youthful ideals.

RELLING. While I remember it, Mr. Werle Junior, forget that foreign word "ideals." Why not use that good old Norwegian word: "lies"?

GREGERS. Do you suggest the two are related?

RELLING. About as closely as typhus and putrid fever.

GREGERS. Dr. Relling, I will not give up until I have rescued Hjalmar Ekdal from your clutches.

RELLING. So much the worse for him. Deprive the average human being of his life-lie, and you rob him of his happiness.

To HEDVIG, *as she enters from the parlour.*

Well, little wild-duck-mother, I'm off downstairs to see if your father's still pondering his great invention on my sofa. *Goes out through front door.*

GREGERS *goes closer to* HEDVIG. I can see it, Hedvig. You haven't done it.

HEDVIG. What? Oh, that thing about the wild duck. No.

GREGERS. Your strength of purpose failed you when the moment for action came, I suppose.

HEDVIG. No, it wasn't that. It was just that when I woke this morning and remembered what we'd been talking about, I thought it all seemed so strange.

GREGERS. Strange?

HEDVIG. I don't know. Yesterday evening, when you first mentioned it, I thought there was something so beautiful in the idea; but when I'd slept on it and thought about it again, it didn't seem so good.

GREGERS. Oh, no. Of course you can't have grown up in this house without some rot setting in.

HEDVIG. I don't care about that. If only Father would come back, I'd—

GREGERS. Oh, if only your eyes could be opened to what really matters in life! If only you had the courage to make your sacrifice truly and joyfully, you'd see—he'd come back to you! But I still believe in you, Hedvig. I believe in you.

He goes out through the front door.

HEDVIG *walks around for a little; then she is about to go into the kitchen when there is a knock on the door of the loft.* HEDVIG *goes over and opens it slightly.* OLD EKDAL *comes out. She closes the door again.*

EKDAL. Hm! It's not much fun having to take my exercise alone.

HEDVIG. Didn't you feel like hunting today, Grandfather?

EKDAL. It's bad weather for hunting today. Dark. You can hardly see your hand in front of your face.

HEDVIG. Don't you ever feel you'd like to shoot something else besides rabbits?

EKDAL. What's wrong with rabbits? Aren't they good enough?

HEDVIG. Yes, but what about—well, the wild duck?

EKDAL *laughs.* Oh, so you're afraid I'll shoot your wild duck, are you? Don't you worry, my child. I'd never do that.

HEDVIG. No, of course, you couldn't. I've heard it's very difficult to shoot wild ducks.

EKDAL. Couldn't? What do you mean? Of course I could.

HEDVIG. How would you go about it, Grandfather? I don't mean with my wild duck, but with other ones?

EKDAL. I'd shoot them under the breast, Hedvig. That's the safest place. And you've got to shoot against the feathers, mind, not with them.

HEDVIG. Do they die then, Grandfather?

EKDAL. You bet they die, if you shoot them properly. Well, I must go in and—hm—clean myself up. You understand—hm?

He goes into his room. HEDVIG *waits a few moments, glances towards the door of the parlour, goes over to the bookcase, reaches up on tiptoe, takes down the double-barrelled pistol from the shelf and looks at it.* GINA *enters from the parlour with her duster and brush.* HEDVIG *quickly puts down the pistol, unnoticed.*

GINA. Don't stand there messing about with your father's things, Hedvig.

HEDVIG *leaves the bookcase.* I only wanted to tidy up a little.

GINA. Go into the kitchen and see if the coffee's still hot. I'll take the tray when I go down.

HEDVIG goes out. GINA begins to sweep and clean the studio. After a few moments, the front door is cautiously opened and HJALMAR looks in. He is wearing his overcoat but is hatless and unwashed. His hair is tousled and his eyes are dull and tired.

GINA *stands with the brush in her hand and looks at him.* Oh. Hullo, Hjalmar. You've come.

HJALMAR *walks in and answers in a flat voice.* I've come—but only to go at once.

GINA. Yes, yes, of course. But, my goodness, look at you!

HJALMAR. At me?

GINA. And your nice winter coat! Well, that's done for.

HEDVIG, *in the kitchen doorway.* Mother, hadn't I better—?

Sees HJALMAR, *gives a cry of joy and runs towards him.*

Oh, Father, Father!

HJALMAR *turns away with a gesture of rejection.* Get away, get away, get away!

To GINA.

Get her away from me!

GINA, *softly.* Go into the parlour, Hedvig.

HEDVIG *goes silently out.*

HJALMAR *feverishly pulls out the drawer of the table.* I must take my books with me. Where are my books?

GINA. What books?

HJALMAR. My scientific books, of course. The technical magazines I need for my invention.

GINA *looks in the bookcase.* Are these the ones, without any covers?

HJALMAR. Of course they are.

GINA *puts a heap of magazines on the table.* Shall I get Hedvig to cut the pages for you?

HJALMAR. I don't want them cut.

Short silence.

GINA. So you're really leaving us, Hjalmar?

HJALMAR, *rummaging among the books.* Have I any choice?

GINA. No, no.

HJALMAR, *vehemently.* I can't go on being pierced to the heart every hour of every day!

GINA. May God forgive you for thinking so vilely of me!

HJALMAR. Give me proof—!

GINA. I think you're the one who needs to do the proving.

HJALMAR. With your past! There are certain things a man has a right to demand—one might be tempted to call them demands of the ideal—

GINA. What about Grandfather? What's going to become of him, poor old man?

HJALMAR. I know my duty. That helpless old man leaves with me. I shall go into town and make arrangements. Hm—

Unwillingly.

Has anyone seen my hat on the stairs?

GINA. No. Have you lost your hat?

HJALMAR. I had it on when I came back last night. Naturally. There can be no doubt about that. But I haven't been able to find it today.

GINA. For mercy's sake, where on earth did you get to with those two scallywags?

HJALMAR. Don't bother me with trivialities. Do you suppose I'm in a mood to recall details?

GINA. Well, I only hope you haven't caught cold, Hjalmar.

Goes out into the kitchen.

HJALMAR *mutters to himself, half audibly and furiously as he empties the drawer beneath the table.* You're a scoundrel, Relling! A cad, that's what you are! Oh, you vile seducer! I wish I could hire someone to stick a knife in your back!

He puts some old letters on one side, finds the letter he tore up yesterday, picks it up and looks at the pieces, then puts it quickly down again as GINA *returns.*

GINA *puts a tray with coffee, etc., on the table.* I've brought you a cup of something warm, in case you feel inclined. And some bread and butter and a bit of cold fish.

HJALMAR *glances at the tray.* Cold fish? Under this roof? Never! I've had no solid food for nearly twenty-four hours, but no matter. My notes! The first chapter of my memoirs! Where's my diary? Where are all my important papers?

Opens the parlour door, but shrinks back.

There she is again!

GINA. But for heaven's sake, the child's got to be somewhere.

HJALMAR. Come out.

He moves aside to make way for her. HEDVIG *enters, frightened.*

HJALMAR, *with his hand on the door handle, says to* GINA. During my last minutes in what *was* my home, I wish to be spared the presence of outsiders.

Goes out into the parlour.

HEDVIG *runs to her mother and asks softly, trembling.* Does he mean me?

GINA. Stay in the kitchen, Hedvig. No, you'd better go to your room.

To HJALMAR, *as she goes in to him.*

Stop rummaging in those drawers. I know where everything is.

HEDVIG *stands motionless for a moment, anguished and bewildered, biting her lips to keep back her tears. Then she clenches her fists convulsively and says quietly.* The wild duck!

She steals over and takes the pistol from the shelf, opens the loft door a few inches, creeps in and pulls it shut behind her. In the parlour offstage, HJALMAR *and* GINA *begin to argue.*

HJALMAR *comes out with some notebooks and old loose papers, which he puts down on the table.* Oh, that old bag's no use. There are hundreds of things I've got to lug away.

GINA *comes after him with the bag.* Well, just take a shirt and a pair of pants with you. You can come back for the rest later.

HJALMAR. Phew! It's so exhausting, all this packing!

Tears off his overcoat and throws it on the sofa.

GINA. And now your coffee's getting cold, too.

HJALMAR. Hm.

Automatically takes a mouthful; then another.

GINA, *dusting the backs of the chairs.* The big difficulty'll be to find another big loft like this for the rabbits.

HJALMAR. What! Do you expect me to drag all those rabbits along too?

GINA. Well, you know Grandfather can't live without his rabbits.

HJALMAR. Well, he'll have to learn. I'm giving up more important things than rabbits.

GINA, *dusting the bookshelves.* Shall I pack the flute?

HJALMAR. No. No flute for me. Give me the pistol, though.

GINA. Are you going to take the pistol?

HJALMAR. Yes. My loaded pistol.

GINA *looks for it.* It's gone. He must have taken it with him.

HJALMAR. Is he in the loft?

GINA. Yes, of course he's in the loft.

HJALMAR. Hm. The lonely old man!

Takes a piece of bread and butter, eats it and empties his cup.

GINA. If only we hadn't let that room, you could have moved in there.

HJALMAR. What! Live under the same roof as—? Never! Never!

GINA. Couldn't you manage in the parlour for a day or two? You'd be alone there.

HJALMAR. Within these walls? Never!

GINA. Well, how about downstairs with Relling and Molvik?

HJALMAR. Don't mention their names to me! The mere thought of them makes me lose my appetite. No, I must go out into the wind and snow, wandering from door to door seeking shelter for myself and my old father.

GINA. But you've no hat, Hjalmar. You've lost your hat.

HJALMAR. Scum! Vice-ridden scum, that's what they are! We must find a hat.

Takes another piece of bread and butter.

Something must be done. I don't intend to die of exposure.

GINA. What are you looking for?

HJALMAR. Butter.

GINA. Coming up right away.

Goes out into the kitchen.

HJALMAR *shouts after her.* Oh, it doesn't matter. I can eat dry bread.

GINA *comes back with a butter-dish.* Here, this is meant to be fresh.

She pours him another cup of coffee. He sits on the sofa, spreads more butter on his bread, and eats and drinks for a few moments in silence.

HJALMAR. Would I really not be bothered by anyone if I stayed a couple of days in that room? Anyone at all?

GINA. No, of course not. Why don't you?

HJALMAR. I can't see any hope of getting all Father's things moved out all at once.

GINA. And don't forget you've got to break the news to him about your not wanting to live with us any longer.

HJALMAR *pushes away his coffee cup.* Yes, there's that too. I've got to dig up all those complications again. I must think things over. I must give myself breathing-space. I can't cope with so many different burdens in one day.

GINA. No, of course not. Especially with the weather what it is.

HJALMAR *touches* WERLE's *letter.* I see that letter's still lying around.

GINA. Yes, I haven't touched it.

HJALMAR. Of course, it's nothing to do with me—

GINA. Well, I certainly don't want to make anything out of it.

HJALMAR. Still, there's no point in letting it get lost. In the confusion of my moving, it might easily—

GINA. I'll see it doesn't.

HJALMAR. Of course, this deed of gift really belongs to Father. It's up to him to decide whether it's to be used or not.

GINA *sighs.* Yes, poor old Father!

HJALMAR. Perhaps for safety's sake—where can I find some glue?

GINA *goes over to the bookcase.* The pot's here.

HJALMAR. And a brush.

GINA. The brush is here, too.

Brings them to him.

HJALMAR *takes a pair of scissors.* Just a strip of paper along the back—

Cuts and glues.

Far be it from me to deprive other people of what belongs to them. Least of all a destitute old man. Or—any other person. There, now! Let that stand for a few minutes. And when it's dry, take it away. I never want to see the thing again. Never!

GREGERS WERLE *enters from the passage.*

GREGERS, *a little surprised.* Oh! Are you here, Hjalmar?

HJALMAR *gets up quickly.* I was overcome by fatigue.

GREGERS. I see you've had breakfast, however.

HJALMAR. The body makes its demands too, you know.

GREGERS. Well, what have you decided?

HJALMAR. For a man like me, there is no choice. I'm just getting my most important belongings together. But that takes time, you know.

GINA, *a little impatiently.* Well, shall I make the room ready or shall I pack your bag?

HJALMAR *gives an annoyed glance at* GREGERS. Pack. *And* make it ready.

GINA *takes the bag.* Well, well. I'll put in a shirt and p— and the other thing.

Goes into the parlour and closes the door behind her.

GREGERS, *after a short silence.* I'd never envisaged it ending like this. Must you really leave your home?

HJALMAR *wanders around restlessly.* Well, what do you want me to do? I wasn't cut out to suffer, Gregers. I must have peace and calm and comfort around me.

GREGERS. Well, why not? Try! It seems to me that now you

have firm ground to build on. Start afresh! And remember, you have your invention to live for too.

HJALMAR. Oh, don't talk about the invention. That may be further off than you think.

GREGERS. Oh?

HJALMAR. Well, dammit, what *is* there for me to invent? Other people have invented almost everything already. It's becoming more and more difficult every day—

GREGERS. But you've put so much work into it.

HJALMAR. It was that drunkard Relling who started me off on it.

GREGERS. Relling?

HJALMAR. Yes. It was he who first made me conscious that I had the talent to make some invention that would revolutionise photography.

GREGERS. I see. So it was Relling.

HJALMAR. Oh, it's made me so happy thinking about it! Not so much for the sake of the invention itself, but because Hedvig believed in it—believed in it as passionately and trustingly as only a child can believe in a thing. What I mean to say is—I was fool enough to delude myself into thinking she believed in it.

GREGERS. Do you seriously believe that Hedvig hasn't been sincere?

HJALMAR. I can believe anything now. Hedvig's the one who stands in my way. Her shadow is going to shut the sunlight out of my life.

GREGERS. Hedvig? Are you talking about Hedvig?

HJALMAR. I loved that child beyond words. I felt so incredibly happy every time I came back to this humble home and she ran to greet me with those sweet eyes peering at me. Oh, what a credulous fool I was! I loved her so, I loved her so. And I dreamed, I deluded myself into believing that she loved me too.

GREGERS. You call that a delusion?

HJALMAR. How can I know? I can't get anything out of Gina—and anyway, she's so totally insensitive to the idealistic aspect of all these complicated— But to you, Gregers, I feel impelled to open my heart. There's this dreadful doubt in my mind that perhaps Hedvig has never really and truly loved me.

GREGERS. Perhaps you may be given proof that she does.

Listens.

What was that? I think I can hear the wild duck crying.

HJALMAR. Yes, that's her quacking. Father's there in the loft.

GREGERS. Is he?

His eyes shine with joy.

I tell you, you may perhaps be given proof that your poor, misjudged Hedvig does love you.

HJALMAR. Oh, what proof can she give me? I couldn't believe anything from those lips.

GREGERS. Hedvig is incapable of deceit.

HJALMAR. Oh, Gregers, that's just what I can't be sure of. Who knows what Gina and that Mrs. Soerby may not have said when they were gossiping up here? And that child keeps her ears open. That deed of gift may not have come as such a surprise to her as she made out. I thought I noticed something odd in her manner.

GREGERS. What on earth has come over you?

HJALMAR. I've had my eyes opened. Just you wait—you'll see. That deed of gift is only the beginning. Mrs. Soerby's always had a soft spot for Hedvig, and now she's in a position to do anything she likes for the child. They can take her from me any moment they want.

GREGERS. Hedvig will never leave you.

HJALMAR. I wouldn't be too sure of that. If they stand there beckoning to her with their hands full of—and I, who loved her so much, so much! I couldn't imagine any greater happiness than to take her gently by the hand and lead her as a man leads a child who is afraid of the dark through a

large, empty room. I can see it now so clearly—the poor
photographer in his attic has never really meant very much
to her. She was just cunning enough to keep on good terms
with him until the time was ripe.

GREGERS. Oh, Hjalmar, you don't believe that.

HJALMAR. The tragedy is that I don't know what to believe—
and that I never will know. Oh, you're too much of an idealist, my dear Gregers. If they came to her with their hands
full of gold and cried to the child: "Leave him! We can
offer you life!"—

GREGERS, *swiftly.* Yes? What do you think she would reply?

HJALMAR. If I were to ask her: "Hedvig, will you sacrifice your
life for me?"—

He laughs scornfully.

Oh, yes! You'd hear what answer she'd give me!

A pistol shot is heard from the loft.

GREGERS *cries joyfully.* Hjalmar!

HJALMAR, *enviously.* Oh, now he's started hunting.

GINA *enters, worried.* Oh, Hjalmar, Grandfather's banging
away in there on his own.

HJALMAR. I'll go and have a look.

GREGERS, *alive, excited.* Wait! Do you know what that was?

HJALMAR. Of course I do.

GREGERS. No, you don't. But I know. It was the proof you
wanted.

HJALMAR. What proof?

GREGERS. A child's sacrifice. She has got your father to shoot
the wild duck.

HJALMAR. Shoot the wild duck?

GINA. What an idea!

HJALMAR. But why?

GREGERS. She wanted to sacrifice for you the most precious of
her possessions, because she thought that then you would
have to love her again.

HJALMAR, *gently, emotionally.* Oh, child, child!

GINA. The things she gets up to!

GREGERS. She only wanted you to love her again, Hjalmar. She couldn't live without it.

GINA, *almost in tears.* There, Hjalmar, you see.

HJALMAR. Where is she, Gina?

GINA *sniffs.* Sitting outside in the kitchen, I suppose, poor child.

HJALMAR *walks across and flings open the kitchen door.* Hedvig, come here. Come and talk to me.

Looks round.

No, she isn't here.

GINA. She must be in her room, then.

HJALMAR, *outside.* No, she isn't there, either.

Comes back.

She must have gone out.

GINA. Well, you didn't want to have her in the house.

HJALMAR. Oh, I wish she'd come home again soon, so that I can tell her! Now everything will be all right, Gregers. Now I think we can start life afresh.

GREGERS, *quietly.* I knew it. Through the child will come resurrection.

OLD EKDAL *appears in the doorway of his room. He is in full uniform, and is busy buckling on his sword.*

HJALMAR, *amazed.* Father! Have you been in there?

GINA. Have you been shooting in your room?

EKDAL, *indignantly, comes closer.* So you go hunting alone now, do you, Hjalmar?

HJALMAR, *confused.* Then it wasn't you who fired that shot in the loft?

EKDAL. Wasn't me? Hm!

GREGERS *cries to* HJALMAR. Hjalmar! She has shot the wild duck herself!

HJALMAR. What's going on round here?

Runs over to the door of the loft, pulls it open, looks in and cries.

Hedvig!

GINA *runs over to the door.* Oh, God! What is it?

HJALMAR *goes inside.* She's lying on the floor.

GREGERS. Lying on the floor? Hedvig?

Joins HJALMAR *inside.*

GINA, *simultaneously.* Hedvig!

Goes into the loft.

Oh, no, no, no!

EKDAL *laughs.* Now she's started hunting too!

HJALMAR, GINA *and* GREGERS *drag* HEDVIG *into the studio. Her right hand is hanging down with the pistol tightly clasped between her fingers.*

HJALMAR, *distraught.* The pistol's gone off! She's shot herself! Call for help! Help!

GINA *runs out into the passage and calls down.* Relling! Relling! Dr. Relling! Come upstairs! As quick as you can!

HJALMAR *and* GREGERS *lay* HEDVIG *on the sofa.*

EKDAL, *quietly.* The forest has taken its revenge.

HJALMAR, *on his knees beside her.* She's coming round now! She'll be all right!

GINA *comes back.* Where's the wound? I can't see anything—

RELLING *hurries in.* MOLVIK *follows, with no waistcoat or tie, and with his coat hanging open.*

RELLING. What's happened?

GINA. They say Hedvig's shot herself.

HJALMAR. Come here and help us.

RELLING. Shot herself!

Pushes the table aside and begins to examine her.

HJALMAR, *lying on the floor, gazes up at him in anguish.* It can't be dangerous? Can it, Relling? She's hardly bleeding at all. It can't be dangerous, can it?

RELLING. How did it happen?

HJALMAR. Oh, how do I know?

GINA. She was going to shoot the wild duck.

RELLING. The wild duck?

HJALMAR. The pistol must have gone off.

RELLING. Hm. I see.

EKDAL. The forest has taken its revenge. But I'm not afraid of it. *Goes into the loft and closes the door behind him.*

HJALMAR. Well, Relling, why don't you say something?

RELLING. The bullet has entered her breast.

HJALMAR. But she'll be all right?

RELLING. Surely you can see that Hedvig is dead.

GINA *bursts into tears.* Oh, my child, my child!

GREGERS, *hoarsely.* The deep blue sea—!

HJALMAR *jumps up.* Yes, yes, she must live! Oh, God bless you, Relling, only for a moment! Only long enough for me to tell her how much I loved her—always—always!

RELLING. The bullet entered her heart. Internal haemorrhage. She died instantaneously.

HJALMAR. And I drove her from me like an animal! And she crept into the loft in terror, and died there—because she loved me!

Sobs.

I can never atone for this—never tell her—!

Clasps his hands and cries upwards.

Oh—You up there—if You exist! Why have You done this to me?

GINA. Hush, hush, don't carry on like that. We had no right to keep her—I suppose—

MOLVIK. The child is not dead, but sleepeth.

RELLING. Rubbish!

HJALMAR *becomes calm, goes across to the sofa and looks down at* HEDVIG, *with folded hands.* How stiff and still she lies!

RELLING *tries to free the pistol from her fingers.* She's holding on to it so tightly. So tightly.

GINA. No, no, Relling, don't break her fingers. Let the pistol stay there.

HJALMAR. Let her keep it.

GINA. Yes, let her. But the child mustn't lie here like a show. We'll take her into her own room. Help me, Hjalmar.

HJALMAR *and* GINA *pick* HEDVIG *up.*

HJALMAR, *as they carry her out.* Oh, Gina, Gina! How shall we live after this?

GINA. We must help each other. Now she belongs to both of us, you know.

MOLVIK *stretches out his arms and mumbles.* Praised be the Lord! To dust thou shalt return! To dust thou shalt return!

RELLING *whispers.* Shut up, man. You're drunk.

HJALMAR *and* GINA *carry the body out through the kitchen door.* RELLING *shuts it behind them.* MOLVIK *slinks out into the passage.*

RELLING *goes over to* GREGERS *and says.* No one's ever going to make me believe that this was an accident.

GREGERS, *who has stood overcome by horror, shaking convulsively.* No one will ever know how this dreadful thing happened.

RELLING. The powder had burned her dress. She must have pressed the pistol against her breast before she fired.

GREGERS. Hedvig has not died in vain. Did you see how grief set free all that is most noble in him?

RELLING. Most men are noble when they stand by a death-bed. But how long do you think this nobility will last?

GREGERS. For as long as he lives. And it will grow, and grow.

RELLING. In nine months, little Hedvig will be nothing more to him than a theme for a recitation.

GREGERS. You dare to say that about Hjalmar Ekdal!

RELLING. Let's talk about it again when the first grasses have withered on her grave. Then you'll hear him gulping about "the child untimely ripped from her father's bosom." You'll see him stewing in emotion and self-admiration and self-pity. Just you wait.

GREGERS. If you are right and I am wrong, life is not worth living.

RELLING. Oh, life would be all right if we didn't have to put up with these damned creditors who keep pestering us with the demands of their ideals.

GREGERS *stares ahead of him.* In that case, I am glad that my destiny is what it is.

RELLING. And what, if I may ask, is your destiny?

GREGERS, *as he goes towards the door.* To be the thirteenth at table.

RELLING *laughs and spits.*

Hedda Gabler

INTRODUCTION

HEDDA GABLER occupies a curious, almost anachronistic position in the Ibsen cycle. He wrote it in 1890, between *The Lady from the Sea* and *The Master Builder*, but if one had to date it from internal evidence one would be tempted to place it ten years earlier, as a companion piece to *A Doll's House, Ghosts* and *An Enemy of the People*. Like them, it is written very simply and directly; we feel, as in those plays, that he is working within an illuminated circle and not, as in the plays of his final period from *The Lady from the Sea* onwards, that he is exploring the darkness outside that circle. At first sight, again, it appears to differ from these final plays in not being an exercise in self-analysis. This, however, is an illusion, for if we examine HEDDA GABLER closely we find that it contains one of the most revealing self-portraits he ever painted. The play might, indeed, be subtitled *Portrait of the Dramatist as a Young Woman*.

The circumstances under which he wrote HEDDA GABLER were as follows. In the summer of 1889, while holidaying at Gossensass in the Tyrol, Ibsen, then aged sixty-one, had become violently infatuated with an eighteen-year-old Viennese girl named Emilie Bardach. After his return to Munich in September, they wrote to each other continuously for four months; then Ibsen broke off the correspondence, and apart from two brief letters towards the end of the year and a third seven years later in acknowledgment of a telegram of congratulations, he did not contact her again. Two years later he was to use this relationship of mutual infatuation as the basis for *The*

Master Builder, but the change it wrought on Ibsen was immediate. For years he had deliberately suppressed his own emotional life, an undersized and ugly man resigned to a loveless marriage; but his encounter with Emilie had awoken him to the realisation that, as Mr. Graham Greene has recently remarked, fame is a powerful aphrodisiac, and he now entered on a series of romantic relationships with women thirty to forty years his junior. (Indeed, the second of these, with the artist Helene Raff, began while he was still corresponding with Emilie.)

It is unlikely, however, that any of these relationships ever resulted in a physical affair, and this meant that, while immensely enriching his work, they also introduced into it a strong undertone of pessimism. In 1887, in a speech in Stockholm, he had startled his audience by describing himself as an "optimist," and *The Lady from the Sea,* written in 1888, had reflected this optimism. "After so many tragedies," Edmund Gosse had written on its appearance, "this is a comedy . . . the tone is quite unusually sunny, and without a tinge of pessimism. It is in some respects the reverse of *Rosmersholm,* the bitterness of restrained and balked individuality, which ends in death, being contrasted with the sweetness of emancipated and gratified individuality, which leads to health and peace." But none of his five subsequent plays could by any possible stretch of the imagination be described as comedies. The theme of HEDDA GABLER, *The Master Builder, Little Eyolf, John Gabriel Borkman,* and *When We Dead Awaken* is, like that of *Rosmersholm,* "restrained and balked individuality," and I do not think there can be much doubt that this stems from the realisation that for various reasons (fear of scandal, sense of duty towards his wife, consciousness of old age, perhaps the consciousness or fear of physical impotence), he, who had suppressed his emotional life for so long, now had the opportunities to fulfil it but was unable to take advantage of them. As a result of his meeting with Emilie Bardach a new glory, but also a new darkness, entered into his work.

He began to plan a new play immediately on his return from Gossensass. Only a week after arriving in Munich, on

October 7, 1889, he wrote to Emilie: "A new poem begins to dawn in me. I want to work on it this winter, transmuting into it the glowing inspiration of the summer. But the end may be disappointment. I feel it. It is my way." A week later, on October 15, he wrote to her: "My imagination is ragingly at work, but always straying to where in working hours it should not. I cannot keep down the memories of this summer, nor do I want to. The things we have lived through I live again and again—and still again. To make of them a poem is for the time being impossible. For the time being? Shall I ever succeed in the future? And do I really wish that I could and would so succeed? For the moment, at any rate, I cannot." However, on November 19 he wrote more cheerfully: "I am greatly occupied with the preparations for my new work. Sit tight at my desk the whole day. Go out only towards evening. I dream and remember and write."

Unfortunately, we do not know whether the play he was working on at this time was in fact HEDDA GABLER. Ibsen left eight sets of rough notes dating from around this period; most of them obviously refer to HEDDA GABLER, but some seem to point towards *The Master Builder* and others towards a third play which he never ultimately wrote, and since these notes are undated we cannot be sure to which of the three projects he was referring in his letters to Emilie. Some scholars think he did not begin to plan HEDDA until April 1890; others believe he had already conceived it as early as February 1889. At any rate, by the spring of 1890 Ibsen's plans for HEDDA were sufficiently advanced for him to express the hope that he would have his first draft ready by midsummer, so that he would be able to work on it during his summer holiday in (again) Gossensass. But on June 29, 1890, he wrote to Carl Snoilsky, the Swedish poet (generally assumed to be the original of Rosmer), that the play had not worked out and that he was staying in Munich until he could get the first draft finished. Perhaps he feared Gossensass might awake disturbing memories.

As things turned out, he did not complete the first draft of even Act 1 until August 10. On August 13 he began Act 2, but early in September he scrapped this, and on September 6 he began a new draft of this act. Things now went better, for by October 7 he had completed the draft not only of Act 2 but also of Acts 3 and 4. The play was at this stage entitled simply HEDDA, and the draft in which it exists bears all the appearance of having been made as a fair copy to send to the printer. But he was not satisfied, and rewrote the play thoroughly, introducing into it for the first time many of its most striking and famous features. This revisionary work occupied him until November 18, and HEDDA GABLER, as he now entitled it, to underline the fact that she was her father's daughter rather than her husband's wife, was published by Gyldendals of Copenhagen on December 16, 1890, only just in time for the Christmas sales—always an important consideration with Ibsen, who depended on book sales in Scandinavia for a large proportion of his income.*

As with every play he wrote after *A Doll's House* in 1879, excepting only the comparatively light and simple *Enemy of the People,* the public reaction was one of utter bewilderment. Halvdan Koht, in his introduction (1934) to the play in the centenary edition of Ibsen's works, has described how Norway received it. "Its only message seemed to be despair. No meaning nor purpose, simply a suicide ending an absolutely pointless life . . . In contemporary criticisms the most common word used to describe the main character is 'puzzling,' 'improbable' or 'incredible.' Readers got the impression that in the concluding line of the play—'But, good God! People don't do such things!'—Ibsen was making fun of them; for it reminded them that too many of them had said just that about Nora's final action in *A Doll's House.* There were things in HEDDA GABLER that seemed almost intended to parody *A Doll's House*—for example, Hedda's lie about having destroyed the manuscript to help her husband, or the curious form of 'comradeship' between man and woman portrayed here." Bredo Morgenstierna wrote in *Aftenposten* of "the obscurity, the eccentric and abnormal psychology, the empty and deso-

---

* His plays, though widely staged, were usually put on for a few performances only. For example, it was not until 1925 that any English production achieved a run of 50 performances.

late impression which the whole picture leaves," while Alfred Sinding-Larsen in *Morgenbladet* described Hedda herself as "a horrid miscarriage of the imagination, a monster in female form to whom no parallel can be found in real life."

Nor, as with some of his plays (e.g., *Ghosts*), were people much enlightened when HEDDA GABLER was performed. At the première on January 31, 1891, at the Residenztheater, Munich, the public whistled. Ibsen was present and was much displeased at the declamatory manner of the actress who played Hedda. On February 10 there was a rather better performance at the Lessing Theater in Berlin, but even here neither the public nor the critics seem to have understood the play. Nor was it a success in Stockholm three days later, while in Copenhagen on February 25 it was a complete fiasco, being greeted by hissing, whistling and laughter. The following evening it was given in Christiania, also inadequately. The first respectable performance of HEDDA GABLER was, improbably, in London (April 20, 1891), where, although it called forth the usual stream of abuse* from the popular newspapers, intelligent opinion was considerably impressed. William Archer, who was often critical of early Ibsen productions in England, described this one as "admirable," and wrote of Elizabeth Robins's Hedda:

* "It was like a visit to the Morgue . . . There they all lay on their copper couches, fronting us, and waiting to be owned . . . There they all were, false men, wicked women, deceitful friends, sensualists, egotists, piled up in a heap behind the screen of glass, which we were thankful for . . . What a horrible story! What a hideous play!" (Clement Scott in the *Daily Telegraph*)

"Hideous nightmare of pessimism . . . the play is simply a bad escape of moral sewage gas . . . Hedda's soul is a-crawl with the foulest passions of humanity." (*Pictorial World*)

"Tedious turmoil of knaves and fools." (*People*)

"Mean and sordid philosophy . . . Insidious nastiness of photographic studies of vice and morbidity." (*Saturday Review*)

"Funereal clown [i.e., Ibsen] . . . For sheer unadulterated stupidity, for inherent meanness and vulgarity, for pretentious triviality . . . no Bostonian novel nor London penny novelette has surpassed *Hedda Gabler*." (Robert Buchanan in *Illustrated London News*)

"I do not hesitate to call her performance in the last act the finest piece of modern tragedy within my recollection. Sarah Bernhardt could not have done this scene better; and it is long since Sarah attempted a scene so well worth doing. . . . From what I hear of representations of *Hedda Gabler* on the Continent, I very much doubt whether it has anywhere been played to such perfection as at the Vaudeville."

Henry James, who had been puzzled by the play on reading it, found the performance gratifyingly illuminating. "The play on perusal," he wrote (*On the Occasion of Hedda Gabler,* 1891), "left one comparatively muddled and mystified, fascinated but—in one's intellectual sympathy—snubbed. Acted, it leads that sympathy over the straightest of roads with all the exhilaration of a superior pace." But he added a gentle rider. "Much more, I confess, one doesn't get from it; but an hour of refreshing exercise is a reward in itself . . . Ibsen is various, and *Hedda Gabler* is probably an ironical pleasantry, the artistic exercise of a mind saturated with the vision of human infirmities; saturated, above all, with a sense of the infinitude, for all its mortal savour, of *character,* finding that an endless romance and a perpetual challenge. Can there have been at the source of such a production a mere refinement of conscious power, an enjoyment of difficulty and a preconceived victory over it?"

There are many people who share James's view of HEDDA GABLER as a brilliant but, for Ibsen, curiously detached, objective, almost brutal "exercise"—a view which has been greatly fostered by the tendency of actresses to portray Hedda as an evil genius, a kind of suburban Lady Macbeth. The opposite view, that it is one of Ibsen's most "committed" plays, has been brilliantly argued by Dr. Arne Duve in his wayward but stimulating book *Symbolikken i Henrik Ibsens Skuespill* (Nasjonalforlaget, Oslo, 1945). Dr. Duve suggests that Hedda represents Ibsen's repressed and crippled emotional life. As a young man, he reminds us, Ibsen had been wildly emotional; at sixteen he had fathered an illegitimate child, and at least once during those early years he became a near-alcoholic and is thought to have attempted suicide. Loevborg and Tesman,

Dr. Duve argues, are aspects of Ibsen's own self; Loevborg is an idealised portrait of himself as he had been in the wild years of his youth, Tesman a *reductio ad absurdum* of what he had chosen to become. Loevborg stands for Ibsen's emotional self, Tesman for his intellectual self. Ibsen was haunted throughout the latter half of his life by the feeling that he had stifled his emotional self and that only his bourgeois and slightly ludicrous intellectual self had lived on. He had persuaded himself to accept this state of affairs, but the encounter with Emilie Bardach seems to have brought all his old feelings of guilt rushing to the surface. Hedda longs to be like Loevborg but lacks the courage; she is repelled by the reality of sex (as Ibsen himself was?) and prefers to experience it vicariously by encouraging Loevborg to describe his experiences to her. Two emotions are dominant in her, the fear of scandal and the fear of ridicule, and Ibsen himself, though always willing to trail his coat in print, seems also to have been privately dominated by these emotions.

But if HEDDA GABLER is in fact a self-portrait, it is certainly an unconscious one—not that that makes it any the less truthful or valuable; rather the reverse. Ibsen's rough preliminary jottings referred to above make it clear that he *intended* the play as a tragedy of the purposelessness of life, and in particular of the purposelessness imposed on women of his time both by their upbringing and by the social conventions which limited their activities. The following extracts will serve as examples:

"1. They aren't all created to be mothers.

2. They all have a leaning towards sensuality, but are afraid of the scandal.

3. They realize that life holds a purpose for them, but they cannot find that purpose."

"Women have no influence on public affairs. So they want to influence individuals spiritually."

"The great tragedy of life is that so many people have nothing to do but yearn for happiness without ever being able to find it."

"Men and women don't belong to the same century."

"There are very few true parents in the world. Most people are brought up by uncles or aunts—neglected or misunderstood or spoiled."

"The play is to be about 'the insuperable'—the longing and striving to defy convention, to defy what people accept (including Hedda)."

"Hedda is typical of women in her position and with her character. One marries Tesman but one titillates one's imagination with Eilert Loevborg. One leans back in one's chair, closes one's eyes and pictures to oneself his adventure. The enormous difference: Mrs. Elvsted 'works to improve him morally,' while for Hedda he is merely a subject for cowardly and tantalising dreams. She lacks the courage to partake actively in such goings-on. Then her confession as to how she really feels. Tied! Don't understand— But to be an object of ridicule! Of ridicule!"

"The daemon in Hedda is that she wants to influence another human being, but once that has happened, she despises him."

"Loevborg has leanings towards Bohemianism. Hedda is also attracted to it, but dares not take the jump."

"It's really a man's life she wants to lead. In all respects. But then scruples intervene. Some inherited—some implanted."

"Remember I was born the child of an old man. And not merely old. Played-out—or anyway, decrepit. Perhaps that's left its mark."

"It is a great delusion that one only loves one person."

"Tesman represents propriety. Hedda represents *ennui*. Mrs. R. [i.e., Mrs. Elvsted] modern nervousness and hysteria. Brack the representative of bourgeois society."

"H.L. [i.e., Loevborg]'s despair arises from the fact that he wants to control the world but cannot control himself."

"Life for Hedda is a farce which isn't worth seeing through to the end."

As usual with Ibsen's plays, certain elements in HEDDA GABLER can be traced to incidents in the lives of people whom he knew personally or had heard or read about. For example, when he visited Norway in 1885 he must have heard of the marriage the previous winter between a famous beauty named Sophie Magelssen and the philologist Peter Groth. Groth had married her on a research grant which he had won in competition with one Hjalmar Falk, whom many thought the better scholar of the two (and who gets a kind of consolatory mention in the play as the dead Cabinet Minister who had previously owned the Tesmans' villa). Neither Tesman nor Loevborg, however, was modelled on either of these two. Ibsen told his son Sigurd that he had based Tesman on Julius Elias, a young German student of literature whom he had got to know in Munich. Elias's great passion was for "putting other people's papers in order"; later he became a distinguished man of letters, and ironically enough it fell to him to put Ibsen's own papers in order when he shared with Halvdan Koht the task of editing the dramatist's literary remains.* Loevborg was closely modelled on a Dane named Julius Hoffory, who was Professor of Scandinavian Philology and Phonetics in Berlin. Hoffory was a gifted but unbalanced man who mixed freely with women of low repute and had once lost the manuscript of a book during a nocturnal orgy. He recognised himself delightedly when HEDDA GABLER appeared, and thereafter adopted Loevborg as his pseudonym. A few years later he became mentally disordered and never fully recovered his sanity.

Miss Tesman, George's aunt, was based on an old lady from Trondhjem named Elise Hokk. Ibsen had met her a number of times during the early seventies in Dresden, where she tended a sick sister for three years until the latter died. He wrote a charming poem in tribute to her in 1874. She is the only character in the play, as far as is known, who was based

---

* In fairness to Elias, it should be stated that Tesman is a much less ridiculous character in the early draft of the play than Ibsen subsequently made him. His maddening repetition of genteel phrases such as "Fancy that!" was added during revision.

on a Norwegian original, and this may have influenced early critics who wrote that HEDDA GABLER was the least Norwegian of Ibsen's plays and that the town (unnamed as usual) in which the action takes place was less suggestive of Christiania than of a Continental capital. William Archer, however, who knew Christiania well, felt sure that Ibsen had that city in mind, and added the interesting comment that Ibsen, although writing in 1890, seemed to have set the play some thirty years earlier. "The electric cars, telephones and other conspicuous factors in the life of a modern capital," he wrote in his introduction (1907) to the English translation by himself and Edmund Gosse, "are notably absent from the play. There is no electric light in Secretary Falk's villa. It is still the habit for ladies to return on foot from evening parties, with gallant swains escorting them. This 'suburbanism' which so distressed the London critics of 1891 was characteristic of the Christiania Ibsen himself had known in the eighteen-sixties—the Christiania of *Love's Comedy*—rather than of the greatly extended and modernised city of the end of the century."

Three further incidents which came to Ibsen's notice found their way into the play. While he was actually working on it, a young married couple came to seek his advice; their happiness, they said, had been ruined because the husband had been hypnotised by another woman. Then there was the unfortunate case of the Norwegian composer Johan Svendsen, whose wife, Sally, in a fit of rage at discovering a letter from another woman hidden in a bouquet of flowers, had burned the score of a symphony which he had just composed. Finally, Ibsen heard of the even more unfortunate incident of the Norwegian lady whose husband had cured himself of drink and had resolved never to touch it again. To see how much power she had over him, she rolled a keg of brandy into his room as a birthday present, and before the day was over he was dead drunk. All these episodes are reflected in HEDDA GABLER.

The original of Hedda herself is not known. She has been rather glibly assumed by some critics to be a portrait of Emilie, on the grounds that both were beautiful and aristocratic and did not know what to do with their lives, and that

Ibsen's description of Hedda (aristocratic face, fine complexion, veiled expression in the eyes, etc.) corresponds to early photographs of Emilie. The same characteristics could, however, be found in the photograph of almost any well-born young lady of the period; the description would apply equally to Queen Alexandra; and few women of Ibsen's time, let alone girls of eighteen, knew what to do with their lives. In any case, the idea of creating such a character had been at the back of Ibsen's mind long before he met Emilie, for his rough notes for *Rosmersholm* (1886) contain a sketch of a girl, intended as Rosmer's elder daughter though he finally decided not to include her in the play, who "is in danger of succumbing to inactivity and loneliness. She has rich talents which are lying unused." On the other hand, Emilie must certainly have been at the back of his mind when he was writing HEDDA GABLER, and it is possible that Hedda may be a portrait, conscious or unconscious, of what Emilie might become in ten years if she did not marry the right man or find a fixed purpose in life. If so, it was a prophecy that came uncomfortably near the truth, for Emilie, though she lived to be eighty-three—she died as late as November 1, 1955—accomplished nothing and never married.

The differences between Ibsen's first draft and his final version as we know it are, as has already been remarked, numerous and revealing. Apart from changing Tesman from an ordinary bourgeois husband into a ninny spoiled (like Hjalmar Ekdal) by loving aunts, he improved him morally, for in the first draft it is Tesman who suggests hiding the manuscript to give Loevborg a fright, and so is partly responsible for the latter's death. Miss Tesman's important account to Bertha in Act 1 of Hedda's life with her father was an afterthought; so were Mademoiselle Danielle, Mrs. Elvsted's abundant hair and Hedda's jealousy of it, the image of the vine-leaves, and Hedda's threat (before the play opens) to shoot Loevborg. Act 1 ends much more feebly in the draft, with no mention of the pistols; and Tesman and Mrs. Elvsted both know of Hedda's former close relationship with Loevborg. Miss Tesman's role is much less

rich than in the final version; she does not realise in Act 1 that
Hedda is going to have a baby, and has a far less effective
scene with Hedda in Act 4. The conversation between Hedda,
Loevborg and Tesman over the photograph album about the
honeymoon contains a direct reference to Gossensass, subsequently deleted. And Brack, in a passage one is rather sorry
to lose, describes sadly to Hedda how three "triangles" of
which he was a part have been broken up during the past six
months—not, as Hedda guesses, by other bachelors but by in-
truders far more destructive to extramarital relationships—
children. Finally, one may note two remarks which Ibsen
originally put into Hedda's mouth but subsequently deleted:
(1) "I can't understand how anyone could fall in love with a
man who isn't married—or engaged—or at least in love with
someone else." (2) "To take someone from someone else—I
think that must be so wonderful!" He saved these lines for a
character, already created in miniature in *The Lady from the
Sea*, to whom he was to allot the principal female role in his
next play two years later—Hilde Wangel in *The Master Builder*.

The repeated references to the "vine-leaves" continues to
puzzle critics, even though William Archer cleared the problem
up fifty years ago. "Surely," he wrote, "this is a very obvious
image or symbol of the beautiful, the ideal aspect of bacchic
elation and revelry . . . Professor Dietrichson relates that
among the young artists whose society Ibsen frequented during his first years in Rome it was customary, at their little
festivals, for the revellers to deck themselves in this fashion.
But the image is so obvious that there is no need to trace it to
any personal experience. The attempt to place Hedda's vine-
leaves among Ibsen's obscurities is an example of the firm reso-
lution not to understand which animated the criticism of the
nineties." Not, alas, only of the nineties. The picture which the
vine-leaves are intended to evoke is that of the young god,
"burning and unashamed," in Hedda's words; as Archer noted,
it was an image Ibsen had used previously in both *Peer Gynt*
and *Emperor and Galilean*.

A point that is sometimes missed in productions of HEDDA
GABLER is the importance of correct casting for Bertha, the

Tesmans' maid. Ibsen never created a role, however tiny, that was not both integral to the play and rewarding to the player, and his servants are no exceptions—one thinks of the two butlers, the superior Pettersen and the inferior Jensen, in *The Wild Duck*, the housekeeper Mrs. Helseth in *Rosmersholm*, and Malene, the sour maid in *John Gabriel Borkman*. Ibsen underlined Bertha's importance in a letter which he wrote to Kristine Steen on January 14, 1891, concerning the casting of the play for Christiania. "Mrs. Wolf," he wrote, "wishes to be released from playing the maid Bertha in my new play, since she is of opinion that this role could be adequately filled by any other member of the company. She is mistaken. There is no one else at the theatre who can perform Bertha as I wish her to be performed. Only Mrs. Wolf can do it. She has evidently not taken the trouble to read the play carefully, or she could hardly fail to appreciate this. George Tesman, his old aunts and Bertha together create a picture of completeness and unity. They have common thoughts, common memories, a common attitude towards life. To Hedda they represent a force foreign and hostile to her and to everything she stands for. The harmony that exists between them must be apparent on the stage. And this can be achieved if Mrs. Wolf plays the part. But only if she does. My respect for Mrs. Wolf's soundness of judgment is too great for me seriously to believe that she regards it as artistically beneath her to create a servant. I did not regard it as artistically beneath me to create this honest, artless old creature. Here in Munich this unpretentious character is to be created by one of the Hoftheater's leading actresses, and she has embraced the task with love and interest. Besides being an actress, she is also an artist. By this I mean that she regards it as a matter of honour not merely to 'give a performance' but to turn a created character into a thing of flesh and blood."

Despite its early failures on the stages of Europe, HEDDA GABLER has come to be accepted as one of the most popular of Ibsen's plays. London has seen no less than eighteen separate productions, a number exceeded only, among Ibsen's other plays, by *A Doll's House* and *Ghosts*. Among the actresses who have played it there are Elizabeth Robins, Eleonora Duse, Mrs. Patrick Campbell, Lydia Yavorska, Jean Forbes Robertson and Peggy Ashcroft. Probably the finest English Hedda, however, was Pamela Brown, who in 1941 at the age of twenty-two gave a performance at the Oxford Playhouse which led James Agate to compare her seriously with the young Sarah Bernhardt. America first saw the play on March 30, 1898, when Elizabeth Robins presented a single performance at the Fifth Avenue Theatre in New York. *The Critic* wrote of this production that "it was, on the whole, the most satisfactory representation of an Ibsen play ever given in this city," and described Miss Robins's performance as "in every way a remarkable achievement." Unfortunately, according to Norman Hapgood in *The Stage in America, 1897–1900*, "it failed to interest the public enough to continue contemplated Ibsen experiments." Blanche Bates played it for a single matinée in Washington in 1900; then in 1903 Minnie Fiske presented it in New York for a whole week to crowded houses, and brought it back to the Manhattan Theatre in November 1904, when it achieved the, by the standard of those days, considerable number of twenty-six performances. The cast included George Arliss as Judge Brack. In 1905 Alla Nazimova played it at the Russian Theatre, New York, in Russian, and the following year she performed it in English, creating a tremendous impression. Subsequent Heddas in New York have included Emily Stevens, Eva Le Gallienne and, in 1960, Anne Meacham, in a production for which this translation was specially commissioned.

M. M.

CHARACTERS

GEORGE TESMAN, research graduate, in cultural history
HEDDA, his wife
MISS JULIANA TESMAN, his aunt
MRS. ELVSTED
JUDGE BRACK
EILERT LOEVBORG
BERTHA, a maid

The action takes place in TESMAN'S *villa in the fashionable quarter of town.*

This translation was commissioned by David Ross and was presented by him at the Fourth Street Theatre, New York, on November 9, 1960, with the following cast:

GEORGE TESMAN	Lester Rawlings
HEDDA	Anne Meacham
MISS JULIANA TESMAN	Lois Holmes
MRS. ELVSTED	Lori March
JUDGE BRACK	Frederick Rolf
EILERT LOEVBORG	Mark Lenard
BERTHA	Elizabeth Colquhoun

Directed by David Ross

ACT ONE

A large drawing room, handsomely and tastefully furnished; decorated in dark colours. In the rear wall is a broad open doorway, with curtains drawn back to either side. It leads to a smaller room, decorated in the same style as the drawing room. In the right-hand wall of the drawing room, a folding door leads out to the hall. The opposite wall, on the left, contains french windows, also with curtains drawn back on either side. Through the glass we can see part of a verandah, and trees in autumn colours. Downstage stands an oval table, covered by a cloth and surrounded by chairs. Downstage right, against the wall, is a broad stove tiled with dark porcelain; in front of it stand a high-backed armchair, a cushioned footrest, and two footstools. Upstage right, in an alcove, is a corner sofa, with a small, round table. Downstage left, a little away from the wall, is another sofa. Upstage of the french windows, a piano. On either side of the open doorway in the rear wall stand what-nots holding ornaments of terra cotta and majolica. Against the rear wall of the smaller room can be seen a sofa, a table, and a couple of chairs. Above this sofa hangs the portrait of a handsome old man in general's uniform. Above the table a lamp hangs from the ceiling, with a shade of opalescent, milky glass. All round the drawing room bunches of flowers stand in vases and glasses. More bunches lie on the tables. The floors of both rooms are covered with thick carpets. Morning light. The sun shines in through the french windows.

MISS JULIANA TESMAN, *wearing a hat and carrying a parasol, enters from the hall, followed by* BERTHA, *who is carrying a bunch of flowers wrapped in paper.* MISS TESMAN *is about sixty-five, of pleasant and kindly appearance. She is neatly but simply dressed in grey outdoor clothes.* BERTHA, *the maid, is rather simple and rustic-looking. She is getting on in years.*

MISS TESMAN *stops just inside the door, listens, and says in a hushed voice.* No, bless my soul! They're not up yet.

BERTHA, *also in hushed tones.* What did I tell you, miss? The boat didn't get in till midnight. And when they did turn up —Jesus, miss, you should have seen all the things Madam made me unpack before she'd go to bed!

MISS TESMAN. Ah, well. Let them have a good lie in. But let's have some nice fresh air waiting for them when they do come down.

Goes to the french windows and throws them wide open.

BERTHA, *bewildered at the table, the bunch of flowers in her hand.* I'm blessed if there's a square inch left to put anything. I'll have to let it lie here, miss.

Puts it on the piano.

MISS TESMAN. Well, Bertha dear, so now you have a new mistress. Heaven knows it nearly broke my heart to have to part with you.

BERTHA *snivels.* What about me, Miss Juju? How do you suppose I felt? After all the happy years I've spent with you and Miss Rena?

MISS TESMAN. We must accept it bravely, Bertha. It was the only way. George needs you to take care of him. He could never manage without you. You've looked after him ever since he was a tiny boy.

BERTHA. Oh, but, Miss Juju, I can't help thinking about Miss Rena, lying there all helpless, poor dear. And that new girl! She'll never learn the proper way to handle an invalid.

MISS TESMAN. Oh, I'll manage to train her. I'll do most of the work myself, you know. You needn't worry about my poor sister, Bertha dear.

BERTHA. But Miss Juju, there's another thing. I'm frightened Madam may not find me suitable.

MISS TESMAN. Oh, nonsense, Bertha. There may be one or two little things to begin with—

BERTHA. She's a real lady. Wants everything just so.

MISS TESMAN. But of course she does! General Gabler's daughter! Think of what she was accustomed to when the General was alive. You remember how we used to see her out riding with her father? In that long black skirt? With the feather in her hat?

BERTHA. Oh, yes, miss. As if I could forget! But, Lord! I never dreamed I'd live to see a match between her and Master Georgie.

MISS TESMAN. Neither did I. By the way, Bertha, from now on you must stop calling him Master Georgie. You must say: Dr. Tesman.

BERTHA. Yes, Madam said something about that too. Last night —the moment they'd set foot inside the door. Is it true, then, miss?

MISS TESMAN. Indeed it is. Just imagine, Bertha, some foreigners have made him a doctor. It happened while they were away. I had no idea till he told me when they got off the boat.

BERTHA. Well, I suppose there's no limit to what he won't become. He's that clever. I never thought he'd go in for hospital work, though.

MISS TESMAN. No, he's not that kind of doctor.

Nods impressively.

In any case, you may soon have to address him by an even grander title.

BERTHA. You don't say! What might that be, miss?

MISS TESMAN *smiles.* Ah! If you only knew!

Moved.

Dear God, if only poor dear Joachim could rise out of his grave and see what his little son has grown into!

Looks round.

But Bertha, why have you done this? Taken the chintz covers off all the furniture!

BERTHA. Madam said I was to. Can't stand chintz covers on chairs, she said.

MISS TESMAN. But surely they're not going to use this room as a parlour?

BERTHA. So I gathered, miss. From what Madam said. He didn't say anything. The Doctor.

GEORGE TESMAN *comes into the rear room, from the right, humming, with an open, empty travelling bag in his hand. He is about thirty-three, of medium height and youthful appearance, rather plump, with an open, round, contented face, and fair hair and beard. He wears spectacles, and is dressed in comfortable, indoor clothes.*

MISS TESMAN. Good morning! Good morning, George!

TESMAN, *in open doorway.* Auntie Juju! Dear Auntie Juju!

Comes forward and shakes her hand.

You've come all the way out here! And so early! What?

MISS TESMAN. Well, I had to make sure you'd settled in comfortably.

TESMAN. But you can't have had a proper night's sleep.

MISS TESMAN. Oh, never mind that.

TESMAN. We were so sorry we couldn't give you a lift. But you saw how it was—Hedda had so much luggage—and she insisted on having it all with her.

MISS TESMAN. Yes, I've never seen so much luggage.

BERTHA, *to* TESMAN. Shall I go and ask Madam if there's anything I can lend her a hand with?

TESMAN. Er—thank you, Bertha; no, you needn't bother. She says if she wants you for anything she'll ring.

BERTHA, *over to right.* Oh. Very good.

TESMAN. Oh, Bertha—take this bag, will you?

BERTHA *takes it.* I'll put it in the attic.

Goes out into the hall.

TESMAN. Just fancy, Auntie Juju, I filled that whole bag with notes for my book. You know, it's really incredible what I've managed to find rooting through those archives. By Jove! Wonderful old things no one even knew existed—

MISS TESMAN. I'm sure you didn't waste a single moment of your honeymoon, George dear.

TESMAN. No, I think I can truthfully claim that. But, Auntie Juju, do take your hat off. Here. Let me untie it for you. What?

MISS TESMAN, *as he does so.* Oh dear, oh dear! It's just as if you were still living at home with us.

TESMAN *turns the hat in his hand and looks at it.* I say! What a splendid new hat!

MISS TESMAN. I bought it for Hedda's sake.

TESMAN. For Hedda's sake? What?

MISS TESMAN. So that Hedda needn't be ashamed of me, in case we ever go for a walk together.

TESMAN *pats her cheek.* You still think of everything, don't you, Auntie Juju?

Puts the hat down on a chair by the table.

Come on, let's sit down here on the sofa. And have a little chat while we wait for Hedda.

They sit. She puts her parasol in the corner of the sofa.

MISS TESMAN *clasps both his hands and looks at him.* Oh, George, it's so wonderful to have you back, and be able to see you with my own eyes again! Poor dear Joachim's own son!

TESMAN. What about me! It's wonderful for me to see you again, Auntie Juju. You've been a mother to me. And a father, too.

MISS TESMAN. You'll always keep a soft spot in your heart for your old aunties, won't you, George dear?

TESMAN. I suppose Auntie Rena's no better? What?

MISS TESMAN. Alas, no. I'm afraid she'll never get better, poor dear. She's lying there just as she has for all these years. Please God I may be allowed to keep her for a little longer. If I lost her I don't know what I'd do. Especially now I haven't you to look after.

TESMAN *pats her on the back.* There, there, there!

MISS TESMAN, *with a sudden change of mood.* Oh but George, fancy you being a married man! And to think it's you who've won Hedda Gabler! The beautiful Hedda Gabler! Fancy! She was always so surrounded by admirers.

TESMAN *hums a little and smiles contentedly.* Yes, I suppose there are quite a few people in this town who wouldn't mind being in my shoes. What?

MISS TESMAN. And what a honeymoon! Five months! Nearly six.

TESMAN. Well, I've done a lot of work, you know. All those archives to go through. And I've had to read lots of books.

MISS TESMAN. Yes, dear, of course.

Lowers her voice confidentially.

But tell me, George—haven't you any—any extra little piece of news to give me?

TESMAN. You mean, arising out of the honeymoon?

MISS TESMAN. Yes.

TESMAN. No, I don't think there's anything I didn't tell you in my letters. My doctorate, of course—but I told you about that last night, didn't I?

MISS TESMAN. Yes, yes, I didn't mean that kind of thing. I was just wondering—are you—are you expecting—?

TESMAN. Expecting what?

MISS TESMAN. Oh, come on George, I'm your old aunt!

TESMAN. Well actually—yes, I am expecting something.

MISS TESMAN. I knew it!

TESMAN. You'll be happy to hear that before very long I expect to become a professor.

MISS TESMAN. Professor?

TESMAN. I think I may say that the matter has been decided. But, Auntie Juju, you know about this.

MISS TESMAN *gives a little laugh.* Yes, of course. I'd forgotten. *Changes her tone.*

But we were talking about your honeymoon. It must have cost a dreadful amount of money, George?

TESMAN. Oh well, you know, that big research grant I got helped a good deal.

MISS TESMAN. But how on earth did you manage to make it do for two?

TESMAN. Well, to tell the truth it was a bit tricky. What?

MISS TESMAN. Especially when one's travelling with a lady. A little bird tells me that makes things very much more expensive.

TESMAN. Well, yes, of course it does make things a little more expensive. But Hedda has to do things in style, Auntie Juju. I mean, she has to. Anything less grand wouldn't have suited her.

MISS TESMAN. No, no, I suppose not. A honeymoon abroad seems to be the vogue nowadays. But tell me, have you had time to look round the house?

TESMAN. You bet. I've been up since the crack of dawn.

MISS TESMAN. Well, what do you think of it?

TESMAN. Splendid. Absolutely splendid. I'm only wondering what we're going to do with those two empty rooms between that little one and Hedda's bedroom.

MISS TESMAN *laughs slyly.* Ah, George dear, I'm sure you'll manage to find some use for them—in time.

TESMAN. Yes, of course, Auntie Juju, how stupid of me. You're thinking of my books. What?

MISS TESMAN. Yes, yes, dear boy. I was thinking of your books.

TESMAN. You know, I'm so happy for Hedda's sake that we've managed to get this house. Before we became engaged she often used to say this was the only house in town she felt she could really bear to live in. It used to belong to Mrs. Falk—you know, the Prime Minister's widow.

MISS TESMAN. Fancy that! And what a stroke of luck it happened to come into the market. Just as you'd left on your honeymoon.

TESMAN. Yes, Auntie Juju, we've certainly had all the luck with us. What?

MISS TESMAN. But, George dear, the expense! It's going to make a dreadful hole in your pocket, all this.

TESMAN, *a little downcast.* Yes, I—I suppose it will, won't it?

MISS TESMAN. Oh, George, really!

TESMAN. How much do you think it'll cost? Roughly, I mean? What?

MISS TESMAN. I can't possibly say till I see the bills.

TESMAN. Well, luckily Judge Brack's managed to get it on very favourable terms. He wrote and told Hedda so.

MISS TESMAN. Don't you worry, George dear. Anyway I've stood security for all the furniture and carpets.

TESMAN. Security? But dear, sweet Auntie Juju, how could you possibly stand security?

MISS TESMAN. I've arranged a mortgage on our annuity.

TESMAN *jumps up.* What? On your annuity? And—Auntie Rena's?

MISS TESMAN. Yes. Well, I couldn't think of any other way.

TESMAN *stands in front of her.* Auntie Juju, have you gone completely out of your mind? That annuity's all you and Auntie Rena have.

MISS TESMAN. All right, there's no need to get so excited about it. It's a pure formality, you know. Judge Brack told me so. He was so kind as to arrange it all for me. A pure formality; those were his very words.

TESMAN. I dare say. All the same—

MISS TESMAN. Anyway, you'll have a salary of your own now. And, good heavens, even if we did have to fork out a little

—tighten our belts for a week or two—why, we'd be happy to do so for your sake.

TESMAN. Oh, Auntie Juju! Will you never stop sacrificing yourself for me?

MISS TESMAN *gets up and puts her hands on his shoulders.* What else have I to live for but to smooth your road a little, my dear boy? You've never had any mother or father to turn to. And now at last we've achieved our goal. I won't deny we've had our little difficulties now and then. But now, thank the good Lord, George dear, all your worries are past.

TESMAN. Yes, it's wonderful really how everything's gone just right for me.

MISS TESMAN. Yes! And the enemies who tried to bar your way have been struck down. They have been made to bite the dust. The man who was your most dangerous rival has had the mightiest fall. And now he's lying there in the pit he dug for himself, poor misguided creature.

TESMAN. Have you heard any news of Eilert? Since I went away?

MISS TESMAN. Only that he's said to have published a new book.

TESMAN. What! Eilert Loevborg? You mean—just recently? What?

MISS TESMAN. So they say. I don't imagine it can be of any value, do you? When your new book comes out, that'll be another story. What's it going to be about?

TESMAN. The domestic industries of Brabant in the Middle Ages.

MISS TESMAN. Oh, George! The things you know about!

TESMAN. Mind you, it may be some time before I actually get down to writing it. I've made these very extensive notes, and I've got to file and index them first.

MISS TESMAN. Ah, yes! Making notes; filing and indexing; you've always been wonderful at that. Poor dear Joachim was just the same.

TESMAN. I'm looking forward so much to getting down to that. Especially now I've a home of my own to work in.

MISS TESMAN. And above all, now that you have the girl you set your heart on, George dear.

TESMAN *embraces her.* Oh, yes, Auntie Juju, yes! Hedda's the loveliest thing of all!

Looks towards the doorway.

I think I hear her coming. What?

HEDDA *enters the rear room from the left, and comes into the drawing room. She is a woman of twenty-nine. Distinguished, aristocratic face and figure. Her complexion is pale and opalescent. Her eyes are steel-grey, with an expression of cold, calm serenity. Her hair is of a handsome auburn colour, but is not especially abundant. She is dressed in an elegant, somewhat loose-fitting morning gown.*

MISS TESMAN *goes to greet her.* Good morning, Hedda dear! Good morning!

HEDDA *holds out her hand.* Good morning, dear Miss Tesman. What an early hour to call. So kind of you.

MISS TESMAN *seems somewhat embarrassed.* And has the young bride slept well in her new home?

HEDDA. Oh—thank you, yes. Passably well.

TESMAN *laughs.* Passably. I say, Hedda, that's good! When I jumped out of bed, you were sleeping like a top.

HEDDA. Yes. Fortunately. One has to accustom oneself to anything new, Miss Tesman. It takes time.

Looks left.

Oh, that maid's left the french windows open. This room's flooded with sun.

MISS TESMAN *goes towards the windows.* Oh—let me close them.

HEDDA. No, no, don't do that. Tesman dear, draw the curtains. This light's blinding me.

TESMAN, *at the windows.* Yes, yes, dear. There, Hedda, now you've got shade and fresh air.

HEDDA. This room needs fresh air. All these flowers— But my dear Miss Tesman, won't you take a seat?

MISS TESMAN. No, really not, thank you. I just wanted to make sure you have everything you need. I must see about getting back home. My poor dear sister will be waiting for me.

TESMAN. Be sure to give her my love, won't you? Tell her I'll run over and see her later today.

MISS TESMAN. Oh yes, I'll tell her that. Oh, George—

Fumbles in the pocket of her skirt.

I almost forgot. I've brought something for you.

TESMAN. What's that, Auntie Juju? What?

MISS TESMAN *pulls out a flat package wrapped in newspaper and gives it to him.* Open and see, dear boy.

TESMAN *opens the package.* Good heavens! Auntie Juju, you've kept them! Hedda, this is really very touching. What?

HEDDA, *by the what-nots, on the right.* What is it, Tesman?

TESMAN. My old shoes! My slippers, Hedda!

HEDDA. Oh, them. I remember you kept talking about them on our honeymoon.

TESMAN. Yes, I missed them dreadfully.

Goes over to her.

Here, Hedda, take a look.

HEDDA *goes away towards the stove.* Thanks, I won't bother.

TESMAN *follows her.* Fancy, Hedda, Auntie Rena's embroidered them for me. Despite her being so ill. Oh, you can't imagine what memories they have for me.

HEDDA, *by the table.* Not for me.

MISS TESMAN. No, Hedda's right there, George.

TESMAN. Yes, but I thought since she's one of the family now—

HEDDA *interrupts.* Tesman, we really can't go on keeping this maid.

MISS TESMAN. Not keep Bertha?

TESMAN. What makes you say that, dear? What?

HEDDA *points.* Look at that! She's left her old hat lying on the chair.

TESMAN, *appalled, drops his slippers on the floor.* But, Hedda—!

HEDDA. Suppose someone came in and saw it?

TESMAN. But Hedda—that's Auntie Juju's hat.

HEDDA. Oh?

MISS TESMAN *picks up the hat.* Indeed it's mine. And it doesn't happen to be old, Hedda dear.

HEDDA. I didn't look at it very closely, Miss Tesman.

MISS TESMAN, *tying on the hat.* As a matter of fact, it's the first time I've worn it. As the good Lord is my witness.

TESMAN. It's very pretty, too. Really smart.

MISS TESMAN. Oh, I'm afraid it's nothing much really.

Looks round.

My parasol? Ah, here it is.

Takes it.

This is mine, too.

Murmurs.

Not Bertha's.

TESMAN. A new hat and a new parasol! I say, Hedda, fancy that!

HEDDA. Very pretty and charming.

TESMAN. Yes, isn't it? What? But Auntie Juju, take a good look at Hedda before you go. Isn't she pretty and charming?

MISS TESMAN. Dear boy, there's nothing new in that. Hedda's been a beauty ever since the day she was born.

Nods and goes right.

TESMAN *follows her.* Yes, but have you noticed how strong and healthy she's looking? And how she's filled out since we went away?

MISS TESMAN *stops and turns.* Filled out?

HEDDA *walks across the room.* Oh, can't we forget it?

TESMAN. Yes, Auntie Juju—you can't see it so clearly with that dress on. But I've good reason to know—

HEDDA, *by the french windows, impatiently.* You haven't good reason to know anything.

TESMAN. It must have been the mountain air up there in the Tyrol—

HEDDA, *curtly, interrupts him.* I'm exactly the same as when I went away.

TESMAN. You keep on saying so. But you're not. I'm right, aren't I, Auntie Juju?

MISS TESMAN *has folded her hands and is gazing at her.* She's beautiful—beautiful. Hedda is beautiful.

Goes over to HEDDA, *takes her head between her hands, draws it down and kisses her hair.*

God bless and keep you, Hedda Tesman. For George's sake.

HEDDA *frees herself politely.* Oh—let me go, please.

MISS TESMAN, *quietly, emotionally.* I shall come and see you both every day.

TESMAN. Yes, Auntie Juju, please do. What?

MISS TESMAN. Good-bye! Good-bye!

She goes out into the hall. TESMAN *follows her. The door remains open.* TESMAN *is heard sending his love to* AUNT RENA *and thanking* MISS TESMAN *for his slippers. Meanwhile* HEDDA *walks up and down the room raising her arms and clenching her fists as though in desperation. Then she throws aside the curtains from the french windows and stands there, looking out. A few moments later,* TESMAN *returns and closes the door behind him.*

TESMAN *picks up his slippers from the floor.* What are you looking at, Hedda?

HEDDA, *calm and controlled again.* Only the leaves. They're so golden. And withered.

TESMAN *wraps up the slippers and lays them on the table.* Well, we're in September now.

HEDDA, *restless again.* Yes. We're already into September.

TESMAN. Auntie Juju was behaving rather oddly, I thought,

didn't you? Almost as though she was in church or something. I wonder what came over her. Any idea?

HEDDA. I hardly know her. Does she often act like that?

TESMAN. Not to the extent she did today.

HEDDA *goes away from the french windows.* Do you think she was hurt by what I said about the hat?

TESMAN. Oh, I don't think so. A little at first, perhaps—

HEDDA. But what a thing to do, throw her hat down in someone's drawing room. People don't do such things.

TESMAN. I'm sure Auntie Juju doesn't do it very often.

HEDDA. Oh well, I'll make it up with her.

TESMAN. Oh Hedda, would you?

HEDDA. When you see them this afternoon invite her to come out here this evening.

TESMAN. You bet I will! I say, there's another thing which would please her enormously.

HEDDA. Oh?

TESMAN. If you could bring yourself to call her Auntie Juju. For my sake, Hedda? What?

HEDDA. Oh no, really Tesman, you mustn't ask me to do that. I've told you so once before. I'll try to call her Aunt Juliana. That's as far as I'll go.

TESMAN, *after a moment.* I say, Hedda, is anything wrong? What?

HEDDA. I'm just looking at my old piano. It doesn't really go with all this.

TESMAN. As soon as I start getting my salary we'll see about changing it.

HEDDA. No, no, don't let's change it. I don't want to part with it. We can move it into that little room and get another one to put in here.

TESMAN, *a little downcast.* Yes, we—might do that.

HEDDA *picks up the bunch of flowers from the piano.* These flowers weren't here when we arrived last night.

TESMAN. I expect Auntie Juju brought them.

HEDDA. Here's a card.

Takes it out and reads.

"Will come back later today." Guess who it's from?

TESMAN. No idea. Who? What?

HEDDA. It says: "Mrs. Elvsted."

TESMAN. No, really? Mrs. Elvsted! She used to be Miss Rysing, didn't she?

HEDDA. Yes. She was the one with that irritating hair she was always showing off. I hear she used to be an old flame of yours.

TESMAN *laughs.* That didn't last long. Anyway, that was before I got to know you, Hedda. By Jove, fancy her being in town!

HEDDA. Strange she should call. I only knew her at school.

TESMAN. Yes, I haven't seen her for—oh, heaven knows how long. I don't know how she manages to stick it out up there in the north. What?

HEDDA *thinks for a moment, then says suddenly.* Tell me, Tesman, doesn't he live somewhere up in those parts? You know —Eilert Loevborg?

TESMAN. Yes, that's right. So he does.

BERTHA *enters from the hall.*

BERTHA. She's here again, madam. The lady who came and left the flowers.

Points.

The ones you're holding.

HEDDA. Oh, is she? Well, show her in.

BERTHA *opens the door for* MRS. ELVSTED *and goes out.* MRS. ELVSTED *is a delicately built woman with gentle, attractive features. Her eyes are light blue, large, and somewhat prominent, with a frightened, questioning expression. Her hair is extremely fair, almost flaxen, and is exceptionally wavy and abundant. She is two or three years younger than* HEDDA. *She is wearing a dark visiting dress, in good taste but not quite in the latest fashion.*

HEDDA *goes cordially to greet her.* Dear Mrs. Elvsted, good morning. How delightful to see you again after all this time.

MRS. ELVSTED, *nervously, trying to control herself.* Yes, it's many years since we met.

TESMAN. And since *we* met. What?

HEDDA. Thank you for your lovely flowers.

MRS. ELVSTED. Oh, please—I wanted to come yesterday afternoon. But they told me you were away—

TESMAN. You've only just arrived in town, then? What?

MRS. ELVSTED. I got here yesterday, around midday. Oh, I became almost desperate when I heard you weren't here.

HEDDA. Desperate? Why?

TESMAN. My dear Mrs. Rysing—Elvsted—

HEDDA. There's nothing wrong, I hope?

MRS. ELVSTED. Yes, there is. And I don't know anyone else here whom I can turn to.

HEDDA *puts the flowers down on the table.* Come and sit with me on the sofa—

MRS. ELVSTED. Oh, I feel too restless to sit down.

HEDDA. You must. Come along, now.

She pulls MRS. ELVSTED *down on to the sofa and sits beside her.*

TESMAN. Well? Tell us, Mrs.—er—

HEDDA. Has something happened at home?

MRS. ELVSTED. Yes—that is, yes and no. Oh, I do hope you won't misunderstand me—

HEDDA. Then you'd better tell us the whole story, Mrs. Elvsted.

TESMAN. That's why you've come. What?

MRS. ELVSTED. Yes—yes, it is. Well, then—in case you don't already know—Eilert Loevborg is in town.

HEDDA. Loevborg here?

TESMAN. Eilert back in town? By Jove, Hedda, did you hear that?

HEDDA. Yes, of course I heard.

MRS. ELVSTED. He's been here a week. A whole week! In this city. Alone. With all those dreadful people—

HEDDA. But my dear Mrs. Elvsted, what concern is he of yours?

MRS. ELVSTED *gives her a frightened look and says quickly.* He's been tutoring the children.

HEDDA. Your children?

MRS. ELVSTED. My husband's. I have none.

HEDDA. Oh, you mean your stepchildren.

MRS. ELVSTED. Yes.

TESMAN, *gropingly.* But was he sufficiently—I don't know how to put it—sufficiently regular in his habits to be suited to such a post? What?

MRS. ELVSTED. For the past two to three years he has been living irreproachably.

TESMAN. You don't say! By Jove, Hedda, hear that?

HEDDA. I hear.

MRS. ELVSTED. Quite irreproachably, I assure you. In every respect. All the same—in this big city—with money in his pockets—I'm so dreadfully frightened something may happen to him.

TESMAN. But why didn't he stay up there with you and your husband?

MRS. ELVSTED. Once his book had come out, he became restless.

TESMAN. Oh, yes—Auntie Juju said he'd brought out a new book.

MRS. ELVSTED. Yes, a big new book about the history of civilisation. A kind of general survey. It came out a fortnight ago. Everyone's been buying it and reading it—it's created a tremendous stir—

TESMAN. Has it really? It must be something he's dug up, then.

MRS. ELVSTED. You mean from the old days?

TESMAN. Yes.

MRS. ELVSTED. No, he's written it all since he came to live with us.

TESMAN. Well, that's splendid news, Hedda. Fancy that!

MRS. ELVSTED. Oh, yes! If only he can go on like this!

HEDDA. Have you met him since you came here?

MRS. ELVSTED. No, not yet. I had such dreadful difficulty find-ing his address. But this morning I managed to track him down at last.

HEDDA *looks searchingly at her.* I must say I find it a little strange that your husband—hm—

MRS. ELVSTED *starts nervously.* My husband! What do you mean?

HEDDA. That he should send you all the way here on an er-rand of this kind. I'm surprised he didn't come himself to keep an eye on his friend.

MRS. ELVSTED. Oh, no, no—my husband hasn't the time. Be-sides, I—er—wanted to do some shopping here.

HEDDA, *with a slight smile.* Ah. Well, that's different.

MRS. ELVSTED *gets up quickly, restlessly.* Please, Mr. Tesman, I beg you—be kind to Eilert Loevborg if he comes here. I'm sure he will. I mean, you used to be such good friends in the old days. And you're both studying the same subject, as far as I can understand. You're in the same field, aren't you?

TESMAN. Well, we used to be, anyway.

MRS. ELVSTED. Yes—so I beg you earnestly, do please, please, keep an eye on him. Oh, Mr. Tesman, do promise me you will.

TESMAN. I shall be only too happy to do so, Mrs. Rysing.

HEDDA. Elvsted.

TESMAN. I'll do everything for Eilert that lies in my power. You can rely on that.

MRS. ELVSTED. Oh, how good and kind you are!
Presses his hands.
Thank you, thank you, thank you.
Frightened.
My husband's so fond of him, you see.

HEDDA *gets up.* You'd better send him a note, Tesman. He may not come to you of his own accord.

TESMAN. Yes, that'd probably be the best plan, Hedda. What?

HEDDA. The sooner the better. Why not do it now?

MRS. ELVSTED, *pleadingly.* Oh yes, if only you would!

TESMAN. I'll do it this very moment. Do you have his address, Mrs.—er—Elvsted?

MRS. ELVSTED. Yes.
Takes a small piece of paper from her pocket and gives it to him.

TESMAN. Good, good. Right, well I'll go inside and—
Looks round.
Where are my slippers? Oh yes, here.
Picks up the package and is about to go.

HEDDA. Try to sound friendly. Make it a nice long letter.

TESMAN. Right, I will.

MRS. ELVSTED. Please don't say anything about my having seen you.

TESMAN. Good heavens no, of course not. What?
Goes out through the rear room to the right.

HEDDA *goes over to* MRS. ELVSTED, *smiles, and says softly.* Well! Now we've killed two birds with one stone.

MRS. ELVSTED. What do you mean?

HEDDA. Didn't you realise I wanted to get him out of the room?

MRS. ELVSTED. So that he could write the letter?

HEDDA. And so that I could talk to you alone.

MRS. ELVSTED, *confused.* About this?

HEDDA. Yes, about this.

MRS. ELVSTED, *in alarm.* But there's nothing more to tell, Mrs. Tesman. Really there isn't.

HEDDA. Oh, yes there is. There's a lot more. I can see that. Come along, let's sit down and have a little chat.
She pushes MRS. ELVSTED *down into the armchair by the stove and seats herself on one of the footstools.*

MRS. ELVSTED *looks anxiously at her watch.* Really, Mrs. Tesman, I think I ought to be going now.

HEDDA. There's no hurry. Well? How are things at home?

MRS. ELVSTED. I'd rather not speak about that.

HEDDA. But my dear, you can tell me. Good heavens, we were at school together.

MRS. ELVSTED. Yes, but you were a year senior to me. Oh, I used to be terribly frightened of you in those days.

HEDDA. Frightened of me?

MRS. ELVSTED. Yes, terribly frightened. Whenever you met me on the staircase you used to pull my hair.

HEDDA. No, did I?

MRS. ELVSTED. Yes. And once you said you'd burn it all off.

HEDDA. Oh, that was only in fun.

MRS. ELVSTED. Yes, but I was so silly in those days. And then afterwards—I mean, we've drifted so far apart. Our backgrounds were so different.

HEDDA. Well, now we must try to drift together again. Now listen. When we were at school we used to call each other by our Christian names—

MRS. ELVSTED. No, I'm sure you're mistaken.

HEDDA. I'm sure I'm not. I remember it quite clearly. Let's tell each other our secrets, as we used to in the old days.

Moves closer on her footstool.

There, now.

Kisses her on the cheek.

You must call me Hedda.

MRS. ELVSTED *squeezes her hands and pats them.* Oh, you're so kind. I'm not used to people being so nice to me.

HEDDA. Now, now, now. And I shall call you Tora, the way I used to.

MRS. ELVSTED. My name is Thea.

HEDDA. Yes, of course. Of course. I meant Thea.

Looks at her sympathetically.

So you're not used to kindness, Thea? In your own home?

MRS. ELVSTED. Oh, if only I had a home! But I haven't. I've never had one.

HEDDA *looks at her for a moment.* I thought that was it.

MRS. ELVSTED *stares blankly and helplessly.* Yes—yes—yes.

HEDDA. I can't remember exactly now, but didn't you first go to Mr. Elvsted as a housekeeper?

MRS. ELVSTED. Governess, actually. But his wife—at the time, I mean—she was an invalid, and had to spend most of her time in bed. So I had to look after the house too.

HEDDA. But in the end, you became mistress of the house.

MRS. ELVSTED, *sadly.* Yes, I did.

HEDDA. Let me see. Roughly how long ago was that?

MRS. ELVSTED. When I got married, you mean?

HEDDA. Yes.

MRS. ELVSTED. About five years.

HEDDA. Yes; it must be about that.

MRS. ELVSTED. Oh, those five years! Especially the last two or three. Oh, Mrs. Tesman, if you only knew—!

HEDDA *slaps her hand gently.* Mrs. Tesman? Oh, Thea!

MRS. ELVSTED. I'm sorry, I'll try to remember. Yes—if you had any idea—

HEDDA, *casually.* Eilert Loevborg's been up there too, for about three years, hasn't he?

MRS. ELVSTED *looks at her uncertainly.* Eilert Loevborg? Yes, he has.

HEDDA. Did you know him before? When you were here?

MRS. ELVSTED. No, not really. That is—I knew him by name, of course.

HEDDA. But up there, he used to visit you?

MRS. ELVSTED. Yes, he used to come and see us every day. To give the children lessons. I found I couldn't do that as well as manage the house.

HEDDA. I'm sure you couldn't. And your husband—? I suppose

being a magistrate he has to be away from home a good deal?

MRS. ELVSTED. Yes. You see, Mrs.—you see, Hedda, he has to cover the whole district.

HEDDA *leans against the arm of* MRS. ELVSTED'S *chair.* Poor, pretty little Thea! Now you must tell me the whole story. From beginning to end.

MRS. ELVSTED. Well—what do you want to know?

HEDDA. What kind of a man is your husband, Thea? I mean, as a person. Is he kind to you?

MRS. ELVSTED, *evasively.* I'm sure he does his best to be.

HEDDA. I only wonder if he isn't too old for you. There's more than twenty years between you, isn't there?

MRS. ELVSTED, *irritably.* Yes, there's that too. Oh, there are so many things. We're different in every way. We've nothing in common. Nothing whatever.

HEDDA. But he loves you, surely? In his own way?

MRS. ELVSTED. Oh, I don't know. I think he just finds me useful. And then I don't cost much to keep. I'm cheap.

HEDDA. Now you're being stupid.

MRS. ELVSTED *shakes her head.* It can't be any different. With him. He doesn't love anyone except himself. And perhaps the children—a little.

HEDDA. He must be fond of Eilert Loevborg, Thea.

MRS. ELVSTED *looks at her.* Eilert Loevborg? What makes you think that?

HEDDA. Well, if he sends you all the way down here to look for him—

Smiles almost imperceptibly.

Besides, you said so yourself to Tesman.

MRS. ELVSTED, *with a nervous twitch.* Did I? Oh yes, I suppose I did.

Impulsively, but keeping her voice low.

Well, I might as well tell you the whole story. It's bound to come out sooner or later.

HEDDA. But my dear Thea—?

MRS. ELVSTED. My husband had no idea I was coming here.

HEDDA. What? Your husband didn't know?

MRS. ELVSTED. No, of course not. As a matter of fact, he wasn't even there. He was away at the assizes. Oh, I couldn't stand it any longer, Hedda! I just couldn't. I'd be so dreadfully lonely up there now.

HEDDA. Go on.

MRS. ELVSTED. So I packed a few things. Secretly. And went.

HEDDA. Without telling anyone?

MRS. ELVSTED. Yes. I caught the train and came straight here.

HEDDA. But my dear Thea! How brave of you!

MRS. ELVSTED *gets up and walks across the room.* Well, what else could I do?

HEDDA. But what do you suppose your husband will say when you get back?

MRS. ELVSTED, *by the table, looks at her.* Back there? To him?

HEDDA. Yes. Surely—?

MRS. ELVSTED. I shall never go back to him.

HEDDA *gets up and goes closer.* You mean you've left your home for good?

MRS. ELVSTED. Yes. I didn't see what else I could do.

HEDDA. But to do it so openly!

MRS. ELVSTED. Oh, it's no use trying to keep a thing like that secret.

HEDDA. But what do you suppose people will say?

MRS. ELVSTED. They can say what they like.

Sits sadly, wearily on the sofa.

I had to do it.

HEDDA, *after a short silence.* What do you intend to do now? How are you going to live?

MRS. ELVSTED. I don't know. I only know that I must live wherever Eilert Loevborg is. If I am to go on living.

HEDDA *moves a chair from the table, sits on it near* MRS.
ELVSTED *and strokes her hands.* Tell me, Thea, how did this
—friendship between you and Eilert Loevborg begin?

MRS. ELVSTED. Oh, it came about gradually. I developed a
kind of—power over him.

HEDDA. Oh?

MRS. ELVSTED. He gave up his old habits. Not because I asked
him to. I'd never have dared to do that. I suppose he just
noticed I didn't like that kind of thing. So he gave it up.

HEDDA *hides a smile.* So you've made a new man of him. Clever
little Thea!

MRS. ELVSTED. Yes—anyway, he says I have. And he's made
a—sort of—real person of me. Taught me to think—and to
understand all kinds of things.

HEDDA. Did he give you lessons too?

MRS. ELVSTED. Not exactly lessons. But he talked to me. About
—oh, you've no idea—so many things! And then he let me
work with him. Oh, it was wonderful. I was so happy to be
allowed to help him.

HEDDA. Did he allow you to help him!

MRS. ELVSTED. Yes. Whenever he wrote anything we always—
did it together.

HEDDA. Like good pals?

MRS. ELVSTED, *eagerly.* Pals! Yes—why, Hedda, that's exactly
the word he used! Oh, I ought to feel so happy. But I can't.
I don't know if it will last.

HEDDA. You don't seem very sure of him.

MRS. ELVSTED, *sadly.* Something stands between Eilert Loevborg and me. The shadow of another woman.

HEDDA. Who can that be?

MRS. ELVSTED. I don't know. Someone he used to be friendly
with in—in the old days. Someone he's never been able to
forget.

HEDDA. What has he told you about her?

MRS. ELVSTED. Oh, he only mentioned her once, casually.

HEDDA. Well! What did he say?

MRS. ELVSTED. He said when he left her she tried to shoot him with a pistol.

HEDDA, *cold, controlled.* What nonsense. People don't do such things. The kind of people we know.

MRS. ELVSTED. No. I think it must have been that red-haired singer he used to—

HEDDA. Ah yes, very probably.

MRS. ELVSTED. I remember they used to say she always carried a loaded pistol.

HEDDA. Well then, it must be her.

MRS. ELVSTED. But Hedda, I hear she's come back, and is living here. Oh, I'm so desperate—!

HEDDA *glances towards the rear room.* Ssh! Tesman's coming. *Gets up and whispers.*

Thea, we mustn't breathe a word about this to anyone.

MRS. ELVSTED *jumps up.* Oh, no, no! Please don't!

GEORGE TESMAN *appears from the right in the rear room with a letter in his hand, and comes into the drawing room.*

TESMAN. Well, here's my little epistle all signed and sealed.

HEDDA. Good. I think Mrs. Elvsted wants to go now. Wait a moment—I'll see you as far as the garden gate.

TESMAN. Er—Hedda, do you think Bertha could deal with this?

HEDDA *takes the letter.* I'll give her instructions.

BERTHA *enters from the hall.*

BERTHA. Judge Brack is here and asks if he may pay his respects to Madam and the Doctor.

HEDDA. Yes, ask him to be so good as to come in. And—wait a moment—drop this letter in the post box.

BERTHA *takes the letter.* Very good, madam.

She opens the door for JUDGE BRACK, *and goes out.* JUDGE BRACK *is forty-five; rather short, but well-built, and elastic in his movements. He has a roundish face with an aristocratic profile. His hair, cut short, is still almost black, and is carefully barbered. Eyes lively and humorous. Thick eye-brows. His moustache is also thick, and is trimmed square at the ends. He is wearing outdoor clothes which are elegant but a little too youthful for him. He has a monocle in one eye; now and then he lets it drop.*

BRACK, *hat in hand, bows.* May one presume to call so early?

HEDDA. One may presume.

TESMAN *shakes his hand.* You're welcome here any time. Judge Brack—Mrs. Rysing.

HEDDA *sighs.*

BRACK *bows.* Ah—charmed—

HEDDA *looks at him and laughs.* What fun to be able to see you by daylight for once, Judge.

BRACK. Do I look—different?

HEDDA. Yes. A little younger, I think.

BRACK. Obliged.

TESMAN. Well, what do you think of Hedda? What? Doesn't she look well? Hasn't she filled out—?

HEDDA. Oh, do stop it. You ought to be thanking Judge Brack for all the inconvenience he's put himself to—

BRACK. Nonsense, it was a pleasure—

HEDDA. You're a loyal friend. But my other friend is pining to get away. Au revoir, Judge. I won't be a minute.

Mutual salutations. MRS. ELVSTED *and* HEDDA *go out through the hall.*

BRACK. Well, is your wife satisfied with everything?

TESMAN. Yes, we can't thank you enough. That is—we may have to shift one or two things around, she tells me. And we're short of one or two little items we'll have to purchase.

BRACK. Oh? Really?

TESMAN. But you mustn't worry your head about that. Hedda says she'll get what's needed. I say, why don't we sit down? What?

BRACK. Thanks, just for a moment.

Sits at the table.

There's something I'd like to talk to you about, my dear Tesman.

TESMAN. Oh? Ah yes, of course.

Sits.

After the feast comes the reckoning. What?

BRACK. Oh, never mind about the financial side—there's no hurry about that. Though I could wish we'd arranged things a little less palatially.

TESMAN. Good heavens, that'd never have done. Think of Hedda, my dear chap. You know her. I couldn't possibly ask her to live like a suburban housewife.

BRACK. No, no—that's just the problem.

TESMAN. Anyway, it can't be long now before my nomination comes through.

BRACK. Well, you know, these things often take time.

TESMAN. Have you heard any more news? What?

BRACK. Nothing definite.

Changing the subject.

Oh, by the way, I have one piece of news for you.

TESMAN. What?

BRACK. Your old friend Eilert Loevborg is back in town.

TESMAN. I know that already.

BRACK. Oh? How did you hear that?

TESMAN. She told me. That lady who went out with Hedda.

BRACK. I see. What was her name? I didn't catch it.

TESMAN. Mrs. Elvsted.

BRACK. Oh, the magistrate's wife. Yes, Loevborg's been living up near them, hasn't he?

TESMAN. I'm delighted to hear he's become a decent human being again.

BRACK. Yes, so they say.

TESMAN. I gather he's published a new book, too. What?

BRACK. Indeed he has.

TESMAN. I hear it's created rather a stir.

BRACK. Quite an unusual stir.

TESMAN. I say, isn't that splendid news! He's such a gifted chap—and I was afraid he'd gone to the dogs for good.

BRACK. Most people thought he had.

TESMAN. But I can't think what he'll do now. How on earth will he manage to make ends meet? What?

As he speaks his last words, HEDDA *enters from the hall.*

HEDDA, *to* BRACK, *laughs slightly scornfully.* Tesman is always worrying about making ends meet.

TESMAN. We were talking about poor Eilert Loevborg, Hedda dear.

HEDDA *gives him a quick look.* Oh, were you?

Sits in the armchair by the stove and asks casually.

Is he in trouble?

TESMAN. Well, he must have run through his inheritance long ago by now. And he can't write a new book every year. What? So I'm wondering what's going to become of him.

BRACK. I may be able to enlighten you there.

TESMAN. Oh?

BRACK. You mustn't forget he has relatives who wield a good deal of influence.

TESMAN. Relatives? Oh, they've quite washed their hands of him, I'm afraid.

BRACK. They used to regard him as the hope of the family.

TESMAN. Used to, yes. But he's put an end to that.

HEDDA. Who knows?

With a little smile.

I hear the Elvsteds have made a new man of him.

BRACK. And then this book he's just published—

TESMAN. Well, let's hope they find something for him. I've just written him a note. Oh, by the way, Hedda, I asked him to come over and see us this evening.

BRACK. But my dear chap, you're coming to me this evening.

My bachelor party. You promised me last night when I met you at the boat.

HEDDA. Had you forgotten, Tesman?

TESMAN. Good heavens, yes, I'd quite forgotten.

BRACK. Anyway, you can be quite sure he won't turn up here.

TESMAN. Why do you think that? What?

BRACK, *a little unwillingly, gets up and rests his hands on the back of his chair.* My dear Tesman—and you, too, Mrs. Tesman—there's something I feel you ought to know.

TESMAN. Concerning Eilert?

BRACK. Concerning him and you.

TESMAN. Well, my dear Judge, tell us, please!

BRACK. You must be prepared for your nomination not to come through quite as quickly as you hope and expect.

TESMAN *jumps up uneasily.* Is anything wrong? What?

BRACK. There's a possibility that the appointment may be decided by competition—

TESMAN. Competition! By Jove, Hedda, fancy that!

HEDDA *leans further back in her chair.* Ah! How interesting!

TESMAN. But who else—? I say, you don't mean—?

BRACK. Exactly. By competition with Eilert Loevborg.

TESMAN *clasps his hands in alarm.* No, no, but this is inconceivable! It's absolutely impossible! What?

BRACK. Hm. We may find it'll happen, all the same.

TESMAN. No, but—Judge Brack, they couldn't be so inconsiderate towards me!
Waves his arms.
I mean, by Jove, I—I'm a married man! It was on the strength of this that Hedda and I *got* married! We ran up some pretty hefty debts. And borrowed money from Auntie Juju! I mean, good heavens, they practically promised me the appointment. What?

BRACK. Well, well, I'm sure you'll get it. But you'll have to go through a competition.

HEDDA, *motionless in her armchair*. How exciting, Tesman. It'll be a kind of duel, by Jove.

TESMAN. My dear Hedda, how can you take it so lightly?

HEDDA, *as before*. I'm not. I can't wait to see who's going to win.

BRACK. In any case, Mrs. Tesman, it's best you should know how things stand. I mean before you commit yourself to these little items I hear you're threatening to purchase.

HEDDA. I can't allow this to alter my plans.

BRACK. Indeed? Well, that's your business. Good-bye.

To TESMAN.

I'll come and collect you on the way home from my afternoon walk.

TESMAN. Oh, yes, yes. I'm sorry, I'm all upside down just now.

HEDDA, *lying in her chair, holds out her hand*. Good-bye, Judge. See you this afternoon.

BRACK. Thank you. Good-bye, good-bye.

TESMAN *sees him to the door*. Good-bye, my dear Judge. You will excuse me, won't you?

JUDGE BRACK *goes out through the hall*.

TESMAN, *pacing up and down*. Oh, Hedda! One oughtn't to go plunging off on wild adventures. What?

HEDDA *looks at him and smiles*. Like you're doing?

TESMAN. Yes. I mean, there's no denying it, it was a pretty big adventure to go off and get married and set up house merely on expectation.

HEDDA. Perhaps you're right.

TESMAN. Well, anyway, we have our home, Hedda. By Jove, yes. The home we dreamed of. And set our hearts on. What?

HEDDA *gets up slowly, wearily*. You agreed that we should enter society. And keep open house. That was the bargain.

TESMAN. Yes. Good heavens, I was looking forward to it all so much. To seeing you play hostess to a select circle! By Jove! What? Ah, well, for the time being we shall have to make do with each other's company, Hedda. Perhaps have Auntie

Juju in now and then. Oh dear, this wasn't at all what you had in mind—

HEDDA. I won't be able to have a liveried footman. For a start.

TESMAN. Oh no, we couldn't possibly afford a footman.

HEDDA. And that thoroughbred horse you promised me—

TESMAN, *fearfully*. Thoroughbred horse!

HEDDA. I mustn't even think of that now.

TESMAN. Heaven forbid!

HEDDA *walks across the room*. Ah, well. I still have one thing left to amuse myself with.

TESMAN, *joyfully*. Thank goodness for that. What's that, Hedda? What?

HEDDA, *in the open doorway, looks at him with concealed scorn*. My pistols, George darling.

TESMAN, *alarmed*. Pistols!

HEDDA, *her eyes cold*. General Gabler's pistols.

She goes into the rear room and disappears.

TESMAN *runs to the doorway and calls after her*. For heaven's sake, Hedda dear, don't touch those things. They're dangerous. Hedda—please—for my sake! What?

ACT TWO

The same as in Act One, except that the piano has been removed and an elegant little writing table, with a bookcase, stands in its place. By the sofa on the left a smaller table has been placed. Most of the flowers have been removed. MRS. ELVSTED's *bouquet stands on the larger table, downstage. It is afternoon.*

HEDDA, *dressed to receive callers, is alone in the room. She is standing by the open french windows, loading a revolver. The pair to it is lying in an open pistol case on the writing table.*

HEDDA *looks down into the garden and calls.* Good afternoon, Judge.

BRACK, *in the distance, below.* Afternoon, Mrs. Tesman.

HEDDA *raises the pistol and takes aim.* I'm going to shoot you, Judge Brack.

BRACK *shouts from below.* No, no, no! Don't aim that thing at me!

HEDDA. This'll teach you to enter houses by the back door. *Fires.*

BRACK, *below.* Have you gone completely out of your mind?

HEDDA. Oh dear! Did I hit you?

BRACK, *still outside.* Stop playing these silly tricks.

HEDDA. All right, Judge. Come along in.

JUDGE BRACK, *dressed for a bachelor party, enters through the french windows. He has a light overcoat on his arm.*

BRACK. For God's sake! Haven't you stopped fooling around with those things yet? What are you trying to hit?

HEDDA. Oh, I was just shooting at the sky.

BRACK *takes the pistol gently from her hand.* By your leave, ma'am.

Looks at it.

Ah, yes—I know this old friend well.

Looks around.

Where's the case? Oh, yes.

Puts the pistol in the case and closes it.

That's enough of that little game for today.

HEDDA. Well, what on earth *am* I to do?

BRACK. You haven't had any visitors?

HEDDA *closes the french windows.* Not one. I suppose the best people are all still in the country.

BRACK. Your husband isn't home yet?

HEDDA *locks the pistol away in a drawer of the writing table.* No. The moment he'd finished eating he ran off to his aunties. He wasn't expecting you so early.

BRACK. Ah, why didn't I think of that? How stupid of me.

HEDDA *turns her head and looks at him.* Why stupid?

BRACK. I'd have come a little sooner.

HEDDA *walks across the room.* There'd have been no one to receive you. I've been in my room since lunch, dressing.

BRACK. You haven't a tiny crack in the door through which we might have negotiated?

HEDDA. You forgot to arrange one.

BRACK. Another stupidity.

HEDDA. Well, we'll have to sit down here. And wait. Tesman won't be back for some time.

BRACK. Sad. Well, I'll be patient.

HEDDA sits on the corner of the sofa. BRACK *puts his coat over the back of the nearest chair and seats himself, keeping his hat in his hand. Short pause. They look at each other.*

HEDDA. Well?

BRACK, *in the same tone of voice*. Well?

HEDDA. I asked first.

BRACK *leans forward slightly*. Yes, well, now we can enjoy a nice, cosy little chat—Mrs. Hedda.

HEDDA *leans further back in her chair*. It seems such ages since we had a talk. I don't count last night or this morning.

BRACK. You mean: *à deux?*

HEDDA. Mm—yes. That's roughly what I meant.

BRACK. I've been longing so much for you to come home.

HEDDA. So have I.

BRACK. You? Really, Mrs. Hedda? And I thought you were having such a wonderful honeymoon.

HEDDA. Oh, yes. Wonderful!

BRACK. But your husband wrote such ecstatic letters.

HEDDA. He! Oh, yes! He thinks life has nothing better to offer than rooting around in libraries and copying old pieces of parchment, or whatever it is he does.

BRACK, *a little maliciously*. Well, that *is* his life. Most of it, anyway.

HEDDA. Yes, I know. Well, it's all right for him. But for me! Oh no, my dear Judge. I've been bored to death.

BRACK, *sympathetically*. Do you mean that? Seriously?

HEDDA. Yes. Can you imagine? Six whole months without ever meeting a single person who was one of us, and to whom I could talk about the kind of things we talk about.

BRACK. Yes, I can understand. I'd miss that, too.

HEDDA. That wasn't the worst, though.

BRACK. What was?

HEDDA. Having to spend every minute of one's life with—with the same person.

BRACK *nods*. Yes. What a thought! Morning; noon; and—

HEDDA, *coldly*. As I said: every minute of one's life.

BRACK. I stand corrected. But dear Tesman is such a clever fellow, I should have thought one ought to be able—

HEDDA. Tesman is only interested in one thing, my dear Judge. His special subject.

BRACK. True.

HEDDA. And people who are only interested in one thing don't make the most amusing company. Not for long, anyway.

BRACK. Not even when they happen to be the person one loves?

HEDDA. Oh, don't use that sickly, stupid word.

BRACK *starts.* But, Mrs. Hedda—!

HEDDA, *half laughing, half annoyed.* You just try it, Judge. Listening to the history of civilisation morning, noon and—

BRACK *corrects her.* Every minute of one's life.

HEDDA. All right. Oh, and those domestic industries of Brabant in the Middle Ages! That really is beyond the limit.

BRACK *looks at her searchingly.* But, tell me—if you feel like this why on earth did you—? Ha—

HEDDA. Why on earth did I marry George Tesman?

BRACK. If you like to put it that way.

HEDDA. Do you think it so very strange?

BRACK. Yes—and no, Mrs. Hedda.

HEDDA. I'd danced myself tired, Judge. I felt my time was up—
Gives a slight shudder.
No, I mustn't say that. Or even think it.

BRACK. You've no rational cause to think it.

HEDDA. Oh—cause, cause—
Looks searchingly at him.
After all, George Tesman—well, I mean, he's a very respectable man.

BRACK. Very respectable, sound as a rock. No denying that.

HEDDA. And there's nothing exactly ridiculous about him. Is there?

BRACK. Ridiculous? N-no, I wouldn't say that.

HEDDA. Mm. He's very clever at collecting material and all that, isn't he? I mean, he may go quite far in time.

BRACK *looks at her a little uncertainly.* I thought you believed, like everyone else, that he would become a very prominent man.

HEDDA *looks tired.* Yes, I did. And when he came and begged me on his bended knees to be allowed to love and to cherish me, I didn't see why I shouldn't let him.

BRACK. No, well—if one looks at it like that—

HEDDA. It was more than my other admirers were prepared to do, Judge dear.

BRACK *laughs.* Well, I can't answer for the others. As far as I myself am concerned, you know I've always had a considerable respect for the institution of marriage. As an institution.

HEDDA, *lightly.* Oh, I've never entertained any hopes of you.

BRACK. All I want is to have a circle of friends whom I can trust, whom I can help with advice or—or by any other means, and into whose houses I may come and go as a—trusted friend.

HEDDA. Of the husband?

BRACK *bows.* Preferably, to be frank, of the wife. And of the husband too, of course. Yes, you know, this kind of—triangle is a delightful arrangement for all parties concerned.

HEDDA. Yes, I often longed for a third person while I was away. Oh, those hours we spent alone in railway compartments—

BRACK. Fortunately your honeymoon is now over.

HEDDA *shakes her head.* There's a long, long way still to go. I've only reached a stop on the line.

BRACK. Why not jump out and stretch your legs a little, Mrs. Hedda?

HEDDA. I'm not the jumping sort.

BRACK. Aren't you?

HEDDA. No. There's always someone around who—

BRACK *laughs.* Who looks at one's legs?

HEDDA. Yes. Exactly.

BRACK. Well, but surely—

HEDDA, *with a gesture of rejection.* I don't like it. I'd rather stay where I am. Sitting in the compartment. *À deux.*

BRACK. But suppose a third person were to step into the compartment?

HEDDA. That would be different.

BRACK. A trusted friend—someone who understood—

HEDDA. And was lively and amusing—

BRACK. And interested in—more subjects than one—

HEDDA *sighs audibly.* Yes, that'd be a relief.

BRACK *hears the front door open and shut.* The triangle is completed.

HEDDA, *half under breath.* And the train goes on.

GEORGE TESMAN, *in grey walking dress with a soft felt hat, enters from the hall. He has a number of paper-covered books under his arm and in his pockets.*

TESMAN *goes over to the table by the corner sofa.* Phew! It's too hot to be lugging all this around.

Puts the books down.

I'm positively sweating, Hedda. Why, hullo, hullo! You here already, Judge? What? Bertha didn't tell me.

BRACK *gets up.* I came in through the garden.

HEDDA. What are all those books you've got there?

TESMAN *stands glancing through them.* Oh, some new publications dealing with my special subject. I had to buy them.

HEDDA. Your special subject?

BRACK. His special subject, Mrs. Tesman.

BRACK *and* HEDDA *exchange a smile.*

HEDDA. Haven't you collected enough material on your special subject?

TESMAN. My dear Hedda, one can never have too much. One must keep abreast of what other people are writing.

HEDDA. Yes. Of course.

TESMAN, *rooting among the books*. Look—I bought a copy of Eilert Loevborg's new book, too.

Holds it out to her.

Perhaps you'd like to have a look at it, Hedda? What?

HEDDA. No, thank you. Er—yes, perhaps I will, later.

TESMAN. I glanced through it on my way home.

BRACK. What's your opinion—as a specialist on the subject?

TESMAN. I'm amazed how sound and balanced it is. He never used to write like that.

Gathers his books together.

Well, I must get down to these at once. I can hardly wait to cut the pages. Oh, I've got to change, too.

To BRACK.

We don't have to be off just yet, do we? What?

BRACK. Heavens, no. We've plenty of time yet.

TESMAN. Good, I needn't hurry, then.

Goes with his books, but stops and turns in the doorway.

Oh, by the way, Hedda, Auntie Juju won't be coming to see you this evening.

HEDDA. Won't she? Oh—the hat, I suppose.

TESMAN. Good heavens, no. How could you think such a thing of Auntie Juju? Fancy—! No, Auntie Rena's very ill.

HEDDA. She always is.

TESMAN. Yes, but today she's been taken really bad.

HEDDA. Oh, then it's quite understandable that the other one should want to stay with her. Well, I shall have to swallow my disappointment.

TESMAN. You can't imagine how happy Auntie Juju was in spite of everything. At your looking so well after the honeymoon!

HEDDA, *half beneath her breath, as she rises*. Oh, these everlasting aunts!

TESMAN. What?

HEDDA *goes over to the french windows*. Nothing.

TESMAN. Oh. All right.

Goes into the rear room and out of sight.

BRACK. What was that about the hat?

HEDDA. Oh, something that happened with Miss Tesman this morning. She'd put her hat down on a chair.

Looks at him and smiles.

And I pretended to think it was the servant's.

BRACK *shakes his head.* But my dear Mrs. Hedda, how could you do such a thing? To that poor old lady?

HEDDA, *nervously, walking across the room.* Sometimes a mood like that hits me. And I can't stop myself.

Throws herself down in the armchair by the stove.

Oh, I don't know how to explain it.

BRACK, *behind her chair.* You're not really happy. That's the answer.

HEDDA *stares ahead of her.* Why on earth should I be happy? Can you give me a reason?

BRACK. Yes. For one thing you've got the home you always wanted.

HEDDA *looks at him.* You really believe that story?

BRACK. You mean it isn't true?

HEDDA. Oh, yes, it's partly true.

BRACK. Well?

HEDDA. It's true I got Tesman to see me home from parties last summer—

BRACK. It was a pity my home lay in another direction.

HEDDA. Yes. Your interests lay in another direction, too.

BRACK *laughs.* That's naughty of you, Mrs. Hedda. But to return to you and Tesman—

HEDDA. Well, we walked past this house one evening. And poor Tesman was fidgeting in his boots trying to find something to talk about. I felt sorry for the great scholar—

BRACK *smiles incredulously.* Did you? Hm.

HEDDA. Yes, honestly I did. Well, to help him out of his misery,

I happened to say quite frivolously how much I'd love to live in this house.

BRACK. Was that all?

HEDDA. That evening, yes.

BRACK. But—afterwards?

HEDDA. Yes. My little frivolity had its consequences, my dear Judge.

BRACK. Our little frivolities do. Much too often, unfortunately.

HEDDA. Thank you. Well, it was our mutual admiration for the late Prime Minister's house that brought George Tesman and me together on common ground. So we got engaged, and we got married, and we went on our honeymoon, and— Ah well, Judge, I've—made my bed and I must lie in it, I was about to say.

BRACK. How utterly fantastic! And you didn't really care in the least about the house?

HEDDA. God knows I didn't.

BRACK. Yes, but now that we've furnished it so beautifully for you?

HEDDA. Ugh—all the rooms smell of lavender and dried roses. But perhaps Auntie Juju brought that in.

BRACK *laughs.* More likely the Prime Minister's widow, rest her soul.

HEDDA. Yes, it's got the odour of death about it. It reminds me of the flowers one has worn at a ball—the morning after. *Clasps her hands behind her neck, leans back in the chair and looks up at him.*

Oh, my dear Judge, you've no idea how hideously bored I'm going to be out here.

BRACK. Couldn't you find some kind of occupation, Mrs. Hedda? Like your husband?

HEDDA. Occupation? That'd interest me?

BRACK. Well—preferably.

HEDDA. God knows what. I've often thought—
Breaks off.

No, that wouldn't work either.

BRACK. Who knows? Tell me about it.

HEDDA. I was thinking—if I could persuade Tesman to go into politics, for example.

BRACK *laughs.* Tesman! No, honestly, I don't think he's quite cut out to be a politician.

HEDDA. Perhaps not. But if I could persuade him to have a go at it?

BRACK. What satisfaction would that give you? If he turned out to be no good? Why do you want to make him do that?

HEDDA. Because I'm bored.

After a moment.

You feel there's absolutely no possibility of Tesman becoming Prime Minister, then?

BRACK. Well, you know, Mrs. Hedda, for one thing he'd have to be pretty well off before he could become that.

HEDDA *gets up impatiently.* There you are!

Walks across the room.

It's this wretched poverty that makes life so hateful. And ludicrous. Well, it is!

BRACK. I don't think that's the real cause.

HEDDA. What is, then?

BRACK. Nothing really exciting has ever happened to you.

HEDDA. Nothing serious, you mean?

BRACK. Call it that if you like. But now perhaps it may.

HEDDA *tosses her head.* Oh, you're thinking of this competition for that wretched professorship? That's Tesman's affair. I'm not going to waste my time worrying about that.

BRACK. Very well, let's forget about that then. But suppose you were to find yourself faced with what people call—to use the conventional phrase—the most solemn of human responsibilities?

Smiles.

A new responsibility, little Mrs. Hedda.

HEDDA, *angrily.* Be quiet! Nothing like that's going to happen.

BRACK, *warily.* We'll talk about it again in a year's time. If not earlier.

HEDDA, *curtly.* I've no leanings in that direction, Judge. I don't want any—responsibilities.

BRACK. But surely you must feel some inclination to make use of that—natural talent which every woman—

HEDDA, *over by the french windows.* Oh, be quiet, I say! I often think there's only one thing for which I have any natural talent.

BRACK *goes closer.* And what is that, if I may be so bold as to ask?

HEDDA *stands looking out.* For boring myself to death. Now you know.

Turns, looks toward the rear room and laughs.

Talking of boring, here comes the Professor.

BRACK, *quietly, warningly.* Now, now, now, Mrs. Hedda!

GEORGE TESMAN, *in evening dress, with gloves and hat in his hand, enters through the rear room from the right.*

TESMAN. Hedda, hasn't any message come from Eilert? What?

HEDDA. No.

TESMAN. Ah, then we'll have him here presently. You wait and see.

BRACK. You really think he'll come?

TESMAN. Yes, I'm almost sure he will. What you were saying about him this morning is just gossip.

BRACK. Oh?

TESMAN. Yes. Auntie Juju said she didn't believe he'd ever dare to stand in my way again. Fancy that!

BRACK. Then everything in the garden's lovely.

TESMAN *puts his hat, with his gloves in it, on a chair, right.* Yes, but you really must let me wait for him as long as possible.

BRACK. We've plenty of time. No one'll be turning up at my place before seven or half past.

TESMAN. Ah, then we can keep Hedda company a little longer. And see if he turns up. What?

HEDDA *picks up* BRACK's *coat and hat and carries them over to the corner sofa.* And if the worst comes to the worst, Mr. Loevborg can sit here and talk to me.

BRACK, *offering to take his things from her.* No, please. What do you mean by "if the worst comes to the worst"?

HEDDA. If he doesn't want to go with you and Tesman.

TESMAN *looks doubtfully at her.* I say, Hedda, do you think it'll be all right for him to stay here with you? What? Remember Auntie Juju isn't coming.

HEDDA. Yes, but Mrs. Elvsted is. The three of us can have a cup of tea together.

TESMAN. Ah, that'll be all right then.

BRACK *smiles.* It's probably the safest solution as far as he's concerned.

HEDDA. Why?

BRACK. My dear Mrs. Tesman, you always say of my little bachelor parties that they should be attended only by men of the strongest principles.

HEDDA. But Mr. Loevborg is a man of principle now. You know what they say about a reformed sinner—

BERTHA *enters from the hall.*

BERTHA. Madam, there's a gentleman here who wants to see you—

HEDDA. Ask him to come in.

TESMAN, *quietly.* I'm sure it's him. By Jove. Fancy that!

EILERT LOEVBORG *enters from the hall. He is slim and lean, of the same age as* TESMAN, *but looks older and somewhat haggard. His hair and beard are of a blackish-brown; his face is long and pale, but with a couple of reddish patches on his cheekbones. He is dressed in an elegant and fairly new black suit, and carries black gloves and a top hat in his hand. He stops just inside the door and bows abruptly. He seems somewhat embarrassed.*

TESMAN *goes over and shakes his hand.* My dear Eilert! How grand to see you again after all these years!

EILERT LOEVBORG *speaks softly.* It was good of you to write, George.

Goes nearer to HEDDA.

May I shake hands with you, too, Mrs. Tesman?

HEDDA *accepts his hand.* Delighted to see you, Mr. Loevborg. *With a gesture.*

I don't know if you two gentlemen—

LOEVBORG *bows slightly.* Judge Brack, I believe.

BRACK, *also with a slight bow.* Correct. We—met some years ago—

TESMAN *puts his hands on* LOEVBORG'S *shoulders.* Now you're to treat this house just as though it were your own home, Eilert. Isn't that right, Hedda? I hear you've decided to settle here again? What?

LOEVBORG. Yes, I have.

TESMAN. Quite understandable. Oh, by the bye—I've just bought your new book. Though to tell the truth I haven't found time to read it yet.

LOEVBORG. You needn't bother.

TESMAN. Oh? Why?

LOEVBORG. There's nothing much in it.

TESMAN. By Jove, fancy hearing that from you!

BRACK. But everyone's praising it.

LOEVBORG. That was exactly what I wanted to happen. So I only wrote what I knew everyone would agree with.

BRACK. Very sensible.

TESMAN. Yes, but my dear Eilert—

LOEVBORG. I want to try to re-establish myself. To begin again —from the beginning.

TESMAN, *a little embarrassed.* Yes, I—er—suppose you do. What?

LOEVBORG *smiles, puts down his hat and takes a package*

wrapped in paper from his coat pocket. But when this gets published—George Tesman—read it. This is my real book. The one in which I have spoken with my own voice.

TESMAN. Oh, really? What's it about?

LOEVBORG. It's the sequel.

TESMAN. Sequel? To what?

LOEVBORG. To the other book.

TESMAN. The one that's just come out?

LOEVBORG. Yes.

TESMAN. But my dear Eilert, that covers the subject right up to the present day.

LOEVBORG. It does. But this is about the future.

TESMAN. The future! But, I say, we don't know anything about that.

LOEVBORG. No. But there are one or two things that need to be said about it.

Opens the package.

Here, have a look.

TESMAN. Surely that's not your handwriting?

LOEVBORG. I dictated it.

Turns the pages.

It's in two parts. The first deals with the forces that will shape our civilisation.

Turns further on towards the end.

And the second indicates the direction in which that civilisation may develop.

TESMAN. Amazing! I'd never think of writing about anything like that.

HEDDA, *by the french windows, drumming on the pane.* No. You wouldn't.

LOEVBORG *puts the pages back into their cover and lays the package on the table.* I brought it because I thought I might possibly read you a few pages this evening.

TESMAN. I say, what a kind idea! Oh, but this evening—?

Glances at BRACK.

I'm not quite sure whether—

LOEVBORG. Well, some other time, then. There's no hurry.

BRACK. The truth is, Mr. Loevborg, I'm giving a little dinner this evening. In Tesman's honour, you know.

LOEVBORG *looks round for his hat.* Oh—then I mustn't—

BRACK. No, wait a minute. Won't you do me the honour of joining us?

LOEVBORG, *curtly, with decision.* No I can't. Thank you so much.

BRACK. Oh, nonsense. Do—please. There'll only be a few of us. And I can promise you we shall have some good sport, as Mrs. Hed—as Mrs. Tesman puts it.

LOEVBORG. I've no doubt. Nevertheless—

BRACK. You could bring your manuscript along and read it to Tesman at my place. I could lend you a room.

TESMAN. By Jove, Eilert, that's an idea. What?

HEDDA *interposes.* But Tesman, Mr. Loevborg doesn't want to go. I'm sure Mr. Loevborg would much rather sit here and have supper with me.

LOEVBORG *looks at her.* With you, Mrs. Tesman?

HEDDA. And Mrs. Elvsted.

LOEVBORG. Oh.

Casually.

I ran into her this afternoon.

HEDDA. Did you? Well, she's coming here this evening. So you really must stay, Mr. Loevborg. Otherwise she'll have no one to see her home.

LOEVBORG. That's true. Well—thank you, Mrs. Tesman, I'll stay then.

HEDDA. I'll just tell the servant.

She goes to the door which leads into the hall, and rings. BERTHA *enters.* HEDDA *talks softly to her and points towards the rear room.* BERTHA *nods and goes out.*

TESMAN, *to* LOEVBORG, *as* HEDDA *does this.* I say, Eilert. This new subject of yours—the—er—future—is that the one you're going to lecture about?

LOEVBORG. Yes.

TESMAN. They told me down at the bookshop that you're going to hold a series of lectures here during the autumn.

LOEVBORG. Yes, I am. I—hope you don't mind, Tesman.

TESMAN. Good heavens, no! But—?

LOEVBORG. I can quite understand it might queer your pitch a little.

TESMAN, *dejectedly.* Oh well, I can't expect you to put them off for my sake.

LOEVBORG. I'll wait till your appointment's been announced.

TESMAN. You'll wait! But—but—aren't you going to compete with me for the post? What?

LOEVBORG. No. I only want to defeat you in the eyes of the world.

TESMAN. Good heavens! Then Auntie Juju was right after all! Oh, I knew it, I knew it! Hear that, Hedda? Fancy! Eilert *doesn't* want to stand in our way.

HEDDA, *curtly.* Our? Leave me out of it, please.

She goes towards the rear room, where BERTHA *is setting a tray with decanters and glasses on the table.* HEDDA *nods approval, and comes back into the drawing room.* BERTHA *goes out.*

TESMAN, *while this is happening.* Judge Brack, what do you think about all this? What?

BRACK. Oh, I think honour and victory can be very splendid things—

TESMAN. Of course they can. Still—

HEDDA *looks at* TESMAN *with a cold smile.* You look as if you'd been hit by a thunderbolt.

TESMAN. Yes, I feel rather like it.

BRACK. There was a black cloud looming up, Mrs. Tesman. But it seems to have passed over.

HEDDA *points towards the rear room.* Well, gentlemen, won't you go in and take a glass of cold punch?

BRACK *glances at his watch.* A stirrup cup? Yes, why not?

TESMAN. An admirable suggestion, Hedda. Admirable! Oh, I feel so relieved!

HEDDA. Won't you have one, too, Mr. Loevborg?

LOEVBORG. No, thank you. I'd rather not.

BRACK. Great heavens, man, cold punch isn't poison. Take my word for it.

LOEVBORG. Not for everyone, perhaps.

HEDDA. I'll keep Mr. Loevborg company while you drink.

TESMAN. Yes, Hedda dear, would you?

He and BRACK *go into the rear room, sit down, drink punch, smoke cigarettes and talk cheerfully during the following scene.* EILERT LOEVBORG *remains standing by the stove.* HEDDA *goes to the writing table.*

HEDDA, *raising her voice slightly.* I've some photographs I'd like to show you, if you'd care to see them. Tesman and I visited the Tyrol on our way home.

She comes back with an album, places it on the table by the sofa and sits in the upstage corner of the sofa. EILERT LOEVBORG *comes towards her, stops and looks at her. Then he takes a chair and sits down on her left, with his back towards the rear room.*

HEDDA *opens the album.* You see these mountains, Mr. Loevborg? That's the Ortler group. Tesman has written the name underneath. You see: "The Ortler Group near Meran."

LOEVBORG *has not taken his eyes from her; says softly, slowly.* Hedda—Gabler!

HEDDA *gives him a quick glance.* Ssh!

LOEVBORG *repeats softly.* Hedda Gabler!

HEDDA *looks at the album.* Yes, that used to be my name. When we first knew each other.

LOEVBORG. And from now on—for the rest of my life—I must teach myself never to say: Hedda Gabler.

HEDDA, *still turning the pages.* Yes, you must. You'd better start getting into practice. The sooner the better.

LOEVBORG, *bitterly.* Hedda Gabler married? And to George Tesman?

HEDDA. Yes. Well—that's life.

LOEVBORG. Oh, Hedda, Hedda! How could you throw yourself away like that?

HEDDA *looks sharply at him.* Stop it.

LOEVBORG. What do you mean?

TESMAN *comes in and goes towards the sofa.*

HEDDA *hears him coming and says casually.* And this, Mr. Loevborg, is the view from the Ampezzo valley. Look at those mountains.

Glances affectionately up at TESMAN.

What did you say those curious mountains were called, dear?

TESMAN. Let me have a look. Oh, those are the Dolomites.

HEDDA. Of course. Those are the Dolomites, Mr. Loevborg.

TESMAN. Hedda, I just wanted to ask you, can't we bring some punch in here? A glass for you, anyway. What?

HEDDA. Thank you, yes. And a biscuit or two, perhaps.

TESMAN. You wouldn't like a cigarette?

HEDDA. No.

TESMAN. Right.

He goes into the rear room and over to the right. BRACK *is sitting there, glancing occasionally at* HEDDA *and* LOEVBORG.

LOEVBORG, *softly, as before.* Answer me, Hedda. How could you do it?

HEDDA, *apparently absorbed in the album.* If you go on calling me Hedda I won't talk to you any more.

LOEVBORG. Mayn't I even when we're alone?

HEDDA. No. You can think it. But you mustn't say it.

LOEVBORG. Oh, I see. Because you love George Tesman.

HEDDA *glances at him and smiles.* Love? Don't be funny.

LOEVBORG. You don't love him?

HEDDA. I don't intend to be unfaithful to him. That's not what I want.

LOEVBORG. Hedda—just tell me one thing—

HEDDA. Ssh!

TESMAN enters from the rear room, carrying a tray.

TESMAN. Here we are! Here come the goodies!

Puts the tray down on the table.

HEDDA. Why didn't you ask the servant to bring it in?

TESMAN *fills the glasses.* I like waiting on you, Hedda.

HEDDA. But you've filled both glasses. Mr. Loevborg doesn't want to drink.

TESMAN. Yes, but Mrs. Elvsted'll be here soon.

HEDDA. Oh yes, that's true. Mrs. Elvsted—

TESMAN. Had you forgotten her? What?

HEDDA. We're so absorbed with these photographs.

Shows him one.

You remember this little village?

TESMAN. Oh, that one down by the Brenner Pass. We spent a night there—

HEDDA. Yes, and met all those amusing people.

TESMAN. Oh yes, it was there, wasn't it? By Jove, if only we could have had you with us, Eilert! Ah, well.

Goes back into the other room and sits down with BRACK.

LOEVBORG. Tell me one thing, Hedda.

HEDDA. Yes?

LOEVBORG. Didn't you love me either? Not—just a little?

HEDDA. Well now, I wonder? No, I think we were just good pals— Really good pals who could tell each other anything.

Smiles.

You certainly poured your heart out to me.

LOEVBORG. You begged me to.

HEDDA. Looking back on it, there was something beautiful and fascinating—and brave—about the way we told each other everything. That secret friendship no one else knew about.

LOEVBORG. Yes, Hedda, yes! Do you remember? How I used to come up to your father's house in the afternoon—and the General sat by the window and read his newspapers—with his back towards us—

HEDDA. And we sat on the sofa in the corner—

LOEVBORG. Always reading the same illustrated magazine—

HEDDA. We hadn't any photograph album.

LOEVBORG. Yes, Hedda. I regarded you as a kind of confessor. Told you things about myself which no one else knew about —then. Those days and nights of drinking and— Oh, Hedda, what power did you have to make me confess such things?

HEDDA. Power? You think I had some power over you?

LOEVBORG. Yes—I don't know how else to explain it. And all those—oblique questions you asked me—

HEDDA. You knew what they meant.

LOEVBORG. But that you could sit there and ask me such questions! So unashamedly—

HEDDA. I thought you said they were oblique.

LOEVBORG. Yes, but you asked them so unashamedly. That you could question me about—about that kind of thing!

HEDDA. You answered willingly enough.

LOEVBORG. Yes—that's what I can't understand—looking back on it. But tell me, Hedda—what you felt for me—wasn't that —love? When you asked me those questions and made me confess my sins to you, wasn't it because you wanted to wash me clean?

HEDDA. No, not exactly.

LOEVBORG. Why did you do it, then?

HEDDA. Do you find it so incredible that a young girl, given the chance to do so without anyone knowing, should want to be allowed a glimpse into a forbidden world of whose existence she is supposed to be ignorant?

LOEVBORG. So that was it?

HEDDA. One reason. One reason—I think.

LOEVBORG. You didn't love me, then. You just wanted—knowledge. But if that was so, why did you break it off?

HEDDA. That was your fault.

LOEVBORG. It was you who put an end to it.

HEDDA. Yes, when I realised that our friendship was threatening to develop into something—something else. Shame on you, Eilert Loevborg! How could you abuse the trust of your dearest friend?

LOEVBORG *clenches his fists.* Oh, why didn't you do it? Why didn't you shoot me dead? As you threatened to?

HEDDA. I was afraid. Of the scandal.

LOEVBORG. Yes, Hedda. You're a coward at heart.

HEDDA. A dreadful coward.

Changes her tone.

Luckily for you. Well, now you've found consolation with the Elvsteds.

LOEVBORG. I know what Thea's been telling you.

HEDDA. I dare say you told her about us.

LOEVBORG. Not a word. She's too silly to understand that kind of thing.

HEDDA. Silly?

LOEVBORG. She's silly about that kind of thing.

HEDDA. And I am a coward.

Leans closer to him, without looking him in the eyes, and says quietly.

But let me tell you something. Something you don't know.

LOEVBORG, *tensely.* Yes?

HEDDA. My failure to shoot you wasn't my worst act of cowardice that evening.

LOEVBORG *looks at her for a moment, realises her meaning and whispers passionately.* Oh, Hedda! Hedda Gabler! Now I see what was behind those questions. Yes! It wasn't knowledge you wanted! It was life!

HEDDA *flashes a look at him and says quietly.* Take care! Don't you delude yourself!

It has begun to grow dark. BERTHA, *from outside, opens the door leading into the hall.*

HEDDA *closes the album with a snap and cries, smiling.* Ah, at last! Come in, Thea dear!

MRS. ELVSTED *enters from the hall, in evening dress. The door is closed behind her.*

HEDDA, *on the sofa, stretches out her arms towards her.* Thea darling, I thought you were never coming!

MRS. ELVSTED *makes a slight bow to the gentlemen in the rear room as she passes the open doorway, and they to her. Then she goes to the table and holds out her hand to* HEDDA. EILERT LOEVBORG *has risen from his chair. He and* MRS. ELVSTED *nod silently to each other.*

MRS. ELVSTED. Perhaps I ought to go in and say a few words to your husband?

HEDDA. Oh, there's no need. They're happy by themselves. They'll be going soon.

MRS. ELVSTED. Going?

HEDDA. Yes, they're off on a spree this evening.

MRS. ELVSTED, *quickly, to* LOEVBORG. You're not going with them?

LOEVBORG. No.

HEDDA. Mr. Loevborg is staying here with us.

MRS. ELVSTED *takes a chair and is about to sit down beside him.* Oh, how nice it is to be here!

HEDDA. No, Thea darling, not there. Come over here and sit beside me. I want to be in the middle.

MRS. ELVSTED. Yes, just as you wish.

She goes round the table and sits on the sofa, on HEDDA's *right.* LOEVBORG *sits down again in his chair.*

LOEVBORG, *after a short pause, to* HEDDA. Isn't she lovely to look at?

HEDDA *strokes her hair gently.* Only to look at?

LOEVBORG. Yes. We're just good pals. We trust each other implicitly. We can talk to each other quite unashamedly.

HEDDA. No need to be oblique?

MRS. ELVSTED *nestles close to* HEDDA *and says quietly.* Oh, Hedda I'm so happy. Imagine—he says I've inspired him!

HEDDA *looks at her with a smile.* Dear Thea! Does he really?

LOEVBORG. She has the courage of her convictions, Mrs. Tesman.

MRS. ELVSTED. I? Courage?

LOEVBORG. Absolute courage. Where friendship is concerned.

HEDDA. Yes. Courage. Yes. If only one had that—

LOEVBORG. Yes?

HEDDA. One might be able to live. In spite of everything.
Changes her tone suddenly.
Well, Thea darling, now you're going to drink a nice glass of cold punch.

MRS. ELVSTED. No, thank you. I never drink anything like that.

HEDDA. Oh. You, Mr. Loevborg?

LOEVBORG. Thank you, I don't either.

MRS. ELVSTED. No, he doesn't, either.

HEDDA *looks into his eyes.* But if I want you to?

LOEVBORG. That doesn't make any difference.

HEDDA *laughs.* Have I no power over you at all? Poor me!

LOEVBORG. Not where this is concerned.

HEDDA. Seriously, I think you should. For your own sake.

MRS. ELVSTED. Hedda!

LOEVBORG. Why?

HEDDA. Or perhaps I should say for other people's sake.

LOEVBORG. What do you mean?

HEDDA. People might think you didn't feel absolutely and unashamedly sure of yourself. In your heart of hearts.

MRS. ELVSTED, *quietly*. Oh, Hedda, no!

LOEVBORG. People can think what they like. For the present.

MRS. ELVSTED, *happily*. Yes, that's true.

HEDDA. I saw it so clearly in Judge Brack a few minutes ago.

LOEVBORG. Oh. What did you see?

HEDDA. He smiled so scornfully when he saw you were afraid to go in there and drink with them.

LOEVBORG. Afraid! I wanted to stay here and talk to you.

MRS. ELVSTED. That was only natural, Hedda.

HEDDA. But the Judge wasn't to know that. I saw him wink at Tesman when you showed you didn't dare to join their wretched little party.

LOEVBORG. Didn't dare! Are you saying I didn't dare?

HEDDA. I'm not saying so. But that was what Judge Brack thought.

LOEVBORG. Well, let him.

HEDDA. You're not going, then?

LOEVBORG. I'm staying here with you and Thea.

MRS. ELVSTED. Yes, Hedda, of course he is.

HEDDA *smiles, and nods approvingly to* LOEVBORG. Firm as a rock! A man of principle! That's how a man should be!
Turns to MRS. ELVSTED *and strokes her cheek.*
Didn't I tell you so this morning when you came here in such a panic—

LOEVBORG *starts*. Panic?

MRS. ELVSTED, *frightened*. Hedda! But—Hedda!

HEDDA. Well, now you can see for yourself. There's no earthly need for you to get scared to death just because—
Stops.
Well! Let's all three cheer up and enjoy ourselves.

LOEVBORG. Mrs. Tesman, would you mind explaining to me what this is all about?

MRS. ELVSTED. Oh, my God, my God, Hedda, what are you saying? What are you doing?

HEDDA. Keep calm. That horrid Judge has his eye on you.

LOEVBORG. Scared to death, were you? For my sake?

MRS. ELVSTED, *quietly, trembling*. Oh, Hedda! You've made me so unhappy!

LOEVBORG *looks coldly at her for a moment. His face is distorted*. So that was how much you trusted me.

MRS. ELVSTED. Eilert dear, please listen to me—

LOEVBORG *takes one of the glasses of punch, raises it and says quietly, hoarsely*. Skoal, Thea!

Empties the glass, puts it down and picks up one of the others.

MRS. ELVSTED, *quietly*. Hedda, Hedda! Why did you want this to happen?

HEDDA. *I*—want it? Are you mad?

LOEVBORG. Skoal to you too, Mrs. Tesman. Thanks for telling me the truth. Here's to the truth!

Empties his glass and refills it.

HEDDA *puts her hand on his arm*. Steady. That's enough for now. Don't forget the party.

MRS. ELVSTED. No, no, no!

HEDDA. Ssh! They're looking at you.

LOEVBORG *puts down his glass*. Thea, tell me the truth—

MRS. ELVSTED. Yes!

LOEVBORG. Did your husband know you were following me?

MRS. ELVSTED. Oh, Hedda!

LOEVBORG. Did you and he have an agreement that you should come here and keep an eye on me? Perhaps he gave you the idea? After all, he's a magistrate. I suppose he needed me back in his office. Or did he miss my companionship at the card table?

MRS. ELVSTED, *quietly, sobbing*. Eilert, Eilert!

LOEVBORG *seizes a glass and is about to fill it.* Let's drink to him, too.

HEDDA. No more now. Remember you're going to read your book to Tesman.

LOEVBORG, *calm again, puts down his glass.* That was silly of me, Thea. To take it like that, I mean. Don't be angry with me, my dear. You'll see—yes, and they'll see, too—that though I fell, I— I have raised myself up again. With your help, Thea.

MRS. ELVSTED, *happily.* Oh, thank God!

BRACK *has meanwhile glanced at his watch. He and* TESMAN *get up and come into the drawing room.*

BRACK *takes his hat and overcoat.* Well, Mrs. Tesman, it's time for us to go.

HEDDA. Yes, I suppose it must be.

LOEVBORG *gets up.* Time for me too, Judge.

MRS. ELVSTED, *quietly, pleadingly.* Eilert, please don't!

HEDDA *pinches her arm.* They can hear you.

MRS. ELVSTED *gives a little cry.* Oh!

LOEVBORG *to* BRACK. You were kind enough to ask me to join you.

BRACK. Are you coming?

LOEVBORG. If I may.

BRACK. Delighted.

LOEVBORG *puts the paper package in his pocket and says to* TESMAN. I'd like to show you one or two things before I send it off to the printer.

TESMAN. I say, that'll be fun. Fancy—! Oh, but Hedda, how'll Mrs. Elvsted get home? What?

HEDDA. Oh, we'll manage somehow.

LOEVBORG *glances over towards the ladies.* Mrs. Elvsted? I shall come back and collect her, naturally.

Goes closer.

About ten o'clock, Mrs. Tesman? Will that suit you?

HEDDA. Yes. That'll suit me admirably.

TESMAN. Good, that's settled. But you mustn't expect me back so early, Hedda.

HEDDA. Stay as long as you c— as long as you like, dear.

MRS. ELVSTED, *trying to hide her anxiety.* Well then, Mr. Loevborg, I'll wait here till you come.

LOEVBORG, *his hat in his hand.* Pray do, Mrs. Elvsted.

BRACK. Well, gentlemen, now the party begins. I trust that, in the words of a certain fair lady, we shall enjoy good sport.

HEDDA. What a pity the fair lady can't be there, invisible.

BRACK. Why invisible?

HEDDA. So as to be able to hear some of your uncensored witticisms, your honour.

BRACK *laughs.* Oh, I shouldn't advise the fair lady to do that.

TESMAN *laughs too.* I say, Hedda, that's good. By Jove! Fancy that!

BRACK. Well, good night, ladies, good night!

LOEVBORG *bows farewell.* About ten o'clock, then.

BRACK, LOEVBORG *and* TESMAN *go out through the hall. As they do so,* BERTHA *enters from the rear room with a lighted lamp. She puts it on the drawing-room table, then goes out the way she came.*

MRS. ELVSTED *has got up and is walking uneasily to and fro.* Oh Hedda, Hedda! How is all this going to end?

HEDDA. At ten o'clock, then. He'll be here. I can see him. With a crown of vine-leaves in his hair. Burning and unashamed!

MRS. ELVSTED. Oh, I do hope so!

HEDDA. Can't you see? Then he'll be himself again! He'll be a free man for the rest of his days!

MRS. ELVSTED. Please God you're right.

HEDDA. That's how he'll come!

Gets up and goes closer.

You can doubt him as much as you like. I believe in him! Now we'll see which of us—

MRS. ELVSTED. You're after something, Hedda.

HEDDA. Yes, I am. For once in my life I want to have the power to shape a man's destiny.

MRS. ELVSTED. Haven't you that power already?

HEDDA. No, I haven't. I've never had it.

MRS. ELVSTED. What about your husband?

HEDDA. Him! Oh, if you could only understand how poor I am. And you're allowed to be so rich, so rich!

Clasps her passionately.

I think I'll burn your hair off after all!

MRS. ELVSTED. Let me go! Let me go! You frighten me, Hedda!

BERTHA, *in the open doorway.* I've laid tea in the dining room, madam.

HEDDA. Good, we're coming.

MRS. ELVSTED. No, no, no! I'd rather go home alone! Now—at once!

HEDDA. Rubbish! First you're going to have some tea, you little idiot. And then—at ten o'clock—Eilert Loevborg will come. With a crown of vine-leaves in his hair!

She drags MRS. ELVSTED *almost forcibly towards the open doorway.*

ACT THREE

The same. The curtains are drawn across the open door-
way, and also across the french windows. The lamp, half
turned down, with a shade over it, is burning on the table.
In the stove, the door of which is open, a fire has been burn-
ing, but it is now almost out.

MRS. ELVSTED, *wrapped in a large shawl and with her feet*
resting on a footstool, is sitting near the stove, huddled in
the armchair. HEDDA *is lying asleep on the sofa, fully*
dressed, with a blanket over her.

MRS. ELVSTED, *after a pause, suddenly sits up in her chair*
and listens tensely. Then she sinks wearily back again and
sighs. Not back yet! Oh, God! Oh, God! Not back yet!

BERTHA *tiptoes cautiously in from the hall. She has a letter*
in her hand.

MRS. ELVSTED *turns and whispers.* What is it? Has someone
come?

BERTHA, *quietly.* Yes, a servant's just called with this letter.

MRS. ELVSTED, *quickly, holding out her hand.* A letter! Give it
to me!

BERTHA. But it's for the Doctor, madam.

MRS. ELVSTED. Oh. I see.

BERTHA. Miss Tesman's maid brought it. I'll leave it here on
the table.

MRS. ELVSTED. Yes, do.

BERTHA *puts down the letter.* I'd better put the lamp out. It's starting to smoke.

MRS. ELVSTED. Yes, put it out. It'll soon be daylight.

BERTHA *puts out the lamp.* It's daylight already, madam.

MRS. ELVSTED. Yes. Broad day. And not home yet.

BERTHA. Oh dear, I was afraid this would happen.

MRS. ELVSTED. Were you?

BERTHA. Yes. When I heard that a certain gentleman had returned to town, and saw him go off with them. I've heard all about him.

MRS. ELVSTED. Don't talk so loud. You'll wake your mistress.

BERTHA *looks at the sofa and sighs.* Yes. Let her go on sleeping, poor dear. Shall I put some more wood on the fire?

MRS. ELVSTED. Thank you, don't bother on my account.

BERTHA. Very good.

Goes quietly out through the hall.

HEDDA *wakes as the door closes and looks up.* What's that?

MRS. ELVSTED. It was only the maid.

HEDDA *looks round.* What am I doing here? Oh, now I remember.

Sits up on the sofa, stretches herself and rubs her eyes.

What time is it, Thea?

MRS. ELVSTED. It's gone seven.

HEDDA. When did Tesman get back?

ELVSTED. He's not back yet.

HEDDA. Not home yet?

MRS. ELVSTED *gets up.* No one's come.

HEDDA. And we sat up waiting for them till four o'clock.

MRS. ELVSTED. God! How I waited for him!

HEDDA *yawns and says with her hand in front of her mouth.* Oh, dear. We might have saved ourselves the trouble.

MRS. ELVSTED. Did you manage to sleep?

HEDDA. Oh, yes. Quite well, I think. Didn't you get any?

MRS. ELVSTED. Not a wink. I couldn't, Hedda. I just couldn't.

HEDDA *gets up and comes over to her.* Now, now, now. There's nothing to worry about. I know what's happened.

MRS. ELVSTED. What? Please tell me.

HEDDA. Well, obviously the party went on very late—

MRS. ELVSTED. Oh dear, I suppose it must have. But—

HEDDA. And Tesman didn't want to come home and wake us all up in the middle of the night.

Laughs.

Probably wasn't too keen to show his face either, after a spree like that.

MRS. ELVSTED. But where could he have gone?

HEDDA. I should think he's probably slept at his aunts'. They keep his old room for him.

MRS. ELVSTED. No, he can't be with them. A letter came for him just now from Miss Tesman. It's over there.

HEDDA. Oh?

Looks at the envelope.

Yes, it's Auntie Juju's handwriting. Well, he must still be at Judge Brack's, then. And Eilert Loevborg is sitting there, reading to him. With a crown of vine-leaves in his hair.

MRS. ELVSTED. Hedda, you're only saying that. You don't believe it.

HEDDA. Thea, you really are a little fool.

MRS. ELVSTED. Perhaps I am.

HEDDA. You look tired to death.

MRS. ELVSTED. Yes. I am tired to death.

HEDDA. Go to my room and lie down for a little. Do as I say, now; don't argue.

MRS. ELVSTED. No, no. I couldn't possibly sleep.

HEDDA. Of course you can.

MRS. ELVSTED. But your husband'll be home soon. And I must know at once—

HEDDA. I'll tell you when he comes.

MRS. ELVSTED. Promise me, Hedda?

HEDDA. Yes, don't worry. Go and get some sleep.

MRS. ELVSTED. Thank you. All right, I'll try.

She goes out through the rear room. HEDDA *goes to the french windows and draws the curtains. Broad daylight floods into the room. She goes to the writing table, takes a small hand mirror from it and arranges her hair. Then she goes to the door leading into the hall and presses the bell. After a few moments,* BERTHA *enters.*

BERTHA. Did you want anything, madam?

HEDDA. Yes, put some more wood on the fire. I'm freezing.

BERTHA. Bless you, I'll soon have this room warmed up.

She rakes the embers together and puts a fresh piece of wood on them. Suddenly she stops and listens.

There's someone at the front door, madam.

HEDDA. Well, go and open it. I'll see to the fire.

BERTHA. It'll burn up in a moment.

She goes out through the hall. HEDDA *kneels on the footstool and puts more wood in the stove. After a few seconds,* GEORGE TESMAN *enters from the hall. He looks tired, and rather worried. He tiptoes towards the open doorway and is about to slip through the curtains.*

HEDDA, *at the stove, without looking up.* Good morning.

TESMAN *turns.* Hedda!

Comes nearer.

Good heavens, are you up already? What?

HEDDA. Yes, I got up very early this morning.

TESMAN. I was sure you'd still be sleeping. Fancy that!

HEDDA. Don't talk so loud. Mrs. Elvsted's asleep in my room.

TESMAN. Mrs. Elvsted? Has she stayed the night here?

HEDDA. Yes. No one came to escort her home.

TESMAN. Oh. No, I suppose not.

HEDDA *closes the door of the stove and gets up.* Well. Was it fun?

TESMAN. Have you been anxious about me? What?

HEDDA. Not in the least. I asked if you'd had fun.

TESMAN. Oh yes, rather! Well, I thought, for once in a while—
The first part was the best; when Eilert read his book to
me. We arrived over an hour too early—what about that,
eh? By Jove! Brack had a lot of things to see to, so Eilert
read to me.

HEDDA *sits at the right-hand side of the table.* Well? Tell me
about it.

TESMAN *sits on a footstool by the stove.* Honestly, Hedda,
you've no idea what a book that's going to be. It's really one
of the most remarkable things that's ever been written. By
Jove!

HEDDA. Oh, never mind about the book—

TESMAN. I'm going to make a confession to you, Hedda. When
he'd finished reading a sort of beastly feeling came over me.

HEDDA. Beastly feeling?

TESMAN. I found myself envying Eilert for being able to write
like that. Imagine that, Hedda!

HEDDA. Yes. I can imagine.

TESMAN. What a tragedy that with all those gifts he should
be so incorrigible.

HEDDA. You mean he's less afraid of life than most men?

TESMAN. Good heavens, no. He just doesn't know the meaning of the word moderation.

HEDDA. What happened afterwards?

TESMAN. Well, looking back on it I suppose you might almost
call it an orgy, Hedda.

HEDDA. Had he vine-leaves in his hair?

TESMAN. Vine-leaves? No, I didn't see any of them. He made
a long, rambling oration in honour of the woman who'd inspired him to write this book. Yes, those were the words
he used.

HEDDA. Did he name her?

TESMAN. No. But I suppose it must be Mrs. Elvsted. You wait and see!

HEDDA. Where did you leave him?

TESMAN. On the way home. We left in a bunch—the last of us, that is—and Brack came with us to get a little fresh air. Well, then, you see, we agreed we ought to see Eilert home. He'd had a drop too much.

HEDDA. You don't say?

TESMAN. But now comes the funny part, Hedda. Or I should really say the tragic part. Oh, I'm almost ashamed to tell you. For Eilert's sake, I mean—

HEDDA. Why, what happened?

TESMAN. Well, you see, as we were walking towards town I happened to drop behind for a minute. Only for a minute —er—you understand—

HEDDA. Yes, yes—?

TESMAN. Well then, when I ran on to catch them up, what do you think I found by the roadside. What?

HEDDA. How on earth should I know?

TESMAN. You mustn't tell anyone, Hedda. What? Promise me that—for Eilert's sake.

Takes a package wrapped in paper from his coat pocket. Just fancy! I found this.

HEDDA. Isn't this the one he brought here yesterday?

TESMAN. Yes! The whole of that precious, irreplaceable manuscript! And he went and lost it! Didn't even notice! What about that? By Jove! Tragic.

HEDDA. But why didn't you give it back to him?

TESMAN. I didn't dare to, in the state he was in.

HEDDA. Didn't you tell any of the others?

TESMAN. Good heavens, no. I didn't want to do that. For Eilert's sake, you understand.

HEDDA. Then no one else knows you have his manuscript?

TESMAN. No. And no one must be allowed to know.

HEDDA. Didn't it come up in the conversation later?

TESMAN. I didn't get a chance to talk to him any more. As soon as we got into the outskirts of town, he and one or two of the others gave us the slip. Disappeared, by Jove!

HEDDA. Oh? I suppose they took him home.

TESMAN. Yes, I imagine that was the idea. Brack left us, too.

HEDDA. And what have you been up to since then?

TESMAN. Well, I and one or two of the others—awfully jolly chaps, they were—went back to where one of them lived, and had a cup of morning coffee. Morning-after coffee—what? Ah, well. I'll just lie down for a bit and give Eilert time to sleep it off, poor chap, then I'll run over and give this back to him.

HEDDA *holds out her hand for the package.* No, don't do that. Not just yet. Let me read it first.

TESMAN. Oh no, really, Hedda dear, honestly, I daren't do that.

HEDDA. Daren't?

TESMAN. No—imagine how desperate he'll be when he wakes up and finds his manuscript's missing. He hasn't any copy, you see. He told me so himself.

HEDDA. Can't a thing like that be rewritten?

TESMAN. Oh no, not possibly, I shouldn't think. I mean, the inspiration, you know—

HEDDA. Oh, yes. I'd forgotten that.

Casually.

By the way, there's a letter for you.

TESMAN. Is there? Fancy that!

HEDDA *holds it out to him.* It came early this morning.

TESMAN. I say, it's from Auntie Juju! What on earth can it be? *Puts the package on the other footstool, opens the letter, reads it and jumps up.*

Oh, Hedda! She says poor Auntie Rena's dying.

HEDDA. Well, we've been expecting that.

TESMAN. She says if I want to see her I must go quickly. I'll run over at once.

HEDDA *hides a smile.* Run?

TESMAN. Hedda dear, I suppose you wouldn't like to come with me? What about that, eh?

HEDDA *gets up and says wearily and with repulsion.* No, no, don't ask me to do anything like that. I can't bear illness or death. I loathe anything ugly.

TESMAN. Yes, yes. Of course.

In a dither.

My hat? My overcoat? Oh yes, in the hall. I do hope I won't get there too late, Hedda? What?

HEDDA. You'll be all right if you run.

BERTHA *enters from the hall.*

BERTHA. Judge Brack's outside and wants to know if he can come in.

TESMAN. At this hour? No, I can't possibly receive him now.

HEDDA. I can.

To BERTHA.

Ask his honour to come in.

BERTHA *goes.*

HEDDA *whispers quickly.* The manuscript, Tesman.

She snatches it from the footstool.

TESMAN. Yes, give it to me.

HEDDA. No, I'll look after it for now.

She goes over to the writing table and puts it in the book-case. TESMAN *stands dithering, unable to get his gloves on.* JUDGE BRACK *enters from the hall.*

HEDDA *nods to him.* Well, you're an early bird.

BRACK. Yes, aren't I?

To TESMAN.

Are you up and about, too?

TESMAN. Yes, I've got to go and see my aunts. Poor Auntie Rena's dying.

BRACK. Oh dear, is she? Then you mustn't let me detain you. At so tragic a—

TESMAN. Yes, I really must run. Good-bye! Good-bye!

Runs out through the hall.

HEDDA *goes nearer.* You seem to have had excellent sport last night—Judge.

BRACK. Indeed yes, Mrs. Hedda. I haven't even had time to take my clothes off.

HEDDA. *You* haven't either?

BRACK. As you see. What's Tesman told you about last night's escapades?

HEDDA. Oh, only some boring story about having gone and drunk coffee somewhere.

BRACK. Yes, I've heard about that coffee party. Eilert Loevborg wasn't with them, I gather?

HEDDA. No, they took him home first.

BRACK. Did Tesman go with him?

HEDDA. No, one or two of the others, he said.

BRACK *smiles.* George Tesman is a credulous man, Mrs. Hedda.

HEDDA. God knows. But—has something happened?

BRACK. Well, yes, I'm afraid it has.

HEDDA. I see. Sit down and tell me.

She sits on the left of the table, BRACK *at the long side of it, near her.*

HEDDA. Well?

BRACK. I had a special reason for keeping track of my guests last night. Or perhaps I should say some of my guests.

HEDDA. Including Eilert Loevborg?

BRACK. I must confess—yes.

HEDDA. You're beginning to make me curious.

BRACK. Do you know where he and some of my other guests spent the latter half of last night, Mrs. Hedda?

HEDDA. Tell me. If it won't shock me.

BRACK. Oh, I don't think it'll shock you. They found themselves participating in an exceedingly animated *soirée*.

HEDDA. Of a sporting character?

BRACK. Of a highly sporting character.

HEDDA. Tell me more.

BRACK. Loevborg had received an invitation in advance—as had the others. I knew all about that. But he had refused. As you know, he's become a new man.

HEDDA. Up at the Elvsteds', yes. But he went?

BRACK. Well, you see, Mrs. Hedda, last night at my house, unhappily, the spirit moved him.

HEDDA. Yes, I hear he became inspired.

BRACK. Somewhat violently inspired. And as a result, I suppose, his thoughts strayed. We men, alas, don't always stick to our principles as firmly as we should.

HEDDA. I'm sure you're an exception, Judge Brack. But go on about Loevborg.

BRACK. Well, to cut a long story short, he ended up in the establishment of a certain Mademoiselle Danielle.

HEDDA. Mademoiselle Danielle?

BRACK. She was holding the *soirée*. For a selected circle of friends and admirers.

HEDDA. Has she got red hair?

BRACK. She has.

HEDDA. A singer of some kind?

BRACK. Yes—among other accomplishments. She's also a celebrated huntress—of men, Mrs. Hedda. I'm sure you've heard about her. Eilert Loevborg used to be one of her most ardent patrons. In his salad days.

HEDDA. And how did all this end?

BRACK. Not entirely amicably, from all accounts. Mademoiselle Danielle began by receiving him with the utmost tenderness and ended by resorting to her fists.

HEDDA. Against Loevborg?

BRACK. Yes. He accused her, or her friends, of having robbed
him. He claimed his pocketbook had been stolen. Among
other things. In short, he seems to have made a bloodthirsty
scene.

HEDDA. And what did this lead to?

BRACK. It led to a general free-for-all, in which both sexes par-
ticipated. Fortunately, in the end the police arrived.

HEDDA. The police too?

BRACK. Yes. I'm afraid it may turn out to be rather an expensive joke for Master Eilert. Crazy fool!

HEDDA. Oh?

BRACK. Apparently he put up a very violent resistance. Hit
one of the constables on the ear and tore his uniform. He
had to accompany them to the police station.

HEDDA. Where did you learn all this?

BRACK. From the police.

HEDDA, *to herself.* So that's what happened. He didn't have a
crown of vine-leaves in his hair.

BRACK. Vine-leaves, Mrs. Hedda?

HEDDA, *in her normal voice again.* But, tell me, Judge, why
do you take such a close interest in Eilert Loevborg?

BRACK. For one thing it'll hardly be a matter of complete in-
difference to me if it's revealed in court that he came there
straight from my house.

HEDDA. Will it come to court?

BRACK. Of course. Well, I don't regard that as particularly
serious. Still, I thought it my duty, as a friend of the family,
to give you and your husband a full account of his nocturnal
adventures.

HEDDA. Why?

BRACK. Because I've a shrewd suspicion that he's hoping to
use you as a kind of screen.

HEDDA. What makes you think that?

BRACK. Oh, for heaven's sake, Mrs. Hedda, we're not blind.

You wait and see. This Mrs. Elvsted won't be going back to her husband just yet.

HEDDA. Well, if there were anything between those two there are plenty of other places where they could meet.

BRACK. Not in anyone's home. From now on every respectable house will once again be closed to Eilert Loevborg.

HEDDA. And mine should be too, you mean?

BRACK. Yes. I confess I should find it more than irksome if this gentleman were to be granted unrestricted access to this house. If he were superfluously to intrude into—

HEDDA. The triangle?

BRACK. Precisely. For me it would be like losing a home.

HEDDA *looks at him and smiles.* I see. You want to be the cock of the walk.

BRACK *nods slowly and lowers his voice.* Yes, that is my aim. And I shall fight for it with—every weapon at my disposal.

HEDDA, *as her smile fades.* You're a dangerous man, aren't you? When you really want something.

BRACK. You think so?

HEDDA. Yes, I'm beginning to think so. I'm deeply thankful you haven't any kind of hold over me.

BRACK *laughs equivocally.* Well, well, Mrs. Hedda—perhaps you're right. If I had, who knows what I might not think up?

HEDDA. Come, Judge Brack. That sounds almost like a threat.

BRACK *gets up.* Heaven forbid! In the creation of a triangle —and its continuance—the question of compulsion should never arise.

HEDDA. Exactly what I was thinking.

BRACK. Well, I've said what I came to say. I must be getting back. Good-bye, Mrs. Hedda.

Goes towards the french windows.

HEDDA *gets up.* Are you going out through the garden?

BRACK. Yes, it's shorter.

HEDDA. Yes. And it's the back door, isn't it?

BRACK. I've nothing against back doors. They can be quite intriguing—sometimes.

HEDDA. When people fire pistols out of them, for example?

BRACK, *in the doorway, laughs.* Oh, people don't shoot tame cocks.

HEDDA *laughs too.* I suppose not. When they've only got one.

They nod good-bye, laughing. He goes. She closes the french windows behind him, and stands for a moment, looking out pensively. Then she walks across the room and glances through the curtains in the open doorway. Goes to the writing table, takes LOEVBORG's *package from the bookcase and is about to leaf through the pages when* BERTHA *is heard remonstrating loudly in the hall.* HEDDA *turns and listens. She hastily puts the package back in the drawer, locks it and puts the key on the inkstand.* EILERT LOEVBORG, *with his overcoat on and his hat in his hand, throws the door open. He looks somewhat confused and excited.*

LOEVBORG *shouts as he enters.* I must come in, I tell you! Let me pass!

He closes the door, turns, sees HEDDA, *controls himself immediately and bows.*

HEDDA, *at the writing table.* Well, Mr. Loevborg, this is rather a late hour to be collecting Thea.

LOEVBORG. And an early hour to call on you. Please forgive me.

HEDDA. How do you know she's still here?

LOEVBORG. They told me at her lodgings that she has been out all night.

HEDDA *goes to the table.* Did you notice anything about their behaviour when they told you?

LOEVBORG *looks at her, puzzled.* Notice anything?

HEDDA. Did they sound as if they thought it—strange?

LOEVBORG *suddenly understands.* Oh, I see what you mean. I'm dragging her down with me. No, as a matter of fact I didn't notice anything. I suppose Tesman isn't up yet?

HEDDA. No, I don't think so.

LOEVBORG. When did he get home?

HEDDA. Very late.

LOEVBORG. Did he tell you anything?

HEDDA. Yes. I gather you had a merry party at Judge Brack's last night.

LOEVBORG. He didn't tell you anything else?

HEDDA. I don't think so. I was so terribly sleepy—

MRS. ELVSTED *comes through the curtains in the open doorway.*

MRS. ELVSTED *runs towards him.* Oh, Eilert! At last!

LOEVBORG. Yes—at last. And too late.

MRS. ELVSTED. What is too late?

LOEVBORG. Everything—now. I'm finished, Thea.

MRS. ELVSTED. Oh, no, no! Don't say that!

LOEVBORG. You'll say it yourself, when you've heard what I—

MRS. ELVSTED. I don't want to hear anything!

HEDDA. Perhaps you'd rather speak to her alone? I'd better go.

LOEVBORG. No, stay.

MRS. ELVSTED. But I don't want to hear anything, I tell you!

LOEVBORG. It's not about last night.

MRS. ELVSTED. Then what—?

LOEVBORG. I want to tell you that from now on we must stop seeing each other.

MRS. ELVSTED. Stop seeing each other!

HEDDA, *involuntarily.* I knew it!

LOEVBORG. I have no further use for you, Thea.

MRS. ELVSTED. You can stand there and say that! No further use for me! Surely I can go on helping you? We'll go on working together, won't we?

LOEVBORG. I don't intend to do any more work from now on.

MRS. ELVSTED, *desperately.* Then what use have I for my life?

LOEVBORG. You must try to live as if you had never known me.

MRS. ELVSTED. But I can't!

LOEVBORG. Try to, Thea. Go back home—

MRS. ELVSTED. Never! I want to be wherever you are! I won't let myself be driven away like this! I want to stay here—and be with you when the book comes out.

HEDDA *whispers*. Ah, yes! The book!

LOEVBORG *looks at her*. Our book; Thea's and mine. It belongs to both of us.

MRS. ELVSTED. Oh, yes! I feel that, too! And I've a right to be with you when it comes into the world. I want to see people respect and honour you again. And the joy! The joy! I want to share it with you!

LOEVBORG. Thea—our book will never come into the world.

HEDDA. Ah!

MRS. ELVSTED. Not—?

LOEVBORG. It cannot. Ever.

MRS. ELVSTED. Eilert—what have you done with the manuscript? Where is it?

LOEVBORG. Oh Thea, please don't ask me that!

MRS. ELVSTED. Yes, yes—I must know. I've a right to know. Now!

LOEVBORG. The manuscript. I've torn it up.

MRS. ELVSTED *screams*. No, no!

HEDDA, *involuntarily*. But that's not—!

LOEVBORG *looks at her*. Not true, you think?

HEDDA *controls herself*. Why—yes, of course it is, if you say so. It just sounded so incredible—

LOEVBORG. It's true, nevertheless.

MRS. ELVSTED. Oh, my God, my God, Hedda—he's destroyed his own book!

LOEVBORG. I have destroyed my life. Why not my life's work, too?

MRS. ELVSTED. And you—did this last night?

LOEVBORG. Yes, Thea. I tore it into a thousand pieces. And scattered them out across the fjord. It's good, clean, salt water. Let it carry them away; let them drift in the current and the wind. And in a little while, they will sink. Deeper and deeper. As I shall, Thea.

MRS. ELVSTED. Do you know, Eilert—this book—all my life I shall feel as though you'd killed a little child?

LOEVBORG. You're right. It is like killing a child.

MRS. ELVSTED. But how could you? It was my child, too!

HEDDA, *almost inaudibly.* Oh—the child—!

MRS. ELVSTED *breathes heavily.* It's all over, then. Well—I'll go now, Hedda.

HEDDA. You're not leaving town?

MRS. ELVSTED. I don't know what I'm going to do. I can't see anything except—darkness.

She goes out through the hall.

HEDDA *waits a moment.* Aren't you going to escort her home, Mr. Loevborg?

LOEVBORG. I? Through the streets? Do you want me to let people see her with me?

HEDDA. Of course I don't know what else may have happened last night. But is it so utterly beyond redress?

LOEVBORG. It isn't just last night. It'll go on happening. I know it. But the curse of it is, I don't want to live that kind of life. I don't want to start all that again. She's broken my courage. I can't spit in the eyes of the world any longer.

HEDDA, *as though to herself.* That pretty little fool's been trying to shape a man's destiny.

Looks at him.

But how could you be so heartless towards her?

LOEVBORG. Don't call me heartless!

HEDDA. To go and destroy the one thing that's made her life worth living? You don't call that heartless?

LOEVBORG. Do you want to know the truth, Hedda?

HEDDA. The truth?

LOEVBORG. Promise me first—give me your word—that you'll never let Thea know about this.

HEDDA. I give you my word.

LOEVBORG. Good. Well; what I told her just now was a lie.

HEDDA. About the manuscript?

LOEVBORG. Yes. I didn't tear it up. Or throw it in the fjord.

HEDDA. You didn't? But where is it, then?

LOEVBORG. I destroyed it, all the same. I destroyed it, Hedda!

HEDDA. I don't understand.

LOEVBORG. Thea said that what I had done was like killing a child.

HEDDA. Yes. That's what she said.

LOEVBORG. But to kill a child isn't the worst thing a father can do to it.

HEDDA. What could be worse than that?

LOEVBORG. Hedda—suppose a man came home one morning, after a night of debauchery, and said to the mother of his child: "Look here. I've been wandering round all night. I've been to—such-and-such a place and such-and-such a place. And I had our child with me. I took him to—these places. And I've lost him. Just—lost him. God knows where he is or whose hands he's fallen into."

HEDDA. I see. But when all's said and done, this was only a book—

LOEVBORG. Thea's heart and soul were in that book. It was her whole life.

HEDDA. Yes. I understand.

LOEVBORG. Well, then you must also understand that she and I cannot possibly ever see each other again.

HEDDA. Where will you go?

LOEVBORG. Nowhere. I just want to put an end to it all. As soon as possible.

HEDDA *takes a step towards him.* Eilert Loevborg, listen to me. Do it—beautifully!

LOEVBORG. Beautifully?

Smiles.

With a crown of vine-leaves in my hair? The way you used to dream of me—in the old days?

HEDDA. No. I don't believe in that crown any longer. But—do it beautifully, all the same. Just this once. Good-bye. You must go now. And don't come back.

LOEVBORG. Adieu, madam. Give my love to George Tesman. *Turns to go.*

HEDDA. Wait. I want to give you a souvenir to take with you.

She goes over to the writing table, opens the drawer and the pistol-case, and comes back to LOEVBORG *with one of the pistols.*

LOEVBORG *looks at her.* This? Is this the souvenir?

HEDDA *nods slowly.* You recognise it? You looked down its barrel once.

LOEVBORG. You should have used it then.

HEDDA. Here! Use it now!

LOEVBORG *puts the pistol in his breast pocket.* Thank you.

HEDDA. Do it beautifully, Eilert Loevborg. Only promise me that!

LOEVBORG. Good-bye, Hedda Gabler.

He goes out through the hall. HEDDA *stands by the door for a moment, listening. Then she goes over to the writing table, takes out the package containing the manuscript, glances inside it, pulls some of the pages half out and looks at them. Then she takes it to the armchair by the stove and sits down with the package in her lap. After a moment, she opens the door of the stove; then she opens the packet.*

HEDDA *throws one of the pages into the stove and whispers to herself.* I'm burning your child, Thea! You with your beautiful wavy hair!

She throws a few more pages into the stove.

The child Eilert Loevborg gave you.

Throws the rest of the manuscript in.

I'm burning it! I'm burning your child!

ACT FOUR

*The same. It is evening. The drawing room is in darkness.
The small room is illuminated by the hanging lamp over the
table. The curtains are drawn across the french windows.*
HEDDA, *dressed in black, is walking up and down in the
darkened room. Then she goes into the small room and
crosses to the left. A few chords are heard from the piano.
She comes back into the drawing room.*

BERTHA *comes through the small room from the right with
a lighted lamp, which she places on the table in front of the
corner sofa in the drawing room. Her eyes are red with crying, and she has black ribbons on her cap. She goes quietly
out, right.* HEDDA *goes over to the french windows, draws
the curtains slightly to one side and looks out into the darkness.*

A few moments later, MISS TESMAN *enters from the hall.
She is dressed in mourning, with a black hat and veil.* HEDDA
goes to meet her and holds out her hand.

MISS TESMAN. Well, Hedda, here I am in the weeds of sorrow.
My poor sister has ended her struggles at last.

HEDDA. I've already heard. Tesman sent me a card.

MISS TESMAN. Yes, he promised me he would. But I thought,
no, I must go and break the news of death to Hedda myself
—here, in the house of life.

HEDDA. It's very kind of you.

MISS TESMAN. Ah, Rena shouldn't have chosen a time like this to pass away. This is no moment for Hedda's house to be a place of mourning.

HEDDA, *changing the subject.* She died peacefully, Miss Tesman?

MISS TESMAN. Oh, it was quite beautiful! The end came so calmly. And she was so happy at being able to see George once again. And say good-bye to him. Hasn't he come home yet?

HEDDA. No. He wrote that I mustn't expect him too soon. But please sit down.

MISS TESMAN. No, thank you, Hedda dear—bless you. I'd like to. But I've so little time. I must dress her and lay her out as well as I can. She shall go to her grave looking really beautiful.

HEDDA. Can't I help with anything?

MISS TESMAN. Why, you mustn't think of such a thing! Hedda Tesman mustn't let her hands be soiled by contact with death. Or her thoughts. Not at this time.

HEDDA. One can't always control one's thoughts.

MISS TESMAN *continues.* Ah, well, that's life. Now we must start to sew poor Rena's shroud. There'll be sewing to be done in this house too before long, I shouldn't wonder. But not for a shroud, praise God.

GEORGE TESMAN *enters from the hall.*

HEDDA. You've come at last! Thank heavens!

TESMAN. Are you here, Auntie Juju? With Hedda? Fancy that!

MISS TESMAN. I was just on the point of leaving, dear boy. Well, have you done everything you promised me?

TESMAN. No, I'm afraid I forgot half of it. I'll have to run over again tomorrow. My head's in a complete whirl today. I can't collect my thoughts.

MISS TESMAN. But George dear, you mustn't take it like this.

TESMAN. Oh? Well—er—how should I?

MISS TESMAN. You must be happy in your grief. Happy for what's happened. As I am.

TESMAN. Oh, yes, yes. You're thinking of Aunt Rena.

HEDDA. It'll be lonely for you now, Miss Tesman.

MISS TESMAN. For the first few days, yes. But it won't last long,
I hope. Poor dear Rena's little room isn't going to stay empty.

TESMAN. Oh? Whom are you going to move in there? What?

MISS TESMAN. Oh, there's always some poor invalid who needs
care and attention.

HEDDA. Do you really want another cross like that to bear?

MISS TESMAN. Cross! God forgive you, child. It's been no cross
for me.

HEDDA. But now—if a complete stranger comes to live with
you—?

MISS TESMAN. Oh, one soon makes friends with invalids. And
I need so much to have someone to live for. Like you, my
dear. Well, I expect there'll soon be work in this house too
for an old aunt, praise God!

HEDDA. Oh—please!

TESMAN. By Jove, yes! What a splendid time the three of us
could have together if—

HEDDA. If?

TESMAN, *uneasily.* Oh, never mind. It'll all work out. Let's hope
so—what?

MISS TESMAN. Yes, yes. Well, I'm sure you two would like to be
alone.

Smiles.

Perhaps Hedda may have something to tell you, George.
Good-bye. I must go home to Rena.

Turns to the door.

Dear God, how strange! Now Rena is with me and with poor
dear Joachim.

TESMAN. Fancy that. Yes, Auntie Juju! What?

MISS TESMAN *goes out through the hall.*

HEDDA *follows* TESMAN *coldly and searchingly with her eyes.*
I really believe this death distresses you more than it does
her.

TESMAN. Oh, it isn't just Auntie Rena. It's Eilert I'm so worried about.

HEDDA, *quickly.* Is there any news of him?

TESMAN. I ran over to see him this afternoon. I wanted to tell him his manuscript was in safe hands.

HEDDA. Oh? You didn't find him?

TESMAN. No. He wasn't at home. But later I met Mrs. Elvsted and she told me he'd been here early this morning.

HEDDA. Yes, just after you'd left.

TESMAN. It seems he said he'd torn the manuscript up. What?

HEDDA. Yes, he claimed to have done so.

TESMAN. You told him we had it, of course?

HEDDA. No.

Quickly.

Did you tell Mrs. Elvsted?

TESMAN. No, I didn't like to. But you ought to have told him. Think if he should go home and do something desperate! Give me the manuscript, Hedda. I'll run over to him with it right away. Where did you put it?

HEDDA, *cold and motionless, leaning against the armchair.* I haven't got it any longer.

TESMAN. Haven't got it? What on earth do you mean?

HEDDA. I've burned it.

TESMAN *starts, terrified.* Burned it! Burned Eilert's manuscript!

HEDDA. Don't shout. The servant will hear you.

TESMAN. Burned it! But in heaven's name—! Oh, no, no, no! This is impossible!

HEDDA. Well, it's true.

TESMAN. But Hedda, do you realise what you've done? That's appropriating lost property! It's against the law! By Jove! You ask Judge Brack and see if I'm not right.

HEDDA. You'd be well advised not to talk about it to Judge Brack or anyone else.

TESMAN. But how could you go and do such a dreadful thing?

What on earth put the idea into your head? What came over you? Answer me! What?

HEDDA *represses an almost imperceptible smile.* I did it for your sake, George.

TESMAN. For my sake?

HEDDA. When you came home this morning and described how he'd read his book to you—

TESMAN. Yes, yes?

HEDDA. You admitted you were jealous of him.

TESMAN. But, good heavens, I didn't mean it literally!

HEDDA. No matter. I couldn't bear the thought that anyone else should push you into the background.

TESMAN, *torn between doubt and joy.* Hedda—is this true? But —but—but I never realised you loved me like that! Fancy—

HEDDA. Well, I suppose you'd better know. I'm going to have— *Breaks off and says violently.*

No, no—you'd better ask your Auntie Juju. She'll tell you.

TESMAN. Hedda! I think I understand what you mean.

Clasps his hands.

Good heavens, can it really be true! What?

HEDDA. Don't shout. The servant will hear you.

TESMAN, *laughing with joy.* The servant! I say, that's good! The servant! Why, that's Bertha! I'll run out and tell her at once!

HEDDA *clenches her hands in despair.* Oh, it's destroying me, all this—it's destroying me!

TESMAN. I say, Hedda, what's up? What?

HEDDA, *cold, controlled.* Oh, it's all so—absurd—George.

TESMAN. Absurd? That I'm so happy? But surely—? Ah, well —perhaps I won't say anything to Bertha.

HEDDA. No, do. She might as well know too.

TESMAN. No, no, I won't tell her yet. But Auntie Juju—I must let her know! And you—you called me George! For the first time! Fancy that! Oh, it'll make Auntie Juju so happy, all this! So very happy!

HEDDA. Will she be happy when she hears I've burned Eilert Loevborg's manuscript—for your sake?

TESMAN. No, I'd forgotten about that. Of course no one must be allowed to know about the manuscript. But that you're burning with love for me, Hedda, I must certainly let Auntie Juju know that. I say, I wonder if young wives often feel like that towards their husbands? What?

HEDDA. You might ask Auntie Juju about that too.

TESMAN. I will, as soon as I get the chance.

Looks uneasy and thoughtful again.

But I say, you know, that manuscript. Dreadful business. Poor Eilert!

MRS. ELVSTED, *dressed as on her first visit, with hat and overcoat, enters from the hall.*

MRS. ELVSTED *greets them hastily and tremulously.* Oh, Hedda dear, do please forgive me for coming here again.

HEDDA. Why, Thea, what's happened?

TESMAN. Is it anything to do with Eilert Loevborg? What?

MRS. ELVSTED. Yes—I'm so dreadfully afraid he may have met with an accident.

HEDDA *grips her arm.* You think so?

TESMAN. But, good heavens, Mrs. Elvsted, what makes you think that?

MRS. ELVSTED. I heard them talking about him at the boarding-house, as I went in. Oh, there are the most terrible rumours being spread about him in town today.

TESMAN. Fancy. Yes, I heard about them too. But I can testify that he went straight home to bed. Fancy that!

HEDDA. Well—what did they say in the boarding-house?

MRS. ELVSTED. Oh, I couldn't find out anything. Either they didn't know, or else— They stopped talking when they saw me. And I didn't dare to ask.

TESMAN *fidgets uneasily.* We must hope—we must hope you misheard them, Mrs. Elvsted.

MRS. ELVSTED. No, no, I'm sure it was he they were talking about. I heard them say something about a hospital—

TESMAN. Hospital!

HEDDA. Oh no, surely that's impossible!

MRS. ELVSTED. Oh, I became so afraid. So I went up to his rooms and asked to see him.

HEDDA. Do you think that was wise, Thea?

MRS. ELVSTED. Well, what else could I do? I couldn't bear the uncertainty any longer.

TESMAN. But *you* didn't manage to find him either? What?

MRS. ELVSTED. No. And they had no idea where he was. They said he hadn't been home since yesterday afternoon.

TESMAN. Since yesterday? Fancy that!

MRS. ELVSTED. I'm sure he must have met with an accident.

TESMAN. Hedda, I wonder if I ought to go into town and make one or two enquiries?

HEDDA. No, no, don't you get mixed up in this.

JUDGE BRACK *enters from the hall, hat in hand.* BERTHA, *who has opened the door for him, closes it. He looks serious and greets them silently.*

TESMAN. Hullo, my dear Judge. Fancy seeing you!

BRACK. I had to come and talk to you.

TESMAN. I can see Auntie Juju's told you the news.

BRACK. Yes, I've heard about that too.

TESMAN. Tragic, isn't it?

BRACK. Well, my dear chap, that depends how you look at it.

TESMAN *looks uncertainly at him.* Has something else happened?

BRACK. Yes.

HEDDA. Another tragedy?

BRACK. That also depends on how you look at it, Mrs. Tesman.

MRS. ELVSTED. Oh, it's something to do with Eilert Loevborg!

BRACK *looks at her for a moment.* How did you guess? Perhaps you've heard already—?

MRS. ELVSTED, *confused.* No, no, not at all—I—

TESMAN. For heaven's sake, tell us!

BRACK *shrugs his shoulders.* Well, I'm afraid they've taken him to the hospital. He's dying.

MRS. ELVSTED *screams.* Oh God, God!

TESMAN. The hospital! Dying!

HEDDA, *involuntarily.* So quickly!

MRS. ELVSTED, *weeping.* Oh, Hedda! And we parted enemies!

HEDDA *whispers.* Thea—Thea!

MRS. ELVSTED, *ignoring her.* I must see him! I must see him before he dies!

BRACK. It's no use, Mrs. Elvsted. No one's allowed to see him now.

MRS. ELVSTED. But what's happened to him? You must tell me!

TESMAN. He hasn't tried to do anything to himself? What?

HEDDA. Yes, he has. I'm sure of it.

TESMAN. Hedda, how can you—?

BRACK, *who has not taken his eyes from her.* I'm afraid you've guessed correctly, Mrs. Tesman.

MRS. ELVSTED. How dreadful!

TESMAN. Attempted suicide! Fancy that!

HEDDA. Shot himself!

BRACK. Right again, Mrs. Tesman.

MRS. ELVSTED *tries to compose herself.* When did this happen, Judge Brack?

BRACK. This afternoon. Between three and four.

TESMAN. But, good heavens—where? What?

BRACK, *a little hesitantly.* Where? Why, my dear chap, in his rooms of course.

MRS. ELVSTED. No, that's impossible. I was there soon after six.

BRACK. Well, it must have been somewhere else, then. I don't know exactly. I only know that they found him. He'd shot himself—through the breast.

MRS. ELVSTED. Oh, how horrible! That he should end like that!

HEDDA, *to* BRACK. Through the breast, you said?

BRACK. That is what I said.

HEDDA. Not through the head?

BRACK. Through the breast, Mrs. Tesman.

HEDDA. The breast. Yes; yes. That's good, too.

BRACK. Why, Mrs. Tesman?

HEDDA. Oh—no, I didn't mean anything.

TESMAN. And the wound's dangerous, you say? What?

BRACK. Mortal. He's probably already dead.

MRS. ELVSTED. Yes, yes—I feel it! It's all over. All over. Oh Hedda—!

TESMAN. But, tell me, how did you manage to learn all this?

BRACK, *curtly.* From the police. I spoke to one of them.

HEDDA, *loudly, clearly.* At last! Oh, thank God!

TESMAN, *appalled.* For God's sake, Hedda, what are you saying?

HEDDA. I am saying there's beauty in what he has done.

BRACK. Hm—Mrs. Tesman—

TESMAN. Beauty! Oh, but I say!

MRS. ELVSTED. Hedda, how can you talk of beauty in connection with a thing like this?

HEDDA. Eilert Loevborg has settled his account with life. He's had the courage to do what—what he had to do.

MRS. ELVSTED. No, that's not why it happened. He did it because he was mad.

TESMAN. He did it because he was desperate.

HEDDA. You're wrong! I know!

MRS. ELVSTED. He must have been mad. The same as when he tore up the manuscript.

BRACK *starts.* Manuscript? Did he tear it up?

MRS. ELVSTED. Yes. Last night.

TESMAN *whispers*. Oh, Hedda, we shall never be able to escape from this.

BRACK. Hm. Strange.

TESMAN *wanders round the room*. To think of Eilert dying like that. And not leaving behind him the thing that would have made his name endure.

MRS. ELVSTED. If only it could be pieced together again!

TESMAN. Yes, fancy! If only it could! I'd give anything—

MRS. ELVSTED. Perhaps it can, Mr. Tesman.

TESMAN. What do you mean?

MRS. ELVSTED *searches in the pocket of her dress*. Look! I kept the notes he dictated it from.

HEDDA *takes a step nearer*. Ah!

TESMAN. You kept them, Mrs. Elvsted! What?

MRS. ELVSTED. Yes, here they are. I brought them with me when I left home. They've been in my pocket ever since.

TESMAN. Let me have a look.

MRS. ELVSTED *hands him a wad of small sheets of paper*. They're in a terrible muddle. All mixed up.

TESMAN. I say, just fancy if we can sort them out! Perhaps if we work on them together—?

MRS. ELVSTED. Oh, yes! Let's try, anyway!

TESMAN. We'll manage it. We must! I shall dedicate my life to this.

HEDDA. *You*, George? Your life?

TESMAN. Yes—well, all the time I can spare. My book'll have to wait. Hedda, you do understand? What? I owe it to Eilert's memory.

HEDDA. Perhaps.

TESMAN. Well, my dear Mrs. Elvsted, you and I'll have to pool our brains. No use crying over spilt milk, what? We must try to approach this matter calmly.

MRS. ELVSTED. Yes, yes, Mr. Tesman. I'll do my best.

TESMAN. Well, come over here and let's start looking at these notes right away. Where shall we sit? Here? No, the other room. You'll excuse us, won't you, Judge? Come along with me, Mrs. Elvsted.

MRS. ELVSTED. Oh, God! If only we can manage to do it!

TESMAN *and* MRS. ELVSTED *go into the rear room. He takes off his hat and overcoat. They sit at the table beneath the hanging lamp and absorb themselves in the notes.* HEDDA *walks across to the stove and sits in the armchair. After a moment,* BRACK *goes over to her.*

HEDDA, *half aloud.* Oh, Judge! This act of Eilert Loevborg's—doesn't it give one a sense of release!

BRACK. Release, Mrs. Hedda? Well, it's a release for him, of course—

HEDDA. Oh, I don't mean him—I mean me! The release of knowing that someone can do something really brave! Something beautiful!

BRACK *smiles.* Hm—my dear Mrs. Hedda—

HEDDA. Oh, I know what you're going to say. You're a bourgeois at heart too, just like—ah, well!

BRACK *looks at her.* Eilert Loevborg has meant more to you than you're willing to admit to yourself. Or am I wrong?

HEDDA. I'm not answering questions like that from you. I only know that Eilert Loevborg has had the courage to live according to his own principles. And now, at last, he's done something big! Something beautiful! To have the courage and the will to rise from the feast of life so early!

BRACK. It distresses me deeply, Mrs. Hedda, but I'm afraid I must rob you of that charming illusion.

HEDDA. Illusion?

BRACK. You wouldn't have been allowed to keep it for long, anyway.

HEDDA. What do you mean?

BRACK. He didn't shoot himself on purpose.

HEDDA. Not on purpose?

BRACK. No. It didn't happen quite the way I told you.

HEDDA. Have you been hiding something? What is it?

BRACK. In order to spare poor Mrs. Elvsted's feelings, I permitted myself one or two small—equivocations.

HEDDA. What?

BRACK. To begin with, he is already dead.

HEDDA. He died at the hospital?

BRACK. Yes. Without regaining consciousness.

HEDDA. What else haven't you told us?

BRACK. The incident didn't take place at his lodgings.

HEDDA. Well, that's utterly unimportant.

BRACK. Not utterly. The fact is, you see, that Eilbert Loevborg was found shot in Mademoiselle Danielle's boudoir.

HEDDA *almost jumps up, but instead sinks back in her chair.* That's impossible. He can't have been there today.

BRACK. He was there this afternoon. He went to ask for something he claimed they'd taken from him. Talked some crazy nonsense about a child which had got lost—

HEDDA. Oh! So that was the reason!

BRACK. I thought at first he might have been referring to his manuscript. But I hear he destroyed that himself. So he must have meant his pocketbook—I suppose.

HEDDA. Yes, I suppose so. So they found him there?

BRACK. Yes; there. With a discharged pistol in his breast pocket. The shot had wounded him mortally.

HEDDA. Yes. In the breast.

BRACK. No. In the—hm—stomach. The—lower part—

HEDDA *looks at him with an expression of repulsion.* That too! Oh, why does everything I touch become mean and ludicrous? It's like a curse!

BRACK. There's something else, Mrs. Hedda. It's rather disagreeable, too.

HEDDA. What?

BRACK. The pistol he had on him—

HEDDA. Yes? What about it?

BRACK. He must have stolen it.

HEDDA *jumps up.* Stolen it! That isn't true! He didn't!

BRACK. It's the only explanation. He must have stolen it. Ssh!

TESMAN *and* MRS. ELVSTED *have got up from the table in
in the rear room and come into the drawing room.*

TESMAN, *his hands full of papers.* Hedda, I can't see properly
under that lamp. Think!

HEDDA. I am thinking.

TESMAN. Do you think we could possibly use your writing
table for a little? What?

HEDDA. Yes, of course.

Quickly.

No, wait! Let me tidy it up first.

TESMAN. Oh, don't you trouble about that. There's plenty of
room.

HEDDA. No, no, let me tidy it up first, I say. I'll take this in
and put them on the piano. Here.

*She pulls an object, covered with sheets of music, out from
under the bookcase, puts some more sheets on top and carries it all into the rear room and away to the left.* TESMAN
*puts his papers on the writing table and moves the lamp
over from the corner table. He and* MRS. ELVSTED *sit down
and begin working again.* HEDDA *comes back.*

HEDDA, *behind* MRS. ELVSTED'S *chair, ruffles her hair gently.*
Well, my pretty Thea! And how is work progressing on
Eilert Loevborg's memorial?

MRS. ELVSTED *looks up at her, dejectedly.* Oh, it's going to be
terribly difficult to get these into any order.

TESMAN. We've got to do it. We must! After all, putting other
people's papers into order is rather my speciality, what?

HEDDA *goes over to the stove and sits on one of the footstools.* BRACK *stands over her, leaning against the armchair.*

HEDDA *whispers.* What was that you were saying about the
pistol?

BRACK, *softly*. I said he must have stolen it.

HEDDA. Why do you think that?

BRACK. Because any other explanation is unthinkable, Mrs. Hedda, or ought to be.

HEDDA. I see.

BRACK *looks at her for a moment*. Eilert Loevborg was here this morning. Wasn't he?

HEDDA. Yes.

BRACK. Were you alone with him?

HEDDA. For a few moments.

BRACK. You didn't leave the room while he was here?

HEDDA. No.

BRACK. Think again. Are you sure you didn't go out for a moment?

HEDDA. Oh—yes, I might have gone into the hall. Just for a few seconds.

BRACK. And where was your pistol-case during this time?

HEDDA. I'd locked it in that—

BRACK. Er—Mrs. Hedda?

HEDDA. It was lying over there on my writing table.

BRACK. Have you looked to see if both the pistols are still there?

HEDDA. No.

BRACK. You needn't bother. I saw the pistol Loevborg had when they found him. I recognised it at once. From yesterday. And other occasions.

HEDDA. Have you got it?

BRACK. No. The police have it.

HEDDA. What will the police do with this pistol?

BRACK. Try to trace the owner.

HEDDA. Do you think they'll succeed?

BRACK *leans down and whispers*. No, Hedda Gabler. Not as long as I hold my tongue.

HEDDA *looks nervously at him*. And if you don't?

BRACK *shrugs his shoulders*. You could always say he'd stolen it.

HEDDA. I'd rather die!

BRACK *smiles*. People say that. They never do it.

HEDDA, *not replying*. And suppose the pistol wasn't stolen? And they trace the owner? What then?

BRACK. There'll be a scandal, Hedda.

HEDDA. A scandal!

BRACK. Yes, a scandal. The thing you're so frightened of. You'll have to appear in court. Together with Mademoiselle Danielle. She'll have to explain how it all happened. Was it an accident, or was it—homicide? Was he about to take the pistol from his pocket to threaten her? And did it go off? Or did she snatch the pistol from his hand, shoot him and then put it back in his pocket? She might quite easily have done it. She's a resourceful lady, is Mademoiselle Danielle.

HEDDA. But I had nothing to do with this repulsive business.

BRACK. No. But you'll have to answer one question. Why did you give Eilert Loevborg this pistol? And what conclusions will people draw when it is proved you did give it to him?

HEDDA *bows her head*. That's true. I hadn't thought of that.

BRACK. Well, luckily there's no danger as long as I hold my tongue.

HEDDA *looks up at him*. In other words, I'm in your power, Judge. From now on, you've got your hold over me.

BRACK *whispers, more slowly*. Hedda, my dearest—believe me —I will not abuse my position.

HEDDA. Nevertheless, I'm in your power. Dependent on your will, and your demands. Not free. Still not free!

Rises passionately.

No. I couldn't bear that. No.

BRACK *looks half-derisively at her*. Most people resign themselves to the inevitable, sooner or later.

HEDDA *returns his gaze*. Possibly they do.

She goes across to the writing table.

HEDDA *represses an involuntary smile and says in* TESMAN's *voice.* Well, George. Think you'll be able to manage? What?

TESMAN. Heaven knows, dear. This is going to take months and months.

HEDDA, *in the same tone as before.* Fancy that, by Jove!

Runs her hands gently through MRS. ELVSTED's *hair.*

Doesn't it feel strange, Thea? Here you are working away with Tesman just the way you used to work with Eilert Loevborg.

MRS. ELVSTED. Oh—if only I can inspire your husband too!

HEDDA. Oh, it'll come. In time.

TESMAN. Yes—do you know, Hedda, I really think I'm beginning to feel a bit—well—that way. But you go back and talk to Judge Brack.

HEDDA. Can't I be of use to you two in any way?

TESMAN. No, none at all.

Turns his head.

You'll have to keep Hedda company from now on, Judge, and see she doesn't get bored. If you don't mind.

BRACK *glances at* HEDDA. It'll be a pleasure.

HEDDA. Thank you. But I'm tired this evening. I think I'll lie down on the sofa in there for a little while.

TESMAN. Yes, dear—do. What?

HEDDA *goes into the rear room and draws the curtains behind her. Short pause. Suddenly she begins to play a frenzied dance melody on the piano.*

MRS. ELVSTED *starts up from her chair.* Oh, what's that?

TESMAN *runs to the doorway.* Hedda dear, please! Don't play dance music tonight! Think of Auntie Rena. And Eilert.

HEDDA *puts her head out through the curtains.* And Auntie Juju. And all the rest of them. From now on I'll be quiet.

Closes the curtains behind her.

TESMAN, *at the writing table.* It distresses her to watch us doing this. I say, Mrs. Elvsted, I've an idea. Why don't you move in with Auntie Juju? I'll run over each evening, and we can sit and work there. What?

MRS. ELVSTED. Yes, that might be the best plan.

HEDDA, *from the rear room.* I can hear what you're saying, Tesman. But how shall I spend the evenings out here?

TESMAN, *looking through his papers.* Oh, I'm sure Judge Brack'll be kind enough to come over and keep you company. You won't mind my not being here, Judge?

BRACK, *in the armchair, calls gaily.* I'll be delighted, Mrs. Tesman. I'll be here every evening. We'll have great fun together, you and I.

HEDDA, *loud and clear.* Yes, that'll suit you, won't it, Judge? The only cock on the dunghill—!

A shot is heard from the rear room. TESMAN, MRS. ELVSTED *and* JUDGE BRACK *start from their chairs.*

TESMAN. Oh, she's playing with those pistols again.

He pulls the curtains aside and runs in. MRS. ELVSTED *follows him.* HEDDA *is lying dead on the sofa. Confusion and shouting.* BERTHA *enters in alarm from the right.*

TESMAN *screams to* BRACK. She's shot herself! Shot herself in the head! By Jove! Fancy that!

BRACK *half paralysed in the armchair.* But, good God! People don't do such things!

Little Eyolf

INTRODUCTION

Ibsen wrote LITTLE EYOLF in Christiania in the summer and autumn of 1894. He was by now sixty-six, and had entered into a mellow, or at any rate comparatively mellow old age. In contrast to the prickly aloofness of his early manhood in Norway and the long years of self-imposed exile in Italy and Germany, we are told that he now partook often and gladly in social life, and that he especially loved the company of young people and children: it amused him, at gatherings, to take them into a corner and entertain them with talk and questioning while their parents sat jealously apart. He said to Caroline Sontum, the wife of one of his doctors, that he "felt the need to be together with young people who would accept him as a friend." He took a close interest in young writers, and enjoyed reading their manuscripts and helping them with advice. As usual since he had reached the age of sixty, he had a young girl who was his special confidante: at this time it was the young pianist Hildur Andersen. He seems, however, to have found his own generation less congenial, and to have felt a certain sense of isolation from Christiania society; and, in particular, from his wife.

He had finished *The Master Builder* in October 1892 and, as was his custom, let his mind lie fallow during the following winter, spring and summer. On September 18, 1893, he wrote to his publisher, Jacob Hegel of Gyldendals: "I have now begun to plan a new dramatic work, which it is my intention to complete during next summer." We hear no further reference to this in his correspondence until June 22, 1894, when he apologised to Gerda Brandes (the wife of the critic Georg Brandes) for having left a letter unanswered for three months: "But today I must and shall write to you, for I have now begun to work seriously on my new play, and so must clear my desk and, as far as possible, my conscience of all other commitments."

We do not know the exact day on which he began, for the first pages of his preliminary draft have not survived, but he completed Act 1 on July 10. The next day he began Act 2, and a fortnight later, on July 25, he was able to write to Hegel: "Yesterday I completed the second act of my new play, and have already today begun work on the third and last act. So I hope to have the final version completed in good time. This of course means that I cannot think of taking any summer holiday this year. But I don't need one. I am very content here, and am happiest when I am working at my desk." The third act he completed on August 7; in other words, each of the last two acts took him (in draft) exactly a fortnight. During the fortnight which he spent on Act 3 he seems also to have found time to make some alterations to Acts 1 and 2, and he proceeded to revise the whole play so thoroughly that nearly three more months elapsed before he was ready, on November 1, to send the play to the printer.

A comparison of the preliminary draft of LITTLE EYOLF with Ibsen's final version is particularly revealing. William Archer summed up the main differences in one of his best critical passages:

"Revision amounted almost to re-invention; and it was the re-invention that determined the poetic value of the play. The poet's original idea (though he doubtless knew very well that this would not be final) was simply to study a rather commonplace wife's jealousy of a rather commonplace child. The lameness of Eyolf proves to have been an afterthought; and as Eyolf is not lame, it follows that the terrible cry of 'The crutch is floating' was also an afterthought, as well as the almost intolerable scene of recrimination between Allmers and Rita as to the accident which caused his lameness. We find, in fact, that nearly everything that gives the play its depth, its horror and its elevation came as an afterthought. The suggestion of the 'evil eye' motive is of the very slightest. Instead of the exquisite beauty of the final scene in its ultimate form, we have a page of almost conventional sentimentalising over Eyolf's continued existence in the hearts of his parents. Instead of telling her the wonderful tale of his meeting with Death in the mountains, Alfred reads to Rita the poem of which Ibsen had written as a first hint for *The Master Builder*.* In no case, perhaps, did revision work such a transfiguration as in LITTLE EYOLF."

As usual, Ibsen changed the names of his characters several times as he progressed with his draft. His original cast list reads as follows:

> HARALD BORGHEJM
> JOHANNE, his wife
> RITA, his sister
> ALFRED, his son, aged 11
> EJVIND ALMER, a road-engineer
> MISS VARG (i.e. WOLF), Johanne's aunt

But by the time father and son make their first appearance (the early pages of the draft are missing), Harald Borghejm has become Hakon Skjoldhejm, an established and famous author now working on his masterpiece. Then, as he is speaking

*
>They dwelt, those two, in so cosy a house
>In autumn and winter weather.
>Then came the fire—and the house was gone.
>They must search the ashes together.
>
>For down in the ashes a jewel lies hid,
>Whose brightness the flames could not smother,
>And search they but faithfully, he and she,
>'Twill be found by one or the other.
>
>But even though they find it, the gem they lost,
>The enduring jewel they cherished—
>She ne'er will recover her vanished faith—
>Nor he the joy that has perished.
>
>   (A. G. Chater's translation)

The only change Ibsen made when he inserted the poem into the first draft of LITTLE EYOLF was to substitute "peace" for "faith" in the penultimate line.

of his determination to abandon his book and dedicate himself to his son, he becomes Dr. Alfred Almer, then Allmer and finally, still in Act 1, Allmers. (Ibsen had been intending for some time to create a character with the Christian name of Alfred, for he had originally given that name to Rosmer, and then to Ragnar Brovik in *The Master Builder*.)

True to his usual custom, he switched the names of the characters as he wrote. Thus Johanne changes to Andrea and then to Rita. As she drops the name of Andrea her sister-in-law (formerly Rita) takes it over, and it is not until Act 3 that the latter becomes Asta. When the father appropriates his son's name of Alfred, a kind of general post takes place; he passes on his old surname of Borghejm to the engineer, who in turn passes on his Christian name, Ejvind, to the son. (At the beginning of this preliminary draft, the engineer and the sister are already engaged.)

The character of Asta may have been based on Ibsen's sister-in-law, Marie Thoresen. Ibsen had long cherished a warm affection for her; like Asta, she was a schoolteacher, and as long ago as 1863 he had written her a poem entitled "With a water-lily"—the flower which, at the end of Act 2, Asta gives to Allmers as a remembrance. The idea of Eyolf's lameness probably sprang from a casual remark which Ibsen put into the boy's mouth in his preliminary draft. Responding to his father's suggestion that they should go together to the mountains next summer, Eyolf (or, as Ibsen called him at this stage, Alfred) asks nervously: "But might I not easily fall and be crippled?" It is possible that Eyolf may be a portrait, conscious or unconscious, of Ibsen himself as a child—the ugly and undersized boy who felt cut off by his temperament from the other village children—and the mock soldier's uniform may reflect Ibsen's old feeling of guilt at not having volunteered to fight for the Danes against the Germans in the Schleswig-Holstein war of 1864.

The Rat Wife is also probably a memory from his childhood in Skien. Her cryptic reference to her sweetheart whom she drowned is clarified in the earlier version:

ALFRED (EYOLF): Why did you leave him?

Miss Varg: Because he had gone away from me. [I loved him so dearly.] Far, far away over the salt waves. But I drew him and drew him home to me again. I almost had him. But then my grasp failed. He was gone for ever.

This passage carries a strong echo of the relationship between Ellida and the Stranger in *The Lady from the Sea*, and it may have been the obviousness of the similarity that caused Ibsen to delete it.

Allmers is another of those "heroes" torn between the demands of his own sensuality and what he feels to be his calling whom Ibsen portrayed so repeatedly in his plays (Brand, Eilert Loevborg, Solness, Rubek); unlike them, but like Rosmer, Gregers Werle, and Earl Skule in *The Pretenders*, he is crippled and rendered impotent by a sense of guilt. Rita is, with the possible exception of Hedda Gabler, the most memorable of those unsatisfied and demanding wives whom we find in every play which Ibsen wrote after his meeting with Emilie Bardach in 1889 (Aline Solness, Gunhild Borkman, Maja Rubek). She is, one might say, Hedda with money and a child; her remark in Act 1 about the possibility of seducing Borghejm from Asta ("So much the better—if I took him from someone else!") had in fact been put by Ibsen into Hedda's mouth four years earlier, though he deleted the line in revision.

The theme of an attraction between half brother and half sister had already been explored in *Ghosts* (Oswald and Regina). Professor Didrik Arup Seip has remarked that the major cause of Allmers's feeling of guilt lies not in Eyolf's lameness, nor in his relationship to Rita, but in his relationship to Asta, and that his realisation of the truth of this relationship, though almost unbearably painful, acts on him like a cure.

LITTLE EYOLF was published by Gyldendals of Copenhagen on December 11, 1894. It had already received the usual public reading in London to secure copyright (at the Haymarket Theatre on December 3), and was staged for the first time at the Deutsches Theater in Berlin on January 12, 1895.

Three days later it was performed in Christiania (at the Christiania Theater), and before the month was out it had also been produced in Bergen, Helsingfors and Gothenburg. Milan and Vienna saw it in February, Copenhagen and Stockholm, in March. Later that spring it was presented in Chicago and Paris, where Lugné-Poë played Allmers.

London had to wait another eighteen months to see LITTLE EYOLF, for it was not staged there until November 23, 1896, with two American actresses, Janet Achurch and Elizabeth Robins, in the parts of Rita and Asta, and Mrs. Patrick Campbell as the Rat Wife. The play evoked from Bernard Shaw not merely one, but two of his most brilliant notices. Five days after the première he wrote:

". . . if you ask me where you can find the Helmer household, the Allmers household, the Solness household, the Rosmer household and all the other Ibsen households, I reply: 'Jump out of a train anywhere between Wimbledon and Haslemere; walk into the first villa you come to; and there you are . . .' LITTLE EYOLF is an extraordinarily powerful play . . . as actual and near to us as the Brighton and South Coast Railway . . . The performance was of course a very remarkable one. When, in a cast of five, you have the three best yet discovered actresses of their generation, you naturally look for something extraordinary. . . . Miss Achurch was more than equal to the occasion. Her power seemed to grow with its own expenditure. The terrible outburst at the end of the first act did not leave a scrape on her voice (which appears to have the compass of a military band) and threw her into victorious action in that tearing second act instead of wrecking her. . . . As Rita she produced almost every sound that a big human voice can, from a creak like the opening of a rusty canal lock to a melodious tenor note that the most robust Siegfried might have envied. She looked at one moment like a young, well-dressed, very pretty woman; at another she was like a desperate creature just fished dripping out of the river by the Thames Police. Yet another moment, and she was the incarnation of impetuous, ungovernable strength. . . .

"I have seen Mrs. Campbell play the Rat Wife twice, once

quite enchantingly and once most disappointingly. On the first occasion Mrs. Campbell divined that she was no village harridan, but the messenger of heaven. She played supernaturally, beautifully. . . . The next time, to my unspeakable fury, she amused herself by playing like any melodramatic old woman, a profanation for which, while my critical life lasts, never will I forgive her. . . .

"The moment I put myself into my old attitude as musical critic, I at once perceive that the performance, as a whole, was an unsatisfactory one. . . . There was nothing like the atmosphere which Lugné-Poë got in *Rosmersholm*. . . . If only the company could keep together for a while! But perhaps that is too much to hope for at present, though it is encouraging to see that the performances are to be continued next week, the five matinées—all crowded, by the way—having by no means exhausted the demand for places."

A fortnight later, on December 12, 1896, Shaw had occasion to write of the play again:

"LITTLE EYOLF, which began at the Avenue Theatre only the other day as an artistic forlorn hope led by Miss Elizabeth Robins, has been promoted into a full-blown fashionable theatrical speculation, with a Morocco Bound syndicate in the background, unlimited starring and bill-posting, and everything complete. The syndicate promptly set to work to shew us how Ibsen should really be done. They found the whole thing wrong from the root up. The silly Ibsen people had put Miss Achurch, an Ibsenite actress, into the leading part, and Mrs. Patrick Campbell, a fashionable actress, into a minor one. This was soon set right. Miss Achurch was got rid of altogether, and her part transferred to Mrs. Campbell. . . .

"Mrs. Patrick Campbell has entered thoroughly into the spirit of the alterations. She has seen how unladylike, how disturbing, how full of horror, even, the part of Rita Allmers is, acted as Miss Achurch acted it. . . . Mrs. Campbell succeeded wonderfully in eliminating all unpleasantness from the play. . . . Her performance was infinitely reassuring and pretty. . . . There was not a taste of nasty jealousy. . . . Goodness gracious, I thought, what things that evil-minded

Miss Achurch did read into this harmless play! And how nicely Mrs. Campbell took the drowning of the child! Just a pretty waving of the fingers, a moderate scream as if she had very nearly walked on a tintack, and it was all over, without tears, without pain. . . . In the third act the smoothness of the proceedings was somewhat marred by the fact that Mrs. Campbell, not knowing her words, had to stop acting and frankly bring the book on the stage and read from it. Now Mrs. Campbell reads very clearly and nicely; and the result of course was that the Ibsenite atmosphere began to assert itself, just as it would if the play were read aloud in a private room. However, that has been remedied, no doubt, by this time; and the public may rely on an uninterruptedly quiet evening."

LITTLE EYOLF had already aroused considerable interest in its printed form. Two years earlier, almost to the day (November 22, 1894), Henry James had written to Elizabeth Robins:

"Heinemann has lent me the proofs of the 2 first acts of the Play—the ineffable Play—and I can't stay my hand from waving wildly to you! It is indeed immense—indeed and indeed. It is of a rare perfection—and if 3 keeps up the tremendous pitch of 1 and 2 it will distinctly stand at the tiptop of his achievement. It's a masterpiece and a marvel; and it *must* leap upon the stage. . . . The inherent difficulties are there, but they are not insurmountable. They are on the contrary manageable—they are a matter of tact and emphasis—of art and discretion. The thing will be a big *profane* (i.e. Ibsen and non-Ibsen *both*) success. The part—*the* part—is Asta—unless it be the Rat-hound in the Bag! What an old woman—and what a Young!"

But three days later, in a letter of apology for having talked indiscreetly about the play "in the despair of a dull dinner—or after-dinner—at Sir Alfred Lyall's," he wrote to Miss Robins:

"I fear, in truth, no harm can be done equal to the harm done to the play by its own most disappointing third act. It came to me last night—and has been, to me, a subject of depressed reflection. It seems to me a singular and almost inexplicable drop—dramatically, *representably* speaking. . . . The worst of it is that it goes back, as it were, on what precedes, and gives a meagreness to that too—makes it less interesting and less significant. . . . I don't see the meaning or effect of Borghejm—I don't see the value or final *function* of Asta. . . . I find the solution too simple, too immediate, too much a harking back, and too productive of the sense that there might have been a stronger one. . . . My idea that Asta was to become an active, *the* active agent is of course blighted." However, he admitted: "Really uttered, *done,* in the gathered northern twilight, with the flag flown and the lights coming out across the fjord, the scene might have a real solemnity of beauty—and perhaps that's all that's required! !" But, he concluded: "I fear Allmers will never be thought an actor manager's part."

James's objections to the third act were, in general, shared by his contemporaries, and by the next generation of readers and theatre-goers. In recent years, however, there has been a growing body of opinion that this act, if properly understood and adequately interpreted, is by no means meagre and that the solution is not, as James thought it, too simple. Supporters of the modern view hold that Ibsen, when he wrote this act, did not envisage it as a happy ending. Devoting themselves to charity, sharing their "gold and green forests" with the poor, will not provide the answer and the peace which Alfred and Rita are seeking. They have reached rock-bottom; but unless they can prove that they have undergone a genuine change of heart, and are prepared to grapple with the realities of life, this will be no solution but merely another, more plausible, but equally insidious "life-lie." They are only at the beginning of their long climb to salvation.

My own belief is that the third act, like the two that precede it, is among the greatest that Ibsen ever wrote, and that in it he achieved exactly what he set out to achieve; namely, to reveal the interior of what, in *Brand,* thirty years before, he had called "the Ice Church"—the interior of a human soul in which love has died—so that, in Rita's words, all that is left to her and Allmers is to "try to fill that emptiness with something. Something resembling love."

LITTLE EYOLF is the most subtle and elusive of all Ibsen's plays, and it does not, at the time of writing, appear to have been adequately produced anywhere outside Scandinavia, if indeed it has ever been adequately produced there. There are several reasons for this besides the false belief in the "happy ending," which, if it is played that way, vitiates much of what has gone before. One is that James's fears concerning the unwillingness of established actors to play Allmers have been proved only too true. There have been several splendid Ritas (notably, in England, Janet Achurch and Jean Forbes Robertson); there has never been an adequate Allmers. "How," asked Bernard Shaw in his review of the first English performance of the play in 1896, "could he recommend himself to spectators who saw in him everything they are ashamed of in themselves?" And James Agate, writing of the performance at the Arts Theatre in 1930, concluded: "The character is deadly anyhow, and should be relegated to the index of the unactable." The character of Allmers is in fact only deadly if, as in common practice, it is romanticised. A romanticised Allmers and a happy ending are burdens that no production of LITTLE EYOLF can hope to survive.

A third consideration which has, until recently, hampered appreciation of the play is its frankness about sex. In this context it is instructive to analyse the reactions of the London press to the productions of 1896, 1928 and 1958. *The Times* expressed itself in the following terms about the 1896 production:

"A perplexing phantasmagoria which still less than the majority of its predecessors deserves the name of a public entertainment. . . . Propriety forbids one to analyse. . . . None of the characters appear quite sane. . . . a set of irresponsible people moved by unaccountable impulses and addicted to fantastic views of duty. There is no knowing what they will do next. They are not amenable to the rules of ordinary human nature. . . . Terribly depressing and lugubrious society. . . . One does not breathe freely until one has escaped from the atmosphere of the theatre into the open air. Gloom, depression, and a sense of the remoteness of the action from all living human interests overcome the spectator, whose abiding impression of the play is that of having seen, in a dream, the patients of a madhouse exercising in their yard."

In 1928 *The Times* saw the play somewhat differently. Analysing the production at the Everyman Theatre, its critic wrote:

"This play is seldom acted, yet how wonderfully actable even a moderately good performance shows it to be. . . . It must then be from its subject that the ordinary playgoer shrinks. He is rarely in the mood to enjoy the 'iron-mouthed' Ibsen's condemnation of just the kind of conjugal love that romantic writers bestow on those whom they destine to live happily ever after. It is a natural hesitancy, but the ordinary playgoer misses much by his unwillingness to risk the possibility of pain, even a queer exhilaration."

By 1958 public opinion was beginning to catch up with LITTLE EYOLF. The production at Hammersmith that spring coincided with the West End presentation of Tennessee Williams's *Cat on a Hot Tin Roof*, and the critics were not slow to compare the two plays, as the following extracts show:

> "It is hard to see why LITTLE EYOLF has so long been left out of the Ibsen repertory. . . . Fresh and pungent, a rare and exciting treat. . . . Its subject is a marriage and it takes that marriage apart about as frankly and twice as truthfully as, say, Tennessee Williams takes apart the marriage of Brick and Maggie the Cat, and it is (written though it was in 1894) just as modern if not more so. . . . The effect is terrific."
>
> (T. C. Worsley in *The New Statesman*)
>
> "This magnificent play . . . so frank about sex that it makes Tennessee Williams look like pap for infants."
>
> (John Barber in *The Daily Express*)
>
> "A rich, rare, late Ibsen."
>
> (Kenneth Tynan in *The Observer*)
>
> "A masterpiece which is rarely done but which is immensely more rewarding to see than to read."
>
> (Alan Dent in *The News Chronicle*)

"A great modern drama which wipes the smile off your face and puts the fear of God into your heart before you can say Tennessee Williams."

(Alan Brien in *The Spectator*)

"This great play's haunting moral beauty . . . A post-Freudian generation will surely marvel at the justness and truth with which this pre-Freudian master picks his symbols."

(Philip Hope-Wallace in *The Manchester Guardian*)

"A horrifying experiment in vivisection, conducted with deadly skill."

(Eric Keown in *Punch*)

But even when public opinion has caught up with the play, and the ending is understood, and Allmers is played with the conflict between sensual imagination on the one side, and intellect plus morality on the other, which the part, like that of Rosmer, demands, two difficulties still remain. One is the title. LITTLE EYOLF is a fine title when one has read or seen the play, but it is not, either in English or in Norwegian, a title likely to lure people into a theatre. Yet one hesitates to rename it simply because, when one has read or seen the play, one despairs of ever finding any other title which could so perfectly pinpoint the twin horns of the dilemma on which the chief characters find themselves impaled. The final obstacle, with all diffidence, is that of translation. LITTLE EYOLF is incomparably the most elusive and difficult of all Ibsen's plays to translate, not excluding *Brand*. Ibsen's characters, especially in his later plays, are inhibited by a deep sense of guilt which makes them evasive in their speech, but none are as evasive as Allmers and Rita, who spend their time circling round a subject which they dread to talk about yet cannot escape from. If one renders these passages too directly, the play becomes a melodrama; if, on the other hand, one takes refuge behind cloudy word-combinations, as, with the greatest respect, Archer did, the thread of the argument gets lost. It is, for example, evident from the reviews of the 1896, 1928, 1930 and even 1945 London productions that many of the critics had not the faintest idea that the shock of Eyolf's fall has rendered Allmers sexually impotent, and unless this fact is made absolutely clear to the audience they can only feel a very restricted sympathy with him.

However, the English public has at last been persuaded to appreciate *Brand*, ninety-four years after Ibsen wrote it, and perhaps it is not too much to hope that before too long they and other audiences may be allowed to see a production of LITTLE EYOLF which will establish it as one of the old master's supreme achievements. Nowhere else does he probe so mercilessly into the complexities of human minds and relationships; it is like a long, sustained and terrifying operation. On the occasion of its first production in England in 1896, William Archer wrote: "I rank the play beside, if not above, the very greatest of Ibsen's works, and am only doubtful whether its soul-searching be not too terrible for human endurance in the theatre."

M. M.

CHARACTERS

ALFRED ALLMERS, a man of property; also of letters; sometime
   supply teacher
RITA, his wife
EYOLF, their son, aged 9
ASTA ALLMERS, Alfred's younger half sister
BORGHEJM, an engineer
THE RAT WIFE

The action takes place on ALLMERS' *estate, by a fjord in west-
ern Norway, a few miles outside town.*

An early version of this translation was broadcast on the B.B.C. Third Programme on February 12, 1956 (repeated on February 17 and June 23 of the same year). The cast was as follows:

ALLMERS	Richard Hurndall
RITA	Maxine Audley
ASTA	Joan Hart
EYOLF	Gabrielle Blunt
RAT WIFE	Mary O'Farrell
BORGHEJM	John Glen

Directed by Peter Watts

It was subsequently presented by Michael Codron Productions, Ltd., at the Lyric Theatre, Hammersmith, on March 11, 1958, with the following cast:

ALLMERS	Robert Eddison
RITA	Heather Chasen
ASTA	Barbara Clegg
EYOLF	John Hall
RAT WIFE	Selma Vaz Dias
BORGHEJM	Michael David

Directed by David William

On April 20, 1958, it was performed on Independent Television (ABC Network), under the title of The Rat Wife:

ALLMERS	Neil McCallum
RITA	Patricia Heneghan
ASTA	Mary Peach
EYOLF	Jimmy Ray
RAT WIFE	Joan Heath
BORGHEJM	John Carson

Directed by Stuart Latham

That version has, however, now been entirely revised and rewritten, so that the text presented here is to all intents and purposes a new translation.

ACT ONE

A handsome and expensively appointed garden room, full of furniture, flowers and plants. Upstage, glass doors open on to a verandah, with a broad view over the fjord. Wooded mountain ranges in the distance. In each of the side walls, there is a door; the one on the right is a double door, set upstage. Downstage right is a sofa, with loose cushions and rugs. Chairs and a small table at the corner of the sofa. Downstage left, a larger table with armchairs around it. On the table stands an open portmanteau. It is early on a summer morning; the sun is shining warmly.

RITA ALLMERS *stands at the table, facing left, unpacking the portmanteau. She is a handsome, blond, Junoesque woman of about thirty, dressed in a light-coloured housecoat.*

After a few seconds, ASTA ALLMERS *enters through the door on the right, dressed in a light brown summer suit, with hat, jacket and parasol. Under her arm she carries a large, locked portfolio. She is slim, of middle height, with dark hair and deep, serious eyes. She is about twenty-five.*

ASTA, *in the doorway.* Good morning, Rita, my dear.

RITA *turns her head and nods.* Why, Asta! Fancy seeing you here so early! What brings you all this way from town?

ASTA *puts her things on a chair by the door.* I felt so restless. I felt I had to come out and see Eyolf today. Little Eyolf. And you, Rita.

She puts her portfolio down on the table by the sofa.

So I caught the steamer and—here I am.

RITA *smiles.* And, quite by accident, you happened to meet someone you knew—a friend—on board?

ASTA, *calmly.* No, as a matter of fact I didn't.

Sees the portmanteau.

Why, Rita, what's that?

RITA *continues unpacking.* Alfred's portmanteau. Don't you recognise it?

ASTA, *happily, going over to her.* You mean Alfred has come home?

RITA. Yes, would you believe it? He arrived quite unexpectedly, by the night train.

ASTA. So that was it. That was what brought me here. But hadn't he written to say he was coming?

RITA. Not a word.

ASTA. Not even a telegram?

RITA. Yes—it arrived an hour before he did. Short and to the point.

Laughs.

Isn't that just like him, Asta?

ASTA. Yes. That's his way. He always was secretive.

RITA. Well, it makes it all the more wonderful to have him home again.

ASTA. I know how you feel.

RITA. A whole fortnight before I was expecting him.

ASTA. And he's well and happy? Not depressed?

RITA *closes the portmanteau and smiles at* ASTA. He looked quite transformed as he came in through the door.

ASTA. He must have been tired, surely?

RITA. Tired? He was ready to drop. Poor darling, he'd come most of the way on foot.

ASTA. That mountain air must have been too sharp for him.

RITA. I don't know. I haven't heard him cough once since he got back.

ASTA. There you are! The doctor was right, after all, to advise him to go on that walking tour.

RITA. Yes. I suppose so, but— You don't know what a dreadful time this has been for me, Asta. I haven't been able to bring myself to talk about it. And you've hardly ever been out to see me.

ASTA. I should have come more often. But—

RITA. No, no—you had your schoolwork to attend to in town. I know.

Smiles.

And our pioneer, our builder of roads—he's been away too, hasn't he?

ASTA. Oh, stop it, Rita.

RITA. Very well. The pioneer is dismissed. Oh, but Asta, how I've missed Alfred! How empty it's been, how desolate! Just as though someone had died here.

ASTA. Rita! He's only been away six or seven weeks—

RITA. Ah, but you must remember that Alfred has never been away from me before. Not even for a day. In all the ten years we've been—

ASTA. But Rita, that's just why I thought it was time he got away this year. He ought to have gone walking in the mountains every summer. That's what he ought to have done.

RITA *smiles.* Ah, it's easy for you to talk. If I were as—sensible as you are, I would have let him go before now—perhaps. But I couldn't, Asta. I couldn't. I felt somehow that if I once let him go, I might never get him back again. You can understand that, can't you?

ASTA. No. But then I don't have anyone I'm afraid of losing.

RITA, *teasingly.* Really? No one at all?

ASTA. Not that I know of.

Quickly.

But, tell me, Rita, where is Alfred? Asleep?

RITA. Asleep? Not he! He got up this morning just as early as ever.

ASTA. He can't have been all that tired, then.

RITA. He was last night, when he arrived. But now he's had Eyolf in with him for—oh, at least an hour.

ASTA. Poor, pale little child! Is he going to be made to study all day again?

RITA *shrugs her shoulders.* Well, you know Alfred wants it that way.

ASTA. Yes, but I think you ought to try to stop him.

RITA, *a trifle impatiently.* Well, really, I can't interfere in these things. Alfred is better qualified to understand these matters than I am. What else would you have Eyolf do? He can't run about and play like other children.

ASTA, *firmly.* I shall speak to Alfred about it.

RITA. Yes, my dear, you do that. Ah, here they are!

ALFRED ALLMERS, *in a summer suit, enters through the door on the left, leading* EYOLF *by the hand.* ALLMERS *is a slim, delicately built man of thirty-six or thirty-seven, with gentle eyes, thinning brown hair and beard, and a serious, thoughtful expression.* EYOLF *wears a suit cut like a uniform, with gold braid and buttons with lions on them. He is lame, and limps with a crutch under his left arm. His leg is paralysed. He is undersized and looks frail, but has fine, wise eyes.*

ALLMERS *lets go of* EYOLF, *comes forward happily and stretches out both his hands to* ASTA. Asta! Asta, my dearest! Are you out here? It's good to see you so soon.

ASTA. I felt I had to. Welcome home.

ALLMERS *clasps her hands.* Thank you.

RITA. Doesn't he look splendid?

ASTA, *looking intently at him.* Wonderful. Wonderful. Your eyes—so sparkling. You must have done a lot of writing while you've been away.

In sudden excitement.

Have you—finished the book?

ALLMERS. The book?

Shrugs his shoulders.

Oh that.

ASTA. I thought it would go easily once you could get away and be alone.

ALLMERS. I used to think so, too. But it didn't turn out that way. If I must confess the truth, I have not written a line.

ASTA. You haven't written—?

RITA. Oh! So that's why I found all those blank sheets of paper in your bag.

ASTA. But my dear Alfred, what on earth have you been doing all this time?

ALLMERS. Walking and thinking. Thinking. Thinking.

RITA *puts her arm round his shoulders.* Thinking a little of us too, I hope.

ALLMERS. Yes, of course. A lot. Every day.

RITA, *gaily, letting go of him.* Well then, everything is as it should be.

ASTA. But did you do no work at all on the book? You look so happy and—contented. We don't often see you like that when you're working—I mean, when your work's not going well.

ALLMERS. Yes, I know. I have been so stupid. Thinking is what matters. What one can manage to put down on paper is insignificant.

ASTA. Insignificant!

RITA *smiles.* Have you gone mad, Alfred?

EYOLF *looks trustingly up at him.* No, Father. What *you* write is important.

ALLMERS *smiles and strokes the boy's hair.* Yes, my son. If you say so. But I tell you, there is one who will come after me and who will do these things better.

EYOLF. Who will that be? Oh, tell me!

ALLMERS. Give him time. He will show himself.

EYOLF. But what will you do when he comes?

ALLMERS. I shall return to the mountains.

RITA. Shame on you, Alfred!

ALLMERS. To the high peaks and the great wide spaces.

EYOLF. Father, don't you think I shall soon be well enough to come with you?

ALLMERS, *ill at ease*. Perhaps, perhaps, my boy.

EYOLF. I think it would be nice if I too could climb mountains.

ASTA, *quickly, changing the subject*. How smart you look today, Eyolf.

EYOLF. Yes, don't you think so, aunt?

ASTA. Yes. Is it for your father's sake that you've put your new clothes on?

EYOLF. Yes. I asked Mother to let me. I wanted Father to see me in them.

ALLMERS, *aside, to* RITA. You shouldn't have given him that kind of suit.

RITA, *aside*. But he begged me so. Again and again. He gave me no peace.

EYOLF. Father, Borghejm has given me a bow. Isn't it wonderful? And he's taught me to shoot with it.

ALLMERS. Yes, that really is a good idea, Eyolf.

EYOLF. Next time he comes, I'm going to ask him to teach me to swim, too.

ALLMERS. To swim? Why do you want to learn to do that?

EYOLF. All the other boys can swim. I'm the only one who can't.

ALLMERS, *moved, puts his arm round the boy's shoulders*. You shall learn anything—anything you want to learn, you shall.

EYOLF. Shall I tell you what I most want to learn, Father?

ALLMERS. What? Tell me.

EYOLF. Most of all I should like to be a soldier.

ALLMERS. Ah, little Eyolf, there are so many other things more worth learning than that.

EYOLF. Yes, but when I grow big I shall have to be a soldier. You know that.

ALLMERS. Yes, yes. We shall see.

ASTA *sits at the table, left.* Eyolf! Come over here and I'll tell you something.

EYOLF *goes over to her.* What is it, aunt?

ASTA. What do you think, Eyolf? I have seen the Rat Wife.

EYOLF. What? Have you seen the Rat Wife? Oh, no, it's not true!

ASTA. Yes, it is. I saw her yesterday.

EYOLF. Where did you see her?

ASTA. On the road, outside the town.

ALLMERS. I saw her too, out in the countryside.

RITA, *seated on the sofa.* Perhaps we shall see her too, then, Eyolf.

EYOLF. Aunt, isn't it strange that she should be called the Rat Wife?

ASTA. People call her that because she goes round the country and drives away all the rats.

ALLMERS. I believe her real name is Mother Lupus.

EYOLF. Lupus? That means a wolf, doesn't it?

ALLMERS *strokes him affectionately on the head.* What a lot of things you know, Eyolf.

EYOLF. Then perhaps it may be true after all that she turns into a werewolf at night. Do you think it is, Father?

ALLMERS. No, I don't think so. Now, why don't you run out and play in the garden?

EYOLF. Oughtn't I to take some of my books with me?

ALLMERS. No, no more books from now on. Run down to the beach and play with the other boys.

EYOLF, *embarrassed.* No, Father. I don't want to go down and play with them today.

ALLMERS. Why not?

EYOLF. Because of my clothes.

ALLMERS *frowns.* Do they make fun of—of your fine clothes?

EYOLF, *evasively.* No, they wouldn't dare to do that. If they did I should beat them.

ALLMERS. Well, then, why—?

EYOLF. I don't like them. And they say I can never become a soldier.

ALLMERS, *with suppressed anger.* Why do they say that?

EYOLF. I think they envy me. They're so poor, Father, that they have to go barefoot.

ALLMERS, *quietly.* Ah, Rita. How this gnaws at my heart!

RITA *rises to calm him.* Now, now, now!

ALLMERS, *grimly.* These boys shall know one day who is the master down there.

ASTA *listens.* Someone is knocking.

EYOLF. It must be Borghejm.

RITA. Come in!

THE RAT WIFE *comes softly in through the door on the right. She is a little, thin, shrivelled old woman, grey-haired, with sharp, piercing eyes, wearing an old-fashioned flowered dress, with a black bonnet and a black cloak with tassels. She carries a large, red umbrella, and from her arm a black bag dangles on a string.*

EYOLF, *clutching* ASTA'S *skirt, whispers.* Aunt! This must be her!

RAT WIFE *curtseys at the door.* Begging your pardon—have your honours any troublesome thing that gnaws here in this house?

ALLMERS. Have we—? No, I don't think so.

RAT WIFE. Ah. I'd be glad to rid you of it, if there was any gnawing thing that troubled you.

RITA. We understand. But we have nothing like that in this house.

RAT WIFE. That's a great pity. For I'm on my round, and who knows when I shall pass this way again? Ah, but I'm tired.

ALLMERS *indicates a chair.* Yes, indeed, you look tired.

RAT WIFE. Poor little creatures. Everyone hates them. After them the whole time. It oughtn't to be tiring, helping them, being kind to them. But it drains a body's strength.

RITA. Sit down and rest yourself, old woman.

RAT WIFE. Thank you, gracious lady. A thousand thanks.

She sits on a chair between the door and the sofa.

The whole night I've been about my business.

ALLMERS. Have you? Where?

RAT WIFE. Over on the islands.

Chuckles.

The people there sent for me. They didn't want to. But they had no choice. They had to bury their teeth in the sour apple.

Looks at EYOLF *and nods.*

Sour apple, little master. Sour apple.

EYOLF, *involuntarily.* Why did they have to—?

RAT WIFE. Have to what, little master?

EYOLF. Bury their teeth in the sour apple?

RAT WIFE. Why, because they couldn't get anything to fill their bellies with. Because of the rats and all the hungry little baby rats, you understand, young master.

RITA. Poor wretched people! Were they so plagued by them?

RAT WIFE. Plagued?

Laughs.

Thousands of them, swarming, teeming.

Smiles with quiet satisfaction.

Up in the beds they crawled and crept the whole night long. They plopped down into the milk churns. And over the floors they hissed and rustled, this way, that way.

EYOLF, *aside, to* ASTA. I never want to go there, aunt.

RAT WIFE. But then *I* came—I and another. And we took them all away with us. The sweet, small creatures. We made an end of every one of them.

EYOLF *shrieks.* Father! Look! Look!

RITA. For God's sake, Eyolf, what's the matter?

EYOLF *points.* Something's struggling in her bag.

RITA *goes left, with a scream.* Ugh! Get rid of her, Alfred.

RAT WIFE *laughs.* Ah, dear lady, don't be afraid of such a harmless little creature.

ALLMERS. What have you got there?

RAT WIFE. It's only Mopsemand.

Unfastens the strings of her bag.

Come up from your darkness, my little lovely.

A SMALL DOG *with a broad black nose sticks its head out of the bag.*

RAT WIFE *nods and beckons to* EYOLF.

Don't be afraid, my little wounded soldier. Come close and stroke him. He won't bite you. Come and stroke him. Come and stroke him.

EYOLF, *close to* ASTA. No. I daren't.

RAT WIFE. Doesn't my young master think Mopsemand has a lovely, gentle face?

EYOLF *points, amazed.* Him?

RAT WIFE. Yes, dearie, him.

EYOLF, *half to himself, staring intently at the dog.* I think he has—the most horrible face I have ever seen.

RAT WIFE *closes her bag.* You'll change your mind, dearie. You'll change your mind.

EYOLF *draws close to her, and strokes the bag lightly.* And at the same time he's beautiful. Beautiful.

RAT WIFE, *solicitously.* But just now he's so tired and full of aches and pains, the poor creature. So dreadfully tired he is.

Looks at ALLMERS.

It drains a body's strength—that kind of game.

ALLMERS. What game?

RAT WIFE. Why—

Laughs.

—follow my leader.

ALLMERS. Ah—and is this dog of yours the one who lures and leads them?

RAT WIFE *nods*. Mopsemand and I, we lead them. We work together, he and I. Easiest thing in the world, you'd think, to watch us. I just tie a string to his collar and lead him three times round the house. While I do this, I play on my pipe. And when they hear me play, up they have to come from the cellars, down from the lofts, out of all their dark holes and crannies—all of them, bless their little hearts.

EYOLF. And then he bites them all to death?

RAT WIFE. No. We just go down to the boat, he and I. And they come after us. The big grown ones, and their little darlings with them.

EYOLF. And then? What happens?

RAT WIFE. Well, we draw away from the land. I pull at the oars, and play on my pipe. And Mopsemand swims behind me.

Her eyes flash.

And all the little creatures that crept and crawled, they follow us further and further out to the deep waters. They have to.

EYOLF. Why do they have to?

RAT WIFE. Because they don't want to. Because they're so afraid of the deep water—that's why they have to swim out to it.

EYOLF. And then they drown?

RAT WIFE. Every single one.

More softly.

And then they've all the dark and quiet and peace they could wish for, little angels. Down there they sleep so sweet, so long a sleep. All the little creatures men hate and persecute.

She gets up.

In the old days I needed no Mopsemand. I used to lure them myself. Alone.

EYOLF. What did you lure?

RAT WIFE. Men. One specially.

EYOLF. Who? Oh, tell me!

RAT WIFE *smiles*. Why, my sweetheart, little lady's man.

EYOLF. Where is he now?

RAT WIFE, *spitefully*. Down among the rats.

Amiably again.

But now it's time for me to be about my business again.
To RITA.

Are you sure you've no work for me today? I could get it
done at once.

RITA. No, thank you. I don't think we need your services today.

RAT WIFE. You think so? Well, one can never be sure. If you
should happen to remember anything that nibbles and
gnaws, creeps and crawls, just send for me and Mopsemand.
Fare ye well!

She goes out through the door, right.

EYOLF, *to* ASTA. Now I've seen the Rat Wife, too!

RITA *goes out on to the verandah and fans herself with her
handkerchief. A moment later* EYOLF *slips unnoticed out
through the door on the right.*

ALLMERS *takes the portfolio from the table by the sofa.* Is this
your portfolio, Asta?

ASTA. Yes. I've got some of those old letters in it.

ALLMERS. Oh, the family letters?

ASTA. Don't you remember? You asked me to go through them
while you were away.

ALLMERS *pats her head.* Did you really manage to find the
time?

ASTA. Yes. I did some of it here and some at home. In town.

ALLMERS. Thank you. Did you find anything of interest in
them?

ASTA, *casually.* Oh, one always finds something of interest in
old letters.

More quietly, serious.

The ones in the portfolio are my mother's.

ALLMERS. You must keep them, of course.

ASTA, *with an effort.* No, I'd like you to look through them too, Alfred. Some time—later. I haven't brought the key of the portfolio with me today.

ALLMERS. Never mind, my dear. I shan't want to read your mother's letters.

ASTA *looks pointedly at him.* One quiet evening I will tell you something they contain.

ALLMERS. Yes, do that. But keep your mother's letters. You haven't so many reminders of her.

Hands the portfolio to ASTA. *She takes it and puts it on the chair, under her overcoat.* RITA *comes back into the room.*

RITA. Ugh! That horrid old woman! She's brought the smell of death into the house.

ALLMERS. She was rather horrible, wasn't she?

RITA. I felt quite ill while she was in the room.

ALLMERS. You know, I can understand that power of compelling and drawing things that she spoke of. Being alone in the mountains, up on those huge, open spaces—one feels that power.

ASTA *glances sharply at him.* What has happened to you, Alfred?

ALLMERS *smiles.* Happened?

ASTA. Something has happened. You're changed. Rita knows it too.

RITA. Yes. I knew at once. But that's good, isn't it, Alfred?

ALLMERS. I hope so. Something good must come from it.

RITA. Something happened to you while you were away. Don't deny it. I can see it.

ALLMERS *shakes his head.* Nothing happened *to* me. But—

RITA, *tensely.* But—?

ALLMERS. *In* me, something happened. A small transformation.

RITA. Oh, God!

ALLMERS *pats her hand reassuringly.* Only for the better, Rita dear. Believe me.

RITA *sits on the sofa.* Now you must tell us all about it. Absolutely everything.

ALLMERS *turns to* ASTA. Yes. Let's sit down, and I'll try to tell you. As well as I can.

He sits on the sofa beside RITA. ASTA *brings forward a chair and sits on it near him. Short pause.*

RITA *looks expectantly at him.* Well?

ALLMERS. When I look back on my life—the road I have taken —these past ten years, it seems almost like a fairy tale, or a dream. Don't you think so, Asta?

ASTA. Yes, I think so. In many ways.

ALLMERS *continues.* When I think what we were, Asta. Two orphans—without a penny.

RITA, *impatiently.* Oh, that's so long ago.

ALLMERS, *not listening.* And now I sit here, comfortable, prosperous. Able to follow my calling: to work and study, just as I please.

Stretches out his hand.

And this unbelievable, unlooked-for happiness we owe to you, my dearest Rita.

RITA, *half in jest, half in spite of herself, smacks his hand.* Now that's enough of that silly talk!

ALLMERS. I mention this only as a kind of preamble.

RITA. Well, let's take it as read.

ALLMERS. Rita—don't think it was the doctor's advice that drove me up to the mountains.

ASTA. Not the doctor?

RITA. What was it, then?

ALLMERS. I couldn't find peace to write any more.

RITA. No peace? But, my dear, who disturbed you?

ALLMERS *shakes his head.* No one disturbed me. I just came

to feel that I was really misusing—well—no, neglecting—my true gifts. That I was wasting time.

ASTA, *her eyes wide.* In writing?

ALLMERS *nods.* Don't you see—I wasn't put here just to write. There must be something I can *do* as well.

RITA. And that was what you were brooding over?

ALLMERS. Yes. Mostly.

RITA. Then that's why you've been so discontented with yourself these last months. And with us, too. Oh, yes you were, Alfred.

ALLMERS, *looking straight ahead.* I sat there bent over my desk, writing, day after day. Nights as well. Writing and writing my great, thick book on *The Responsibility of Man.* Hm!

ASTA *puts her hand on his arm.* But, my dear—that book is your life's work.

RITA. Yes, you've said so often enough.

ALLMERS. It was going to be. Or so I thought. From the time I grew up.

With a warm expression in his eyes.

Then you made it possible for me to devote myself to it, my dearest Rita.

RITA. What nonsense you talk!

ALLMERS *smiles at her.* You with "your gold and your green forests"—

RITA, *half smiling, half vexed.* If you go on talking like that I shall smack you!

ASTA *stares at him, worried.* But the book, Alfred?

ALLMERS. Somehow it began to seem less and less important. And the claim of higher duties began to fill my mind.

RITA *takes his hand, her eyes radiant.* Alfred!

ALLMERS. I am thinking of Eyolf, my dear.

RITA *lets go his hand.* Oh. Eyolf.

ALLMERS. He is always in my mind. Since that tragic fall from the table— And especially now that we know he can never be cured—

RITA. But you do everything you can for him, Alfred.

ALLMERS. As a schoolmaster, perhaps. But not as a father. From now on I want to be a father to Eyolf.

RITA *stares at him and shakes her head.* I don't think I quite understand you.

ALLMERS. I mean I am going to do everything in my power to help him to come to terms with the irrevocable, and live with it.

RITA. But Alfred, thank God I don't think Eyolf feels so deeply about it.

ASTA, *emotionally.* Yes, Rita. He does.

ALLMERS. Yes; you may be sure he feels it deeply.

RITA, *impatiently.* But, Alfred, what more can you do for him?

ALLMERS. I want to try to reveal the potential of the dreams which are dawning in his childish mind. To nurture those high hopes so that they flower and come to fruition.

With increasing ardour, rising to his feet.

I want to do more than that. I want to help him to shape his ambitions towards goals that lie within his reach. As he is now, he longs only for the things he can never attain. I want to put happiness within his grasp.

He paces once or twice up and down the room. ASTA *and* RITA *watch him.*

RITA. Shouldn't you take these things more calmly, Alfred?

ALLMERS *stands at the table on the left and looks at them.* Eyolf shall take up my life's work. If he so wishes. Or he may choose to attempt something which shall be completely and entirely his. Perhaps that would be best. In any case, I shall write no more.

RITA *rises.* But, Alfred dearest—can't you work both for yourself and for Eyolf?

ALLMERS. No! Impossible! In this matter, I cannot divide myself. Therefore I prefer to yield. Eyolf shall be the one of our family to fulfil himself. And it shall be my task to bring him to self-fulfilment.

ASTA *has risen and goes over to him.* It has been a hard struggle for you, Alfred. To come to this decision.

ALLMERS. It has. Here, at home, I would never have been able to conquer myself. I would never have been able to force myself to renounce anything. Not in this house.

RITA. Was that why you went away this summer?

ALLMERS, *his eyes shining.* Yes! I climbed up into an infinite solitude. I saw the sun rise above the mountain tops. I felt —nearer the stars—almost as if I understood them, and belonged with them. Then I was—able to do it.

ASTA *looks at him sadly.* But will you never carry on with *The Responsibility of Man?*

ALLMERS. No, never. I have told you I cannot divide myself between two tasks. I shall fulfil my ideal of human responsibility through my own life.

RITA, *with a smile.* Do you really believe you will be able to stay faithful to such high ideals in this house?

ALLMERS *takes her hand.* With your help, Rita.

Stretches out his other hand.

And with yours, Asta.

RITA *withdraws her hand.* Then you can divide yourself, after all.

ALLMERS. But, my dearest—

RITA *turns away from him and goes to the french windows. There is a quick tap on the door and* BORGHEJM *comes briskly in. He is a young man of thirty odd, with a bright, cheerful face and an easy, upright bearing.*

BORGHEJM. Good morning, good morning, Mrs. Allmers.

Stops short with delight as he sees ALLMERS.

Well, well! What's this? Home again already, Mr. Allmers?

ALLMERS *shakes his hand.* Yes. I came home last night.

RITA, *gaily.* His leave was up, Mr. Borghejm.

ALLMERS. Rita's joking.

RITA *comes towards them.* Joking? It's the truth. His leave had expired.

BORGHEJM. You keep your husband on a tight rein, Mrs. Allmers.

RITA. I insist on my rights. In any case, everything has to come to an end some time.

BORGHEJM. Oh, not everything—I hope. Good morning, Miss Allmers.

ASTA, *avoiding his eyes.* Good morning.

RITA *looks at* BORGHEJM. Not everything, did you say?

BORGHEJM. I do believe there is at least one thing in this world which need not come to an end.

RITA. I see. You're thinking of love, and that kind of thing.

BORGHEJM. I am thinking of all that is lovely and unforgettable—

RITA. And that will never end? Yes, let us hope so for all our sakes.

ALLMERS *goes over to them.* I suppose you will soon have finished this road you've been building here?

BORGHEJM. I have finished it. Yesterday. It's taken a long time. Thank heaven that came to an end!

RITA. And that's why you are so cock-a-hoop this morning?

BORGHEJM. Yes.

RITA. Well, I must say—!

BORGHEJM. What, Mrs. Allmers?

RITA. That's not very nice of you, Mr. Borghejm.

BORGHEJM. Oh? Why not?

RITA. Well, it means you won't be seeing very much more of us.

BORGHEJM. No, that's true. I hadn't thought of that.

RITA. Still, I suppose you'll be able to visit us now and then.

BORGHEJM. I'm afraid that won't be possible. For a long time.

ALLMERS. Oh? Why not?

BORGHEJM. I've just been given an important new contract which I have to start work on at once.

ALLMERS. No, have you?

Presses his hand.

I'm delighted to hear it.

RITA. Congratulations, Mr. Borghejm, congratulations.

BORGHEJM. Sssh! I'm not meant to be talking about it yet. But I can't keep it to myself. It's a big road that's to be built up in the north. Mountains to negotiate. Extraordinary obstacles to overcome.

Exclaims.

Oh, it's a marvellous life to be a maker of new roads!

RITA *smiles and looks teasingly at him.* Is it just this new road that brings you out here to see us today in such high spirits?

BORGHEJM. No, not only that. The whole future seems so full of hope and promise.

RITA, *in the same tone as before.* Perhaps there's something even more marvellous lying ahead?

BORGHEJM *glances at* ASTA. Who knows? When fortune comes, she comes like the spring floods.

Turns to ASTA.

Miss Allmers, shall we two take a little stroll together? As usual?

ASTA, *quickly.* No. No, thank you. Not now. Not today.

BORGHEJM. Ah, please! Just for a few minutes. I've so many things I want to say to you before I go.

RITA. Something else you mustn't talk about yet, perhaps?

BORGHEJM. I—er—

RITA. Well, things that cannot be talked about may sometimes be whispered.

Aside to ASTA.

Go with him, Asta.

ASTA. But, Rita—

BORGHEJM, *pleadingly.* Miss Asta—remember this will be our last walk together.

ASTA *takes her hat and parasol.* Well, let us take a short stroll in the garden then.

BORGHEJM. Thank you—thank you!

ALLMERS. You might keep an eye on Eyolf while you're down there.

BORGHEJM. Eyolf? Why, yes. Where is Eyolf today? I've brought something for him.

ALLMERS. He's playing somewhere down there.

BORGHEJM. Really? So he's started to play now? He usually just sits indoors reading.

ALLMERS. I'm going to change all that now. I want him to spend a lot of time out of doors.

BORGHEJM. Quite right! Let him have his share of the free air too, poor little fellow! Good God, it's the best thing we can do in this blessed world. I sometimes think our whole life is a game. Come, Miss Asta.

BORGHEJM *and* ASTA *go out on to the verandah and down into the garden.*

ALLMERS *stands looking after them.* Rita, do you think there is anything between those two?

RITA. I don't know what to think. I used to believe there was. But Asta's been behaving so strangely these last weeks—almost as though she'd become a stranger to me.

ALLMERS. Really? While I've been away, you mean?

RITA. Yes, these last weeks.

ALLMERS. You don't think she's really interested in him?

RITA. Not seriously. Not with her heart and soul—ruthlessly. No, I don't think she's seriously interested in him now. *Looks searchingly at him.* Would it upset you if she was?

ALLMERS. Not upset me, exactly. I can't deny that it would worry me a little, though.

RITA. Worry you?

ALLMERS. Remember I am responsible for Asta. And for her happiness.

RITA. Nonsense! Responsible? Asta isn't a child. She's old enough to know whom to choose for herself, I should have thought.

ALLMERS. Yes, let us hope she is, Rita.

RITA. I see no harm in Borghejm.

ALLMERS. No, my dear, neither do I. Rather the reverse. And yet—

RITA *continues*. And I should be very happy to see him and Asta married.

ALLMERS, *not pleased*. Would you? Why?

RITA, *with increasing emotion*. Because she'd have to go far away with him, and then she could never come and visit us again!

ALLMERS *stares amazed at her*. What? You mean you want to be rid of Asta?

RITA. Yes, Alfred, yes!

ALLMERS. But why—?

RITA *throws her arms passionately round his neck*. Then I would have you to myself at last! No—not even then! Not to myself!

She begins to cry hysterically.

Oh, Alfred, Alfred! I can't let you go!

ALLMERS *frees himself gently*. Rita, my dear. Be reasonable.

RITA. No, I don't want to be reasonable. I only want you. Nothing else, in all the world.

Throws herself again round his neck.

I want you, you, you!

ALLMERS. Let me go! You're strangling me!

RITA *releases him*. I wish I could!

She looks at him with flashing eyes.

Oh, if only you knew how I have hated you—

ALLMERS. Hated me?

RITA. Yes. When you sat alone in there, brooding over your work. Deep into the night.

Complainingly.

So long, and so late, Alfred. Oh, how I've hated that work of yours!

ALLMERS. But now I am finished with it.

RITA *laughs jarringly.* And now you are preoccupied with something even more hateful.

ALLMERS. Hateful? You call our child hateful?

RITA, *violently.* I do! For what he has done to us! Your book had no face, no voice, but this child is a living wall between us.

Her voice rises.

I won't stand for it, Alfred! I won't stand for it, I tell you!

ALLMERS *looks steadily at her, then says quietly.* Sometimes you almost frighten me, Rita.

RITA. I often frighten myself. Don't rouse the demon in me, Alfred.

ALLMERS. In heaven's name—do I do that?

RITA. Yes! When you tear the holy bond that joins us.

ALLMERS. Rita, be reasonable. It's your child—our only child— we're talking about.

RITA. The child is only half mine.

Bursts out.

But you—you shall be mine—all mine—only mine! I demand it. It's my right.

ALLMERS *shrugs his shoulders.* My dear Rita, it's no use demanding. These things can only be given freely.

RITA. And from now on you are unable to do that?

ALLMERS. Yes. I must divide myself between Eyolf and you.

RITA. But if Eyolf had never been born?

ALLMERS, *defensively.* That would have been different. Then I would have had only you to love.

RITA, *quietly, trembling*. Then I wish to God I had never borne him!

ALLMERS. Rita! You don't know what you're saying!

RITA. I gave birth to him in unimaginable pain. But I endured it gladly—for your sake.

ALLMERS, *warmly*. Yes, yes. I know you did.

RITA. But that's over and done with. I want to *live*. With you. Just you and I. I can't be just a mother. Eyolf's mother and nothing else. I will not, I tell you—I cannot. I want to be everything to you. To you, Alfred.

ALLMERS. But you are, Rita. Through the child—

RITA. Oh! Sickening stale phrases! No, that's not for me. I was made to bear your child; but not to act the mother to it. You must take me as I am, Alfred.

ALLMERS. But you were always so fond of Eyolf.

RITA. I pitied him. Because you gave him no love or kindness; made him read until his eyes ached; hardly spent an hour with him.

ALLMERS *nods slowly*. I was blind. I had not yet come to realise—

RITA. But now you have?

ALLMERS. Yes; at last. Now I see that the highest duty open to me in this world is to be a true father to Eyolf.

RITA. And to me? What are you going to be to me?

ALLMERS, *gently*. I shall go on loving you, Rita. With all my soul.

He tries to take her hands.

RITA *avoids him*. I'm not interested in your soul! I want you —all of you—to myself—the way it used to be in those first, few, unforgettable years—

Viciously.

I will never let myself be fobbed off with the scraps of love.

ALLMERS, *gently*. Surely there is enough happiness to share between the three of us?

RITA, *contemptuously*. Then you can't want much.

Sits at the table, left.

Listen.

ALLMERS *comes closer.* Well? What is it?

RITA *looks up at him with a dull glow in her eyes.* When I got your telegram last night—

ALLMERS. Yes?

RITA. I dressed in white—

ALLMERS. Yes. I noticed you were wearing white when I arrived.

RITA. I let down my hair—

ALLMERS. It smells so sweetly—

RITA. So that it streamed down over my back and shoulders—

ALLMERS. I know. I know. Oh, you were beautiful, Rita.

RITA. I put rose-coloured shades over both lamps. We were alone—just you and I awake in the whole house. And there was champagne on the table.

ALLMERS. I didn't have any.

RITA, *bitterly.* True; you didn't. "The champagne stood there, but who raised his glass?" As the poet said.

She gets up from the armchair, goes as though tired to the sofa and half sits, half lies on it.

ALLMERS *goes across and stands in front of her.* I was full of serious thoughts. I was determined to speak to you about our future. And, above all, about Eyolf.

RITA *smiles.* And so you did, my dear.

ALLMERS. No. I wasn't able to. You started to undress yourself.

RITA. Yes. And while I undressed myself, you talked about Eyolf. Remember? You asked me how little Eyolf's stomach was.

ALLMERS. Rita!

RITA. And then you lay down in your bed. And slept like a child.

ALLMERS *shakes his head.* Rita.

RITA *lies down full length and looks up at him.* Alfred?

ALLMERS. Yes?

RITA. "The champagne stood there, but who raised his glass?"

ALLMERS, *in a hard voice.* I left it—untouched.

He turns from her and goes to the french windows. RITA *lies for some seconds motionless, her eyes closed.*

RITA *suddenly leaps to her feet.* But let me tell you something, Alfred.

ALLMERS *turns at the window.* What?

RITA. Don't be too sure of yourself.

ALLMERS. Sure of myself?

RITA. You take things too much for granted. You're too sure that you have me.

ALLMERS *comes closer.* What do you mean?

RITA, *with trembling lips.* I have never been unfaithful to you, Alfred—even in my thoughts—not for a moment—

ALLMERS. I know, Rita. I know you so well—

RITA, *with flashing eyes.* But if you should spurn me—

ALLMERS. Spurn you? I don't understand what you mean—

RITA. You don't know what I might do if—

ALLMERS. If?

RITA. If I should ever believe that you no longer cared for me— loved me as you used to do—

ALLMERS. But, my dearest Rita—people change with the years —and it must happen to us also—it does to everyone.

RITA. Not to me. And I won't have any change in you either. I couldn't stand it. I want to keep you all to myself.

ALLMERS *looks troubled at her.* Your jealousy is terrible—

RITA. I can't change. I am what I am.

Threateningly.

If you divide yourself between me and anyone else—

ALLMERS. Well?

RITA. I would have my revenge on you, Alfred.

ALLMERS. How could you have your revenge?

RITA. I don't know. Yes. I do know.

ALLMERS. How?

RITA. I would throw myself into the arms of the first man who comes along.

ALMERS *looks warmly at her, and shakes his head.* That you could never do—my proud, faithful, honest Rita!

RITA *puts her arms round his neck.* Oh, you don't know what I could do, if you stopped loving me.

ALLMERS. Stopped loving you? How can you say such a thing?

RITA, *half laughing, lets him go.* I could, for example, spread my nets for that builder of roads who is walking in our garden.

ALLMERS, *relieved.* Thank heavens! For a moment I thought you were being serious.

RITA. So I am. Why not him? As well as the next man?

ALLMERS. But—! In any case, he's already—

RITA. So much the better! If I took him from someone else. That's exactly what Eyolf has done to me.

ALLMERS. How can you say that Eyolf has done that?

RITA *points her finger at him.* You see! You see! As soon as you even mention Eyolf's name, your voice becomes soft and trembles.

Threateningly, clasping her hands together.

Oh, I am almost tempted to wish that—oh, well—!

ALLMERS *looks at her, frightened.* What would you wish, Rita?

RITA, *violently, moves away from him.* No, no, no! I won't tell you. Ever.

ALLMERS *goes closer to her.* Rita, I beg of you, for both our sakes—do not let yourself be tempted to anything evil.

BORGHEJM *and* ASTA *come up from the garden. Both are disturbed, but controlled. They look serious and downcast.* ASTA *remains on the verandah.* BORGHEJM *comes into the room.*

BORGHEJM. Well, Miss Allmers and I have taken our last walk together.

RITA *looks at him in surprise.* You won't be—taking a longer journey?

BORGHEJM. I shall, yes.

RITA. Alone?

BORGHEJM. Yes, alone.

RITA *glances at* ALLMERS. You hear that, Alfred?

Turns to BORGHEJM.

I wouldn't mind betting some evil eye has played you a trick here.

BORGHEJM *stares, amazed.* Evil eye?

RITA *nods.* Yes.

BORGHEJM. Do you believe in the evil eye, Mrs. Allmers?

RITA. I am beginning to. Or anyway in the evil that lies in a child's eye.

ALLMERS, *shocked, whispers.* How can you—?

RITA, *half aloud.* It is you who are making me like this, Alfred.

Confused shouts and screams are heard in the distance, down by the water.

BORGHEJM *goes to the french windows.* What is that noise?

ASTA, *on the verandah.* Look at all those people running out on the jetty.

ALLMERS. What is it?

Glances out.

Those guttersnipes up to something again, I suppose.

BORGHEJM *shouts down from the verandah.* Hi, you boys! What's going on down there?

Several voices are heard simultaneously, making indistinct reply.

RITA. What are they saying?

BORGHEJM. They say a child has been drowned.

ALLMERS. A child drowned?

ASTA, *uneasily.* A little boy, they say.

ALLMERS. But they can all swim.

RITA *cries suddenly in fear.* Where is Eyolf?

ALLMERS. Don't worry. Eyolf's playing in the garden.

ASTA. No. He wasn't when we were there.

RITA *clasps her hands to her head.* Don't let it be him!

BORGHEJM *listens and shouts down.* Whose child is it, did you say?

Indistinct voices are heard. BORGHEJM *and* ASTA *utter a suppressed cry and run down through the garden.*

ALLMERS, *in anguish.* It isn't Eyolf. It isn't Eyolf, Rita.

RITA, *on the verandah, listening.* Hush! Be quiet! Let me hear what they are saying.

She listens for a moment, then gives a dreadful scream and turns back into the room.

ALLMERS. What did they say?

RITA *sinks down into the armchair.* They said: "The crutch is floating."

ALLMERS, *stunned.* No! No!

RITA. Eyolf! Eyolf! Oh, God! They must save him!

ALLMERS, *distraught.* They must, they must! So precious a life! So precious a life!

He runs down through the garden.

ACT TWO

A small, narrow glen in the forest on ALLMERS' *estate, down by the shore. On the left, old, tall trees lean over the scene. Down the slope in the background a stream gushes, losing itself among the stones on the edge of the wood. A path winds alongside the stream. To the right stand a few trees, through which the fjord can be seen. In the foreground can be seen the corner of the boathouse, with a boat drawn up. Beneath the old trees on the left stands a table, with a bench and a few chairs, all made of slender birchwood. It is a heavy day, pregnant with rain, and with low, drifting clouds.*

ALFRED ALLMERS, *dressed as before, is seated on the bench, with his arms resting on the table. His hat lies in front of him. He is motionless, staring abstractedly out over the water. After a few moments,* ASTA ALLMERS *comes down the path. She is carrying an open umbrella.*

ASTA *comes quietly up to him.* You ought not to sit here in this grey weather, Alfred.

ALLMERS *nods slowly.*

ASTA *shuts her umbrella.*

I've been looking for you for such a long time.

ALLMERS, *expressionlessly.* Thank you.

ASTA *moves a chair and sits next to him.* Have you been sitting here long? The whole time?

ALLMERS *does not at first reply. Then he says.* No. I don't understand it. It seems so—impossible. All this.

ASTA *puts her hand on his arm.* Poor Alfred.

ALLMERS *stares at her.* Has it really happened, Asta? Or have I gone mad? Or am I dreaming? Oh, if only it were a dream! How beautiful if I could wake up now!

ASTA. I wish I had the power to wake you.

ALLMERS *stares out over the water.* How merciless the fjord looks today. Lying there so heavy . . . drowsy. Lead-grey, with flashes of yellow . . . reflecting the rain clouds.

ASTA. Alfred, you mustn't sit here staring at the fjord.

ALLMERS, *not listening.* On the surface, yes. But deep down, there is the undertow.

ASTA, *frightened.* For God's sake, don't think of that!

ALLMERS *looks mildly at her.* You think he lies out here, don't you, Asta? But he doesn't. You needn't fear that. Remember how strong the current is here. Out to the open sea.

ASTA *throws herself sobbing over the table, her hands covering her face.* Oh God! God!

ALLMERS. That is why little Eyolf has been taken so far—far away from us now.

ASTA. Don't talk like that, Alfred.

ALLMERS. You can work it out, you're so clever with figures. Twenty-eight hours, twenty-nine—let me see, let me see.

ASTA *screams and puts her hands over her ears.* Alfred!

ALLMERS *presses his fist hard against the table.* But can you see the meaning of it?

ASTA. Of what?

ALLMERS. Of what has been done to me and Rita.

ASTA. The meaning of it?

ALLMERS, *impatiently.* Yes, the meaning. There must be some meaning in it. Life, creation, Providence—have they no meaning, no purpose at all?

ASTA. Oh, Alfred, how can we tell the purpose of these things?

ALLMERS *laughs bitterly.* No, no, indeed. Perhaps it's all haphazard. Things take their own course, like a wrecked ship drifting. Perhaps that's how it is. It seems so, anyway.

ASTA, *quietly.* What if it only seems?

ALLMERS, *sharply.* Oh? Perhaps you can give me a better answer? For my part, I see none.

More gently.

Here is Eyolf, on the threshold of discovering life. Potent with promise—such rich promise. He was to fill my life with pride and joy. And then it only needs a crazy old hag to come to the house and dangle a dog in a sack—

ASTA. But, Alfred, we don't know for certain *how* it happened.

ALLMERS. Oh, yes. We know. The boys saw her row out over the fjord. They saw Eyolf standing alone on the end of the jetty, staring after her. Suddenly he—seemed to become giddy. And then he fell—and disappeared.

ASTA. I know. But—

ALLMERS. She dragged him down into the deep. I'm sure of it.

ASTA. But, my dear—why should she?

ALLMERS. Exactly. Why should she? It can't be retribution; there's nothing to atone for. Eyolf never did her any harm. Never shouted abuse at her, never threw a stone at her dog. He had never set eyes on her or the dog before yesterday. So it can't be retribution. How senseless it is; how absolutely meaningless, Asta. And yet it seems to serve the purposes of Providence.

ASTA. Have you talked about this with Rita?

ALLMERS *shakes his head.* I seem to find it easier to talk to you about it. As about everything else.

ASTA *takes her sewing things and a small package wrapped in paper from her pocket.* ALLMERS *sits watching her abstractedly.*

ALLMERS. What's that you have there, Asta?

ASTA, *taking his hat.* Only some crepe.

ALLMERS. Is it necessary?

ASTA. Rita asked me to do it. May I?

ALLMERS. I see. By all means.

She begins to sew the crepe on to his hat.

ALLMERS. Where is Rita?

ASTA. Walking in the garden, I believe. Borghejm is with her.

ALLMERS, *mildly surprised.* Oh? Is Borghejm out here today?

ASTA. Yes. He came by the noon train.

ALLMERS. Oh, I didn't expect him to take the trouble.

ASTA, *as she sews.* He was very fond of Eyolf.

ALLMERS. Borghejm is good and loyal.

ASTA, *warmly.* Yes. You are right. He is loyal.

ALLMERS *looks at her.* You are fond of him, aren't you?

ASTA. Yes. I am fond of him.

ALLMERS. But you can't—make up your mind to—?

ASTA *cuts him short.* Oh, Alfred, don't let's talk about it.

ALLMERS. Very well. Only—tell me why—

ASTA. Oh, no, please don't ask me, Alfred. It's too distressing for me to talk about. Here, your hat's ready.

ALLMERS. Thank you.

ASTA. Now give me your left arm.

ALLMERS. Are you going to put crepe on that, too?

ASTA. It's usual.

ALLMERS. As you wish.

She moves her chair closer to him and begins to sew crepe on to his left sleeve.

ASTA. Keep your arm still. Otherwise I shall prick you.

ALLMERS, *with a little smile.* This is like old times.

ASTA. Yes, isn't it?

ALLMERS. You used to sit like this mending my clothes when you were a little girl.

ASTA. I wasn't very good at it.

ALLMERS. I remember, the first thing you ever sewed for me was a piece of black crepe.

ASTA. Oh?

ALLMERS. On my student cap. When Father died.

ASTA. Did I really? I don't remember.

ALLMERS. Of course not. You were only a child then.

ASTA. Yes, I was only a child.

ALLMERS. Then, two years later—when your mother died—you sewed a big black band on my arm.

ASTA. I thought you ought to have one.

ALLMERS *pats her hand.* Yes, yes, quite right. And afterwards, when we two were left alone in the world—have you finished already?

ASTA. Yes.

She gathers her sewing things together.

It turned out to be a happy time for us after all, Alfred. Just the two of us.

ALLMERS. Yes, it did. It was a hard struggle, though.

ASTA. It was for you.

ALLMERS, *livelier.* It was a struggle for you too, Asta.

Smiles.

Dear, faithful—Eyolf.

ASTA. Oh, don't remind me of that silly nonsense about the name.

ALLMERS. If you had been a boy, you would have been called Eyolf.

ASTA. If—yes. But then when you went to university—

She smiles involuntarily.

To think you could have been so childish.

ALLMERS. *I* was childish?

ASTA. Yes, now I look back on it. You were ashamed of not having any brother, only a sister.

ALLMERS. No, it was you who were ashamed.

ASTA. A little, perhaps. I felt—I don't know—somehow sorry for you.

ALLMERS. Yes, you must have done. You got out the old clothes I'd worn as a boy—

ASTA. Your best Sunday clothes. Do you remember that blue blouse? And the knee breeches?

ALLMERS, *his eyes linger on her.* How well I remember how you looked! When you put them on and walked round in them.

ASTA. I only did it when we were alone at home together.

ALLMERS. How solemn we were, and how seriously we took ourselves! And I would always call you Eyolf.

ASTA. Alfred, you haven't said anything about this to Rita, have you?

ALLMERS. I believe I mentioned it to her once, yes.

ASTA. Oh, Alfred! How could you?

ALLMERS. You know how it is. One tells one's wife everything —practically everything.

ASTA. I suppose one does.

ALLMERS, *as though suddenly waking, clasps his forehead and leaps to his feet.* Good God! How can I sit here and—!

ASTA *rises, concerned.* What is it?

ALLMERS. I almost forgot him. I forgot him—completely.

ASTA. Eyolf?

ALLMERS. I was sitting here, absorbed in my memories. And he wasn't there.

ASTA. No, Alfred, you're wrong! Little Eyolf was there, in everything we said.

ALLMERS. He was not. He slipped right out of my mind. Out of my thoughts. I didn't see him for a moment while we were talking. All that while I forgot him completely.

ASTA. You must have some rest from your grief.

ALLMERS. No, no. That is just what I mustn't have. I have no right to it; and no heart for it, either.

Walks across right.

There is no place for me but the place where he lies, drifting down there in the dark.

ASTA *goes after him and holds him back.* Alfred! Alfred! Don't go near the fjord.

ALLMERS. I must go to him. Let me go, Asta. Let me get to the boat.

ASTA, *in terror.* No, Alfred, no! Don't go near the fjord!

ALLMERS, *yielding.* No, no; I won't. Just leave me alone.

ASTA *leads him back to the table.* You must let your mind rest, Alfred. Come and sit down with me again.

ALLMERS *is about to sit on the bench.* Very well. As you wish, Asta.

ASTA. No, not there.

ALLMERS. Yes, let me sit here.

ASTA. No. When you sit there, you look over the—
Presses him down on to a chair, facing left.
Like that, now. That's better, isn't it?
Sits on the bench.
Now. Let's go on with what we were talking about before.

ALLMERS, *breathing audibly.* It was good to forget these sorrows for a moment.

ASTA. You must forget, Alfred.

ALLMERS. But don't you think me weak and unfeeling to be able to do so?

ASTA. Oh, no! One cannot circle round the same thought for ever.

ALLMERS. I can't, anyway. Before you came down to me just now, I was sitting here tormented by this haunting, gnawing grief—

ASTA. Yes?

ALLMERS. And then—can you believe it, Asta?—hm—

ASTA. What?

ALLMERS. In my agony, I suddenly found myself wondering what there was going to be for dinner today.

ASTA, *soothingly.* As long as it gave you comfort—

ALLMERS. Comfort? Yes, that is what I seemed to find.

Reaches out his hand to her across the table.

What a blessing I have in you, Asta. It gives me such joy. Joy—in my sorrow—

ASTA *looks seriously at him.* Your greatest source of happiness should be Rita.

ALLMERS. Of course. But Rita is not of my blood. It is not the same as having a sister.

ASTA, *tensely.* Is that how you feel, Alfred?

ALLMERS. Yes. Our family is—something apart.

Jokingly.

Our Christian names always begin with a vowel. Do you remember how we used to talk about it? And all our relations are equally poor. And our eyes are all the same colour.

ASTA. But—I—

ALLMERS. Ah, Asta, you are your mother's child. You don't really look like one of us. Not even like Father. And yet—

ASTA. Yes—?

ALLMERS. I was thinking that our life together has somehow made you and me resemble each other—in our outlook and temper, I mean.

ASTA, *moved.* No, Alfred. It's I who've grown to resemble you. I owe everything to you—everything I value in the world.

ALLMERS *shakes his head.* You owe me nothing, Asta. On the contrary—

ASTA. Yes, Alfred. I owe you everything. You should know that. No sacrifice has been too great—

ALLMERS. Sacrifice! What nonsense you talk, Asta. I have simply—loved you. Ever since you were a small child.

Short pause.

Besides, I always felt there was so much I had to make amends for. Not so much for what I'd done, as for Father.

ASTA. Father—! What do you mean?

ALLMERS. Father was never very kind to you.

ASTA. You mustn't say that.

ALLMERS. It's true. He never loved you. As he should have done.

ASTA, *defensively*. Perhaps not as much as he loved you. But that was only to be expected.

ALLMERS. He was often unkind to your mother, too. During their last years together.

ASTA, *quietly*. You must remember Mother was so very much younger than he.

ALLMERS. Do you think they weren't suited to each other?

ASTA. I think perhaps not.

ALLMERS. And yet Father was always so kind and generous to everyone else—

ASTA, *quietly*. Mother wasn't always as she should have been.

ALLMERS. Your mother?

ASTA. Perhaps not always.

ALLMERS. To Father?

ASTA. Yes.

ALLMERS. I never noticed anything.

ASTA *rises, trying not to cry*. Oh, Alfred. Let the dead rest in peace.

She crosses right.

ALLMERS *rises*. Yes, let them rest.

Clasps his hands.

But the dead will not give us peace. Day and night they haunt us.

ASTA. It will seem less painful as time goes by.

ALLMERS. It must—mustn't it? But how I shall survive these first, ghastly days, I cannot imagine.

ASTA *puts her hands on his shoulders*. Go up to Rita. I beg you.

ALLMERS *frees himself*. No, no! Don't ask me to do that! I can't, don't you understand! I can't!

More calmly.

Let me stay here with you.

ASTA. All right. I won't leave you.

ALLMERS *takes her hand and holds it tightly.* Thank you.

Glances out for a moment across the fjord.

Where is my little Eyolf now?

Smiles bitterly.

Can you answer me that, my big, wise Eyolf?

Shakes his head.

No. No one in the whole world can tell me that. I know only the one dreadful certainty, that I no longer have him.

ASTA *glances up left, and withdraws her hand.* They are coming now.

RITA *comes down the path, with* BORGHEJM *following her. She is wearing dark clothes, with a veil over her face. He carries an umbrella.*

ALLMERS *goes to meet her.* How are you, Rita?

RITA *walks past him.* Need you ask?

ALLMERS. Why have you come down here?

RITA. Only to look for you. What are you doing?

ALLMERS. Nothing in particular. Asta came down to sit with me.

RITA. Yes, but what were you doing before Asta came? You've been away from me the whole morning.

ALLMERS. I've been sitting here, looking out over the water.

RITA *shudders.* How can you!

ALLMERS, *impatiently.* I prefer to be alone now.

RITA, *walking about relentlessly.* Sitting in the same spot like a statue.

ALLMERS. I have no reason to go anywhere.

RITA. I can't stand it anywhere. Least of all here. With the fjord practically lapping one's feet.

ALLMERS. That's why I sit here. Because it is so near the fjord.

RITA, *to* BORGHEJM. Don't you think he should come up with the rest of us?

BORGHEJM, *to* ALLMERS. I think it would be better for you.

ALLMERS. No. Let me stay where I am.

RITA. In that case I shall stay with you.

ALLMERS. As you please. You stay too, Asta.

ASTA *whispers to* BORGHEJM. Let's leave them alone together.

BORGHEJM *nods.* Miss Allmers, shall we take a stroll along the shore? For the very last time.

ASTA *takes her umbrella.* Yes, let's.

ASTA *and* BORGHEJM *go out together behind the boathouse.* ALLMERS *walks around for a little, then sits down on a stone under the trees downstage left.*

RITA *comes closer and stands in front of him with her hands folded.* Alfred, is it possible that we have lost Eyolf?

ALLMERS. We must accustom ourselves to the thought.

RITA. I can't. I can't. That dreadful sight—I shall never forget it as long as I live.

ALLMERS *looks up.* What sight? What have you seen?

RITA. I didn't see it myself. Only heard about it. Oh!

ALLMERS. You might as well tell me.

RITA. I went with Borghejm down to the jetty—

ALLMERS. Why did you go there?

RITA. I wanted to question the boys about how it had happened.

ALLMERS. We know.

RITA. We know more now.

ALLMERS. What?

RITA. It isn't true that he disappeared at once.

ALLMERS. They say that now?

RITA. Yes. They say they saw him lying on the bottom. Deep down in the clear water.

ALLMERS, *bitterly.* And they didn't save him?

RITA. I don't suppose there was anything they could do.

ALLMERS. They can swim. All of them.

RITA. They say he lay on his back. With his eyes wide open.

ALLMERS. With his eyes open? And quite still?

RITA. Yes, quite still. Then something came and carried him out towards the sea. They call it the undertow.

ALLMERS *nods slowly*. And that was the last they saw of him?

RITA. Yes.

ALLMERS. And no one will ever see him again.

RITA. Day and night I shall see him lying there.

ALLMERS. With his eyes wide open.

RITA. Yes. With those large, open eyes. I can see them now.

ALLMERS *rises slowly and looks quietly but menacingly at her*. Were they evil eyes, Rita?

RITA *turns pale*. Evil?

ALLMERS *goes close to her*. Were they evil eyes staring up from the sea bed?

RITA *shrinks from him*. Alfred!

ALLMERS *follows her*. Answer me! Were the child's eyes evil?

RITA *screams*. Alfred! Alfred!

ALLMERS. Now it is as you wished, Rita.

RITA. I? What did I wish?

ALLMERS. That Eyolf should be out of the way.

RITA. Never for one moment did I wish that! I wished that he might not stand between us—yes—but—

ALLMERS. Well, he won't now, will he?

RITA, *quietly, to herself*. Perhaps now more than ever.

Shudders.

Oh, that dreadful sight!

ALLMERS *nods*. Yes. The evil eye of a child.

RITA *shrinks away from him fearfully*. Alfred! Leave me alone. You frighten me. I've never seen you like this before.

ALLMERS, *hard and cold*. Grief makes one cruel.

RITA, *frightened but still defiant*. Yes. It has made me so too

ALLMERS *goes right, and looks out over the fjord.* RITA *sits at the table. Short pause.*

ALLMERS *turns his head towards her.* You never loved him. Not really.

RITA, *cold and controlled.* Eyolf would never allow me to make him wholly mine.

ALLMERS. Because you never really wanted him.

RITA. You are wrong. I did want him. But someone stood between us. From the first.

ALLMERS *turns so that he stands facing her.* You mean I stood between you?

RITA. Oh, no. Not in the beginning.

ALLMERS *goes closer.* Who, then?

RITA. His aunt.

ALLMERS. Asta?

RITA. Yes. Asta stood like a wall between Eyolf and me.

ALLMERS. You feel that?

RITA. Yes. Asta made him hers—right from the time it happened. The accident—

ALLMERS. If she did, she did it out of love.

RITA, *violently.* Exactly. And I am not prepared to share with anyone. Not in love.

ALLMERS. You and I ought to have shared him. In love.

RITA *looks scornfully at him.* We? If it comes to that, you never really loved him either, Alfred.

ALLMERS. *I* never loved him?

RITA. No. You were only in love with your book. About—responsibility.

ALLMERS, *firmly.* I was—preoccupied with that, it is true. But I gave it up. For Eyolf's sake.

RITA. But not because you loved him.

ALLMERS. What do you mean?

RITA. You gave it up because you were eaten up with self-distrust. You had begun to doubt whether you had any great calling to live for after all.

ALLMERS, *searchingly*. Did I give you any cause to think that?

RITA. Oh, yes—in small things. And when you needed something new to occupy yourself with. I dare say I wasn't enough for you any longer.

ALLMERS. It is the law of change, Rita.

RITA. That was why you wanted to make poor little Eyolf into a child prodigy.

ALLMERS. That's not true. I wanted to make him—happy. That is all.

RITA. But not because you loved him. Look into yourself.

With a certain shyness.

And think of all that you have buried there, and would like to forget.

ALLMERS *avoids her eyes*. You're trying to avoid the issue.

RITA. So are you.

ALLMERS *looks thoughtfully at her*. If you are right in what you are thinking, our child never really belonged to us.

RITA. No. We never loved him.

ALLMERS. And yet we sit here bitterly mourning his loss.

RITA, *bitterly*. Yes. Isn't it odd? That we are sitting here mourning a little stranger boy.

ALLMERS. Rita, for God's sake. Don't call him a stranger.

RITA *shakes her head*. We never won his love, Alfred. Neither you, nor I.

ALLMERS. And now it's too late. Too late.

With sudden violence.

It's you who are guilty!

RITA *rises*. I?

ALLMERS. Yes! It's your fault that he became what he was! It's your fault he couldn't save himself when he fell into the water!

RITA, *defensively*. Alfred! Don't blame me for that!

ALLMERS. I do, I do! You know it's true! It was you who left that helpless baby unattended on the table—

RITA. He lay there so comfortably among the cushions. And slept so sweetly. And you had promised to keep an eye on him.

ALLMERS. That's right.

Lowers his voice.

And then you came—and tempted me in to you.

RITA, *defiantly.* Be a man and admit that you forgot the child and everything else!

ALLMERS, *with suppressed fury.* By God, you are right!

More quietly.

I forgot the child. In your arms.

RITA. Alfred—that's vile!

ALLMERS, *quietly.* In that moment, you condemned little Eyolf to death.

RITA. You too! You too! If I am guilty, so are you!

ALLMERS. Oh, very well, if you wish. We are both guilty. So there was retribution in Eyolf's death after all.

RITA. Retribution?

ALLMERS, *more controlled.* Yes. A judgment on you and me. Now we have what we deserve. While he lived, our cowardly, furtive consciences would not let us love him because we could not bear to look at the—thing he carried.

RITA, *quietly.* The crutch.

ALLMERS. Yes. That. And what we call our loss, our grief, is merely the gnawing of our consciences. Nothing more.

RITA, *helplessly.* Alfred—this can only lead us into despair— perhaps beyond—into madness. We can never undo what has been done.

ALLMERS, *in a quieter mood.* I dreamed of Eyolf last night. I thought I saw him coming up from the jetty. He could run like other boys. Nothing had happened to him. Nothing at all. This stifling existence was only a dream, I thought. Oh, Rita, how I praised and thanked—

Stops himself.

RITA. Whom?

ALLMERS, *evasively.* Whom?

RITA. Whom did you praise and thank?

ALLMERS. I told you, I was dreaming—

RITA. The One in Whom you do not believe?

ALLMERS. It just happened like that. I was asleep, I tell you.

RITA. You should not have sowed the seeds of doubt in me, Alfred.

ALLMERS. Would I have done better to let you continue through life believing in empty illusions?

RITA. It would have been better for me. I should at least have been able to turn somewhere for comfort. Now I have nowhere.

ALLMERS *looks at her closely.* If you were given the choice now—if you could follow Eyolf to—to where he now is—

RITA. Yes?

ALLMERS. If you could be sure you would find him again. Know him—understand him—

RITA. Yes, yes?

ALLMERS. Would you leap the gulf to join him? Leave all this? Renounce life? Would you do that, Rita?

RITA, *quietly.* You mean—now?

ALLMERS. Yes. Today. Now. Answer me. Would you?

RITA, *hesitantly.* Oh, I don't know, Alfred. I think I would choose to stay here with you for a while.

ALLMERS. For my sake?

RITA. Yes. Only for your sake.

ALLMERS. But afterwards? Would you? Answer me.

RITA. Oh, what can I say? You know I could never leave you. Never.

ALLMERS. But suppose I were to go to join Eyolf—and suppose you knew for sure that you would meet both him and me there? Then would you come to join us?

RITA. I should like to. With all my heart. But—

ALLMERS. But—?

RITA. I don't think I could. No, no—I simply couldn't. No, not even for the promise of heaven.

ALLMERS. Neither could I.

RITA. No, Alfred. You couldn't do it either, could you?

ALLMERS. No. This is where we belong. Here on earth. Living.

RITA. Yes. Here is the kind of happiness we understand.

ALLMERS. Oh, happiness—happiness—

RITA. You mean we shall never find happiness again? But suppose—? No. I daren't say it.

ALLMERS. Say it, Rita. Say it.

RITA, *hesitantly.* Couldn't we try to—? If only we could forget.

ALLMERS. Forget Eyolf?

RITA. No. Forget ourselves. Our guilt.

ALLMERS. Is that what you want?

RITA. Yes. If it's possible.

In a sudden outburst.

I can't bear this much longer, Alfred. Can't we find something to make us forget?

ALLMERS. What?

RITA. We could travel. Go far away.

ALLMERS. Go away? You are never happy anywhere but here.

RITA. Well, we could invite people here. Keep open house. Throw ourselves into some activity which would deaden—

ALLMERS. That kind of life is not for me. No, rather than that I would try to take up my work again.

RITA, *acidly.* Your book? Which has stood for so many years like a wall between us?

ALLMERS, *slowly, looking coldly at her.* There will always be a wall between you and me from now on.

RITA. Why?

ALLMERS. Who knows whether large child-eyes do not watch us night and day?

RITA, *softly, shuddering.* Alfred!

ALLMERS. Our love has been a consuming fire. Now it has burned itself out.

RITA. Burned out!

ALLMERS, *in a hard voice.* It is already burned out in one of us.

RITA, *as though turned to stone.* And you dare say that to me!

ALLMERS, *more gently.* It is dead, Rita. But something has taken its place—a sharing of guilt and remorse—a sharing in which there is perhaps a new beginning—a resurrection—

RITA, *violently.* Resurrection! What do I care about resurrection!

ALLMERS. Rita!

RITA. I am flesh and blood! I cannot drowse my life away like a fish! To be walled up for the rest of my life in a cell of guilt and remorse! With a man who is no longer mine, mine, mine!

ALLMERS. It had to end some time, Rita.

RITA. Had it to end like this? A love that began as consumingly as ours did?

ALLMERS. My first feeling for you was not love, Rita.

RITA. What was it, then?

ALLMERS. Fear.

RITA. That I can understand. But if that was so, how did I manage to win you?

ALLMERS. You were so—so consumingly beautiful, Rita.

RITA. Was it only that? Answer me, Alfred. Was there nothing else?

ALLMERS, *reluctantly.* Yes. There was something else.

RITA. I can guess what it was. My gold and my green forests, I think you called them. Aren't I right, Alfred?

ALLMERS. Yes.

RITA. How could you? How could you do it?

ALLMERS. I had Asta to think of.

RITA. Oh, yes—Asta! So it was Asta who brought us together!

ALLMERS. She knew nothing. She has no inkling of it even now.

RITA. None the less, it was Asta.

Smiles scornfully.

No. It was little Eyolf. Yes, Alfred. Little Eyolf.

ALLMERS. Eyolf?

RITA. You used to call her Eyolf, didn't you? I seem to remember you telling me so once—in a quiet moment.

Comes closer.

Do you remember that moment, Alfred?

ALLMERS *shrinks from her.* I remember nothing! I don't want
to remember!

RITA, *following him.* It was that moment when your other little Eyolf became a cripple.

ALLMERS *supports himself against the table.* The retribution.

RITA. Yes. The retribution.

ASTA *and* BORGHEJM *come back past the boathouse. She has
some water lilies in her hand.*

RITA, *controlled.* Well, Asta. Have you and Mr. Borghejm said
everything you had to say to each other?

ASTA. Oh, yes—I think so.

She puts down her umbrella and lays the flowers on a chair.

BORGHEJM. Miss Allmers has been very quiet during our walk.

RITA. Really? Alfred and I have said enough to each other—

ASTA *looks tensely from one to the other.* Yes?

RITA. To last us for the rest of our lives. Come now, let's go
up to the house. Alfred and I need company from now on.
We can't be alone now.

ALLMERS. You two go ahead. Asta, I must have a word with
you alone.

RITA. Indeed? Well, come with me then, Mr. Borghejm.

RITA *and* BORGHEJM *go out.*

ASTA. Alfred, what's been happening?

ALLMERS. I can't stand it here any longer.

ASTA. Here? You mean with Rita?

ALLMERS. Yes. Rita and I cannot go on living together.

ASTA *shakes his arm.* Alfred, you mustn't say such dreadful things.

ALLMERS. It is true. Living together makes us both evil and detestable.

ASTA. I'd never realised—

ALLMERS. Nor had I. Until today.

ASTA. And now you want to—yes, what do you really want, Alfred?

ALLMERS. To get away from this place. Far away from it all.

ASTA. And live on your own?

ALLMERS *nods.* Yes. As I used to.

ASTA. But you can't live alone.

ALLMERS. I did once.

ASTA. You mean in the old days? But then you had me with you.

ALLMERS *tries to take her hand.* Yes, Asta. And now I want to come home to you again.

ASTA *avoids his hand.* To me? No, no, Alfred. That's quite impossible.

ALLMERS. Because of Borghejm.

ASTA, *emotionally.* No, you are wrong. It's not because of him.

ALLMERS. I am glad. Then I return to you, my dear, my dearest sister. I want to come home to you to be cleansed and purified from my life with—

ASTA. Alfred! It's a sin—

ALLMERS. No. I have sinned against her. But not in this. Remember, Asta! Do you remember how our life used to be? Was it not one long ecstasy of dedication?

ASTA. Yes, Alfred. But we can't relive the past.

ALLMERS, *bitterly.* You mean my marriage has unfitted me for that kind of life?

ASTA, *calmly*. No, I don't mean that.

ALLMERS. Then let us live again as we used to.

ASTA, *firmly*. We cannot do that, Alfred.

ALLMERS. We can. Love between brother and sister is the one relationship which does not obey the law of change.

ASTA, *quietly, trembling*. But if that should turn out not to— be our relationship?

ALLMERS, *amazed*. Not our—? What do you mean?

ASTA. My mother's letters—the ones in the portfolio—

ALLMERS. Well? What of them?

ASTA. Read them—when I have gone.

ALLMERS. Why?

ASTA, *with an effort*. Well, you'll find that—

ALLMERS. Yes?

ASTA. That I have no right to bear your father's name.

ALLMERS. Asta!

ASTA. Read the letters. Then you will see. And understand— and perhaps be able to forgive—my mother too.

ALLMERS. I don't understand this. I can't credit it. Asta! You mean you're not—?

ASTA. You are not my brother, Alfred.

ALLMERS, *quickly, defiantly, looking her in the eyes*. Well? What difference does that make? None at all.

ASTA *shakes her head*. It changes everything, Alfred. Our relationship is not that of brother and sister.

ALLMERS. But it is still sacred. It will always remain sacred.

ASTA. Now it must obey the law of change.

ALLMERS *looks searchingly at her*. You mean—?

ASTA, *quietly, warmly*. Please don't say anything more. My dearest—my dearest!

She takes the flowers from the table.

Do you see these water lilies?

ALLMERS *nods slowly.* They are the sort that shoot up to the surface from the depths.

ASTA. I gathered them from the lake. Where it flows out into the fjord.

Holds them out.

Would you like them, Alfred?

ALLMERS *takes them.* Thank you.

ASTA, *with tears in her eyes.* Take them as a last greeting from—from little Eyolf.

ALLMERS *looks at her.* From Eyolf out there? Or from you?

ASTA, *quietly.* From us both.

She takes her umbrella.

Come. Let us go up to Rita.

She goes up the path.

ALLMERS *takes his hat from the table and whispers.* Asta. Eyolf. Little Eyolf—!

He follows her up the path.

ACT THREE

A shrub-covered mound in ALLMERS' *garden. In the background, a sheer cliff, with a railing along its edge and steps on the left leading down. A broad view with the fjord lying deep below. Close by the railing stands a flagstaff, with a line but no flag. In the foreground on the right is a summerhouse, covered with creepers and wild vine. A bench stands outside it. It is late on a summer evening; the sky is clear. Dusk is falling.*

ASTA *is seated on the bench, her hands in her lap. She is wearing outdoor clothes and hat; her parasol is at her side, and she carries a small travelling bag slung from her shoulder on a strap.*

BORGHEJM *climbs up backstage left. He, too, carries a travelling bag slung from his shoulder, and a rolled-up flag over his arm.*

BORGHEJM *catches sight of* ASTA. Ah, here you are.

ASTA. I thought I would sit here and look out over the fjord for the last time.

BORGHEJM. How lucky for me I came here too.

ASTA. Have you been searching for me?

BORGHEJM. Yes. I wanted so much to get the chance to say au revoir. Not good-bye, I hope.

ASTA *smiles.* You are very persistent.

BORGHEJM. You have to be to be a road builder.

ASTA. Did you see anything of Alfred? Or Rita?

BORGHEJM. Yes, I saw them both.

ASTA. Together?

BORGHEJM. No. Apart.

ASTA. What are you going to do with that flag?

BORGHEJM. Mrs. Allmers asked me to come and hoist it.

ASTA. Hoist it—now?

BORGHEJM. To half-mast. Let it hang there night and day, she said.

ASTA *sighs*. Poor Rita. And poor Alfred.

BORGHEJM, *busying himself with the flag*. Have you really the heart to leave them? I ask because I see you are dressed for a journey.

ASTA, *in a low voice*. I have to go.

BORGHEJM. Of course, if you must—

ASTA. You are going tonight, too?

BORGHEJM. Yes. I, too, must go. I shall be catching the train. Will you be on it?

ASTA. No. I shall be taking the steamer.

BORGHEJM, *with a glance at her*. Ah. Not the same way, then?

ASTA. No.

She sits watching him while he hoists the flag to half-mast. When he has finished he goes over to her.

BORGHEJM. Miss Asta—you cannot imagine how deeply little Eyolf's death grieves me.

ASTA *looks up at him*. I know it does.

BORGHEJM. It hurts so much. You see, it's not in my nature to mourn.

ASTA *turns her eyes towards the flag*. Time will heal it. As it heals all things. All sorrows.

BORGHEJM. All? Do you believe that?

ASTA. They pass like summer showers. When you are far away from here, then—

BORGHEJM. It will have to be far.

ASTA. And you have your big new road to think about.

BORGHEJM. Yes. But no one to help me with it.

ASTA. Oh, you'll have many people to help you.

BORGHEJM *shakes his head.* No one to share the excitement and the joy of the work. And that's what one most wants to share.

ASTA. What about the sweat and the toil?

BORGHEJM. Ah—that one can endure alone.

ASTA. But the joy must be shared.

BORGHEJM. Yes. What is the use of finding happiness if one cannot share it with anyone?

ASTA. Perhaps you are right.

BORGHEJM. Of course one can enjoy happiness alone for a while. But not for long. No, happiness cannot really be enjoyed except by two people.

ASTA. Two? Why not three, or five, or ten?

BORGHEJM. Ah—that's a different sort of happiness. Miss Asta —couldn't you bring yourself to share the joys and triumphs of life—and the sweat and toil, too—with just one person?

ASTA. I have tried it—once.

BORGHEJM. Have you?

ASTA. Yes. All the years my brother—all the years Alfred and I lived together.

BORGHEJM. Oh, your brother? But that's quite different, surely. I would call that peace rather than happiness.

ASTA. Anyway, it was wonderful.

BORGHEJM. There, now! Even that seemed wonderful! But suppose now—just suppose he had not been your brother—

ASTA *almost rises, but controls herself.* Then we would never have lived together. I was a child at the time. And he was little more than a child.

BORGHEJM, *after a moment.* Were they so wonderful, those years?

ASTA. Yes. Oh, yes. They were.

BORGHEJM. You had moments of real happiness and ex-hilaration?

ASTA. Oh, yes. So many. So many.

BORGHEJM. Tell me about them, Miss Asta.

ASTA. Oh, they were only little things.

BORGHEJM. Such as?

ASTA. Such as the time Alfred passed his matriculation. He'd done so well. And by and by he got a post at a school. Or when he was working at his thesis. And read it to me. And then it got printed in a periodical.

BORGHEJM. Yes. I can imagine it must have been a lovely, peaceful life. A brother and sister, sharing each other's happiness.

Shakes his head.

I don't know how your brother ever brought himself to let you go.

ASTA. He got married, you know.

BORGHEJM. That must have been difficult for you.

ASTA. Yes. At first. I thought I'd lost him.

BORGHEJM. But luckily you hadn't.

ASTA. No.

BORGHEJM. All the same, how could he? Marry, I mean. When he could have gone on living with you.

ASTA, *to herself*. The law of change, I suppose.

BORGHEJM. The law of change?

ASTA. It's Alfred's phrase.

BORGHEJM. Pah! A stupid law. I don't believe in it.

ASTA *rises*. Not now, perhaps. You may come to believe in it in time.

BORGHEJM. I? Never!

Earnestly.

But listen to me, Miss Asta—be sensible for once—about all this, I mean—

ASTA *interrupts him*. Please, please don't let's discuss it any further.

BORGHEJM. Yes, Asta! I can't let you go as easily as that. Your

brother has chosen his own way of life. He is quite happy
without you. He does not even miss you. Then this—this
thing happened which altered everything for you—

ASTA *starts.* What do you mean?

BORGHEJM. The death of his child. What did you think I
meant?

ASTA *recovers her composure.* Little Eyolf. Yes.

BORGHEJM. Now there is nothing to keep you here any longer.
No little crippled child who needs your love. No duties,
nothing—

ASTA. Mr. Borghejm, please! Don't make it so hard for me.

BORGHEJM. I must. I would be mad if I did not. Any day now
I shall leave town. I may not have an opportunity to see you
there before I go. I may not see you again for years. Who
knows what may happen before we meet again?

ASTA *smiles.* So you are afraid of the law of change?

BORGHEJM. Oh, no I'm not!

Laughs bitterly.

In any case, what change have I to be afraid of? In you,
I mean. It's clear you don't really care for me.

ASTA. You know I do.

BORGHEJM. Not enough. Not the way I want you to.

More violently.

In God's name, Asta—Miss Asta—can't you see how wrong
you're being? Just over the horizon a whole lifetime of happiness may be lying in wait for us—and we are simply letting
it lie there. Don't you think we're going to regret it, Asta?

ASTA, *quietly.* I don't know. I only know that we have to let
it lie there waiting.

BORGHEJM. Then I must build my roads alone?

ASTA, *warmly.* Oh, if only I could share it with you—the work
and the joy—

BORGHEJM. Would you? If you could?

ASTA. Yes. I would.

BORGHEJM. But you can't?

ASTA *looks down.* Would you be content with only part of me?

BORGHEJM. No. I must have all of you.

ASTA *looks at him and says quietly.* Then I cannot.

BORGHEJM. Then good-bye, Miss Asta.

He turns to go. ALLMERS *climbs up from the back, left.* BORGHEJM *pauses.*

ALLMERS, *as he reaches the top of the steps, points and says quietly.* Is Rita down there in the summerhouse?

BORGHEJM. No, there's no one here but Miss Asta.

ALLMERS *comes forward.*

ASTA *goes towards him.* Shall I go down and look for her? And get her to come up here?

ALLMERS. No, no, no—don't bother.

To BORGHEJM.

Did you hoist the flag?

BORGHEJM. Yes. Your wife asked me to. That was why I came up here.

ALLMERS. And you're leaving us tonight?

BORGHEJM. Yes. Tonight I really am leaving you.

ALLMERS, *with a glance at* ASTA. You have found a good travelling companion, I trust?

BORGHEJM *shakes his head.* I am travelling alone.

ALLMERS, *startled.* Alone?

BORGHEJM. Quite alone.

ALLMERS, *abstractedly.* Oh, really?

BORGHEJM. And I shall stay alone.

ALLMERS. It is horrible to be alone. The thought of it chills my blood.

ASTA, *uneasily.* Don't talk like that.

ALLMERS. But if you are not going with—why not stay out here with me and Rita?

ASTA. No Alfred, I can't. I must get back to town now.

ALLMERS. But only to town, Asta. You hear?

ASTA. Yes.

ALLMERS. And promise me you'll come out here soon again.

ASTA, *quickly.* No, I can't promise that. Not for a while.

ALLMERS. As you wish. We'll meet in town, then.

ASTA. But Alfred, you must stay here with Rita now.

ALLMERS *turns to* BORGHEJM. I think you're probably lucky to be travelling alone.

BORGHEJM. What on earth do you mean?

ALLMERS. You never know whom you may meet. On the journey.

ASTA. Alfred!

ALLMERS. The right travelling companion. When it's too late.

ASTA, *quietly, trembling.* Alfred! Alfred!

BORGHEJM *looks from one to the other.* What do you mean? I don't understand—

RITA *climbs up from the back, left.*

RITA. Why are you all leaving me?

ASTA *goes to meet her.* You said you wanted to be alone—

RITA. I know. But I daren't. It's getting so dark. I seem to see great open eyes staring at me.

ASTA, *gently.* What if they are, Rita? You shouldn't be afraid of those eyes.

RITA. I don't know how you can say that.

ALLMERS, *urgently.* Asta, I beg you. Please. Stay here—with Rita.

RITA. Yes. And with Alfred, too. Please stay, Asta.

ASTA, *fighting with herself.* Oh! I would so gladly—

RITA. Well then, stay. Alfred and I cannot face our grief alone. Our bereavement.

ALLMERS. Why not say the gnawing of our consciences?

RITA. Whatever you call it—we two can't face it alone. Asta, I beg you with all my heart. Stay here and help us. Be to us what Eyolf was.

ASTA *shrinks.* Eyolf!

RITA. You'd like her to stay, wouldn't you, Alfred?

ALLMERS. If she can, and if she wants to.

RITA. You used to call her your little Eyolf, didn't you?

Takes ASTA's *hand.*

From now on you shall be *our* Eyolf, Asta. Eyolf, as you used to be.

ALLMERS, *controlling his emotions.* Stay—and share our life, Asta. With Rita. With me. Your—brother.

ASTA *withdraws her hand and says with decision.* No. I can't.

Turns to BORGHEJM.

When does the steamer leave?

BORGHEJM. Any minute now.

ASTA. Then I must go aboard. Are you coming with me?

BORGHEJM. Am I—? Yes, yes, yes!

ASTA. Come along, then.

RITA, *slowly.* Oh. I see. Well, in that case—

ASTA *throws her arms round* RITA's *neck.* Thank you, Rita. For everything.

Goes over to ALLMERS *and clasps his hand.*

Good-bye, Alfred. Good-bye.

ALLMERS, *quietly.* What is this, Asta? Are you running away?

ASTA. Yes, Alfred. I am.

ALLMERS. From me?

ASTA *whispers.* From you—and from myself.

ALLMERS *shrinks.* Ah—!

ASTA hurries out. BORGHEJM *waves his hat and follows her.* RITA *leans against the porch of the summerhouse.* ALLMERS *walks to the railing and stands there, looking down. Pause.*

ALLMERS, *with forced composure.* Here's the steamer, Rita. Come and look.

RITA. I dare not look at it.

ALLMERS. Dare not?

RITA. No. It has a red eye. And a green eye also. Great glaring eyes.

ALLMERS. You know they are only lanterns.

RITA. They will always be eyes to me. They stare and stare out of the darkness. And—into the darkness, too.

ALLMERS. Now she is coming alongside.

RITA. Where will they be mooring her this evening?

ALLMERS *comes near her.* At the jetty, as usual, my dear—

RITA *draws herself up.* How can they moor her there?

ALLMERS. You know they have to.

RITA. But it was there that Eyolf—! How can they do it?

ALLMERS. Life is pitiless, Rita.

RITA. People are pitiless. They don't consider anyone. Neither the living nor the dead.

ALLMERS. You're right. Life goes on, just as if nothing had happened.

RITA. Nothing has happened. To the rest of the world. Only to you and me.

ALLMERS, *his pain reawakening.* Rita—how meaningless it was, the pain of bearing him. For now he is gone—without a trace.

RITA. Only the crutch was saved.

ALLMERS. Be quiet! I never want to hear that word!

RITA. I can't bear the thought that he's gone from us.

ALLMERS, *coldly and bitterly.* You managed well enough without him while he was alive. Whole days would pass without your seeing him.

RITA. Only because I knew I could see him any time I wanted.

ALLMERS. Yes. That's how we wasted the few years we had with little Eyolf.

RITA *listens.* Listen, Alfred. It's tolling again.

ALLMERS *glances out over the fjord.* That's the steamer sounding its bell. It is ready to leave.

RITA. I don't mean that bell. All day this bell's been ringing in my ears. Ah! There it is again!

ALLMERS *goes to her.* You are mistaken, Rita.

RITA. No. I hear it so clearly. It sounds like a funeral bell. Slowly—slowly. Always the same words.

ALLMERS. Words? What words?

RITA *nods in time with the syllables.* "The-crutch-is-float-ing. The-crutch-is-float-ing." Surely you can hear it?

ALLMERS *shakes his head.* I hear nothing. There is nothing to hear.

RITA. Oh, you can say what you like. I hear it clearly.

ALLMERS *looks out over the railing.* Now they are aboard, Rita. Now the ship is steaming towards town.

RITA. Can you really not hear it? "The-crutch-is-float-ing. The-crutch—"

ALLMERS *comes towards her.* You mustn't stand here listening to something that isn't there. I tell you, Asta and Borghejm are aboard now, and on their way. Asta has gone.

RITA *glances timidly at him.* Then you will soon be gone too, Alfred?

ALLMERS, *quickly.* What do you mean?

RITA. You will be following your sister.

ALLMERS. Has Asta said anything to you?

RITA. No. But you told me yourself that it was for Asta's sake you married me.

ALLMERS. Yes. But you have bound me to you. By the years we have lived together.

RITA. Ah! In your eyes I am not so—so consumingly beautiful as I was once.

ALLMERS. Perhaps the law of change will hold us together, in spite of everything.

RITA *nods slowly.* A change is taking place in me. Oh, God! It hurts me so!

ALLMERS. Hurts?

RITA. Yes. Like a birth.

ALLMERS. That is what it is. A birth. Or a resurrection. A transition. To another way of living.

RITA *stares sadly ahead of her.* Yes. But it means the wreck of all life's happiness.

ALLMERS. In that wreck lies our victory.

RITA, *violently.* Oh—words! Good God, we are human! Flesh and blood!

ALLMERS. We are also kin with the sea and the sky, Rita.

RITA. You, perhaps. Not I.

ALLMERS. You, too. More than you know.

RITA *takes a step towards him.* Tell me, Alfred. Couldn't you think of taking up your work again?

ALLMERS. That work you hate so much?

RITA. I am humbler now. I am ready to share you with your book.

ALLMERS. Why?

RITA. So that I may keep you here. Near me.

ALLMERS. I can be of little help to you, Rita.

RITA. But perhaps I could help you.

ALLMERS. To work, you mean?

RITA. No. To live.

ALLMERS *shakes his head.* I have no life left to live.

RITA. To endure the years that remain, then.

ALLMERS, *almost to himself.* I think it would be best for both of us if we were to part.

RITA. Whom would you go to? Asta?

ALLMERS. No. Not Asta. I shall never see her again.

RITA. Where, then?

ALLMERS. Up into my solitude.

RITA. The mountains?

ALLMERS. Yes.

RITA. But these are only daydreams, Alfred. You couldn't live up there.

ALLMERS. Perhaps. But that is where I long to go. To the mountains.

RITA. Why?

ALLMERS. I want to tell you something.

RITA. Something that happened to you up there?

ALLMERS. Yes.

RITA. Something you kept from Asta and me?

ALLMERS. Yes.

RITA. Oh, why do you keep everything to yourself? You shouldn't.

ALLMERS. Sit down and I'll tell you about it.

RITA. Yes. Tell me.

She sits on the bench by the summerhouse.

ALLMERS. I was alone up there. In the heart of the high mountains. Suddenly I came to a large, desolate lake. And I had to cross that lake. But I couldn't, for there was no one there, and no boat.

RITA. What happened then?

ALLMERS. I went all alone, with no one to guide me, into a side valley. I thought that way I might be able to push forward over the heights and between the peaks, and so come down on the other side of the lake.

RITA. And you got lost?

ALLMERS. Yes. I lost all sense of direction, for there was no kind of road nor path there. I walked all day—and all night, too. I began to think I would never find my way back.

RITA. I know your thoughts were with us.

ALLMERS. No; they were not. It was strange. Both you and Eyolf had drifted far, far away from me. And Asta too.

RITA. Then what were you thinking about?

ALLMERS. Nothing. I struggled along the deep crevasses, exulting in the peace and serenity of being in the presence of death.

RITA *jumps to her feet*. It's horrible! How can you use such words about it!

ALLMERS. But that was how I felt. I had no fear. I felt that

Death and I walked side by side like two good fellow travellers. It all seemed so natural. So logical. After all, in my family we do not live to be old—

RITA. Don't talk any more about it, Alfred. You are alive.

ALLMERS. Yes. Quite suddenly, I found I was there. On the other side of the lake.

RITA. That must have been a night of terror for you, Alfred. But now that it's over, you won't admit it to yourself.

ALLMERS. That night resolved me. I turned back and came home. To Eyolf.

RITA, *quietly.* Too late.

ALLMERS. Yes. For my fellow traveller came and claimed him. And then he suddenly seemed loathsome to me—and life too—this damned existence we dare not tear ourselves away from. We are earthbound Rita, you and I.

RITA. Yes! You're the same, aren't you?

Comes towards him.

Oh, let us live our lives together. As long as we can.

ALLMERS *shrugs his shoulders.* Live?

Laughs.

What for? Our lives are empty wastes. Whichever way I look.

RITA. Oh, Alfred. Sooner or later you will leave me. I feel it. I can see it in your eyes. You will leave me.

ALLMERS. You mean, when my fellow traveller comes for me?

RITA. No. Worse. Of your own free will. Because it's only when you are here with me that your life is meaningless. Answer me! Isn't that what you think?

ALLMERS *looks her in the eyes.* And if I do?

Angry, spiteful voices are heard raised against each other in a hubbub from far below.

ALLMERS *goes to the railing.*

RITA. What's that? *Cries.* Oh, they've found him!

ALLMERS. He will never be found.

RITA. Then why are they shouting?

ALLMERS *comes forward.* They're only fighting. As usual.

RITA. Down by the shore?

ALLMERS. Yes. The whole of that damned village ought to be cleared. Now the men have come home—drunk, of course. Someone's beating his children. Listen to them yelling! And his wife shouting for someone to save them—

RITA. Oughtn't we to get someone to go down and help them?

ALLMERS. Help them? They were the ones who let Eyolf drown. No, let them perish—as they let Eyolf perish.

RITA. You mustn't talk like that, Alfred. Or even think it.

ALLMERS. How else can I think? All those old shacks ought to be demolished.

RITA. What would happen to those poor people?

ALLMERS. They'd have to go somewhere else.

RITA. And the children?

ALLMERS. Does it matter where they lead their miserable lives?

RITA, *quietly, reproachfully.* You are making yourself hard, Alfred.

ALLMERS. I have a right to be hard. A duty.

RITA. A duty?

ALLMERS. My duty towards Eyolf. He must not lie unavenged. So. There it is, Rita. I advise you to think it over. Have that village levelled to the ground—when I am gone.

RITA. When you are gone?

ALLMERS. At least it will give you something to occupy yourself with. And you'll need that.

RITA, *with decision.* You're right. I shall need something. But can you guess what I am going to do? When you are gone.

ALLMERS. Well? Tell me.

RITA. The moment you leave me, I shall go down there and bring all those poor, neglected children up to this house.

ALLMERS. What do you want them here for?

RITA. I want to make them mine.

ALLMERS. You?

RITA. Yes. From the day you leave they shall all live here. As if they were mine.

ALLMERS. In our little Eyolf's place?

RITA. Yes. They shall live in Eyolf's room—look at his books—play with his toys.

ALLMERS. But this is absolute madness. There's no one in the world less suited than you to such work.

RITA. Then I shall have to teach myself. Work; and learn.

ALLMERS. If you really mean this, Rita, a great change must indeed have taken place in you.

RITA. It has, Alfred. You have seen to that. You have left me empty, and I must try to fill that emptiness with something. Something resembling love.

ALLMERS *stands in thought for a moment, looking at her.* It's true we haven't done much for those poor people down there. Have we?

RITA. We haven't done anything for them.

ALLMERS. Hardly thought of them.

RITA. Not with compassion, anyway.

ALLMERS. We who had the gold and the green forests.

RITA. We closed our doors to them. And our hearts, too.

ALLMERS *nods.* No wonder they wouldn't risk their lives to save little Eyolf.

RITA, *quietly.* Ask yourself, Alfred. Are you sure—quite sure—we would have risked ours?

ALLMERS. Rita! Can you doubt it?

RITA. Oh, Alfred. We are so earthbound, you and I.

ALLMERS. Well, what do you intend to do for these wretched children?

RITA. To begin with, I shall have to try to make life less hard for them.

ALLMERS. If you can do that, Eyolf will not have been born in vain.

RITA. And will not have been taken from us in vain.

ALLMERS *looks at her*. Don't deceive yourself, Rita. You are not doing this out of love.

RITA. No. I'm not. Not yet, anyway.

ALLMERS. Why are you doing it, then?

RITA. I have so often heard you talking to Asta about human responsibility—

ALLMERS. The book you hated so much.

RITA. I hate it still. But I sat there and listened to you talking. And now I want to try to carry on from there—in my own way.

ALLMERS *shakes his head*. For the sake of that unfinished book?

RITA. No. I have another reason.

Quietly, with a sad smile.

I want to placate the eyes that stare at me.

ALLMERS *looks at her*. Will you let me stay with you, Rita?

RITA. Would you like to?

ALLMERS. Yes. If I was sure that I could help you.

RITA, *hesitantly*. You would have to go on living here.

ALLMERS, *quietly*. Let us see if we cannot make it work.

RITA, *almost inaudibly*. Yes, Alfred. Let us see.

Both are silent for a few moments. Then ALLMERS *walks over to the flagstaff and hoists the flag to the top.* RITA *stands by the summerhouse watching him quietly.*

ALLMERS *comes back to her*. We have a long day ahead of us, Rita.

RITA. You will see. A Sunday calm will fall on us now and then.

ALLMERS, *quietly, moved*. Then, perhaps, we shall sense their spirits beside us.

RITA *whispers*. Spirits?

ALLMERS. Yes. Perhaps they will come to visit us. The ones we have lost.

RITA *nods slowly.* Our little Eyolf. And your big Eyolf, too.

ALLMERS. Perhaps now and then, on our way, we shall catch a glimpse of them.

RITA. Where shall we look, Alfred?

ALLMERS, *his eyes meet hers.* Upwards.

RITA. Yes. Upwards.

ALLMERS. Up towards the mountains. Towards the stars. And the great silence.

RITA *stretches out her hand towards him.* Thank you.

NOTE ON THE TRANSLATION

The Pillars of Society is a fairly straightforward play to translate; the chief problems are Hilmar Toennesen and Lona Hessel. Hilmar talks in a fanciful manner, overloaded with adjectives and ridiculous flights of imagination, like Hjalmar
Ekdal in *The Wild Duck*. Lona has a breezy, slangy way of
talking which contrasts markedly with the prim speech of the
local inhabitants, and since she has spent the past fifteen years
in America I have tried to make her talk like an American.

The Wild Duck presents repeated difficulties to the translator. Hjalmar, Gregers and Gina have particularly idiosyn-
cratic styles of speech which are most awkward to render.
Hjalmar talks pretentiously, like Hilmar Toennesen, but much
more so; he is perpetually starting sentences he cannot finish,
mixing his metaphors, wandering into cliché, indulging in ex-
travagant romanticising and self-pity. It is always tempting
when dealing with a ridiculous character to pare down his
absurdities, but it is a temptation that must be resisted; his
ridiculousness must be given full play; it is a baroque part
for a baroque actor. Gregers is part political fanatic, part evan-
gelist, and has acquired the worst rhetorical characteristics of
both. He, like Hjalmar, is full of other people's phrases. Gina
is even more of a problem. Her speech is lower-class, and
lower-class dialogue is especially difficult to translate because
any real equivalent in English has strong regional associations.
A Norwegian woman cannot talk Cockney or North Country,
and one is forced to compromise with a rough unlocalised
speech which necessarily loses some of the richness of the

original. In the Norwegian she frequently lapses into mala-propisms (*pigstol* for *pistol, den intricata fordringen* for *den ideala fordringen,* the ideal demand, etc.) but malapropisms in English are death to any dialogue except that of farce, and I have not tried to convey them. The phrase *havsens bund* which Gregers uses in Act 3 to describe the bottom of the sea, and which Hedvig says is the phrase she always calls to mind when she thinks of the loft, presents considerable dif-ficulties. It has overtones of both infinity and oblivion; Gregers mutters it hoarsely to himself in the last act when he realises that Hedvig is dead, and in that context it epitomises the choice she has made. In Norwegian it is an antique phrase, some-thing like "the vasty deep," but there is no equivalent in Eng-lish with both the antiquity and the overtones; I have chosen to sacrifice the antiquity and call it "the deep blue sea." The overriding essential is that its significance should be clear when Gregers uses it at the climax of the play.

The main problem in *Hedda Gabler* is to contrast the snob-bish and consciously upper-class speech of Hedda and Judge Brack with the naïve and homely way of talking shared by Miss Tesman, Bertha and George Tesman. Hedda is a Gen-eral's daughter and lets no one forget it. George Tesman has unconsciously acquired the nanny-like mode of speech of the old aunts who brought him up. He addresses Aunt Juliana as *Tante Julle,* a particularly irritating and babylike abbreviation which drives Hedda mad every time he uses it. The last straw is when he asks her to address the old lady by it too. To render this as Aunt Julie, as has usually been done, is completely to miss the point; it must be a ridiculous nickname such as Juju. When Brack tells Hedda where Loevborg has shot himself, he must make it clear to her that the bullet destroyed his sexual organs; otherwise Hedda's reaction makes no sense. To translate this as "belly" or "bowels" is again to miss the point, yet Brack must not use the phrase "sexual organs" directly; he is far too shrewd a *roué* to speak so bluntly to a lady. What he says is: "In the—hm—stomach. The—lower part." I have altered the name of the red-haired singer from Mademoiselle Diana, which is difficult to say in English and has an improbable ring about it, to Mademoiselle Danielle.

Little Eyolf presents difficulties of interpretation beside which even those of *The Wild Duck* or *Brand* seem comparatively minor. There is scarcely a page in the last two acts which is not a translator's nightmare. The characters are perpetually sidestepping the issue, but in a way that leaves their real meaning clear. All the time they are shifting position like skilled stalkers, and each shift must be plotted. Another problem is following Ibsen's subtle changes of pace. No one knew better than he the art of pacing his dialogue; to read any of his mature plays in the original is like watching an orchestra obey the beat of a conductor, and correct pacing is more essential to the translation (and staging) of *Little Eyolf* than of any other work he wrote.

I gladly acknowledge my debt to Mr. Casper Wrede for much minute and valuable criticism in respect of the translations of *The Wild Duck* and *Little Eyolf*.

M. M.

ANCHOR BOOKS

Drama (continued)

Drama (continued). Music

PEER GYNT—Henrik Ibsen, Michael Meyer, trans., A215d

SHAKESPEARE—Mark Van Doren, A11

SHAKESPEARE OUR CONTEMPORARY—Jan Kott, trans. by Boleslaw Taborski, A499

SIX PLAYS OF PLAUTUS—Lionel Casson, trans., A367

SIX PLAYS OF STRINDBERG—Elizabeth Sprigge, trans., A54

THE SON OF A SERVANT: The Story of the Evolution of a Human Being (1849–1867)—August Strindberg, trans. by Evert Sprinchorn, A492a

SOPHOCLES' OEDIPUS THE KING AND OEDIPUS AT COLONUS—A New Translation for Modern Audiences and Readers by Charles R. Walker, A496

STUDIES IN SEVENTEENTH-CENTURY FRENCH LITERATURE—Jean-Jacques Demorest, ed., A503

THEATRE OF THE ABSURD—Martin Esslin, A279

THEORIES OF COMEDY—Paul Lauter, ed., A403

TUDOR PLAYS: An Anthology of Early English Drama—ed. by Edmund Creeth, AO-1

WHEN WE DEAD AWAKEN AND THREE OTHER PLAYS—Henrik Ibsen, Michael Meyer, trans., A215b

MUSIC

BEETHOVEN'S LETTERS, JOURNALS AND CONVERSATIONS—Michael Hamburger, ed., A206

BRAHMS: HIS LIFE AND WORK—Karl Geiringer, A248

COMPOSER'S WORLD—Paul Hindemith, A235

DARWIN, MARX, WAGNER—Jacques Barzun, A127

AN ELIZABETHAN SONGBOOK—Noah Greenberg, W. H. Auden and Chester Kallman, A56

PUCCINI LIBRETTOS—In New English Translations by William Weaver with the Original Italian, A531

RING OF WORDS: An Anthology of Song Texts—ed. and trans. by Philip L. Miller, A428

VERDI LIBRETTOS—William Weaver, trans., A342

ANCHOR BOOKS

FICTION

CLASSICS AND HUMANITIES